# Love That Produces Hope

## The Thought of Ignacio Ellacuría

María Pilar Aquino

Gregory Baum

Antonio González

Roger Haight, S.J.

Martin Maier

J. Matthew Ashley

Kevin F. Burke, S.J.

Gustavo Gutiérrez, O.P.

Robert Lassalle-Klein

Johann Baptist Metz

Jon Sobrino, S.J.

Aquiline Tarimo, S.J., and William O'Neill, S.J.

Edited by

*Kevin F. Burke, S.J., and Robert Lassalle-Klein*

A Michael Glazier Book

**LITURGICAL PRESS**

Collegeville, Minnesota

www.litpress.org

A Michael Glazier Book published by Liturgical Press

Cover design by David Manahan, O.S.B. Photo of Ignacio Ellacuría provided by the editors.

ISBN 13: 978-0-8146-5217-6
ISBN 10: 0-8146-5217-4

1    2    3    4    5    6    7    8

**Library of Congress Cataloging-in-Publication Data**

Love that produces hope : the thought of Ignacio Ellacuría / María Pilar Aquino
    . . . [et al.] ; edited by Kevin F. Burke and Robert Lassalle-Klein.
        p.    cm.
    "A Michael Glazier book."
    Includes bibliographical references and index.
    ISBN 0-8146-5217-4
    1. Ellacuría, Ignacio.    I. Aquino, María Pilar.    II. Burke, Kevin F.
III. Lassalle-Klein, Robert Anthony

BX4705.E46L68    2005
230'.2'092—dc22

                                                                2004020498

# Contents

## Part Two: Reception of Ellacuría's Thought

# Acknowledgments

The proceeds from this volume will go to the Archbishop Oscar Romero Pastoral Center to honor the six Jesuits and two lay companions assassinated there on November 16, 1989, by soldiers acting under orders from the highest levels of the Salvadoran military. The eight martyrs include Fr. Ignacio Ellacuría, s.j., president of the University of Central America; Fr. Ignacio Martin-Baro, s.j., university vice president and director of the university's Institute of Public Opinion; Fr. Segundo Montes, s.j., director of the university's Human Rights Institute and superior of the Jesuit community; Fr. Amando Lopez, s.j., professor of theology, and former president of the University of Central America in Managua; Fr. Joaquin Lopez y Lopez, s.j., national director of Fe y Alegría, an education and direct-service program for El Salvador's poor children; Fr. Juan Ramon Moreno, s.j., assistant director of the newly constructed Archbishop Oscar Romero Pastoral Center, and the Department of Pastoral Theology; Elba Ramos, cook for one of the Jesuit communities, and her sixteen-year-old daughter, Celina, who planned to be married the following year.

We wish to express our gratitude to all those who helped make this volume possible. Above all, we acknowledge our debt to Ignacio Ellacuría and those who gave their lives with him. We thank Jon Sobrino, Dean Brackley, Rodolfo Cardenal, and countless other individuals at the University of Central America and the Archbishop Oscar Romero Pastoral Center in San Salvador. We also wish to thank all of the authors and translators who contributed to this volume; their wisdom, care, and insight have profoundly enriched our understanding of Ellacuría's thought and importance. Special thanks go to Matt Ashley for his advice and encouragement in the initial stages of this project and throughout, and to our assistants, Joanne Doi, Karen Enriquez, and Emily Rauer, for their many hours of research on the footnotes and bibliography; to Jerome Post for his assistance to Robert Lassalle-Klein with the Spanish translation of several chapters; and to Anna Bonta for her assistance on the translation of Martin Meier's chapter. We are grateful to Mark Twomey and Linda Maloney at Liturgical Press, whose faithful patience, assistance, and support helped sustain this project to its completion; and to colleagues at the Jesuit School of Theology at Berkeley, DePaul University, Holy Names University, and the Weston Jesuit School of Theology for the invaluable critical feedback and institutional support. Finally, we are thankful for the unflagging support of our families and communities, especially Lynn Lassalle-Klein and the Weston Jesuit Community, who have supported us and this project through weekends and vacations for several years.

Kevin F. Burke, s.j., and Robert Lassalle-Klein, editors

# A Note on Citations

The bibliography of Ignacio Ellacuría contains several distinctive features. We call attention to the most important of these in order both to facilitate the reader's use of the bibliography. We also wish to explain the system we adopted to cross-reference translations, and to coordinate the citations from the various chapters of this book among themselves and with the bibliography.

(1) With one exception, all of Ellacuría's writings were originally published as essays. The exception is his book *Filosofía de la realidad histórica* (1990), unfinished at the time Ellacuría was murdered. This manuscript was edited by his student and friend, Antonio González, and posthumously published. González uses Ellacuría's previously published essay, "El objeto de la filosofía (1981)," as a prologue/conclusion of the book. Ellacuría published two collections of essays in book form during his lifetime: *Teología política* (1973) [in English, *Freedom Made Flesh,* (1976)] and *Conversión de la Iglesia al Reino de Dios* (1984). All the chapters in these two collections were published previously in various venues. Therefore, our citations always include the specific essay and not merely the title of a collection. These collections, along with several other collections that Ellacuría coedited (i.e., *Mysterium Liberationis,* 1990) or jointly-authored (i.e., *Iglesia de los pobres y organizaciones populares,* 1979), whether published in his lifetime or posthumously, are likewise cited by year of publication in the bibliography.

(2) Many of Ellacuría's essays were published in multiple venues: journals, books, magazines, theological dictionaries, newsletters, formal or informal publications of the UCA, etc. Sometimes he published the same essay with two different titles; at other times he published a section of a longer essay as an essay in its own right. To create a bibliography

that includes an accurate publication history, we have arranged all the entries in Ellacuría's bibliography by year of publication rather than in alphabetical order. The various venues in which a piece has been published are noted in the entry, along with changes in titles and other idiosyncratic elements.

(3) UCA Editores, the publishing arm of the UCA, has been steadily publishing the collected works of Ignacio Ellacuría since his death. Twelve volumes have appeared to date: *Filosofía de la realidad histórica* (1990); *Veinte años de historia en El Salvador (1969–1989),* 3 volumes (1991); *Escritos filosóficos,* 3 volumes (1996, 1999, 2001); *Escritos universitarios* (1999); *Escritos teolóicos,* 4 volumes (2000, 2001). These critical editions make an outstanding contribution to future scholarship, providing uniform access to Ellacuría's previously published writings as well as a substantial number of pieces that were previously unpublished. All of the individual essays, collections of letters, outlines, etc., as they appear in the table of contents of these twelve volumes are reflected in this bibliography. Whenever possible, we locate previously unpublished works according to the year they were written. We are indebted to the editors of the collected works both for making these works available and for clarifying the publication histories of Ellacuría's writings.

(4) Ellacuría subdivided his bibliography according to the various academic disciplines he was engaging: theology, philosophy, and politics. We have adopted that convention here, with several additional features. We have expanded his original threefold classification into five sections: Early Writings, Philosophical Writings, Theological Writings, Political Writings, and University Writings. A limited number of essays cross over into two classifications. In those cases, the full citation is given under one classification, but the entry also appears in an abbreviated form under the other relevant classification. In addition, we have gathered all of Ellacuría's writings translated into English in a sixth section located at the end of the bibliography. These entries are arranged according to the year the English translation was first published. They reference the Spanish original by title and year of publication, and they note multiple publications in English.

(5) Our contributors made use of the various versions of Ellacuría's writings as these were available to them or for reasons of their own. Sometimes our authors cite a work in its original Spanish publication. Sometimes they cite a later collection or other publication. Sometimes they cite a translation of the essay. Sometimes they do all three. In order to reflect the sources as our contributors used them, we have kept their ci-

tations intact; thus, we did not impose a system of standardized citations on the chapter notes. However, whenever authors cited only a collection and not an essay by name (e.g., *Conversión de la Iglesia al Reino de Dios*), we put both the essay title and the collection title in the original citation. Furthermore, to assist readers interested in tracing or comparing the sources used by different contributors, we developed a system of cross-references in the citations. Readers will recognize this system whenever a citation includes an element placed within square brackets. Our system of citations follows these protocols: first, the contributing author's original citation is reproduced; second, if that citation is to a secondary Spanish publication, the original Spanish source and date is noted in order to help readers locate the piece in the bibliography; third, if a work cited in Spanish has appeared in English translation, the English translation appears in square brackets; fourth, when the contributor's citation is to an English translation, the Spanish original appears in square brackets.

(6) We developed a system of abbreviations for the books, collections, and major journals in which Ellacuría's writings appear. These are gathered in the table of abbreviations below. Likewise, we abbreviated the longer titles of a select group of frequently cited essays. All the entries included in the table of abbreviations note the year of publication. Readers who wish to locate the full bibliographical reference for any work cited can do so by year of publication.

Kevin F. Burke, s.j., and Robert Lassalle-Klein, editors

# Abbreviations of Ellacuría's Writings

## Books, Collections, and Major Journals

| | |
|---|---|
| CIRD | Ellacuría, *Conversión de la Iglesia al Reino de Dios* (1984) |
| ECA | *Estudios Centroamericanos* (periodical, El Salvador) |
| EF | Ellacuría, *Escritos filosóficos*, 3 Vols. (1996, 1999, 2001) |
| ET | Ellacuría, *Escritos teolóicos*, 4 Vols. (2000, 2001) |
| ETM | Ellacuría, *Ignacio Ellacuría: Teólogo mártir por la liberación del pueblo* (1990) |
| EU | Ellacuría, *Escritos universitarios* (1999) |
| FMF | Ellacuría, *Freedom Made Flesh* (1976) |
| FRH | Ellacuría, *Filosofía de la realidad histórica* (1990) |
| IPOP | Ellacuría, *Iglesia de los pobres y organizaciones populares* (1979) |
| ML/ MLT | Sobrino and Ellacuría, *Mysterium Liberationis* (1990/English trans., 1993) |
| RLT | *Revista Latinoamericana de Teología* (periodical, El Salvador) |
| ST | *Sal Terrae* (periodical, Spain) |
| TP | Ellacuría, *Teología política* (1973) |
| TSSP | Hassett and Lacey, *Towards a Society That Serves Its People* (1991) |
| VA | Ellacuría, *Veinte años de historia en El Salvador (1969–1989)*, 3 Vols. (1991) |

## Frequently Cited Essays

1975 "Antropología"    "La antropología filosófica de Xavier Zubiri"
1975 "Hacia una fundamentación"    "Hacia una fundamentación
        filosófica del método teológico latinoamericano"

1975 "Tesis sobre teología"   "Tesis sobre la posibilidad, necesidad y sentido de una teología latinoamericana"

1976 "Propiedad"   "La historización del concepto de propiedad como principio de desideologización"

1977 "Sacramento histórico"   "Iglesia de los pobres, sacramento histórico de la liberación"

1978 "Bien común"   "Historización del bien común y de los derechos humanos en una sociedad dividida"

1978 "Por qué muere Jesús"   "Por qué muere Jesús y por qué le matan"

1978 "Teología como praxis"   "La teología como momento ideológico de la praxis eclesial"

1979 "Fundamentación biológica"   "Fundamentación biológica de la ética"

1981 "Lugar teológico"   "Los pobres, 'lugar teológico' en América Latina"

1981 "Nueva obra"   "La nueva obra de Zubiri: 'Inteligencia Sentiente'"

1981 "Verdadero pueblo"   "El verdadero pueblo de Dios según Monseñor Romero"

1982 "Discurso de graduación"   "Discurso de graduación en la Universidad de Santa Clara, 12 de junio de 1982"

1983 "Aproximación"   "Aproximación a la obra completa de Xavier Zubiri"

1985 "Función liberadora"   "Función liberadora de la filosofía"

1987 "Religiones abrahámicas"   "Aporte de la teología de la liberación a las religiones abrahámicas en la superación del individualismo y del positivismo"

1987 "Teología frente al cambio"   "La teología de la liberación frente al cambio socio-histórico de América Latina"

1988 "Reduccionismo"   "La superación del reduccionismo idealista en Zubiri"

1989 "Derechos humanos"   "Historización de los derechos humanos desde los pueblos oprimidos y las mayorías populares"

1989 "Utopía y profetismo"   "Utopía y profetismo desde América Latina: un ensayo concreto de soteriología historíca"

1991 "Lectura"   "Lectura Latinoamericana de los Ejercicios Espirituales de San Ignacio"

# Introduction

*Robert Lassalle-Klein*

> It is not easy to know how to keep on hoping, and we must all answer
> this question in our own way. It seems that everything is against hope.
> But for me at least, where I see there has been great love, I see hope
> being born again. This is not a rational conclusion. Perhaps it is not even
> theological. It is simply true: love produces hope, and great love produces
> great hope.[1]

> Jon Sobrino, *Companions of Jesus: The Jesuit Martyrs of El Salvador*

Fr. Ignacio Ellacuría, S.J., was among the most exceptional of a remarkable generation of mid-twentieth-century Spanish Jesuits sent to
serve the Catholic Church of Latin America. His riveting biography and
brilliant writings embody the transformations and tensions that re-
shaped the life of the Catholic Church among the "crucified peoples"[2] of
Central America during the last half of the twentieth century. *Love That
Produces Hope: The Thought of Ignacio Ellacuría* brings together some of the
world's leading authorities on key aspects of the Spaniard's thought. All
who have contributed to this volume are convinced of the far-reaching
significance at the dawn of the third millennium of Ellacuría's still little-
known writings, and the grace-filled intellectual and personal transformations they embody. The editors also believe that the book serves as an
outstanding introduction to the life and thought of Ignacio Ellacuría,
while offering new insights and important texts to the scholarly reader.

## The Need for a Critical Introduction to Ellacuría's Life and Thought

Ellacuría was the primary target in the brutal assassination of six Jesuits and two women by government troops at the University of Central America (UCA) in San Salvador on November 16, 1989. The United Nations Commission on the Truth for El Salvador states that the crime was commissioned late November 15 when the chief of staff and other leaders of the armed forces of El Salvador ordered members of an elite U.S.-trained battalion "to kill Father Ellacuría and to leave no witnesses."[3] Around 2:30 A.M., Ellacuría and four fellow Spanish-born Jesuit priest-academics were executed with machine guns as they lay face down in the grass behind the Jesuit residence of the University of Central America. One neighbor reports that "just before the gunfire" she heard "rhythmic whispering, like a psalmody of a group in prayer."[4] Minutes later, a mother and daughter who had sought refuge in the Jesuit residence were repeatedly shot as they huddled in each others' arms. The brutality ended with the murder of a seventy-one-year-old Salvadoran-born Jesuit priest in his room.

Those interested in Latin American religion know Ellacuría as among the most original and important philosophers and theologians produced by twentieth-century Latin American liberation thought. Outside of Latin America, Ellacuría is known mainly through his pervasive influence on the work of his friend and collaborator, Fr. Jon Sobrino, S.J., the Continent's leading author on Jesus Christ. Educators know Ellacuría as the genius behind what Sobrino has called the most important advance in the idea of the Christian university since Cardinal John Henry Newman.[5] Political observers know of Ellacuría's singular role as El Salvador's leading public intellectual in promoting dialogue and negotiations during the fratricidal civil war (1980–92) that coincided with his decade as president of the UCA (1979–89). Each year, a growing list of publications and dissertations in various languages cite the far-reaching implications of Ellacuría's reinterpretation of several defining currents of late twentieth-century thought from a Catholic, Latin American, liberationist perspective.

Despite this growing interest, however, the actual content and significance of Ellacuría's thought is not well known in the English-speaking world. This is due in part to the breadth and complexity of Ellacuría's vast corpus, which spans philosophy, theology, political affairs, human rights, literature, spirituality, the nature of the university, and geopolitical issues of war and peace. Over fifteen years after his death, multivolume collections of his writings continue to appear, gradually making them available to the general public. Many, however, are only available in Spanish.

For readers in the United States and Europe, Ellacuría's written reflections on his transformative journey "from Portugalete to San Salvador"[6] offer an additional hurdle. For they present uncomfortable moral and intellectual challenges to the devastating impact of First World policies and patterns of consumption on what Ellacuría called the "vast majorities"[7] of the less developed countries. Today, much of the world chafes before the unrivaled projection of U.S. and European cultural, economic, and military interests around the globe. Even Europe protests the unapologetic unilateralism that currently drives the foreign policy of the world's last remaining superpower. Thus, fifteen years after Ellacuría's untimely death, American and European readers are likely to find his breathtaking vision of the twentieth century more challenging than ever.

This book, then, is designed to fill the much-needed role of a broad-ranging, international, critical introduction to the life and thought of Ignacio Ellacuría, s.j.[8] Its purpose will have been served if questions are raised that lead readers to look beyond this volume into the actual writings themselves. The most complete and up-to-date bibliography in English on Ellacuría's writings (published and unpublished) has been provided with this volume expressly for that purpose.

## Highlights from Ellacuría's Personal and Intellectual Biography

This section can treat only the bare essentials of Ellacuría's personal and intellectual biography. Fortunately, Jon Sobrino's important essay includes fascinating biographical details and personal recollections of conversations and events shared by these closest of Jesuit friends and collaborators over many years. Part One also includes major essays outlining Ellacuría's "critical and creative"[9] (one could add postcolonial and postmodern) dialogue with the defining currents of Western and Latin American cultural and social scientific thought. Part Two is comprised of essays by theologians and philosophers from around the world that outline the importance of Ellacuría's insights for their own culturally contextualized interpretations of Christian tradition.

Jon Sobrino reports that "Ellacuría used to say he was impressed by five people during his life: his novice master, Fr. Elizondo, at the human, spiritual level; Espinoza Pólit, his humanities professor in Ecuador; Angel Martínez, the poet; Karl Rahner as a theologian at Innsbruck; and Xavier Zubiri in Spain, the subject of his doctoral dissertation in philosophy."[10] Fr. Rudolfo Cardenal, s.j.,[11] who lived with Ellacuría during the final decade of his life, follows this pattern, crediting the teachers who "established the fundamentals around which Ellacuría shaped his life and his praxis."[12] This section will build on that tradition, adding biographical information, my own insights, and additional figures at the end.

*Miguel Elizondo, s.j.:* Ignacio Ellacuría was born November 9, 1930, in Portugalete,[13] the heart of the Basque country, on the Northern (Atlantic) Coast of Spain. The fourth of six children, and five sons, in 1940 he was sent to southern Navarro, one hundred and forty three miles from home, for studies at the Jesuit high school in Tudela, Spain.[14] Here, young Ignacio began the study of the classics of Western literature, his knowledge of which, including Greek and Latin, would impress later mentors in the humanities,[15] and philosophy.[16] He also nurtured what became a lifelong passion for soccer.[17]

Reserved and intense, Ellacuría was not invited to a meeting of promising recruits by the spiritual father of the senior class at Tudela.[18] Still, he graduated at age sixteen and became the fourth of five brothers to enter the seminary. Young Ignacio entered the Jesuit novitiate at Loyola on September 14, 1947, the ancestral home of Ignatius Loyola, founder of the Jesuits. There he made the famous thirty-day silent retreat known as the Spiritual Exercises of St. Ignatius, under the direction of Fr. Miguel Elizondo, s.j., then master of novices. The first of his great teachers, Elizondo would mentor Ellacuría in a vigorous and thoroughly updated version of Ignatian spirituality.

After only one year in the novitiate, Ellacuría volunteered, with five other novices, to accompany Fr. Elizondo on an exciting new mission to open the doors of the first-ever novitiate for the Society of Jesus in Central America. Elizondo sought to instill both the freedom and the deep spirituality of St. Ignatius Loyola in his novices. He encouraged them to interiorize the spirituality of their yearly retreat encounter with the Spiritual Exercises through study of the founding history and documents of the Society of Jesus, and by using their own judgment in adapting to the new surroundings. This seemed better to Elizondo than depending on Spanish convention regarding "the many things they were supposed to do in order to be a good Jesuit—the many rules to obey, virtues to practice, devotions to keep, and so on, in order to reach what one can consider essential in the vocation of the Society."[19]

Elizondo is revered for his work as the spiritual director of the final stage of Jesuit formation for Latin America through three decades after Vatican II. Looking back on the challenge of forming mainly Spanish novices to serve in the Americas, Elizondo recalls being guided by Ignatius's motto *Ad majorem Dei gloriam* (for the greater glory of God). He says, "I felt totally free of my past, of my antecedents as a Jesuit and as a novice master, although I was a 'novice' in that myself."[20] Fr. Cesar Jerez, s.j., the native-born and much-loved provincial of Central America during its first persecutions and martyrdoms, said shortly before his death that Elizondo "taught us not to be afraid."[21]

This would prove to be a valuable quality. For on December 24–31, 1969, Elizondo and his former protégé, Ellacuría, led the Jesuits of Central America through the Spiritual Exercises of St. Ignatius as they sought to discern "the call" of the Society of Jesus in Central America after Vatican II (1962–5).[22] Elizondo immersed his colleagues and former novices in a profound appropriation, based on the latest research, of the founding traditions of Jesuit spirituality.[23] Ellacuría electrified the gathered priests, brothers, and seminarians with the bold new Jesuit apostolic vision emerging after the 1968 meeting of Latin American Bishops in Medellín, Colombia.[24] And together, they created an acute awareness of standing at the threshold of what Ellacuría's teacher, Karl Rahner, called the third "great epoch"[25] in the history of Christianity. In the end, the days of prayer and discernment during the Christmas holiday of 1969 led the Jesuits of Central America to embrace the option for the poor outlined the previous year by the Latin American bishops at Medellin. It was a choice that would catalyze an entire generation of Central American Jesuits, while leading to the death of Ellacuría and several others gathered there.[26]

*Aurelio Espinoza Pólit, s.j.:* In September 1949, Ellacuría took vows of poverty, chastity, and obedience in the Society of Jesus with five classmates in San Salvador. Shortly thereafter, the newly minted Jesuit "scholastic" left with his classmates for undergraduate studies in classics and philosophy at the Universidad Católica del Ecuador in Quito. There Ellacuría met Fr. Aurelio Espinoza Pólit, s.j. (1894–1961), and Fr. Angel Martínez, s.j. (1899–1971). Dr. Héctor Samour, dean of Human and Natural Sciences, and chair of the Department of Philosophy at the UCA, notes that Ellacuría studied the emerging synthesis of Thomas Aquinas with the modern philosophy of Kant, Husserl, and Heidegger known as transcendental Thomism. However, he insists that "the roots of . . . [Ellacuría's] philosophical thought must be sought in the hu-

manistic and philosophical studies in Quito, especially in . . . the teaching of Aurelio Espinoza Pólit and Angel Martínez Baigorri."[27]

Espinoza Pólit was Ellacuría's first great teacher in the humanities.
Cardenal writes, "President of the Universidad Católica, occasional poet,
and advisor for cultural affairs to the Ecuadorian government, Aurelio
Espinoza was a world renowned authority on Sophocles and Virgil, and,
more importantly still, a humanist in the full sense of the term."[28] The
young student and his teacher soon developed a great appreciation for
each other. During five years in Quito (1950–5), Ellacuría would button-
hole recently arrived Jesuit students exhorting them "not to waste the
opportunity to be with a great man," claiming that by "devoting themselves" to Espinoza Pólit, they would pick up by simple osmosis the demanding essentials of Jesuit intellectual formation.[29]

In an encomium dated two weeks after the death of his first academic mentor,[30] Ellacuría says the renowned man of letters believed
education "was rooted in the person and not in ideas."[31] Espinoza insisted that "the letter never reproduces the person." He therefore strove
"to put his students in . . . immediate and total contact . . . with the
richest classical personalities" by attempting to "recreate" the historical
situations that made "the written work . . . possible."[32] Ellacuría recalls
that Espinoza's classes were "really creative, without prepared schemas,"
a "spiritual adventure" wherein students and teacher "searched for the
new and deeper insight," and the "unexpected discovery."[33] In discussion, the teacher preferred "education to erudition, the living form to the
material contents."[34] Ellacuría says this pedagogy fostered an "integral
human formation by means of culture,"[35] which transmitted a deeply
sacramental view of the world wherein one "does Christianity" by "creating what is human."[36]

Cardenal finds it significant that Ellacuría's classes likewise emphasized "the importance of learning to think and to find the necessary
data."[37] Building on the work of Héctor Samour,[38] Cardenal suggests
that it was Espinoza Pólit who first led Ellacuría "to teach his students
to learn from reality," and to the conviction that "books were just useful
instruments"[39] in the service of this larger goal. Samour also asserts that
Espinoza nurtured Ellacuría's "lack of satisfaction with scholasticism as
a disembodied and intellectualist form of thought," and convinced him
of "the need to humanize and reorient it toward the existential and vital
problematic of concrete human beings."[40]

Curiously, however, Ellacuría himself places the emphasis elsewhere.
He focuses on the importance of Espinoza Pólit as a "national figure" in

the intellectual and cultural life of Ecuador. And he offers Pólit as a model for the solution to "the problem" of the Latin American intellectual, that is, "how to combine the most serious intellectual work . . . with attention to multiple problems, and the ability to transcend one's own specialization. . . ."[41]

Pólit's parting gift to his student in 1955 was the recommendation that "upon returning to El Salvador, he should found a library containing everything related to the country."[42] Cardenal, now vice president of the UCA, claims this was the initial inspiration for what became the renowned Salvadoran collection of the university's library, and its Center for Documentation and Research Support. Writing at the beginning of his own career, Ellacuría's description of Espinoza Pólit provides a map of his own future in El Salvador:

> Having gained prestige in a specialization in the humanities, and later in the wider circle of literature and education, the road was opened so that his powerful personality could impact the masses, and outstanding individuals. He was a man truly on the cutting edge of ideas. Thus, personal contact elevated the admiration and influence created by his teaching . . . [and] his actions in shaping the future [of Equador.][43]

He continues that, "though his works could be highly praised," a portrait of "the personality and the meaning of the life of Father Espinoza Pólit" would more accurately focus on "the Christian and priestly meaning that constituted the highest and total significance of his existence."[44] It is interesting that Ellacuría's own life would be evaluated almost thirty years later in terms similar to those he used for Espinoza Pólit.[45]

*Angel Martínez, s.j.:* Toward the end of this period, Ellacuría came to know his third great teacher, Fr. Angel Martínez Baigorri, s.j.[46] We are indebted to Cardenal and Samour for their attention to this figure. Though two articles and several letters appear in his collected works, Ellacuría's "sporadic but very intense"[47] correspondence with the Spanish poet goes virtually unmentioned in the other testimonies, recollections, and biographical fragments produced by his contemporaries.

Those familiar with Ellacuría's later work will not be surprised that Cardenal (based partly on research by Samour) concludes that "Angel Martínez showed him the path of reaching what is ultimate through things."[48] Ellacuría's 1954 letter to the poet says he learned, "how, by going deeper into the reality of things . . . one gets to deep emotions that grab hold of our entire being and enable it to manifest the impact of those things on our very soul."[49] This material is historically significant, for it reveals a young man in his early twenties, over a decade before meeting Rahner and Zubiri, who already "wanted to find a philosophy that could simultaneously respond to the ultimate questions, while dealing with the everyday problems of humanity."[50]

Cardenal, however, finds it "surprising" to have discovered an "identification so profound and intimate"[51] in the correspondence. He draws attention to the 1954 letter, where Ellacuría writes, "your life echoes in mine, in its deepest and most spiritual dimensions."[52] This impression is confirmed by notes taken days after Ellacuría's first powerful encounter with Angel Martínez. The young Spaniard writes, "During the five days I was with him, I realized that he is possibly the only person who has made me forget myself—my worries, my tendencies, and even my passions—and who has been able to get my whole being to focus on the object he discussed."[53] Ellacuría quotes this passage a year and a half later in a letter to Martínez. But he inserts a mysterious speculation that the older poet, "knows something, or suspects it from the violent way that I always clench myself." And he predicts that Martínez will eventually, "figure out what this personal phenomenon potentially implies about the person who produced it." [54]

Ellacuría's closest friend recalls that he "was not given to demonstrations of intimacy."[55] Yet the first letter states, "I am desiring more and more of your letters, which say many things that also belong to me, but which I do not know how to express, if you do not awaken them from within me."[56] He says the Jesuit's poems repeatedly appear in "my meditations," expressing "what I live ineffably." And he confesses from El Salvador, "my most intimate being shares some of the things that belong to you."[57] Clearly, this is a young man in the spell of the sensuous verse and the charismatic personality of the older poet.

Héctor Samour draws our attention to the impact of Ellacuría's encounter with Angel Martínez on the Spaniard's later philosophical and theological thought. He asserts that Ellacuría believes:

> Just as the poetry of Angel Martínez is vital and essential, so philosophy should also be vital and essential. . . . A philosophy that tries to respond to the vital problems of being human . . . [will] represent a "liberation from the slavery in which we live, the slavery in which we are kept by things, and the most superficial, carnal part of ourselves." This effort to investigate the essence of what is real implies a liberation of the human person "that is neither misled by fruitless solipsism, nor gets lost or alienated from itself—becoming one more thing—amidst that 'other' that surrounds us."[58]

In the end, this relationship is also important for the rare glimpse it provides of the youthful passions, worries, emotional struggles, and inspirations that shaped Ellacuría's famously forceful personality.

At the age of twenty-five, Ellacuría returned in 1955 to work for three years in a Central American Jesuit apostolate. He taught Thomistic philosophy at the San Salvador seminary, San José de la Montaña, throughout this middle period of Jesuit formation. Cardenal says Ellacuría also spoke with the diocesan seminarians about "existential trends" in philosophy. Living with them virtually year round, however, he reports that, "For Ellacuría, the biggest problem was entertaining them during the weekend."[59] Thus the youthful Jesuit staff "would organize hikes to the San Salvador volcano, to Lake Illopango, or to the swimming pool at the Externado San Jose, the Jesuit High School." Cardenal observes that, though Ellacuría was "hard and demanding," he inspired the students to create a small classics library using their own money.

Ellacuría also found time during this period to publish in the same journals as his mentor, Angel Martínez. He wrote five articles for the prestigious Central American Studies, which would later become the flagship publication of the University of Central America under his direction.[60] Cardenal adds that "older and more experienced Jesuits" took note of Ellacuría's increasing publications and public presentations with a combination of "admiration"[61] and "a certain amount of jealousy."[62]

*Karl Rahner, s.j.:* Ellacuría left San Salvador to study for the master's in theology from 1958–62 with the Jesuit faculty at Innsbruck, Austria. Given the ambivalence that Ellacuría manifests about this period of his Jesuit formation, it is interesting that Aurelio Pólit cautions the recently arrived student:

> I think it is a tremendous advantage that you will be in a position to profit from all the German contributions to science and criticism. But I would consider it a disaster if you so subordinate yourself to its influence that you lose your freedom of spirit, and the clear-headed trust in your own judgment and the aesthetic perspective that we Latinos bring.[63]

Cardenal reports that Austria seemed "cold and gloomy" to Ellacuría, who "missed the spirit of the Central American [Jesuit] community in Ecuador," and his friends who were "spread all over Europe."[64] In a twist on national stereotypes, certain students called Ellacuría "the Sun King"[65] for his aloof and ironic brilliance, and the Spanish-speaking (and Latin American) enclave that formed around him. The group made no secret of "its discontent with . . . the antiquated restrictions on the daily life of the theologian, and the surprisingly poor quality of instruction."[66]

On the other hand, with one German and two Austrians, they demonstrated a holy enthusiasm for soccer, forming a Jesuit team that won the Austrian national university championship, much to the horror of their superiors at Innsbruck and Rome. The Spaniard maintained a lifelong devotion to the sport, later organizing weekend Jesuit matches at the UCA, and combing the sports section for news of his favorite teams. Ellacuría later recalled with good humor "how he had to defend the theologate soccer team to the Jesuit superiors."[67] Their reaction, however, was not so positive. Despite having excelled in classes, won a national championship, and been a leader among the Latin Americans, the local superior's final evaluation complains, "though he is exceedingly talented, his character is potentially difficult, his . . . critical attitude is constant, he is not open to others, and he separates himself from the community with a small group in which he exercises a strong influence."[68] It is worth noting that Ellacuría's frustration with the "preconciliar structures" at Innsbruck between 1958–62 was hardly unique among students of that period.

Cardenal recalls that Ellacuría used to say, "the only thing that made the [Innsbruck] theologate worthwhile was the opportunity to study with Rahner."[69] Thus, the Spaniard took various courses during these years with Fr. Karl Rahner, S.J., his fourth great teacher. In October 1961, Rahner was appointed private advisor to Cardinal Franz König of Vienna for the upcoming Second Vatican Council. He soon emerged as perhaps the "most powerful"[70] theological *periti* of Vatican II. Martin Maier, S.J., suggests, "one can imagine that Rahner frequently shared his thoughts about the preparations for . . . [the council] with his class" during those years, including "the young Ellacuría."[71]

Ellacuría was deeply moved by Rahner, both as a theologian and as a Christian. In an open letter to Ellacuría dated a year after the assassinations, Jon Sobrino recalls, "I remember one day in 1969 you told me . . . your great teacher Karl Rahner bore his doubts with great elegance, which made you say that faith was not something obvious for you either, but rather a victory."[72] Ellacuría also clearly saw his own work as a development of Rahner's. His earliest and most significant theological statements are explicitly framed as interpretations of what he learned from this great theologian of the council. He presents the key talk of the 1969 retreat as a "small attempt" to apply Rahner's categories to the "mundane reality [of the Third World], and to conceive of it in theological terms."[73] And the English forward to Ellacuría's first book (1973) describes the author (with his approval, one supposes) as a "former student of Karl Rahner," whose book represents "a synthesis" that "has tried to combine the insights of Rahner with those of the Theology of Liberation."[74]

Commentators have not sufficiently emphasized the significance of the fact that Ellacuría frames his entire theological project as a "theology of sign,"[75] his own development of Rahner's "theology of symbol."[76] Ellacuría claims that "God revealed himself in history, not directly, but in a sign . . . the humanity of Jesus."[77] In this, he reinterprets Rahner's famous assertion that "the incarnate word is the absolute symbol of God in the world."[78] But the emphasis has been shifted from "symbol" to "sign," in part, to cohere with the Council's mandate to "the Church . . . of reading the signs of the times and of interpreting them in light of the Gospel (*Gaudium et spes* 4)." Ellacuría then argues that the "mission of the Church" is to be "a sign, and only a sign, of the God who has revealed himself in history . . . of Jesus, the Lord, the Revealer of the Father."[79]

In a previously unpublished and uncited document, Ellacuría vehemently insists that his work cannot be properly understood apart from the Rahnerian "theology of sign" that frames it. Written a year after the 1973 publication of *Teología Política,* this letter successfully defends the book against criticisms expressed in writing by the office of the apostolic nuncio in San Salvador. Ellacuría's argument is that the unnamed reviewer, "ignores and passes over what is essential in my work: salvation in history is a sign of the plenitude of a salvation that is meta-historical." Then he adds the remarkable (for our purposes) assertion,

> Not to have understood this theology of sign, which dominates the entire publication . . . presupposes a serious lack of depth in the interpretation and the evaluation of my work. Everything that is presented as salvation in history . . . is regarded as a sign of the history of salvation. It comes from that, and it moves toward that. My work tries to demonstrate the connection between the sign and what constitutes it as a sign.[80]

These words serve as a clue and a caution for interpreters of the many signs that dominate the rest of Ellacuría's theological career regarding the unifying importance he assigns to this Rahnerian framework. Ellacuría shapes the 1969 province retreat with the Ignatian exhortation that, "The Province should be the efficacious sign of [the] Christ experienced in the Exercises."[81] He dedicates the next twenty years (1969–89) to variations on the claim that, through its "option for the poor,"[82] the church becomes a "sacramental" and "mediating sign"[83] of the ongoing presence of Jesus Christ to the "crucified peoples"[84] of a broken world.[85] And Jon Sobrino says Ellacuría himself was finally transformed by the personal implications of his famous claim that the principle sign of the times "by whose light all the others should be discerned and interpreted . . . is . . . the crucified people."[86] Indeed, Sobrino argues that Ellacuría came to believe that "the foundation of his life, his vocation as a Jesuit, and deeper still, as a human being" was "to take the crucified people down from the cross."[87]

*Xavier Zubiri:* Ellacuría was ordained a priest on July 26, 1961, during his final year at Innsbruck. Six weeks later, while visiting his family in Bilbao, Spain, he decided to seek out the famous Spanish philosopher Xavier Zubiri at his home. Ellacuría had written several unanswered letters to the philosopher, and in a letter to his provincial, says he went there to tell him "that I wanted to do a doctoral dissertation with him and about him." The surprise visitors were met by the Spaniard's sister-in-law, who said that Zubiri was at Mass, and "didn't usually receive visitors." She added, however, that Zubiri had a standing exception for priests, and when Zubiri returned, Ellacuría recalls that he greeted them "with great simplicity and spontaneity." Seeing "the moment was ripe," the young man made his request, which "sat well," and even "flattered" the philosopher. He recalls that Zubiri then inquired, "what would I claim?" Ellacuría continues, "I quickly replied that I saw in him a model of the intersection between the classical and the modern, between the essential and the existential." Zubiri liked this answer, for "He smiled and said that this had actually been the goal of his work. Then he promised to put himself entirely at my disposal for whatever I needed."[88]

Cardenal says that "Zubiri was so impressed with his new disciple that he immediately wrote to his wife to say he had met 'a brilliant young Jesuit' who even knew Greek, the language in which he was weakest."[89] During the Franco Regime, Zubiri had severed all direct ties with the university, and determined "never to direct another thesis."[90] However, he steadfastly supported Ellacuría through "problems with the academic authorities . . . who rejected the idea of writing a dissertation about a living philosopher." Ellacuría eventually found a faculty member willing to direct, but not interfere, with the writing of the dissertation. He presented the outline to Zubiri in October 1963, and defended *La principalidad de la esencia en Xavier Zubiri* at the University of Complutense, in Madrid in 1965. Near the end of this process, Ellacuría made the Spiritual Exercises of St. Ignatius in Ireland, and took final vows in the Society of Jesus on February 2, 1965.

It is interesting that both teacher and student shared a predilection for theology, and an interest in Rahner. In their first conversation Zubiri spoke at great length about theology and his desire to spend two years with Rahner at Innsbruck, and two more studying Scripture in Jerusalem.[91] Zubiri dedicated the introduction of an unpublished monograph on God to Rahner, and it appears as the conclusion to his final book, *El Hombre y Dios*.[92] Cardenal adds that Zubiri once confessed that theology "satisfied him more than philosophy."[93] For his part, Ellacuría completed the courses for a doctorate in theology at the University of Comillas in Madrid in 1965, and the partial draft of a proposal for a dissertation in theology.[94]

After two more years with Zubiri, however, it was determined that Ellacuría would be sent to the University of Central America in San Salvador, which had opened its doors a year earlier. On January 29, 1967, while this decision was being discussed, Zubiri wrote that his collaboration with Ellacuría was, "unsurpassed and irreplaceable. Nobody understands me like you, and only you have my full trust."[95] Later that year Zubiri wrote personally to Fr. Pedro Arrupe, s.j., superior general of the Jesuit Order, requesting that Ellacuría be missioned to work with Zubiri full time in Spain. Arrupe was "very impressed" by the letter, and approved the request. But superiors in San Salvador did not agree. As a compromise, it was decided that Ellacuría would return to work with Zubiri in Madrid for three or four months each year.

Ellacuría wrote in 1968, summarizing the current state of their collaboration in theology, that "all the materials are ready for you to begin publishing, and for me to do the dissertation in theology."[96] But Ellacuría never wrote the dissertation, and Zubiri died September 21, 1983, still editing the manuscript on the philosophy of God, *El hombre y Dios*. Ellacuría finished editing the manuscript, did an introduction, and published the book posthumously in 1984. As Zubiri's closest collaborator and intellectual heir, he was named first director of the Xavier Zubiri Foundation in Madrid, and promoted distribution and understanding of Zubiri's writings around the world. Not surprisingly, many Latin American Jesuit seminarians from this period have studied Zubiri's work.

More than anyone else, Xavier Zubiri shaped the sweeping Christian historical realism of Ignacio Ellacuría. But Ellacuría's posthumously published magnum opus, *Philosophy of Historical Reality*, moves definitively beyond the work of his mentor by making "historical reality"[97] the proper object of his work in philosophy and theology. [98] Ellacuría explicitly accepts the systemic hypothesis of Zubiri's philosophy of science that, "All worldly reality constitutes a single complex and differentiated physical unity."[99] And he builds carefully on Zubiri's philosophical integration of the theory of evolution, analyzing matter, biological life, sentient life, and human history (in its personal and social dimensions), as subsystems of the more comprehensive reality of the cosmos.

However, he shifts the emphasis from Zubiri's more abstract focus on the unity of the material cosmos, to his own concentration on "historical reality" as the object of philosophy and theology. Ellacuría justifies this move with the argument that "historical reality is where reality is 'more,' . . . both 'more its own,' and 'more open.'"[100] It is here that reality becomes decisively human, in his view. And he believes that philosophy and theology have the duty to explore the limits and possibilities of the human freedom this entails. Indeed, it is on this point (which is derived from Zubiri) that Ellacuría will focus his most creative efforts.

This important theoretical development explains how Ellacuría moves beyond Zubiri and Rahner precisely by grounding his philosophical and theological work in a specific historical reality, that of Latin America. Interestingly enough, it is this move that allows him to treat the "option for the poor" made by the church in Latin America as a "concrete universal,"[101] (in Rahner's sense of the term) of significance for the whole church. It also grounds his prophetic cry that the "crucified people"[102] of the Third World constitute the "principle . . . sign of the times" orienting the "universal historical mission" of the church in world today. Many commentators believe the substance of this position has been explicitly confirmed by the Social Encyclicals of Pope John Paul II.

*Archbishop Oscar Romero and the People of El Salvador:* These, then, are the five teachers who Ignacio Ellacuría believed shaped the fundamentals of his life and thought. During the final decade of his life, however, Ellacuría began to insist on the importance of Archbishop Oscar Romero and the Salvadoran people in this pedagogy of transformation. In 1985 Ellacuría presented a posthumous doctorate to the archbishop on behalf of the UCA. He insists:

> no one doubted who was the teacher, and who was the assistant; who was the pastor setting the direction, and who was the implementor; who was the prophet revealing the mystery, and who was the follower; who was the one who encouraged, and who was the one encouraged; who was the voice, and who was the echo.[103]

But what was it that the UCA learned from Romero? Jon Sobrino says, "the UCA learned how to fulfill its mission as a Christian university by watching what it meant to run the Archdiocese from the perspective of solidarity with the poor."[104] And Ellacuría says the 1985 award represents "a commitment to do in our university way what he did as a pastor."[105]

In a liturgy celebrated at the university a few days after the assassination of Archbishop Romero on March 24, 1980, Ellacuría outlines what he believes the UCA learned from its self-proclaimed mentor.[106] First, Romero showed the UCA how "to historicize the force of the Gospel"[107] in a Salvadoran context. Second, Archbishop Romero showed the UCA how to empower "the poor to historicize [their own] salvation."[108] Third, Romero modeled growth as a religious leader because he humbly "changed his situation, so that what had been an opaque, amorphous and ineffective word, became a torrent of life to which the people drew near in order to quench their thirst." [109] And fourth, he says the archbishop's death taught the university to look to the Salvadoran people for the salvation preached by their mentor. Why? Because thousands of common Salvadorans were now "disposed to follow his footsteps, knowing that the Archbishop . . . was an exemplary follower of Jesus."[110]

Archbishop Oscar Romero, then, touched both the mind and the heart of Ignacio Ellacuría. He was the great mentor in faith who taught this remarkable intellectual to find God in common people of El Salvador. I will say no more about this here, as the first two articles make similar claims about what Ellacuría learned both from Romero and the people of El Salvador. We should notice, however, that the two are linked. For, more than anyone else, it was Archbishop Romero who taught Ignacio Ellacuría to see God's grace in the ever-increasing capacity of the common people of El Salvador to realize their hopes, dreams, and aspirations for a more just and humane future.

Thirty-five years after following his first great teacher to Central America, Ellacuría would recall with apparent humor that his affirmative response to the invitation of Miguel Elizondo reflected, more than anything else, the fact that "back then we had a very simple understanding of obedience."[111] Ellacuría says, "It wasn't a sacrifice or heroism."[112] And he adds, "I have never regretted having begun an American life." However, it is worth nothing that, like the Castilian accent he retained throughout his life, this phrase betrays the ongoing influence of Spain on Ignacio Ellacuría thirty-five years after his formative journey from Portugalete to San Salvador. North American readers will notice that Ellacuría does not think of his "American" life in reference to the U.S. And Central Americans will wonder why he eschews the more geographically specific "Latin" or "Central" American modifiers. From either angle, however,

Ellacuría's sense that he is living an "American life" carries the echo of a distinctively Spanish worldview.

My point is that Ellacuría lived his entire adult life at the crossroads of Spain and El Salvador. Viewed correctly, this aspect of Ellacuría's intellectual and personal biography makes the transformations he experienced all the more remarkable and interesting. It is no secret that friends and foes alike identified Ellacuría with the sometimes overbearing influence of Spanish Jesuits on the Society of Jesus in Central America.[113] Five of the six murdered priests, all of whom played important roles at the University, were Spanish. Yet, within two years of the assassinations, many younger Jesuits (though loyal to the ideals of the martyrs) called openly for reduced Spanish influence in key Jesuit positions in order to promote the "Central-Americanization" of the province.[114] It is likewise significant that, by the end of his second year as President of the University of Central America, and seven years after becoming a Salvadoran citizen, Ellacuría had spent only thirteen of his fifty-two years in the country!

These details can help us to appreciate that Ignacio Ellacuría is best understood as a genuine bridge figure. He was among the most brilliant of a generation of mid-twentieth-century Spanish Jesuits sent to serve the Catholic Church of Latin America. But he is loved and remembered mainly for having embraced, and been transformed by, a lifetime of sharing the suffering, hopes, and aspirations of the "crucified people" of El Salvador.

## The Essays

Part One of *Love That Produces Hope* approaches the thought of Ignacio Ellacuría in terms of its sources. Each article examines how Ellacuría appropriates and advances the interpretation of a particular source. And each author strives to situate his or her discussion at the intersection of the personal and intellectual strands of Ellacuría's biography. What emerges is an account of the Spaniard's efforts to "apprehend and face up to"[115] the historical reality of El Salvador and Latin America, and the formative impact of these efforts on Ellacuría's philosophical and theological thought. Part Two then presents the attempts of leading theologians and ethicists from several continents to appropriate Ellacuría's achievements as a resource for confronting their own historical realities. Together, the essays suggest the tremendous potential of Ellacuría's thought for communities living with the Christian tradition at the beginning of its third millennium.

The opening essays by Jon Sobrino, s.j., and Gustavo Gutierrez explicitly emphasize the importance of knowledge about Ellacuría as a person for understanding his contributions as an intellectual. These very personal reflections are historically significant both for the claims they make, and their authorship. The remaining articles in Part One focus on key intellectual sources and interlocutors that shape Ellacuría's corpus. Matthew Ashley examines Ellacuría as a major interpreter of the Spiritual Exercises of St. Ignatius. Robert Lassalle-Klein shows how Ellacuría reinterprets both phenomenology and the work of Xavier Zubiri in his proposals for a truly Latin American philosophy and theology of liberation. Martin Maier, s.j., makes new and important claims about the relationship of Ellacuría and Karl Rahner. And Antonio Gonzalez, s.j., whom Ellacuría considered his most brilliant student, critically examines his teacher's philosophy of liberation. Each essay shows how Ellacuría significantly advances the scholarly interpretation of his sources by historicizing them. Taken together, they provide a powerful introduction to Ellacuría's sources, and the complex interrelationship of the personal and intellectual dimensions of his journey from Spain to El Salvador.

Part Two then extends the process, showing how others are interpreting Ellacuría in historical contexts around the globe. The first essay by Kevin Burke, s.j., outlines Ellacuría's remarkable "historical soteriology." Burke looks at how this aspect of his theology emerges from and clarifies key questions confronting the Latin American church after the Bishops' Conference at Medellín, Colombia, in 1968. Roger Haight, s.j., follows with an essay examining the fundamental claims behind what he calls Ellacuría's "ecclesiology from below." He uses these to develop five original principles that structure Haight's own approach to this theme. In the third essay, María Pilar Aquino examines Ellacuría's ideas on the theological meaning of persecution and martyrdom as an expression of liberating Christian faith. Reflecting on the struggles of women and men in Mexico, Guatemala, and on the U.S.-Mexico border, she emphasizes the importance of eschatological hope in animating real communities of faith in their daily struggle for justice.

Gregory Baum then analyzes Ellacuría as a prophet of Catholic social teaching, a martyr for Medellín's option for the poor, and a pastor moved by the suffering of his people. In the next essay Aquiline Tarimo, s.j., from Tanzania, Africa, collaborates with U.S. theologian William O'Neill, s.j., to explore the remarkable promise of Ellacuría's work relating human rights and the common good. The article illustrates what the authors see as the potential contribution of Ellacuría's work for contemporary social ethics in Africa, and the ongoing "struggle of life against death" of the African Church. The collection ends with a brief, but poignant, personal reflection by Johann Baptist Metz. This is appropriate, for Metz's famous challenge to Rahner, like his "political theology," explicitly influenced Ellacuría's early work.[116] Here Metz shares his belief that the dangerous memory of Ellacuría's "Christianity of political compassion," both manifests and nurtures a "mysticism of open eyes."

As the title indicates, Jon Sobrino believes that the remarkable journey of Ignacio Ellacuría from Spain to El Salvador was characterized by "love that produces hope." The following pages, written by an outstanding international panel, are an invitation to readers to make up their own minds about this, and a host of other issues. Like any true "sign of the times," however, the thought of Ignacio Ellacuría ultimately points beyond itself. Likewise, the editors hope that this collection draws the reader's attention to the ongoing passion of Ellacuría's beloved "crucified peoples." For, like Archbishop Oscar Romero, Ignacio Ellacuría found hope in his faith that God's grace sustains the tenacious struggle of millions of men, women, and children to nurture those they love in the face of poverty, and an uncertain future at the dawn of Christianity's tragically conflicted third millennium.

---

[1] Jon Sobrino, "El asesinato-martirio de los jesuitas salvadoreños," *RLT,* no. 18 (1989) 304. ["Companions of Jesus," trans. Dinah Livingstone, in Jon Sobrino, Ignacio Ellacuría, and others, *Companions of Jesus: The Jesuit Martyrs of El Salvador,* (New York: Orbis, 1990) 56.]

[2] This image appeared in print for the first time in 1978 in an article by Ellacuría (below). It is most likely based on a famous homily delivered the year before by Archbishop Oscar Romero after the assassination of Fr. Rutilio Grande, s.j. Archbishop Romero told the terrorized peasants, "You are the image of the pierced savior." Archbishop Oscar Romero, "Homilia en Aguilares" (19-6-1977), *La voz de los sin voz: La palabra viva de Monseñor Oscar Arnulfo Romero* (San Salvador: UCA Editores, 1980) 208. See Ignacio Ellacuría, "The Crucified People," in *Mysterium Liberationis* (New York: Orbis, 1993) 580–604, trans. P. Berryman and R. Barr from "El pueblo crucificado, ensayo de soteriologia historica," originally published in I. Ellacuría and others, *Cruz y resurrección: anuncio de una Iglesia nueva* (Mexico City: CTR, 1978) 49–82; collection hereafter cited as *MLT* (English translation) and *ML* (Spanish original).

[3] United Nations, "Report of the Commission on the Truth for El Salvador," *From Madness to Hope: The 12-Year War in El Salvador* (March 15, 1993) 50.

⁴ Martha Doggett, *Death Foretold: The Jesuit Murders in El Salvador* (Washington, D.C.: Georgetown University, Lawyers Committee for Human Rights, 1993) 282, and 68; henceforth cited as Doggett, *Death Foretold*.

⁵ This is the thesis of Jon Sobrino, s.j., in "Companions of Jesus," 38.

⁶ Rudolfo Cardenal, s.j., "De Portugalete a San Salvador: de la mano de cinco maestros," in J. Sobrino, R. Alvarado, eds., *Ignacio Ellacuría, 'Aquella libertad esclarecida,'* (San Salvador: UCA Editores, 1999) 42–58, henceforth cited as "De Portugalete."

⁷ This phrase appears repeatedly. For two important examples see (1) Ignacio Ellacuría, "Is a Different Kind of University Possible?" in J. Hasset and H. Lacey, eds., *Towards a Society That Serves Its People* (Washington, D.C.: Georgetown University Press, 1991) 189, trans. P. Berryman from "Diez años después: ¿es posible una Universidad distinta?" *ECA*, nos. 324–5 (1975) 605–28; collection henceforth cited as *TSSP*; (2) "The Crucified People," 580 [*MLT*, vol. 2, 189].

⁸ Kevin F. Burke, s.j., has written an excellent monograph introducing the thought of Ignacio Ellacuría entitled *The Ground Beneath the Cross: The Theology of Ignacio Ellacuría* (Washington, D.C.: Georgetown University Press, 2000).

⁹ Ellacuría used these words to outline principles for a "truly Latin American philosophy," and to define the role of the University of Central America as a "critical and creative conscience" for El Salvador; see Ignacio Ellacuría, Rev. José María Gondra, s.j. "Discurso de la Universidad Centroamericana José Simeón Cañas en la Firma del Contrato con el BID," in *Planteamiento Universitario, 1989* (San Salvador: UCA Editores, 1989) 12. (This speech was written by Ignacio Ellacuría and delivered by Jose Maria Gondra in 1970; it has been mistakenly attributed to Rev. Luis Achaerandio, s.j.). See also Ignacio Ellacuría, "Función liberadora de la filosofía," *ECA* 40, no. 435 (1985) 47.

¹⁰ Interview with Jon Sobrino by Robert Lassalle-Klein and Barry Stenger (San Salvador: UCA, January 29, 1992) 4.

¹¹ Rudolfo Cardenal, "Ser jesuita hoy en El Salvador," *ECA*, nos. 493–4 (1989) 1013–21, henceforth cited as Cardenal "Ser jesuita hoy." For revised and expanded versions of this article, see "Ignacio Ellacuría (1930–1989)," http://www.uca.edu.sv/martires/new/ella/fella.htm (San Salvador, septiembre 1999), henceforth cited as Cardenal, "Ignacio Ellacuría." See also Cardenal, "De Portugalete"; Teresa Whitfield, *Paying the Price: Ignacio Ellacuría and the Murdered Jesuits of El Salvador* (Philadelphia: Temple University Press, 1994) 15–7.

¹² Cardenal, "De Portugalete," 43.

¹³ Cardenal, "Ser jesuita hoy," 1013.

¹⁴ Ibid.

¹⁵ Whitfield, 25.

¹⁶ Cardenal, "Ignacio Ellacuría," 4.

¹⁷ Ibid., 6; and Cardenal, "Ser jesuita hoy," 1017.

¹⁸ José Ellacuría, in a talk at the UCA, San Salvador, November 15, 1990. Cited in Whitfield, 16; Cardenal, "Ignacio Ellacuría," 1.

¹⁹ Interview with Fr. Miguel Elizondo (1990), cited in Whitfield, 22; see also 21–4.

²⁰ Whitfield, 21.

²¹ Interview with Cesar Jerez (1991), cited in Whitfield, 24.

²² Ignacio Ellacuría, "Presentacion," in "Reunion-Ejercicios de la Viceprovincia Jesuitica de Centroamerica, Diciembre 1969," *Reflexion teologico-espiritual de la Compañia de Jesus en Centroamerica, II* (San Salvador: Archives of the Society of Jesus, Central American Province, Survey S.J. de Centroamérica, diciembre 1969) 1, henceforth cited as "Reunion-Ejercicios, 1969." Juan Hernandez Pico asserts that this discussion, and a corresponding proposal developed at the Province Congregation of 1970, contributed seminal ideas to what eventually became the famous "Decree Two: The Jesuits Today" of the worldwide 32nd General Congregation of the Society of Jesus, Dec. 2, 1974–March 7, 1975; see Juan Hernandez Pico, *Historia Reciente de la Provincia de Centroamerica (1976–1986)* (San Salvador: Ediciones Cardoner, 1991) 9–10; henceforth cited as Pico, *Historia Reciente.*

²³ Elizondo delivered the following talks: "The Theological and Spiritual Meaning of a Communal Meeting of the Vice-Province"; "The First Week as the Indispensable Beginning of Conversion"; "The Ignatian Vision of the Following of Christ"; "Prayer in the Society of Jesus." See "El Sentido Teológico y Espiritual de una Reunión Comunitaria de la Vice-provincia," "La Primera Semana como comienzo indispensable de conversion," "La vision ignaciana del seguimiento de Cristo," and "La Oración en al Compañia de Jesús" in "Reunion-Ejercicios, 1969," 31, 37–45, 46–57, 76–83, 88–95.

²⁴ Ellacuría delivered the following talks: "The Goal and the Meaning of the Meeting"; "Our Collective Situation Seen from the Perspective of the First Week"; "The Problem of Translating the Spirit of the Exercises to the Vice-Province"; "The Third World as the Optimal Place for the Christian Life of the Exercises." See "Finalidad y Sentido de la Reunión," "Nuestra situación colectiva vista desde la perspective de la Primera Semana," "El problema del traslado del espíritu de los Ejercicios a la Vice," "El Tercer Mundo como lugar óptimo de la vivencia cristiana de los Ejercicios" in "Reunion-Ejercicios, 1969," 31, 32–6, 58–71, 99–115, 124–38.

²⁵ Karl Rahner, "Basic Theological Interpretation of the Second Vatican Council," in *Concern for the Church: Theological Investigations XX* (New York: Crossroad, 1981) 82.

²⁶ For a detailed analysis of this meeting see Robert Lassalle-Klein, *Blood and Ink* (New York: Crossroads, forthcoming).

²⁷ Héctor Jesús Samour Canán, "Voluntad de liberación: Génesis y constitución del proyecto de filosofía de liberación de Ignacio Ellacuría" (San Salvador: University of Central America José Simeón Cañas, doctoral thesis) 25; henceforth cited as Samour, "Voluntad de liberación."

²⁸ Cardenal, "De Portugalete," 44.

²⁹ Ibid.

³⁰ Espinoza Pólit was born July 11, 1894, and died January 21, 1961. The encomium is dated February 5, 1961 from Innsbruck, Austria, where Ellacuría was nearing the end of his studies in theology with his fourth great teacher, Karl Rahner.

³¹ Ignacio Ellacuria, "El P. Aurelio Espinosa Pólit, s.j." *Escritos filosóficos,* vol. 1 (San Salvador: UCA Editores, 1996) 530; originally published in *ECA,* no. 178 (1963) 21–4; henceforth cited as "Espinoza Pólit."

³² Ibid., 530.

³³ Ibid., 530.

³⁴ Ibid., 529.

[35] Ibid., 531.

[36] Ibid., 532.

[37] Cardenal, "Ser jesuita hoy," 1014.

[38] Samour, "Voluntad de liberación," 26–7.

[39] Cardenal, "Ser jesuita hoy," 1014.

[40] Samour, "Voluntad de liberación," 24.

[41] "Espinoza Pólit," 527, 525.

[42] Ibid.

[43] "Espinoza Pólit," 532.

[44] "Espinoza Pólit," 532.

[45] See the essay in this volume by Jon Sobrino, "Ignacio Ellacuría as a Human Being and a Christian," henceforth cited as Sobrino, "Human Being and Christian;" originally published as Jon Sobrino, "Ignacio Ellacuría, el hombre y el cristiano. 'Bajar de la cruz al pueblo crucificado,'" *RLT,* nos. 32–3 (1994) 131–61, 215–44.

[46] Ignacio Ellacuría, "Angel Martínez Baigorri, s.j.," in *Escritos filosóficos,* vol. 1, 117; collection henceforth cited as *EF;* essay henceforth cited as "Angel Martínez."

[47] Cardenal, "De Portugalete," 48.

[48] Ibid., 50.

[49] Ignacio Ellacuría, "Carta de I. Ellacuría a A. Martínez" (Ecuador, Julio de 1954), in *Escritos filosóficos,* vol. 1, no. 201; Ellacuría's letters to Martínez cited with place and date of composition as "Carta a Martínez."

[50] Cardenal, "De Portugalete," 50.

[51] Ibid., 48.

[52] Ellacuría, "Carta a Martínez" (Ecuador, Julio de 1954) 199; cited (n.p.) in Cardenal, "De Portugalete," 48.

[53] Ellacuría, "Angel Martínez," 118.

[54] Ellacuría, "Carta a Martínez" (San Salvador, 11 de febrero de 1956) 211.

[55] Sobrino, "Ignacio Ellacuría, the Human Being and the Christian," in *Love That Produces Hope,* 1.

[56] Ellacuría, "Carta a Martínez" (Ecuador, Julio de 1954) 202.

[57] Ellacuría, "Carta a Martínez" (San Salvador, August 2, 1955) 209.

[58] Samour, "Voluntad de liberación," 32. The quotations from Ellacuría are taken from Ellacuría, "Angel Martínez," 155, 157.

[59] Cardenal, "Ser jesuita hoy," 1014–5.

[60] See the entries for these years in Ellacuría's bibliography below.

[61] Cardenal, "Ser jesuita hoy," 1015.

[62] Cardenal, "Ignacio Ellacuría," 5.

[63] Letter from Aurelio Pólit to Ignacio Ellacuría, 1958. Quoted in Cardenal, "Ignacio Ellacuría," 5.

[64] Cardenal, "Ignacio Ellacuría," 5.

[65] Victor Codina, "Ignacio Ellacuría, teologo y martir," *Revista Latinoamericana de Teologia,* no. 21 (September–December 1990) 263. Cited in Cardenal, "Ignacio Ellacuría," 28.

[66] Cardenal, "Ser jesuita hoy," 1015

[67] Ibid.

[68] Cardenal, "Ignacio Ellacuría," 6.

[69] Cardenal, "Ser jesuita hoy," 1015. Cardenal adds, however, that Ellacuría was also impressed by Hugo Rahner and Andres Jurgmann.

[70] See Herbert Vorgrimler, *Understanding Karl Rahner: An Introduction to His Life and Thought* (New York: Crossroad, 1986) 99, trans. John Bowden from *Karl Rahner verstehen. Eine Einführung in sein Leben und Denken* (Freiburg: Verlag Herder, 1985).

[71] Maier, "Karl Rahner: The Teacher of Ignacio Ellacuría," in *Love That Produces Hope,* 125.

[72] Jon Sobrino, "Ignacio Ellacuría, el hombre y el cristiano." "Bajar de la curz al pueblo crucificado" II, *Revista Latinoamericano de teología,* no. 33 (1994) 241; see below Sobrino, "Ignacio Ellacuría, the Human Being and the Christian," 59 (*RLT,* no. 33, 241).

[73] Ellacuría, "El Tercer Mundo Como Lugar Optimo de la Vivencia Cristiana de los Ejercicios," in "Reunion-Ejercicios, 1969," 2.

[74] Laurence A. Egan, M.M. "Forward," in Ignacio Ellacuría, *Freedom Made Flesh: The Mission of Christ and His Church* (Maryknoll, N.Y.: Orbis, 1976) viii, trans. John Drury from *Teologia politica* (San Salvador: Ediciones del Secretariado Social Interdiocesano, 1973); original collection henceforth cited as *TP,* English translation as *FMF.*

[75] Ignacio Ellacuría, *TP,* esp. 9–10, 44–69 [*FMF,* 15–8, 82–126]. See also Ignacio Ellacuría, "Repuesta crítica a 'Nota sobre la publicación *Teología política* del Reverendo Padre Ignacio Ellacuría, s.j.'" (San Salvador: Archivos Ignacio Ellacuría, April 24, 1974), henceforth cited as Ellacuría, "Repuesta crítica."

[76] Karl Rahner, "Theology of the Symbol," *Theological Investigations,* IV (Baltimore: Helicon Press, 1966) 221–52.

[77] Ellacuría, *TP,* 9 [*FMF,* 18].

[78] Rahner, "Theology of the Symbol," 237.

[79] Ellacuría, *TP,* 48 [*FMF,* 89].

[80] Ellacuría, "Repuesta crítica," 6–7.

[81] "El Problema del Traslado del Espiritu de los Ejercicios a la Vice-provincia," in "Reunion-Ejercicios," 6.

[82] Ignacio Ellacuría, "Aporte de la teología de la liberación a las religiones Abráhamicas en la superación del individualismo y del positivismo," *RLT,* no. 10 (1987) 9, 15; henceforth cited as "Religiones Abráhamicas."

[83] Ellacuría, *TP,* 47–8 [*FMF,* 87–9]; and "Fe y Justicia," in I. Ellacuría and others, eds., *Fe, Justicia y Opcion por los Oprimidos* (Bilbao, Spain: Editorial Desclée de Brouwer, 1980) 23.

[84] Ellacuría, "El pueblo crucificado," 49–82 [*MLT,* 580–604].

[85] Ellacuría makes analogous claims regarding "Latin American theology"; the "Christian University" and its graduates; Archbishop Oscar Romero; Latin American philosophy; the "Abrahamic religions"; those who "seek truth"; advocates of human rights, and so on. See Ignacio Ellacuría, "Hacia una fundamentacion del metodo teologico Latinoamericano," *ECA,* nos. 322–3 (1975) 409–25, henceforth cited as "Hacia una fundamentación;" "Tesis sobre la posibilidad, necesidad y sentido de una teologia Latinoamericana," *Teologia y mundo contemporaneo: homenaje a Karl Rahner,* A. Vargas Machua, ed. (Madrid: Ediciones Cristiandad, 1975) 325–50; "Diez años despues;

¿es posible una universidad distinta?" *ECA,* nos. 324–5 (1975) 605–28; "La inspiracion Cristiana de la UCA en la docencia," *Planteamiento universitario 1989* (San Salvador, El Salvador: Universidad Centroamericana Jose Simeon Canas, febrero 1989) 195–200; "Monsenor Romero, un enviado de Dios para Salvador a su pueblo," *Sal Terrae,* no. 811 (1980) 825–32 and *RLT,* no. 19 (1990) 5–10; "Funcion liberadora de la filosofia," *ECA,* no. 435 (1985) 45–64; "Religiones Abráhamicas," 3–27; "Voluntad de fundamentalidad y voluntad de verdad: conocimiento-fe y su configuración histórica," *RLT,* no. 8 (1986) 113–32; "Human Rights in a Divided Society," in A. Hennelly and J. Langan, eds., *Human Rights in the Americas: The Struggle for Consensus* (Washington, D.C.: Georgetown Univ. Press, 1982) 52–65.

[86] Ignacio Ellacuría, "Discernir el signo de los tiempos," *Diakonía* 17 (1981) 58, 59.

[87] Sobrino, "Ignacio Ellacuría as a Human Being and a Christian," 5 (*RLT,* no. 33, p. 240).

[88] Ignacio Ellacuría, "Entrevista con Zubiri (San Sebastián, 8 de septiembre de 1961)," in *EF,* vol. 2, 26.

[89] Cardenal, "Ignacio Ellacuría," 6.

[90] Cardenal, "De Portugalete," 53.

[91] Ellacuría, "Entrevista con Zubiri (San Sebastián, 8 de septiembre de 1961)," in *EF,* vol. 2, 20.

[92] Ignacio Ellacuría, "Presentacion," in Xavier Zubiri, *El hombre y Dios* (Madrid, Spain: Alianza Editorial, 1984) ix. Ellacuría explains that it was his editorial decision to append this introduction as the conclusion to Zubiri's posthumously published *El hombre y Dios.*

[93] Cardenal, "De Portugalete," 55.

[94] Ignacio Ellacuría, "Estado actual de la teología fundamental" (San Salvador: Archivos Ignacio Ellacuría, n.d.). Cited in Rocío de los Reyes Ramírez, Archivo de Ignacio Ellacuría (Seville, Spain: Universidad Internacionál de Andalucía) 77.

[95] Ignacio Ellacuría, "Carta de I. Ellacuría a X. Zubiri (29 de jenero de 1967)," *EF,* vol. 2, 59.

[96] Ignacio Ellacuría, "Carta de I. Ellacuría a X. Zubiri (15 de agosto de 1968)," *EF,* vol. 2, 65.

[97] Ignacio Ellacuría, *Filosofía de la realidad histórica* (San Salvador: UCA Editores, 1990) 42; henceforth cited as *FRH.*

[98] Ellacuría substitutes "historical reality" for Zubiri's more abstract "unity of *intramundane* reality"; see ibid., 30, 25.

[99] Ellacuría, *FRH,* 31.

[100] Ibid.

[101] Karl Rahner, *Spirit in the World* (New York: Continuum, 1968, 1994) 124, and "The Orientation Towards Universality in the Particular and Successful History of Revelation," in *Foundations of Christian Faith* (New York: Crossroad, 1978) 161. See Ellacuría, *FMF* 145, 146 [*TP,* 80].

[102] Ellacuría, "Discernir 'El signo' de los tiempos," 58, 59.

[103] Ignacio Ellacuría, "La UCA ante el doctorado concedido a Monseñor Romero," *ECA,* no. 437 (1985) 168; *Escritos Universitarios* (San Salvador: UCA Editores, 1999) 232.

[104] Interview of Jon Sobrino by Robert Lassalle-Klein, May 8, 1994, 4.

[105] Ellacuría, "La UCA ante el doctorado concedido a Monseñor Romero," 167.

[106] This detail provided by Jon Sobrino in "Ignacio Ellacuría as a Human Being and a Christian," 57.

[107] Ignacio Ellacuría, "Monseñor Romero, un enviado de Dios para salvar a su pueblo," *RLT,* no. 19 (1990) 6.

[108] Ibid., 7.

[109] Ibid., 8.

[110] Ibid., 10.

[111] Cardenal, "De Portugalete," 43.

[112] "El volcán jesuita: entrevista con el Padre Ellacuría, Rector de la Universidad Centroamericana," *ABC,* Madrid, March 28, 1982; cited in Whitfield, 17; Whitfield cited in Cardenal, "De Portugalete," 44.

[113] November 13, 1989, three days before the assassinations, "La Prensa Gráfica" stated "it is of the utmost urgency that the Jesuits are thrown out of the country," and falsely charges "[t]he Spanish Jesuit priest, Ignacio Ellacuría" with making the University a guerrilla arms depot. See Doggett, *Death Foretold,* 309.

[114] This issue is mentioned as the central challenge facing the province in the brief history by Juan Hernandez Pico; see Pico, *Historia Reciente,* 3. See also, "Interview of Jesuits in Formation," by Robert Lassalle-Klein, (San Salvador, July, 1994).

[115] Ellacuría says that "the formal structure of intelligence and its differentiating function . . . is not to understand and grasp meaning, but to apprehend reality and to face up to that reality." Ellacuría, "Hacia una fundamentacion," 419.

[116] In the 1969 Jesuit retreat, Ellacuría indirectly acknowledges the influence of Metz's critique of Rahner: "A short time ago a group of young German theologians wrote to Karl Rahner asking him to stop his abstractions and to reflect on concrete reality, about which he has always reflected, but particularly on this worldly reality, and to conceive of it in theological terms. That is the small attempt that I am making here." Ellacuría, "El tercer mundo como lugar optimo de la vivencia christiana de Los Ejercicios," in "Reunion-Ejercicios," 128. For related references to Rahner see *TP,* 58; "Religiones Abráhamicas"; "La teología de la liberación frente al cambio socio-histórico de América Latina," *RLT,* no. 12 (1987) 241–64.

Part One

# Sources of Ellacuría's Thought

# Chapter 1

# Ignacio Ellacuría, the Human Being and the Christian: "Taking the Crucified People Down from the Cross"*

*Jon Sobrino, S.J.*

The figure of Ignacio Ellacuría, in its tremendous wealth, can be examined from a variety of perspectives. Ellacuría emerged as an important *public personality,* intellectual, philosopher, and theologian beginning in the 1970s. During the 1980s he was president of the University of Central America (UCA), and was known for his role as a mediator and negotiator in El Salvador's political process. But underlying everything, through it all, and manifested there, was Ignacio Ellacuría, the *person,* the human being, and the Christian.

Though one's person and their public personality cannot be adequately distinguished, we focus on his person in this article, first of all because this is what we were asked to do, but also because it seems extremely useful and beneficial for several reasons.

*First,* knowledge about him as a person enables one to better understand and appreciate Ellacuría's intellectual achievement, and his sociopolitical impact as a public personality. It also stimulates and

* Translated by Robert Lassalle-Klein.

1

facilitates the study of his work and his cause, all of which the world needs today.

To understand this adequately one must accept, on the one hand, who he came to be as a person. This was expressed—in Rahner's sense of the term—in the public personality. It is also true, on the other hand, that Ellacuría's achievement can survive independently of the knowledge we might have of him as a person.[1] Indeed, as he himself used to say, following Zubiri, human actions, in addition to operating *opus operantis,* become *opus operatum,* actions that are objectified in history.[2] However, it is also true that since the events of his life are recent, knowledge of Ellacuría as a person can serve as an indispensable hermeneutical principle for understanding his thought, and the meaning it gave to his praxis.

To give some important examples, the meanings Ellacuría attributed to concepts like realism, mediation, revolution, the church of the poor, persecution, prophecy, and so on, are better understood in reference to the concrete details of who he was as a person, who he was in his deepest reality. This is even truer of limit concepts such as utopia, the "more" of history, the following of Christ, faith in God, and so on.[3] Even if we admit, then, the necessary circularity and mutual reference between the person and the public personality, I believe that in order to deeply understand Ellacuría's thought and praxis it is necessary, and certainly very helpful, to understand the precise nature of his life as a person and as a Christian.

Ellacuría's way of being, existentially and concretely, freely and consciously chosen over the course of a lifetime, brings us to the same conclusion. Antonio González has said, drawing a parallel to Socrates, "what distinguishes the intellectual work of Ignacio Ellacuría does not consist so much in his having placed the historical praxis of liberation at the center of his philosophical reflections, but rather in having made philosophy a constitutive element of a life dedicated to liberation."[4] In other words, his intellectual and political work for liberation is an expression, and an important one, but in the end, only an expression of something more fundamental in Ellacuría. It is an expression, we might say, of the *unum necesarium:* his personal dedication to the task of liberating the oppressed.

The *second* reason for turning to Ellacuría, the person, is to avoid two dangers: distorting the overall picture, and manipulating the deepest truth about Ellacuría—which would tend to distance us existentially not only from his person, but also from his cause.

It is dangerous to focus too quickly on what can be praised or criticized in his life as an intellectual, for which he is usually admired due to the extraordinary depth of his Zubirian theory, or his theology of liberation. I speak of danger, because an over hasty focus on his work as an intellectual can lead to reductionism, and may function existentially as a subtle excuse for not doing—in our own way and with our more limited abilities—what he did with his exceptional philosophical and theological talent. I am referring to the well-known mechanism of admiration in order to avoid imitation, or, in religious language, of canonizing—sanctifying—in order to create distance. I fear this happens frequently to Ellacuría.

It is likewise dangerous to concentrate too quickly on his political praxis. That usually leads to its distortion and even manipulation in the service of movements and processes, of whatever variety.[5] These approaches have sometimes made it seem that Ellacuría allowed his analysis and praxis to be guided by whether and how historical processes—accepting ethical and Christian norms—might benefit the poor and oppressed common majorities, and by nothing more. I believe the most efficacious way to avoid that type of manipulation is to return to who he was as a person.

The *third* reason is of a different nature. It is beneficial and even necessary to remember him as a person because this becomes good news more easily than his thought or praxis considered in themselves, something humanizing in principle for all.

In this quite trivialized and gray world, without utopias or dreams, it is important to meet persons who communicate light and inspiration by their way of being. This makes us able to be human and Christian. These persons must be sought out like the precious pearl, and thanks should be given when they are found. John XXIII, Archbishop Romero, and Father Arrupe were these types of persons. While they were perhaps not "perfect in all things," they indeed showed themselves to be "human." They have communicated truth, dignity, hope, love, and a meaning for life.

So, I speak of Ignacio Ellacuría in these terms as well. This is necessary, for the world in which we live does not seem to have the least interest in introducing or offering us persons like him, or the others we have mentioned. These people are good news because each of them, in their own particular way, communicates light and inspiration. Together they help purify the air we inhale, not so much the body, but the human spirit. The ecological problem is global, and for that reason a proper ecology of the spirit is needed. Persons like Ellacuría make an important contribution to the construction of this ecology of the spirit, introducing a meaning for life and faith into the environment.

These personal values, the roots of his person, will be examined in what follows. We will do this from the dual perspective of what is human and what is Christian, showing that both converge in his person. But they do not intersect as a simple juxtaposition, forming a whole by mere addition of externals, one upon another. Rather, they form an essentially mutual reference, one to the other, as he himself theoretically understood this relationship. What is Christian, both in history and as transcendent, is historicized and must be historicized in what is human to become real. On the other hand, what is human is always, and in essence, open to the "more," to the transcendent. Indeed, it encounters its historical fulfillment—this was the substance of Ellacuría's faith—in what is Christian, understood in terms of Jesus of Nazareth.

In studying the person of Ellacuría, we focus neither on his character, nor the qualities and limitations of his temperament.[6] Rather, we focus on what Ellacuría left behind that is objectively beneficial and liberating for our country, the church, and the Society of Jesus. In a way of speaking used frequently here, we focus on a tradition that is simultaneously human and Christian. This is something objective and positive—a physical track carved in history—that Ellacuría helped to generate. And its mere existence helps us travel along it. This tradition, in any case, lives on as a demand and an invitation to us to follow it.

Finally, this article is based on certain personal memories I recount in the form of brief reflections. These are illustrated with significant quotes from Ellacuría that allow him to speak for himself. The great richness of his person has not made the selection of relevant material easy. I have let myself be guided by what seems most useful for the world today. The memories upon which these reflections are based come from the sixteen years I lived with him. Since those years—1974 to 1989—were extremely dense historically, and since he was not at all given to pretense, I believe I can say that I came to know him well, including the deepest dimensions of his person.

## Part I: The Human Being

### 1. Taking the Crucified People Down from the Cross

If anything in Ellacuría forcefully drew my attention from the very first, it was his passion for service. His fundamental or perhaps transcendental question was always "what should I do?" This was his historical embodiment of the typically Ignatian desire "to seek God's will in all things, and carry it out." The question he asked in everyday practice (at the categorical level one could say) so as not to avoid or dilute what he had to do, was also typical of St. Ignatius: "Where am I going, and why?" The core of his actions was, finally, service; likewise the essence of the Ignatian ideal, "to love and serve God in all things."

In my opinion, this was the foundation of his life, and his vocation as a Jesuit, and deeper still, as a human being: knowing you are called to serve, using all your talents, even your defects, to serve in the best way possible, and staying faithful to the end.[7] With no exaggeration and strictly speaking, his life was a decentered life, a life of service *for* others, and, more and more, service *from the place of* others. This emerged from the reality that it was others who both gave meaning to his life, and who taught him how to serve.

He not only dedicated his life to service, but throughout he constantly asked himself, as one who knew he was called, what this service meant concretely. Slowly he came to understand that it was not just any service, but a specific service: *to take the crucified people down from the cross.* This is what we want to study below.

### 1.1. The Root of Everything: The Suffering of the Victims

Ellacuría was not at all the sentimentalist. But his life was indeed poured out in compassion, understood in a very specific sense: (a) as a (re)action, not just a feeling in the strict sense, (b) to the suffering of victims, especially the historical victims, (c) which involves taking their side and joining in their struggle for liberation from their victimizers, (d) historicized in the lived reality of the victim and their suffering, and (e) all because of the mere fact that such suffering exists.[8] Such compassion, as we said, must be historicized. Ellacuría basically historicized it in the form of justice, both because there are great multitudes of wounded lying in the road—entire peoples, millions of human beings, "broken and wasted," as he said—and because their wounds have been caused by injustice, above all, by structural injustice.

I want to insist, however, that the origin of all this lies neither in a disembodied categorical imperative, nor in an aesthetic attraction to putting some theory of justice into practice. Its origin lies in the fact that Ellacuría was moved to the depths by the sight of a people prostrate, oppressed, deceived, ridiculed—in the forceful terms he always used. He reacted to this, not just by way of lament. Indeed, he never made peace with the pain it implies, as postmodernism tends to do today (even when it does so with a good conscience) when it argues that one must accept fragmentation, or as neoliberalism does when it insists there is no other solution.

In this sense and for this reason, I would like to say that from the start Ellacuría was, and remained to the end, a radical. The suffering of victims has deep roots, and it is these roots that must be pulled out (no small thing), and replaced by others that produce life and fraternity. This is why to the end of his days he rebelled against "the geoculture of despair and the theology of inevitability,"[9] so regnant today. Thus, in his last public speech in Barcelona on November 6, 1989, a kind of last will and testament, he spoke the following words:

> It is from this universal and solidarity-based perspective of the common majorities that the problematic of a new historical project emerges. This project, which is continually pointing from prophetic denunciation and utopian affirmation toward a process of revolutionary change, consists in reversing the principal sign shaping the civilization of the world.[10]

Such talk about *revolution,* which is to say, about radical transformations, and about *reversing history,* or a 180-degree turn in history, is not something frequently heard these days. That is why—to truly understand who Ignacio Ellacuría was—we begin with these words, which might also serve as a conclusion. We do this as a way of insisting that what he said so vigorously at the end of his life, is what gave meaning to his whole life: the struggle to reverse a history of inhumanity.

This radical attitude does not reflect some youthful flippancy, or the irresponsibility of someone who was just an academic. Rather, it was the fruit of his seriousness about reality. This is why Ellacuría demanded from the intellectual, and analogously from everyone else, the following four things—I cite from memory. Ellacuría demands *objectivity* in order to come closer to reality, to grasp it, and to analyze it just as it is. It is here, of course, that the option for the poor originates as an objective demand of reality. He demands *realism,* so that we will take steps that are adapted to reality, and therefore possible. Ellacuría understands these as *steps,* however. By definition they are to be achieved and then *overstepped,* in order to arrive at what is really intended, and must never be lost from sight. He demands *prophecy* to denounce the evils of reality—without compromising oneself—and because evil presents itself as an ultimate. Finally, he requires *utopia* to indicate what the rejection of various evils is pointing to and the horizon for personal and social fulfillment.

Ellacuría's genius, in my opinion, is that he insists on the need for these four things, and realizes them simultaneously. But it must be insisted that what moved, lent force, and gave direction to each, and what existentially drove him to combine them all, was the pain that the suffering of the victims caused him. It was a suffering that he never minimized, and with which he never made peace. It was fundamental and foundational in the life of Ellacuría. We will examine this in what follows.

Above all, Ellacuría stayed close to, and always tried to keep his eyes on, reality. This is not at all obvious among those who belong to the middle class, among those who work professionally at universities, and among those who have institutional responsibility in the Church and religious life.[11] What he saw was the *true* reality, that is, reality as it is. In fact, this was Ellacuría's chief interest as a philosopher. Affected to the core by this true reality, he formulated it in many and varied ways. He understood it, above all, as an inhuman poverty, cruel and unjust death for the majorities. He expressed this in Christian language of unrivaled power—and, in my view, unrivaled rigor—to communicate the radical and ultimate character of how he viewed and judged reality.

> Among the many signs that constantly appear, some calling for attention and others barely noticeable, there is one in every age that is most important, by whose light all the others should be discerned and interpreted. This sign is always the historically crucified people, whose permanent character includes the ever-distinctive historical form of their crucifixion. This crucified people is the historical succession of the servant of Yahweh, from whom the sin of the world continues to take away all human form, and whom the powers of this world dispossess of everything, seizing even their lives, above all their lives.[12]

This theological way of thinking about reality—calling the poor of this world the suffering servant of Yahweh or comparing them to Christ crucified—shows the power and the mood of Ellacuría the theologian. But it also shows his perception of the tragedy of reality: death, the terrible pain of the victims of this world. This is how Ellacuría saw the true reality of our world. Conceptualizing reality in Christian language raises it to the level of a theological concept. Above all, however, it lays a radical judgment on our world, one that is not at all postmodern or even guided by modernity. This world is sin, radical negativity, a radical negation of the will of God, and the highest manifestation of the rejection of God. This world is the historical appearance of the servant of Yahweh as suffering servant and the appearance of Christ as crucified.

He also insists philosophically on the de-ideologizing and unmasking character that reality, concealed, should have. Here Ellacuría protests against Heidegger that, "perhaps instead of asking why there is being rather than nothingness, he should have been asking why there is nothingness—no being, no reality, no truth, etc.—instead of being."[13] The first impact that reality makes is that of radical negativity.

One may or may not share Ellacuría's theological and philosophical analysis. But what cannot be doubted is the impact the tragedy of this world had on him. He said in 1989 on the occasion of the fifth centennial, in authentic and prophetic language, that what happened five centuries before was not a discovery, but rather a cover-up. Putting it in historical terms, he added that the Latin American people, first by the Spaniards and Portuguese, and now by North Americans, "have been abandoned like a Christ."[14]

## 1.2. The Passion for Justice

Shortly after their deaths, there was a desire to honor the UCA martyrs in a Christian ceremony. The intention was to attribute to each—since there were eight—the Beatitude that best fit them. Without exception the Beatitude attributed to Ellacuría was "blessed are those who hunger and thirst for justice." It was the right choice.

Justice was Ellacuría's obsession, because it corresponded to his innate sense of fairness, and perhaps also to his temperament as a fighter and challenger. For him, it was not a question only of eliminating or alleviating poverty. Rather it was about really changing an antagonistic world, divided between the impoverished and those who impoverish others, between victims and executioners. It is a world that represents the greatest human failure, the very self-destruction of the human family, and the greatest failure of the creator God.[15] That is why he spoke about the reality of the poor, neither frivolously nor lightly, as the reality of "crucified peoples." He did so in order to express that entire peoples are dying and, moreover, they are unjustly condemned to death by other human beings.

Looking at the real world, Ellacuría certainly supported any good work that might alleviate human suffering. The pain and the death of millions of victims at the hands of a few moved him to prioritize not just any action, though it might be good, but specifically love and compassion that is directed toward the oppressed majorities, that is, justice. This efficacious love for the majorities (and not an elitist or superior spirit) is what guided his choices about what he must do, and what motivated the great deeds to which he aspired and the relationships he developed, when necessary, with the powerful in history.

Thus, the primacy he gave to justice led him to favor the type of praxis that had the greatest effect on structures. Likewise, he supported works and activities that had direct contact with the poor. But he privileged those that had a potentially significant effect on the majorities. That was the reason for his admiration and support, and affection as well, for Rutilio Grande and the team in Aguilares. It was his personal way of historicizing the well-known words of St. Ignatius, "the more universal the good, the more divine."

Ellacuría also insisted on the dialectical relationship, mutually exclusive and antagonistic, between justice and injustice. This is why by the end of the 1960s he spoke about the need not only for development but also, formally, for liberation. He saw it as the correlative of oppression and as necessary for justice to become real. He did this even before what was being developed in Brazil and the Southern Cone became popularized in Central America. In existential terms, and to express the antagonism between justice and injustice, he spoke early on about the unavoidable vulnerability to persecution in the fight against injustice. This antagonism also led him to speak about the distinction and the opposition between the gods who favor this or that: the God of life versus the idols of death.[16]

Finally, Ellacuría saw justice as a key reality—not the only reality, certainly—from which to understand and construct the fundamental content of his theology. Its content was the reign of God, the reign of a sufficient and dignified life for the poor and—having eradicated oppression and repression—a reign of fraternity for all. This was what the prophets of the Old Testament and Jesus of Nazareth announced, and what liberation theology understands it to be today.

> What Jesus came to announce and realize, that is, the Reign of God, is what must become the unifying objective of all Christian theology, as well as Christian morality and pastoral work. What true followers of Jesus should pursue is the maximum realization possible of the Reign of God in history.[17]

### 1.3. The University in the Service of Liberation

Ellacuría was certainly an exceptional fighter and theoretician for justice. In my view, his most original and creative work was not in this area, however, but rather in two other things. The first was his ability to imagine any personal or institutional reality in terms of its potential for the promotion of justice. The second was his way of letting the suffering of victims become an absolute. He allowed it to interrogate processes of liberation, so prolonged and changing, so that they might seek the best solutions from the point of view of this suffering. This is what I want to demonstrate in this and the following sections, focusing on two important examples: his theory of the university, and his accompaniment of the El Salvadoran process. Let us look at the first.

Ellacuría felt that everyone, persons and institutions, should place themselves at the service of justice. In the Third World, and certainly in El Salvador, he believed justice must pass through the historical door of liberation.[18] This meant that, for Ellacuría, the university professional, this generic demand was concretized existentially in how the university should understand itself in terms of liberation and its service of liberation.[19]

How to bring the university and liberation together is not at all clear. History shows that the university has not even theoretically been conceived in terms of the perspective and the end of justice and liberation. But even if the essential relation of the university and liberation were accepted theoretically, a difficult problem remains. How is the specific character of the university to be placed at the service of liberation in such a way that it serves liberation without doing violence to or losing its character as a university? Ellacuría saw the task, then, as looking for a way to make the *university* and *liberation* intersect. To this he added the need to rethink both the *political dimension* of the university, so evident given the explosive historical situation, and—as a Jesuit who had been given a university mission—the *Christian inspiration* of the university. Let us look at the basic elements of his response.

(a) Ellacuría insisted that what had to be placed at the service of the liberation of the popular majorities was a *university* and not something else, that is, an institution for which the cultivation of rational knowledge and, in some way, culture, is essential. That is why he insisted on the need for generating knowledge. The idea was to come to know reality, its positive dimensions, its problems, and above all causes and solutions, through research. All this was to be communicated in teaching, so that what should be taught in and through each course was the national reality. He also used to say, "other universities can better us in other fields, but nobody should know more about the reality of our country than the UCA."

He was also convinced that a university, while remaining a university, could be helpful to the process of liberation. This is because reason, as theoretical and practical, prophetic and utopian reason, is useful and many times irreplaceable in order to achieve the kind of truth that should guide processes of liberation. Between the university, which exercises reason, and a process of liberation demanded by reality, not only does no opposition exist, but there is a convergence.

(b) The source of this conviction would have to be studied, but it was certainly very profound.[20] Perhaps it came from a personal experience that the truth always illuminates and enlivens, even though it may also plunge us into doubts and questions. In my opinion, however, it grew from verifying through reason how the truth of reality is established and how solutions emerge. In this way the specific processes of liberation come to be based on solid ground. Conversely, I believe it grew from showing how, without reason, grave errors are committed by letting oneself be carried away in such serious affairs simply by enthusiasm and a good heart, or by dogmatic prejudices. This was confirmed for him by historical evidence that it is the powerful and the oppressors who crush reason and suffocate truth. It is the poor and oppressed who fear neither reason nor truth. They want it to be proclaimed and consider it in their favor.

The former was denounced by Paul's words, "Woe unto those who crush the truth with injustice!" (Rom 1:16). The apostle also denounces the pervasive dehumanization that accompanies the primitive deeds involved in crushing the truth. This was the general reality in our country when institutionalized lies, which created further dehumanization, proliferated. The latter assertion about the poor, which seems more unthinkable a priori, was also our overall experience. When Archbishop Romero told the truth, the poor were joyful, even when they were also criticized, because they felt that the truth defended them.

Ellacuría was able, therefore, to show that the same people who crushed the truth were those who oppressed the poor. The same people who hoped for liberation from oppression were those who hoped that truth would be liberated. Thus, even before thinking about how to place the university concretely at the service of liberation, Ellacuría intuited its tremendous possibilities. These would increase—so he thought and argued—if the university remained a university. In this sense, he saw a convergence, an affinity even, between the specific reality of the university and the processes of liberation. He saw a *convergence*, because the truth that seeks and finds reason is itself historically liberating. He saw an *affinity*, since both must pass through a process of liberation. Attaining truth presupposes a process of passing, not only from ignorance to knowledge, but from lies to the truth. It passes from a truth that is crushed, to a truth that is liberated.[21]

(c) To seek and to find truth through reason, and to proclaim it through the word, is a task that belongs to the university. Moreover, it places the university in a situation of being able to recognize reality as a reality of the poor, and to make, ethically, an opinion for the poor. This is what emerges, according to Ellacuría, from the right use of reason in the university.

In addition, Ellacuría insisted in a new way on the reality of the university as a social force and on the responsibilities that follow:

> The university is a social reality and a social force historically impacted by the society in which it lives. And it is destined to illuminate and transform, as the social force that it is, that reality in which it lives, by which it lives, and for which it should live. It is from this character that the fundamental question arises: what does it mean to serve, in a university manner, by facilitating the transformative illumination of the contextual reality, the society and the people where the university is situated?[22]

Faced with this demand by reality, Ellacuría emphasized first of all that the university must respond and that this response can and must come from the university as a whole. Through rational truth and the accumulation of true knowledge, the university can project itself outward and become a critical and constructive, a prophetic and utopian, conscience for society. It can influence the collective consciousness, as well as those movements and groups leading processes of liberation, toward shaping a just society. This task, which he pioneered in the theory of the university, is what he called social projection.

(d) Lastly, Ellacuría saw in this understanding of the university, the possibility of reformulating what should be its *political* dimension and its *Christian* inspiration. We have already said that, given the explosive situation in the country, it was inevitable that they should ask how the university would exercise political influence. Given that the UCA was under the direction of the Jesuits—and their belief in the liberating potential of Christian faith—it was likewise inevitable they should ask how and in what sense the university was going to be Christian. Both aspects, the political dimension and Christian inspiration, are difficult to theorize and to handle in themselves. In addition, universities are inclined to claim they have found solutions—facile and finally false—for this problem. Given all this, Ellacuría developed a new theory regarding the political dimension and the Christian inspiration of the university. But before doing that, he unmasked a general fallacy: his idea was that the political and the Christian do not become strictly university realities simply because they occur *at* the university.

Put graphically, a meeting or a religious event is often understood as a university activity because it takes place *at* the university. Following this reasoning, the university might think that it is complying with its political and Christian mission when, for example, activities of political parties or revolutionary groups physically and geographically take place *at* the university, or when Christian liturgies are celebrated *at* the university.

The question is not whether both political and religious activities are in fact, or potentially, good. Nor is the idea that they should not be performed on the university campus. Ellacuría was questioning whether the "geographical" approach was the correct way to relate the university to what is political and Christian, and whether it adequately fulfilled the double responsibility of the university in this regard. He thought, rather, that this relationship could not be based on the simplistic assumption that what occurs spatially at the university—in a categorical *ubi*—is therefore strictly part of the university. He believed, instead, that this relationship has to be based on the specific reality of the university: on a substantive *quid*.

(e) The proper association of the university and politics will be achieved, then, when the political dimension is derived from those very functions that are specific to the university. That is why Ellacuría asserted polemically that, "while every public university action is in some way or another, and in some measure or another, a political action, still not every political action physically undertaken at the university or by members of the university is an action of the university."[23]

The solution lies, then, in understanding the relationship of the political to what belongs specifically to the university.

> A university elaborates its fundamental political character in a university manner when, among its diverse functions—teaching, research and social projection—it gives the highest rank to social outreach, so that it ultimately guides the others, even though it is regulated by them. Of course, this is not just any social outreach, but one that gives priority to the radical transformation of the established disorder of structural injustice.[24]

(f) This same lens helps us to understand what constitutes the Christian inspiration of the university. This is decided not by what is done *at* the university that is explicitly religious (liturgies, Christian education, attention to orthodoxy), good things, but things that can be done, in fact and legitimately, outside the university. Rather, it is decided by how the fundamental functions of the university, research, teaching, and social projection, are permeated with Christian spirit. According to the theology of liberation and Ellacuría's own theology, this is possible in the measure that the university as a whole places its social influence at the service of building the reign of God, actualized through a preferential option for the poor. In this sense, and without the slightest rhetorical exaggeration, Ellacuría tried to historicize at the university the same mission that Archbishop Romero carried out in a pastoral context.

Ellacuría wrote copiously about these things: the mission of the university to build the reign of God and doing so through a preferential option for the poor. We reproduce here only two paragraphs of a famous talk given when the University of Santa Clara awarded him a doctorate *honoris causa* in 1982. Regarding the construction of the reign of God, he offered the following programmatic description:

> We desire that the Reign of God become more and more present among humanity. . . . Immersed in this reality (of the Third World), trapped by it, we ask what to do as a university? And we answer, above all, from an ethical position: transform it, do everything possible so that good overcomes evil, liberty overcomes oppression, justice overcomes injustice, truth overcomes lies, love overcomes hate. Without this commitment, and without such a decision, we do not understand the validity of the university and, even less, the validity of a university inspired by Christianity.[25]

Referring to the option for the poor, Ellacuría paraphrased that day the well-known words of Archbishop Romero: "These sermons are intended as the voice of this people. They are intended as the voice of those who have no voice."[26] This is exactly what Ellacuría thought the university had to be.

> A university of Christian inspiration is one that focuses all its university activity . . . within the illuminating horizon of the meaning of a Christian preferential option for the poor. . . . The university must intellectually incarnate itself among the poor in order to be the science of those who have no voice. It must do this to be intellectual support for those who, in their very reality, possess truth and reason, though at times as rubble, but who have no academic reasons to justify and legitimate their truth and their reason.[27]

### 1.4. The Adaptation of Praxis and a Constant Plea

(a) Ellacuría had a passionate commitment to justice, and that is why he was a prophet and a utopian. For the same reason he had an obsession for finding what is fitting, that is, for adapting to reality and its real possibilities. This did not make him an opportunist, a crude pragmatist, or a simple practitioner of the art of the possible, something to which neither his temperament, his love for the majorities, nor his Christian faith, would endear him. And this is worth clarifying, because there are some who have recently tried to present him as such. It is one thing to study and to act on reality so that it yields *["para que éste de de sí"]* as much as it can. This approach establishes and maintains a clear horizon—a utopian horizon—of what you want to achieve, always evaluating what has been achieved from the perspective of that horizon. But it is something else, somewhere between resignation and irresponsibility, to simply accept what can and cannot be done.

The first attitude actively seeks solutions, and understands the possible "steps" as that which can be achieved. But it also sees those steps, as we have said, as the means to move beyond the present situation and toward a utopian horizon. The second can degenerate into an attitude of "that's the way things are," with a concomitant tendency to inaction. It can end up really privileging the few, for whom the status quo is very good, and into abandoning the many for whom these same things are very bad.

This is why it does not seem very accurate to fundamentally describe Ellacuría as a realist or a practitioner of the art of the possible—though words are not what count here. He seems rather to have been an active seeker of real approaches and solutions compatible with reality, but always situated on the utopian horizon that reality itself demands. On this point he was exceptional. It can be argued whether he always hit the mark or not, but it seems to me there is no doubt (a) that he always sought solutions actively and creatively, anticipating those that others proposed; (b) that although he was familiar with and made use of political theories, he did not mechanically follow any recipe; and (c) that he kept his own council no matter what the attacks were from the right and without acting to attain approval from the left.

(b) Examples of this include his many talks with persons and institutions, politicians, union leaders, diplomats, officers and fighters of the FMLN, bishops, papal nuncios, priests and religious, women from committees of mothers of the disappeared, nongovernmental organizations, President Cristiani in the last months, and a very long et cetera. The purpose of this ceaseless activity was to encourage all these persons and institutions to objectively contribute toward positive steps in the process.

At the very least—and in this Ellacuría can certainly be called a realist—he sought to "moderate" the most reactionary elements among the government, politicians, oligarchs, and military leaders in order to rationalize as much as possible the power they enjoyed or to reduce their irrationality to a minimum.

Another example of this was his continued openness, which was thoughtful, carefully weighed, and always measured against the demands and possibilities of reality, to change, to move ahead, and to encourage others to move ahead. He used to say, "a leader is the one who goes on ahead," exploring the paths that are best suited to reality, though this might mean abandoning old, familiar paths and setting off toward other new and unfamiliar paths.

Thus, in the early 1970s he supported the beginning of talks on agrarian reform and went against the left to support the timid attempt by President Molina at reform. Yet he later criticized President Molina in one of his most brilliant and prophetic editorials, "At your orders, My Capital!" which was the eventual motive for the explosion of a large bomb at UCA.

Also during the 1970s, he followed the elections—1972 and 1977—very closely. He had studied their possibilities and limits beforehand, and he later denounced them as fraudulent. In those years he also defended the principle behind and many of the actual activities of the community-based movements. He always supported the fundamental justice of their cause, and defended them when their most elemental rights were violated. Yet he criticized them for their errors and their reductionism.

In 1979 he supported—like Archbishop Romero—the bloodless coup d'état of October 15, challenging the left, which gave almost no opportunity to the government junta. And he later denounced the Armed Forces and the Christian Democrats for having prostituted the best intentions behind the coup.

At the end of 1980, the country was in the midst of an open savagery and at the beginnings of the war that the FMLN was about to undertake. Yet he concluded—with the greatest objectivity possible and with fear and trembling; I remember it well—that the situation was such that the solution could only be of a military-political character.

Yet by February of 1981, only one month after the failed final offensive, in Managua where he was in exile, he said that nobody was going to win the war and that the solution was negotiation. This did not gain him much sympathy at the time, not from the right, of course—"how can you negotiate with criminals?"—but not from the left either. Nonetheless, Ellacuría continued to promote this direction, and to seek the support of the third force, so misunderstood by the left, by working toward the goal of negotiations until the end of his life.

(c) As we have already said, one may or may not agree with the specifics of Ellacuría's political analyses and experts will have to analyze the correctness of his decisions. We have recalled them to emphasize something important about him as a person: faced with the tragedy of the majorities, he believed one must leave the many comforts of body and soul toward which academics and clergy tend to gravitate, shielding themselves with what seem to be good reasons, in order to give themselves wholly to the search for a solution. To be in the right, or at least on the way toward a solution, one must a priori abandon all dogmatism. This implied above all—rather than looking to the government, the FMLN, the manual for the revolution, or the American embassy—a continual examination of how the common majorities are faring. As Archbishop Romero said, "the Church will support one or another political process, depending on how it affects the people."

The reason why Ellacuría, who was so solidly structured in his way of thinking and not given to irresponsible whims, should change and seek new paths for solutions, and why he did it so often "alone," may be due in part to his defiant and, at times, even arrogant temperament. But it would be wrong to look for the explanation for this constant willingness to explore simply in his temperament. We have to look, I believe, in the depths of the person who, asking himself as a human being what to do for his country, was also questioning what to do with himself in this world of injustice.

At this personal level, Ellacuría heard the cries of the poor, and answered in the most appropriate way he could. But this answer had its process; and here we must insist that few people take the risk to change in these matters. Judging from its duration (some twenty years), its complexity (the need to take into account more and more factors), and the cost (jobs, persecution, frequent solitude, and finally death), one can infer the personal depths touched by the cries of the poor.

In Valladolid in 1982, again in exile, Ellacuría gave a presentation that ended with words which, although he was not given to speaking of himself with this type of language, could be accurately interpreted as autobiographical. They can be understood as a description of the effect on him of living in the midst of a world of victims.

> The only thing I would ask—because the word demand sounds too strong—is two things: that you look with your eyes and heart at these

peoples who are suffering so much—some from poverty and hunger, others from oppression and repression. Then (since I am a Jesuit), I would bid you pray the colloquy of St. Ignatius from the first week of the Exercises[28] before this crucified people, asking yourself: What have I done to crucify them? What am I doing to end their crucifixion? What should I do so that this people might rise from the dead?[29]

Looking back, thinking about Ellacuría the theoretician, the Rahnerian and Zubirian, one who knew and appreciated some of the contributions of Marxism, tireless seeker of rationality, I believe that his only really unchangeable historical truth during the many years of searching, his sole existential "dogma," so to speak, was the reality of the crucified people and the requirement to take them down from their cross.

## 2. Intelligence in the Service of Justice

Ignacio Ellacuría, this Good Samaritan and man of justice, practiced compassion above all using intelligence, as we have said. But we want to dwell on this a bit in order to go more deeply into and to understand the ultimate dimension of his compassion. It may also help, though it is not the central point of our discussion, anyone who considers themselves a "professional intellectual" (especially one with postmodern pretensions) to see how intelligence can and must be placed at the service of reality, justice, and liberation. In other words, we want to see how Ellacuría's work as an *intellectual* expressed the dedication of his *person* to a cause that had logical priority over merely advancing knowledge. We also want to explore how this story can help other thinkers, academics and scientists, to be, as we say, liberation philosophers; liberation engineers, physicians and economists; liberation lawyers, historians and writers . . .

### 2.1. The Noetic, Ethical, and Praxis-Oriented Dimensions of Intelligence

We have already said that, from an existential perspective, what was most decisive for Ellacuría was not simply the exercise of his intelligence—truly prodigious—but rather the dedication of himself and his intelligence to the service of liberation. He introduced this *dedication* to liberation, a dimension that should be present at all levels of the person, into his understanding of what actually constitutes the exercise of intelligence. He defined the formal structure of intelligence as "apprehending reality and facing up to that reality." [30]

Ellacuría studied how and in what forms this "facing up to" reality could happen. He concluded that it happens at the *noetic* level, assuming that we are incarnated in reality; at the ethical level, assuming that intelligence is interrogated by reality and must respond to its demand; and at the level of *praxis,* carrying the weight of real tasks. This is what he himself says in precise and densely compacted words, in what has become a classic text:

> This act of facing up to real things as real has a threefold dimension. It involves realizing the weight of reality, which implies a being-in the reality of things, and not merely a being-before the idea of things, or a being-in their meaning. It presumes a "real" being-in the reality of things, which in its active character of being-in-existence is quite the opposite of being thing-like and inert, and implies being among them through their material and active mediations. It involves shouldering the weight of reality, an expression that points to the fundamentally ethical character of intelligence, which has not been given to humanity so that it might evade its real obligations, but rather so that it might shoulder upon itself the weight of what things really are, and what they really demand. And it involves taking charge of the weight of reality, an expression that points to the praxis-oriented character of intelligence, which only complies with what it is, including its character as something that knows reality and comprehends its meaning, to the degree it undertakes really doing something.[31]

According to Ellacuría, then, it is not adequate to say that the ultimate goal of theology is to advance knowledge—even though this is good and a necessary aspect of the ultimate goal. Rather, the latter consists in taking charge of that reality in the most suitable manner possible, which in theological language implies "the fullest realization possible of the Reign of God." This is why Ellacuría formally defines theology as the "ideological moment of an ecclesial and historical praxis."[32]

## 2.2. The Task of Theology in Light of the Poor

This end—the "for" of theology—is already known. But one must add something that Ellacuría likewise developed in depth: the "from," that is, the location of the theological task. Determining this place is of the greatest importance, since, depending whether one or another place is chosen, the sources of theological knowledge will produce different results. Therefore, for Ellacuría,

> The poor in Latin America are a theological place inasmuch as they constitute the most extreme and scandalous prophetic and apocalyptic presence of the Christian God, and consequently the privileged location for

praxis and Christian reflection. We see and feel this in historical reality, and in the processes Latin America is living through. And we verify it again in the interpretation we give, from that place, of the word of God and the whole history of salvation.[33]

What is stated here in theoretical terms, he also examined historically. He used to ask, for example, how it is possible that a topic as historically and theologically central as liberation, which even the two Vatican Instructions of 1984 and 1986 on the theology of liberation[34] recognize as central to the revelation of God, could have been ignored in theology for centuries. It is even ignored by the leading edge of European theology, which is so scientific and so endowed with every kind of resource.[35]

His answer is that what has made the rediscovery of liberation possible is the place where theological reflection has occurred. If liberation has been recovered in Latin America as something central to God's revelation and the Gospel of Jesus, this has happened because it is an impoverished continent. And Ellacuría added, polemically and dialectically, that, "the proper place for it (liberation) to appear is the place of the poor and dispossessed, not that of the rich who dispossessed them, who were inclined instead not to see and even to obscure justice and the need for liberation."[36] Putting it in personal terms, especially when he spoke in Spain and other countries of the First World, he used to say, "we the liberation theologians are not more intelligent than other theologians, nor do we have more resources, rather, the opposite is often the case. But what has happened is that we are in the appropriate place to think about the Christian faith: a world of the poor."

Let us say in concluding this section that Ellacuría, when he spoke of the place of theology, distinguished between physical places, which could be various (a university, a seminary, a curia, base communities, and so on), and the real location, which had to be the place of poverty. Physical places provide advantages and disadvantages for the work of theological reflection, but all of them should be filled with the reality of poverty, and in any of them the theologian must be impacted by this reality.

Ellacuría especially appreciated two *physical* locations for doing theology: the university (for the possibilities of doing structural analyses, the interdisciplinary nature, and the rigor, despite the danger of a physical distancing from reality), and the base communities (due to the immediacy of the reality of life and faith, and the quality of their hope and commitment unto martyrdom, despite the danger of immediacy). He wanted both places to join forces in making room for and analyzing the reality of poverty. To those who did not accept the base communities as a place to do theology, he used to say that the communities contributed more light for understanding any theological content (which is more important), than the content itself. To those who criticized the university as a place for theology because it was distanced from reality, he used to say that "we do theology *at* a desk, but not *from* a desk."

## 2.3. An Integral Theological Approach

With these commitments regarding the place and purpose of theology, we can characterize Ellacuría's approach to the intellectual and specifically theological endeavor, comparing it with other approaches and other conventional ways of doing theology. To put it in simple and graphic terms, we can compare the origins of Western thought and its various pre-Socratic, Socratic, and Aristotelian-analytic expressions, to the intellectual approach of Ellacuría.

Doing theology for the purpose described above is, first of all, an expression of the *Socratic* dimension[37] of the intellectual task, that is, facing up to reality in order to transform it, and its dominions in order to combat them. As in the case of Socrates, Ellacuría's martyrdom shows there is a way of using intelligence for the purpose of directly influencing reality, really transforming persons and structures. This is done so that the change being sought, liberation, becomes not only a possible effect of the work of philosophy and theology, but rather their explicit purpose, and normative for the intellectual task.

Second, doing theology from the place we have described—although the parallel is less precise—is also a way of recovering the *pre-Socratic* dimension of the intellectual task, because of the position of immediacy with reality and of openness to the novelty of history. This means facing up to reality theoretically, when by definition there are not yet texts to rely on. Instead one must read reality and what it says, the signs of the times.[38] This is the case when prior concepts and theories that are adequate and appropriate for the interpretation of reality cannot be presupposed (because they are dated).

Moreover, reality simply unfolds as it unfolds. It does not fit itself to what manuals of whatever type say about it. It does not even fit into the most lucid prognoses, as has occurred in practice in all processes of liberation. Therefore, it is also necessary to accept and face this fact honestly. And this supposes what we have called the pre-Socratic attitude: we cannot presuppose adequate preexisting categories for analyzing what is a changing reality; instead we must actively and creatively seek them out.

Lastly, Ellacuría strongly insisted on the analytic—let us say *Aristotelian*[39]—dimension of the theological task, for which he demonstrated an exceptional talent. Even more, he insisted on the tremendous need for, and always promoted the development of, rigorous disciplines at UCA, without which neither justice, nor development, nor liberation, can be effectively advanced. However, Ellacuría also thought that, left to its own inertia and without being joined to the other two dimensions, purely analytic intelligence has no reason to humanize humanity, or to transform society in the right direction. This is demonstrated above all by the immense accumulation of knowledge in persons and institutions in the First World, which has often served not the interests of liberation, but rather oppression.

In summary, we can say that these three dimensions can be clearly seen in Ellacuría's intellectual work. The *pre-Socratic* dimension is somehow expressed in the immediacy with which he faced reality, above all the suffering reality of the crucified peoples. It is expressed in the openness to change and to seeking new conceptual categories, without presupposing he still had adequate categories at hand to take on the novelty of the processes underway. The *Aristotelian,* analytic dimension is expressed in his theoretical analyses of every type, theological, philosophical, political, religious, and his use of Rahner, Zubiri, and Marx, for which he is best known by outsiders. Lastly, the *Socratic* dimension is expressed in the will to transform reality, shouldering its weight, without avoiding the consequences of directly facing up to the powers of the world. This implied, like Socrates, being accused of corrupting the citizenry and of atheism, and being brought to trial.

Ellacuría's holistic and new theoretical explanation of the role of intelligence has its roots in Zubiri and Marx. But the existential rediscovery of its ethical and praxis-related dimensions is rooted, we think, in the depths of his response as a person to the pleas of the crucified people.

### 3. A Utopian-Prophetic Vision of Reality

#### 3.1. The Need for Prophecy and Utopia Today

Today, especially in the First World, neither philosophers nor most theologians speak of prophecy, much less utopia. This is not accidental, for they do not depend exclusively or even principally on personal attitudes, but rather on objective realities. They do not want to speak about prophecy because they would have to ask themselves about reality's evils, to denounce them, and at least let the question arise regarding who is responsible for the worldwide catastrophe in which we live. Neither does anyone speak of utopia, because unlimited progress, and unlimited freedom—not to mention unlimited wealth and pleasure—have not been realized in this world, nor can they be realized, as was hoped. Since the First World, specifically Europe, thinks that it is "the measure of all things"—what the Greeks claimed regarding the human person—it authoritatively declares that it is no longer time to speak of prophecy or utopia.

Ellacuría, however, in his last theological article—a kind of last will and testament written a few months before he was assassinated—wrote precisely about "Utopia and Prophecy from Latin America."[40] Also, it should be emphasized that he did not write the piece simply to include one of the subjects needed, so to speak, to round off and leave for posterity a complete and finished philosophical and theological system. He did not limit himself, as often happens, to dialoguing with what other thinkers have said about prophecy and utopia. Rather, he wrote the piece as a human being and a Christian, to express the victims' pain and to denounce poverty, repression, and murder. He wrote to express hope and to announce the possibility of life. Finally, he wrote with conviction and daring to express his own vision of what is ultimate in reality. Ellacuría had the audacity, until the end of his days, to say that there is an ultimate evil that must be prophetically denounced and an ultimate hope that must be announced in a utopian manner.

It is impossible to summarize this long piece here. But we will cite the opening words, positively and polemically, that illuminate the place and the way of approaching this subject:

> In order to achieve the proper union of utopia and prophecy, one must be situated in the proper historical place. Every intersection of these two human and historical dimensions must be "situated" at precise geo-social coordinates in order to be realistic and fruitful. Lacking this, the inescapable force of the principle of reality dissipates, and utopia and prophecy become a mental game, rather than something real. But some places are more conducive to the emergence of prophetic utopians or utopian prophets. It is said that in decadent cultures there is no longer a place for prophecy and utopia, but only for pragmatism and egotism, for the quantitative verification of results, for the scientific computation of cost and benefit and, in the best of cases, for the institutionalization, legalization, and ritualization of the spirit that renews all things. Whether or not this situation is inevitable, there nevertheless remain places where hope is not merely the result of infinitesimal calculations, but

rather of hoping, and "giving hope" in spite of all dogmatic judgements
that close down the future of the utopian project and the struggle. One
of these places is Latin America.[41]

We want to offer some important reflections as a comment on this
text. Above all, Ellacuría's understanding of prophecy should not be discerned simply in terms of his personal temperament. Though he may
have had a difficult character, he did not hate anybody, as he said pub-
licly on television with great sincerity. But neither did he hate utopia,
though he was not at all the fanciful dreamer. Prophecy and utopia appear to be, rather, demands made by reality itself, which, as Rahner said,
struggles to speak. What is specific to Ellacuría is the idea that reality
does not struggle to speak the same way in each place, nor does it express the same outcries and hopes.

As for its content, the text says—and this is probably the most original part of his vision—that both things have to be seen as mutually ref-
erential, in a dialectical interrelationship. One refers to, and must refer
to, the other in a precise way: there *has* to be utopia because prophecy
tells us that there is evil to overcome, and there *can* be prophecy because utopia tells us that there is the possibility of good. In this sense, it
can certainly be said that Ellacuría establishes a true "realism"—above
all as a method. This has nothing to do with the simple acceptance of
the possibilities that things offer, but rather with a real way, through
negation and affirmation, of making reality give more of itself. This is
why he says that prophecy must be used as a method, and utopia as a
horizon,[42] so that in the union of both we know where we must go and
what we must do.

Lastly, the text insists that even though the mutual reference of utopia
and prophecy can be theoretically established, the problem is to find the
place in which each of them, and their mutual reference, are possible. This
place, consistent with what we have seen above, is Latin America, a world
of the poor. It was from this place that Ellacuría prophetically denounced
the evils of our world and the solution they offer us, and from which he
outlined, in a utopian manner, a true solution.

### 3.2. Prophecy: We Are in a Bad Way
### and We Are Being Offered a Bad Solution

We have already seen Ellacuría's verdict regarding the reality of
this world as objectified sin. I would now like to add two things to this
judgment.

(a) In addition to its murder of victims, the powers of this world hide their deeds with a gigantic cover-up and live in self-deception, especially in the First World. To overcome this, Ellacuría asked—and offered—the First World the opportunity to look face to face at the true reality of the world, which is mainly the Third World. "The exteriority of the Third World thus reveals and denounces the interiority of the First World. But this is something we do not want to see, because it could lead us either to insanity or to conversion from a whole way of being and doing."[43]

He repeated the same idea in the form of a metaphor. The First World can see itself, as if in a rear view mirror, by looking at the Third World and its disfigured but true reality. He suggests that the First World achieves this perspective by examining what it produces: a crucified people. He said the same thing, using the metaphor of stool analysis: if you want to know the state of health of the patient, you have to do an analysis of their feces. What this analysis shows is the tragedy of the Third World, which indicates the degree of health of the First World that produced it.

This is well understood and there is no need to dwell on it. However, I would like to clarify two things. First, the depth of Ellacuría's denunciation emerges from considering the evils of our reality as *sin*, reflecting their ultimate dimension. He does not treat them merely as limitations, partial failures, failed but necessary steps toward a better future, and so on, as philosophers and ideologies might. In my opinion, the main force of his denunciation comes from the objectivity of the analysis and from the (Christian) interpretation of these evils as an ultimate reality.[44] Second, his prophetic denunciation was mainly directed against objective and structural realities and the groups responsible for them, rather than against specific persons. That is, the purpose of the denunciation was to unmask realities that should be transformed. His motivation was to defend the victims, not the desire to insult an adversary, though Ellacuría could be biting in his denunciations.

(b) While the preceding is important, perhaps what was most characteristic about Ellacuría's prophetic dimension—precisely because what most interested him was solution of the problems—was the uncommon strength and rigor of his denunciations and exposés, not only of the evils of our reality, but also of the *solutions* being proposed to us to alleviate those evils. He examined the many solutions being presented to us as attractive, even ideal, and in any case as inevitable—which, coincidentally, would make any prophetic denunciation useless and meaningless.

In today's antiprophetic environment, Ellacuría, in one of his last talks, spoke words that few people would dare utter, even though they are still valid. "From my point of view—and this may be simultaneously somewhat prophetic and paradoxical—the United States is in a much worse situation than Latin America. Because the United States has a solution, but, in my opinion, it is a bad solution, both for them and for the world in general."[45]

This solution, which Ellacuría denounced as "a civilization of capital," is the neoliberal, democratic society that today they propose and impose on us like vassals. They do this with claims that the model has resolved the basic problems in the countries of Southeast Asia and is the only viable solution. Nonetheless, Ellacuría said that it is a bad solution, because it cannot be universalized and is, therefore, by definition, not a solution for the entire human family. This makes it an immoral solution according to the principle of Kant, which holds that what cannot be made universal is not moral.

Ellacuría insisted that the resources simply do not exist on the planet for everyone to live as the United States, the European Community, or even the four Asian Dragons. If this is true, then the solution we are offered implies a tragic choice regarding which peoples are going to live, which are going to die, and what percentage of the population in the poor countries—40, 50, or 60 percent—is going to survive. Also, who makes the choice, if the life and death of human beings is not to be left to the heartlessness of the market? If it is not possible to guarantee the minimum standard for life, then, once more, only the few will enjoy the benefits of this supposedly more civil and more democratic society. This is a contradiction and it leaves the very idea of the human family even more compromised.

This evil solution must be prophetically denounced and countered with a true solution. That solution must be sought, Ellacuría thought, along very different and even contrary paths.

### 3.3. Utopia: A Civilization of Poverty

Even if the solution they want to impose on us should prove viable from an economic point of view, Ellacuría did not consider it desirable. He used to say that the theoretical conceptualization of a true solution was easy, but that putting it into practice would be extremely difficult, "utopian" really—something that has no place in our world. A true solution like this required not only reforms, but "conversion and transformation, . . . another inspiration contrary to the present one, . . . a change of mentality and a change in the direction of history."[46] He called this solution a "civilization of work" and, in a more original turn of phrase, a "civilization of poverty."

As I understand it, this last phrase[47] and what is behind it, is an original creation Ellacuría worked out theoretically over the years.[48] He attributed great importance to it. That is because he thought that it was the only way of making "a civilization of work" real in our world, and of historicizing a "civilization of love"—to which, of course, the popes call us [in their social encyclicals].

As I recall, he wrote about this for the first time in a 1982 article on unemployment for the journal *Concilium*.[49] Later, in 1983, he raised the subject in connection to what should be the mission of the Society of Jesus, which was going to have its General Congregation that year.[50] Finally, he returned to the subject in the 1989 article, "Utopia and Prophecy," cited above.

The 1982 article offered a programmatic vision for

> a civilization of poverty, in which poverty would no longer be the privation of what is necessary and basic through the historical actions of social groups or classes, and nations or coalitions of nations. This civilization of poverty refers to a universal state of things in which the satisfaction of basic necessities, the freedom of personal choice, and an environment of personal and communal creativity, are guaranteed. Such an environment would create the proper conditions for the emergence of new forms of life and culture, new relationships with nature, other humans, oneself, and God.[51]

These words are utopian, and there is not much analysis in them. They say powerfully that our present civilization is not civilized, because it has not provided all men and women with the aforementioned goods. This is an example of how the place of utopia is the same as that of prophecy. Nonetheless, in the same article, he points to two important things. First, not only is our present civilization not civilized; but further, the reason is that it is a civilization of wealth. In Christian terms, Ellacuría is emphasizing that we live in a world of sin,[52] a reality "made still worse by the fact that the First World calls itself Christian, the fruit of a Christian civilization, and a missionary of the gospel it carried to the Third World as one more ingredient of colonization."[53] Second, this problem is deeper than it seems, because it becomes a question of "believing not only in a new world economic order . . . but in a new civilization."[54]

In the 1983 article he insists that this civilization is both a historical necessity (given the correlation between worldwide resources and population) and an opportunity for the spirit to grow. It would thereby unmask the generally accepted assumption that Western civilization, though it may have failed in other areas, at least has not failed in cultivating the spirit.

> This poverty is what actually creates space for the spirit. The spirit will no longer find itself suffocated by the anxiety to have more than the other, by the concupiscent anxiety of a desire to possess every kind of superfluous object, while the majority of humankind lacks what is necessary to live. In this space the spirit will be able to flourish, including the immense spiritual and human wealth of the poor, and the peoples of the Third World. Today that spirit is being drowned by destitution, and the imposition of cultural models that, though more developed in some respects, are not, thereby, more fully human.[55]

In the 1989 article he further specifies the dialectical opposition of a civilization of poverty to a civilization of wealth, and the antagonistic forces of each.

> A civilization of poverty . . . founded on a materialist humanism, and transformed by Christian light and inspiration, rejects the accumulation of capital as the mover of history, and the possession-enjoyment of wealth as the principle of humanization. It makes the universal satisfaction of basic needs the principle for development, and the growth of shared solidarity the ground for humanization.
>
> A civilization of poverty is so named in order to highlight the contrast with a civilization of wealth, not to assert universal impoverishment as an ideal for life. . . . The intention here is to highlight the dialectical relationship of wealth and poverty, not poverty itself. In a world sinfully configured by the forces of capital and wealth, it is necessary to create a different force to salvifically overcome it.[56]

These words need no comment. However, it is certainly good to insist that what Ellacuría here calls utopia is not merely the possibility of *life* for the majorities, but rather the possibility of *civilization*. It is the possibility of a way of life that is really human and fraternal. That is why these words also constitute a prophetic denunciation of a civilization of wealth, which not only does not generate life for all, but does not civilize human beings nor humanize them.

Ellacuría grew more and more aware of the importance of civilization, and not just the dimensions of economic production and distribution. Correspondingly, he became increasingly interested in every type of manifestation of the spirit. As an important example, in describing the poor he insisted on the material reality of their need, on the historical reality of their having been impoverished, on their potential for becoming aware and organizing politically. However, to all this he added the need and the possibility of being imbued with and generating spirit, so one of his most profound utopian phrases spoke of the "the poor with spirit."[57]

He reflected on this utopia theoretically, but also in terms of the needs and possibilities of the Salvadoran reality. Consistent with the aforementioned realism, which became a central preoccupation during his final years, this is what he said in his talk in Barcelona:

> Another fundamental step remains. It is the creation of economic, political, and cultural models that make it possible for a civilization of work to take the place of a civilization of capital. And it is here that intellectuals of every type, critical theorists of reality, are presented with a challenge and task that cannot be avoided. Critique and destruction do not suffice. Instead, what is needed is a constructive proposal that provides a real alternative.[58]

On the other hand, Ellacuría elaborated utopia in terms of what the reality of El Salvador was giving of itself. He saw the seeds—certainly imperfect and often bearing no fruit—of a civilization of poverty in the various achievements of the people and the church in El Salvador: grassroots organizations rather than traditional political parties, attempts at a grassroots and communitarian economy, the construction of a church of the poor. He also saw values being created that were closer to a civilization of poverty than a civilization of wealth. Using our own words, we might describe them as: the spirit of community *versus* isolationist individualism that easily degenerates into egotism; celebration *versus* irresponsible diversion that degenerates into alienation; openness *versus* cruel ethnocentrism that degenerates into a lack of understanding of the suffering of others; creativity *versus* servile imitation, that easily degenerates into the loss of one's identity; compromise *versus* mere tolerance that degenerates into indifference; and faith *versus* crude positivism and pragmatism, that degenerate into lack of meaning in life, and so on.

## 3.4. The Hope That Does Not Die

I have suggested that Ellacuría thought it was better not to have a solution, than to have a bad solution. However, Ellacuría himself maintained a utopian hope for a solution, and the following even more utopian foundational belief, until the end of his life. He writes:

> All the martyrial blood that has been shed in El Salvador and throughout Latin America, far from creating discouragement and despair, infuses our people with a new spirit of struggle and a new hope. In this sense, if we are neither a "new world" nor a "new continent," we are clearly and verifiably—though maybe not for outsiders—a continent of hope. This is an extremely interesting sign from a future society facing other continents that do not have hope. Indeed, the only thing they have is fear.[59]

Ellacuría directly opposed, then, not only a civilization of wealth, but its present-day historical companions: despair, fear, and the sense of frustration and inevitability. That is to say, he opposed a culture without prophecy and without utopia. He both argued and embodied the belief that it is worth living and dying for the prophetic-utopian alternative.

None of this is easy to put into practice, since this type of more human and more Christian life is of no interest to the system. That is why it is habitually delegitimated in theory and, when it is embodied, is usually historically persecuted. Though difficult, it is possible, necessary, and good to live in this way. Those who live in abundance and take life for granted do not understand this. But it is understood by those for whom life, a life with the minimum of possibilities and dignity, is precisely what cannot be taken for granted. They understand what a civilization of poverty is about and what is at stake. They understand that many human beings have generously given their lives for this utopia.

*   *   *

To conclude this introduction to the human being who was Ignacio Ellacuría, to his hopes and his commitments, we return to some key ideas from his talk in Barcelona:

> There is much that remains to be done. Only in a utopian and hope-filled manner, can one believe in and be willing to attempt, in the company of all the poor and oppressed of the world, to reverse history, to subvert it, and launch it in another direction. . . . Our civilization is seriously ill, and in order to save it from an ominous and fatal end, we must attempt to change it from within. Helping, like prophets and utopians, to nourish and provoke a collective consciousness of the need for substantial change, is already in itself an important first step.[60]

# Part II: The Christian

## 1. The Historical Effect of His Christianity

Everything we have talked about—service, justice, prophecy, utopia, and so forth—is, of course, or can be, a reality that is clearly Christian. But Ellacuría also frequently spoke explicitly about Christianity, and he did so as a Christian. He did this not only when he was writing theology, but rather in conversations, in talks about the reality of our country, and in relation to ideologies such as Marxism. So Christianity was very present to him. Let us examine in what it consists for Ignacio Ellacuría.

### *1.1. Christianity as a Reality That Shaped Him as a Person*

To introduce us to Ellacuría as a Christian, I would like to begin with a statement he made that drew my attention. Ellacuría was not given at all to pious language, nor did he speak easily about his own faith. So he was not one of those persons who, according the Gospel, is always crying out "Lord, Lord." Rather, he was one of those who went to work in the fields to do the will of God. He was not given to poetic or paradoxical language, apart from rationality. Indeed, just the opposite.

Ellacuría frequently used expressions like "Christianity is this or that . . ."; "Christians should be the first to . . ."; "but the most Christian thing is . . . " We have seen that at times he made clearly utopian-prophetic statements with little apparent rational argumentation. But these were central affirmations of the Christian faith: "it is better to give than to receive," "the servant brings salvation," "one can live like a resurrected person in history," and so on. This shows that Christianity was very real for Ellacuría, something whose historical and transcendental elements have the capacity to shape a person and, indirectly, peoples and societies as well. For that reason, let us examine what he understood by *Christianity [lo cristiano]*, an expression that goes beyond mere doctrine and routine, and was existentially important to him.

(a) Christianity is something real that consists in an overall way of being, seeing, acting, hoping, and celebrating. It is seen in persons and, by analogy, in human groups and societies. The first is expressed in the following of Jesus and in the configuration of human beings to his image. The second is expressed as a society shaped according to the ideal of the reign of God.

(b) The specific Christianity that existentially influenced Ellacuría has its guiding and motivating principle in the tradition originating in Jesus of Nazareth. It has been historicized and lived in community by the people of God throughout the centuries—under the influence of the Spirit. It has been revitalized by the best Christians, the saints, a St. Ignatius Loyola or a St. Francis of Assisi, an Archbishop Romero or a Fr. Arrupe, to name some people Ellacuría used to mention. This does not mean that Ellacuría did not accept, and even praise, many other Christian things: dogmatic tradition, liturgical and sacramental life, ecclesial institutions, and so on. But he saw Jesus and the tradition about Jesus that has endured throughout history as fundamental. He did not think that Jesus, and following Jesus, were all of what Christianity is. But he did regard them existentially as fundamental.

(c) Lastly, Christianity has its own identity and specific characteristics, although Ellacuría found that they shared some elements with modernity, grassroots movements, and Marxism.[61] He emphasizes this theoretically not for reasons of pure orthodoxy, but because he thought these overlaps were real and that keeping them alive was beneficial for all. In operative terms, then, he used to say that a Christian has no reason for an inferiority complex if he or she tries to live their faith in line with the Gospel. But neither should they have a superiority complex, especially here in Latin America, where at the beginning of the liberation movements, a Marxist commitment and ethics "aroused a certain embarrassment and inferiority complex among Christians because it supposed a neglect of something essential to the faith."[62]

Ellacuría reflected upon and wrote copiously about the nature and specificity of Christianity. We have recently published his theological writings in four volumes at *UCA Editores*. There he analyzes a great variety of topics like the reign of God, the historical Jesus, the church of the poor, the following of Christ, spirituality, basic Christian communities, and many others.

I will not treat these topics in what follows. Instead, let us focus on how Christianity shaped Ellacuría as a person. This is clear in Ellacuría's vision and his attitude toward certain key negative and positive historical realities or, in the language of Christian tradition, toward the *mysterium iniquitatis* and the *mysterium salutis*. This approach, though indirect, will enable us to get close to Ellacuría as a Christian. I believe it is one of the best ways to come to know him as a person, and not just to analyze his theological texts.

## 1.2 *The* Mysterium Iniquitatis

### 1.2.1. Sin

Ellacuría was convinced not only that there are limits in the world, failed attempts at evolution, disasters. Such expressions help to show the negativity of history. Rather Ellacuría repeatedly and radically used the word *sin* that brings us to his Christian vision of the negativity of history. We will analyze it in three points.

(a) By using the Christian terminology of sin, Ellacuría situates the negativity of history in an ultimate context. In using the term, he is declaring negativity to be something radical because it is rooted in history, something other schools of thinking do not do. And, *sub specie contrarii,* he is pointing to a theological dimension. He used to say that the incarnation is the Son becoming flesh in history, citing Rahner. But—he would add as a fundamental point—the Son becomes flesh in a history of sin.

(b) In addition to insisting that sin is a kind of ultimate, he also insisted that sin should not only be forgiven in the subjectivity of the sinner, but it should be pulled up by its roots in history. This picks up both the Gospel tradition of welcoming the sinner and the prophetic tradition of eliminating the sin. The second is what makes it necessary to fight sin—overcoming alienation, toppling structures, and so on, in the language of modernity—all of which implies the use of some kind of external force to eliminate sin. Ellacuría was not especially original in this, nor was he expressing anything specifically Christian. But by saying it, he undermined a false pacifism that appeared to be Christian and he recovered the struggling character of faith. In practice, he demonstrated great creativity in his specific proposals about how to fight sin.

(c) By insisting on the need to struggle against sin, Ellacuría was transcending postmodernity and drawing from the vision of modernity. He added something that modernity always ignores or passes over lightly: in order to overcome sin one must shoulder its weight, which is something specifically Christian. In other words, sin must not only be fought from the outside. It must also be combated from within, shouldering its weight, and being willing to be crushed by it. This should not be understood simply as the necessary social cost that must be paid so that progress or a revolution can succeed. Ellacuría accepted this as something specifically Christian. Without trying to defend it, he used to refer to the songs of the Suffering Servant of Yahweh who, in succumbing to the power of sin, overcomes it.

> The servant will justify many because he bore the weight of their crimes.
> . . . The Lord himself takes on this situation: he takes on himself the weight of our crimes. . . . Only by means of a difficult act of faith is the

author of the servant song able to discover that which is perceived as its exact opposite through the eyes of history.[63]

This was not pious exaggeration, clearly seen from how often and how naturally he repeated the idea that one must shoulder the weight of sin. I remember his talk of September 19, 1989, on the honorary doctorate awarded to President Oscar Arias, in the presence of President Cristiani, the United States ambassador, and other political figures. Ellacuría, in the middle of a deep political analysis, unexpectedly and quite naturally spoke the following words: "The pain has been great, and the bloodshed has been great. But the classic *theologumenon, nulla redemptio sine efussione sanguinis,* is still there to remind us that the people's salvation and liberation come about through very painful sacrifices."[64]

Ellacuría used these words as a direct reminder that the steps to peace were not taken only by famous people and by political gestures, but that the pain and the blood shed by the people had been equally or even more important. In this context, he unexpectedly referred to the Christian dimension and cited the well-known phrase: without blood, there is no redemption. In our terminology, if one does not shoulder the weight of sin, it is not eradicated. Ellacuría was not sanctioning a glorification of suffering, masochism, or a form of Anselm's theology of atonement. Rather, he was expressing his deep Christian conviction: to effect salvation, one must be willing to bear the weight of sin.

### 1.2.2. Violence

Ellacuría also analyzed one of the most grievous historical forms in which negativity is expressed: *violence.* Faced with violence, he came up with an appropriate definition: the unjust use of force. He developed a hierarchy of violence that follows Medellín: there is an original violence that takes two forms: structural injustice—truly institutionalized violence—plus the repressive violence used to maintain it; and there is violence that responds to the original violence, a revolutionary violence. He analyzed the possible legitimacy and illegitimacy of violence as a response, and under what conditions it substantially follows traditional theological doctrine. Additionally, as a personal contribution, he insisted—and here he was a realist—on "humanizing" violence, minimizing it, and using the principle of proportionality to determine the response. Above all, he tried to prevent violence before it erupted, and to stop it once it exploded.[65]

In this discussion, Ellacuría thought and acted like someone responsible to all of humanity. He made significant contributions in this arena that we have discussed elsewhere.[66] In summary, we can say, on the one hand, that Ellacuría was not an out-and-out pacifist, especially after war had broken out. Rather, he insisted on the absolute necessity of combating injustice. On the other hand, however, he also insisted that violence is a great evil in itself, even violence that manages to be legitimate. He stressed the terrible negative side effects it produces. To the fanatics of violence and those who wanted to create a mystique of violence, he said, "violence is always an evil, greater than we think."[67] In the graphic language to which he was given, especially on television, he said things such as: "only pacifists should go to war," in order to express how careful we must be in accepting violence, even legitimate violence. He said, "we should cry when we announce that we have inflicted so many casualties on the enemy," in order to express how far violence should be from becoming a mystique.

Nevertheless, in this paragraph, I want to insist that Ellacuría also proposed and offered something specifically Christian in response to violence, even when it was a legitimate violence responding to injustice. This Christian approach amounted to a particular way of fighting and a commitment to turn around violence. This is what Ellacuría wrote a few months before he was murdered:

> It would seem from a more Christian point of view, one committed to evangelical perfection in following the historical Jesus, that Christians should not use violence. I am speaking of those who are self-consciously Christian in their way of being and acting, since they are amongst the first, and the most vulnerable, in the fight against every form of injustice. This does not mean that a Christian should always and in every case reject violence. But the Christian as such does not ordinarily give his or her specific witness through violence. And it does not mean that the Christian wants to leave the "dirty" work to others, while they remain "pure" and do not dirty their hands. It is more a question of the most appropriate and complete way giving witness to the fact that life is more important than death, that love is above hate. This attitude is acceptable and effective when the Christian risks even martyrdom in order to defend those who are poorest and to combat oppressors with the testimony of his or her words and life.[68]

What Ellacuría is saying in this paragraph—expressed in torturous prose oscillating between what a Christian may do and his own reflections—is that a Christian, like everybody, has to fight and struggle against all forms of injustice. What is specifically Christian resides (a) in using means that, in themselves, express the supremacy of life over death, and (b) in the fact that Christians themselves are ready to be "the first and most vulnerable . . . even to martyrdom," which gives them credibility in the eyes of others. What we have already said must also be added: Christians must shoulder the weight of violence, thereby collapsing its lethal structure, which is to say, redeeming it.

This phrase, "redeeming violence," expresses what is perhaps most specific to the Christian response to violence. This redemption attempts to bring about events that not only delay the spiral of violence, but which, as foundational events, overcome the very roots of violence. This is the saving value of shouldering the weight of unjust violence. By doing this without defenses, it also becomes a way of redeeming the *hubris* and even the mystique of violence. Likewise, perhaps, the salvific dimension of the Cross of Jesus can be interpreted from this perspective—as Paul seems to do—as an event that, metaphorically speaking, allows violence to vent its force against Jesus until it is exhausted. Perhaps this is how the dynamic of violence can be undone.

### 1.2.3. Power

I would like to speak of Ellacuría's thoughts about *power*. He always talked in personal and direct terms about how dangerous power is, usually adding that this included being president of the UCA. Getting and keeping power often involves serious physical and moral harm, and its use habitually generates many other evils. That is why he considered power an evil, albeit inevitable, a kind of lesser evil always needing historical redemption. This means that reason must guide the use of power to the greatest extent possible, in order to minimize its negative side effects. This conclusion flowed from Ellacuría's observations of history, but it was also based on his Christian faith. Consider his commentary on the passage about the temptations of Jesus:

> It is interesting to emphasize the diabolical interpretation of the power and the glory of the kingdoms of this world. This is especially true in Luke's account, where the evangelist emphasizes that these have been given over to the devil. The point is that they are not diabolical in themselves, but historically they have become so.[69]

This also explains his vision of the world of politics. Ellacuría was not an anarchist at all, either by disposition or by belief. He accepted the need and the inevitability of the existence of politics, including its greater or lesser capacity for good. He saw in politics and political parties a proclivity for evil that comes with seeking and holding onto power. This is why, with a historical rationality ultimately guided by a Christian utopian vision, he favored the efforts of other types of institutions and organizations like the church, religious communities, universities, unions, grassroots movements, and so on. Such institutions by their nature exert their influence more from the social realm than the political. He also tried to generate values grounded in the social realm: truth, hope, reconciliation, a sense of community and celebration, spirituality, and art. These can become social forces and, in this sense, forms of power.

Ellacuría sought these values rather than others grounded in politics, because in the latter, the political party tends to place itself above the interests of the majorities. In any case, Ellacuría saw the social arena as more consonant with the humanizing possibilities of Christianity. That is why he encouraged grassroots movements to stay the way they were, and not to fall into becoming political parties. Their best contribution would be as movements:

> I am not denying the right and the advantages that may come from establishing a political front. What is being questioned is the order of priorities: the grass roots organization or the political front. No doubt the dynamics of each may be different, if not contradictory. But regardless, priority has to be given to the grass roots organization, and not to the political front. . . . The social arena is more basic than the political, even though in the present moment the political arena may be more important than the social.[70]

This way of interpreting and acting in response to the negative dimension of history, sin, violence, and power, demonstrates how deep was the Christian influence on Ellacuría.

## *1.3.* Mysterium Salutis

We have just noted with what depth Ellacuría considered and critiqued the negativity of this world as a *mysterium iniquitatis* that must be fought, and whose weight must be shouldered to defeat it. However, from the Christian point of view, he also saw reality as positive, as a *mysterium salutis* that shoulders our weight as well. Ellacuría reminds me of a phrase Rahner used in his final years: "The Gospel is a heavy light burden; the more you carry it, the more it carries you." My point is that Ellacuría also found a reality in Christianity that can mold us to the positive dimension of reality.

*1.3.1. Hope for Salvation*

This appears especially in Ellacuría's hope that, despite evil, there is the possibility of *salvation*, a salvation that must become real now in history. This is a fundamental affirmation for Ellacuría. It is utopian in the sense already mentioned, which is not naïve. It is made possible by Christianity, and it must never be taken for granted.

From the beginning of his work in El Salvador, Ellacuría emphasized the reality of salvation. He coined the famous phrase: "The history of salvation is a salvation in history."[71] The intent of this phrase is clearly to historicize salvation, to make God's salvation real in the world. I want to emphasize his insistence on the hope that salvation is possible, and his contribution to making that hope present among the other topics in theology. Though it seems simple to say, this is still a confession of faith, or at least of hope, since the expectation of historical salvation in this world is not at all reasonable. That is especially true for Ellacuría, who was not at all naïve and, for that reason, did not accept the salvation that some, both right and left, dogmatically and mechanically predicted. The roots of his hope for salvation, and his commitment to work and struggle for it to the end had a different source: his Christianity.

It is important to remember that two of his most important articles cited above, "The Crucified People," written originally in 1978, and "Utopia and Prophecy," written in 1989, are subtitled respectively, "An Essay on Historical Soteriology," and "A Concrete Essay on Historical Soteriology." The first article was especially notable from the point of view of salvation. To seriously accept that a crucified people contributes something good to this world is anything but evident. Nonetheless, that was the faith that led Ellacuría to seriously investigate in what historical sense this crucified people brings salvation. He developed the idea in many ways, showing how this people is "a light to the nations," as Isaiah claims (42:6 and 49:6), and historicizing it for today as a road to truth and utopia, a force for conversion, something that supports others in the faith, and so on.

The second article ends programmatically—like a last will and testament—with a hymn to the church of the poor that brings salvation:

> The church of the poor is set up as a new heaven. . . . The utopian affirmation of a church that looks like the new heaven of a civilization of poverty is an undeniable claim of the signs of the times. It represents the soteriological force of the Christian faith historicized in new human beings who continue to steadfastly proclaim an always greater—though always obscure—future. And they do this because, beyond the coming historical futures, God the savior, God the liberator, can be seen.[72]

This soteriological force, the hope it generates, and the vision of reality it assumes, is essential to a reality always full of possibilities beyond what we can make it produce. In his own life, Ellacuría gave exceptional testimony to this hope. He never stopped working for salvation. He adapted to reality, yes, but he never lost sight of utopia. This is so rare, when we see how quickly some people accept the limitations of reality and forget the hope that salvation is possible. This hope expresses Ellacuría's Christian core very well.

Ellacuría worked to the end of his life so that historical salvation would become a reality. He did this not just for loyalty to Kantian ethical imperatives. He did it, rather, from Christian conviction, and finally, from a faith commitment. As he says so beautifully, "he glimpsed God the Savior."

### 1.3.2. Poverty

One can see the influence of his Christianity on Ellacuría's view of *poverty* as well. He often said that Christianity believes wealth is the great temptation. He once said on television, to everyone's surprise, "politicians, soldiers, and priests should leave their jobs with less money than when they began." More folly than utopia, this statement was meant to emphasize the constant temptation of wealth, and those who are most susceptible to it, though they are precisely the ones who should be serving the country. This story aside, let us focus on Ellacuría's thoughts on poverty.

In his proposal on the need for a civilization of poverty, Ellacuría argues on the one hand that it is "a historical necessity," based on reasons "that have more to do with the relationship between world resources and universal welfare."[73] But he also insists, without defending it, that from a Christian perspective:

> The Third World may become the natural place for the Christian faith. . . . It makes it easier to live out the spirit of the Gospel, by which one does not need to have much, in order to be much. . . . And it facilitates the beginnings of a civilization of poverty fully consistent with the preaching of Jesus. . . . Such a civilization would be open to the transcendent, and most especially to the Christian form of transcendence revealed in Jesus of Nazareth, who made himself equal to the poor in order to manifest in a new way the glory of God.[74]

Ellacuría was not preaching poverty, nor did he want to "divvy up destitution." He saw something positive in poverty, and it flowed from his acceptance of the Gospel. It is true that, up to a point, a rational case can be made for the benefits of poverty. But in the end, the praise of poverty is definitely evangelical *madness*. On its own merits, such praise is indefensible, though the saints have shown poverty can be humanizing.

Ellacuría also learned from the Gospel about the mutually exclusive, antagonistic dynamic of wealth and poverty—see, for example, what the *Magnificat* and the Beatitudes-woes of Luke say about poverty and wealth. He also learned from the *Spiritual Exercises* of St. Ignatius, especially the meditation on the two standards,[75] about the "elemental" character of wealth and poverty that lead, by their nature, to the various vices and virtues.

Finally, Ellacuría's typically Christian appreciation for poverty is seen in the way he distances himself from Marxist analyses of poverty and the poor. Christianity "does not admit that the proletariat alone is the principal subject of liberation or, much less, the principal addressee of liberation."[76] It insists, rather, that anyone who is poor possesses a salvific potential. It insists that Christianity constantly proclaim that the poor are especially beloved by God because they are poor.

### 1.3.3. Integral Liberation

Finally, it is important to say that Ellacuría, with many others, contributed to and promoted liberation. He insisted, and not as a matter of routine, that this liberation must be integral. Moreover, he derived this not only from normal fidelity to the magisterium of the church, which speaks about liberation in this manner, but also from what is simply Christian.

In the article on liberation cited above, he writes, "liberation from sin, death and the law is an essential part of the proposal for *integral liberation*, as it must be seen from the perspective of Christian faith."[77] He approaches the integral nature of liberation from another point of view with the following words:

> Liberation is, above all, a liberation from the basic necessities. If they are not safely satisfied, these needs do not allow one to speak of a human life, much less of the life of dignity deserved by the children of God to whom the Creator gave a common and communicable material world. . . . Liberation is, in the second place, a liberation from the fantasies and realities that frighten and terrify a human person. . . . This is what should be called liberation from repression. . . . Presupposing (and simultaneous with) these two forms of liberation, is personal and collective liberation from all forms of dependency [that] take away one's liberty when they are interiorized. . . . And finally, there is liberation from oneself, that is, from oneself as an absolutely absolute reality, which one is not, and which engenders idolatry.[78]

This insistence on liberation, and the hope for salvation as unavoidable, totalizing, and rooted in the underside of history, ultimately came to Ellacuría from the Christian tradition. It helped him see that reality is also a *mysterium salutis,* or, in Latin American terms, a *mysterium liberationis.*

## 1.4. Christianity's Potential

This way of framing and approaching important historical realities, sin as an ultimate and the need to shoulder its burden, the hope for salvation, the benefits of poverty, the radical distrust of power, and so forth, shows how Christianity shaped Ellacuría as a person. One could find elements in philosophy and ideology to argue this rationally, something that Ellacuría also did. In my opinion, it was his Christianity and, finally, Christian tradition, that sustained the radical and coherent character of his position.

There were certainly Christian witnesses like John XXIII, Archbishop Romero,[79] and Fr. Arrupe[80]—whom he loved and revered—who moved him to think in this way and to act accordingly. He was born and raised in this tradition. He had to deal with doubts and criticisms, theories and questions of practice. To put it simply, I think nothing helped him like Christianity to understand himself and to understand history, to become a person and make history a human history.

For Ellacuría, Christian faith does not invalidate philosophies and ideologies. However, at key moments in life, and when faced with important realities, Christian faith seemed to act for him as a kind of *reservoir of truth.* This is a place not many philosophies and ideologies reach, or even aspire to. He drew light and daring from it. On the one hand, he insisted that neither the faith, nor even the church, Christianity that is, could by themselves make the totality of liberation real. On the other hand, however, he was convinced that its contribution is irreplaceable:

> It makes no sense to object that the social teaching of the church or liberation theology does not offer fully operational solutions for humanity's problems. This lack does not imply that its historical contribution is useless, or that others can replace it. Integral liberation cannot be achieved using only the instruments offered by faith; however it cannot be achieved without them. The integral character of liberation demands this presence of faith.[81]

This conviction, in my opinion, is an important expression of Ellacuría's faith. I close by saying that Ellacuría located the fundamental mission of the church precisely in making the potential of Christian tradition fruitful. He called this, beautifully, her maternity:

The maternal nature of the church refers to her role as a midwife for humanity and holiness, as midwife for new impulses and ideas supporting liberation. And this character belongs to those to whom God has given it through the Spirit of Christ. . . . With the church being formed into a people of God more by her maternal than her magisterial forces, she will be in a better position to make her contribution to the liberation of humanity and history.[82]

## 2. Faced with the Mystery of God

The Christian dimension that shaped the most significant realities of Ellacuría's life was suffused with transcendence as well. To my knowledge, he analyzed this in greater detail in his philosophical than in his theological discourses. Whatever the case, one must emphasize that Ellacuría ignored neither history nor transcendence. He did not separate or confuse them either, maintaining a deep faithfulness to Chalcedon. Rather, he reformulated their relationship as *a transcendence within history,* so that history is understood as continuing to produce more from within itself.

### 2.1. History Is Pregnant with the "More"

In my opinion, Ellacuría was convinced of the existence of transcendence, and certainly of its manifestation in history. His theoretical vision and the direction of his praxis were always faithful to this "more" that he found in history. He tried personally to respond to, and to fit into, a history that is always pregnant with the "more." He was influenced in this by Zubiri's principle that "reality gives more of itself," and, above all, by the Ignatian *"magis."* According to Ignatius, it is not enough to do things well, but they must be done "for the *greater* glory of God." Nonetheless, what is fundamental is Ellacuría's deep conviction of that reality cannot be understood without accepting some form of transcendence.

If this is true, a final question remains, the deepest question. We have already said that Ellacuría was influenced and shaped as a person by his acceptance of the *mysterium iniquitatis* and the *mysterium salutis* that permeate history. It remains to be seen how Ellacuría's faith in the mystery of God lies behind this—the *Deus semper maior,* in the language of transcendence, the God of Jesus, in biblical terms. These were both phrases he often used.

Describing his personal faith is not an easy task. Certainly, God and Christ are frequently and profoundly treated in his writings. We are aware that he knew and thoroughly appreciated Zubiri's thought on God,[83] and that he wrote a magisterial philosophical article on faith.[84] In his theological thought, historical salvation is the actualization of the transcendent, "as a greater presence of the God who is always greater."[85] In sermons and talks, he spoke of God naturally. As far as he was able, he spoke favorably of pastoral work, especially with poor and simple people, because he believed their faith in God gives them clarity, strength, energy, and dignity.[86] He celebrated and participated in the Eucharist with devotion, and presided at the Mass we celebrated at UCA a few days after Archbishop Romero was assassinated. Visibly shaken by emotion, he spoke these famous words: "in Archbishop Romero, God visited El Salvador." These words, which I have cited so many times as Ellacuría's eulogy for Archbishop Romero, I bring up now as an expression of Ellacuría's own faith. In effect, Ellacuría, disinclined to using the name of God frivolously, or to using Archbishop Romero's name frivolously, was saying—testifying really—that he found the presence of that mysterious reality we call God in Archbishop Romero.

Having said all this, it is also true that it is not easy to find words to describe Ellacuría's faith, or that of any other person. It is even more difficult in his case, because his character was not given to demonstrations of intimacy and sentimental talk. For that reason, what follows is instead my perception of his faith and my honest conviction, based more on intuition from prolonged personal contact than on reflections about texts Ellacuría left us. I would like to add that it is based on what I have received from Ellacuría in the form of faith.

Changing our method, then, and without quoting him or basing my reflections on his writing, I will attempt to articulate what was, in my opinion, the mystery of God for Ellacuría. I will do so in reflections based on personal memories.

## 2.2. His Fascination with Jesus, Sacrament of the Mystery of God

My first reflection has to do with *Jesus of Nazareth*. It is clear to me that Jesus held a powerful attraction for Ellacuría. This was obvious from the way Ellacuría spoke of him, and not only when he argued about the historical Jesus as a theologian to convince an adversary where the church and the Society of Jesus should go. I think this attraction focused on the following: first, the mission of Jesus, the announcement and the construction of the reign of God for the poor, the defense of the weak, marginalized and victims, and the denunciation of oppressors and power elites of every kind. Second, there was an attraction to Jesus' way of being, his attitudes toward life and death, his honesty about truth, his compassion, his perseverance to the end, and his availability to God.

What is important is not the details, but the overall impact. This Jesus, the one from Nazareth who was not a philosopher like Zubiri, nor a theologian like Rahner, nor an economist like Marx, held a tremendous fascination for Ellacuría. Ellacuría did not express this in flowery words. A member of his audience recalls how one day Ellacuría became deeply moved as he spoke of Jesus:

> In a non-majors course on theology, Fr. Ellacuría was analyzing of the life of Jesus. Suddenly the rationality disappeared and his heart began to overflow. He said: "The fact is that Jesus had the justice to go to the depths, while at the same time he had the eyes and the heart of compassion to understand human beings." Then Ellacu became silent. And he ended, saying of Jesus: "He was a great man."[87]

I am personally convinced that Jesus of Nazareth made a great impact on Ellacuría, and exercised a fascination that is difficult to put into words. My impression is that a different Ellacuría would appear when he spoke about Jesus, and this speaking about Jesus made him feel and express himself in a different way than usual. This could be seen when he spoke of Jesus in relation to the Exercises of St. Ignatius, or to liberation theology. I remember his emotion—so peaceful—when he spoke of Jesus as the sacrament of God, following his admired teacher Rahner. In my opinion Ellacuría wanted to communicate something like what is said in the letter to Titus: the supreme goodness, kindness, and humanity of God our savior has appeared in our history in a human being.

## 2.3. Standing Before God with the Faith of Archbishop Romero

The second reflection involves *the mystery of God,* definitive for anyone's faith. I often think what faith is like for people, especially those who have been significant for my own faith, Pedro Arrupe, Archbishop Romero, and others. That is why I have also asked myself, what was Ellacuría's faith like? What problems did he have and how did he approach them? What was the mystery of God for him and, especially, what sustained his faith in that mystery, at once so luminous and so obscure? In thinking about this, two things always occur to me. One is that Ellacuría's faith had to pass through some type of darkness. The other is that, motivated as he was by honesty to reality and an original fidelity—to reality, to tradition, to faith, and finally to himself—he lived and remained attentive to a mystery, the mystery of God.

I believe this mystery, which as a mystery is "something that one must simply let be," was a reality in his life. Perhaps his relationship to this mystery could be described in the following words: it is necessary to let God be God, and it is good for human beings to let God be God. Perhaps it could be expressed in the hope with which he ended his last theological article: "beyond the successive historical futures that lie ahead, one can catch a glimpse of God the savior, God the liberator." Whatever the case, Ellacuría needed to come to terms with God, and he did.

This is what I tried to put into words, but not to explain, in the letter I wrote to Ellacuría one year after he was assassinated, reproduced at the end of this article. I would like to add a brief thought, more of an intuition really. It has great significance for me. For I lived many years with Ellacuría and, after asking myself many times what his faith was like, I finally articulated for myself what it was that finally kept him alive, and what led him to give up his life and accept death naturally.

This reflection deals with the impact of Archbishop Romero on Ellacuría's faith. In his talk when UCA posthumously awarded Romero a doctorate *honoris causa*, Ellacuría said the following:

> It has been said maliciously that our university manipulated Archbishop Romero. It is time to say publicly and solemnly that this was not so. Certainly, Archbishop Romero asked for our collaboration on many occasions. And this represented, and will always represent, a great honor because of whom it was who asked, and the reasons he asked it. . . . But in all these collaborations there was no doubt who was the teacher and who was the assistant, who was the pastor giving the instructions and who carried them out, who was the prophet getting to the bottom of the mystery and who was the follower, who was the motivator and who was the one being motivated, who was the voice and who was the echo.[88]

It was unusual for Ellacuría to refer to anyone as he did when he used to say, "Archbishop Romero was ahead of us." On the other hand, this was said with total sincerity, and not as a concession to the laudatory style of an honorary doctorate. The following is surprising as well. Ellacuría was known to be critical. Rare were the persons, even if Ellacuría liked and sincerely admired them, who were not the object of his criticism at some time. But Archbishop Romero was the only person I never heard him criticize. He admired him extraordinarily and praised him with total sincerity.[89]

For me, this means that Ellacuría saw in the archbishop, in who he was as a whole, something very special that fascinated him. The praise and gratitude expressed in his talk reflect the beneficial impact Archbishop Romero had not only on the UCA, but also on the deepest dimensions of Ellacuría as a person. Ellacuría seems to have been saying that to live near the reality of Archbishop Romero, near his commitment to the poor and his faith in God, was, to put it simply, to live in the presence of truth. He did not offer this as a generic thesis, but as his own existential reality.

I have no doubt that Ellacuría was really and existentially affected by Archbishop Romero, and in a different way than Rahner or Zubiri had affected him. The archbishop's prophetic character and compassion, his utopian vision and freedom, left their mark on Ellacuría. In my opinion, however, what was deepest and most specific was something else: the profound faith of Archbishop Romero, the unpretentious faith in the mystery of God the archbishop expressed so naturally, and that radiated from his person.[90]

As I have already stated, after the assassination of Archbishop Romero, Ellacuría said, "in Archbishop Romero, God visited El Salvador." These words were not spoken in a studied attempt to say something memorable that would bring him notoriety. They emerged as words of tremendous affection, admiration, and gratitude. Above all, they were spontaneous, coming from the depths of his being. Perhaps without meaning to, Ellacuría was also saying something deep and significant about himself. Therefore, they introduce us to the mystery of Ignacio Ellacuría himself: in our history, in spite of everything, and against all hope, one can often see God's footsteps.

For Ellacuría, such people as Archbishop Romero became like the face of God in our world, a face that was finally more *fascinans* than *tremens*. Moreover, in the presence of Archbishop Romero he felt smaller, he who was not used to that. It was a smallness that does not humiliate, but rather increases and confers dignity. He felt supported in his faith by the faith of the archbishop. Thus, it was Ellacuría, who in almost everything else was the leader and supported others, who felt himself supported by others in faith.[91] This is one of the inherent elements of his faith, dialectically united to his solitude and his unique responsibilities.

In conclusion, I would say that Ellacuría encountered a man of God in Archbishop Romero, and that he encountered God in this man. Truth and prophecy, compassion, justice, utopia and grace, and the elusive integration of it all that flowered so limitlessly in Archbishop Romero, brought Ellacuría, inexplicably, into the presence of God. I believe that, for Ellacuría, Archbishop Romero realized the aspiration we all carry within: that God is good, and that it is good that there is a God. What he encountered in a personal and exceptional way in Archbishop Romero, he also saw in some of the simple people he knew: in the poverty, the simplicity, the hope, and the dignity of this people he saw the mysterious traces of God. In the crucified peoples above all, he encountered the sacrament of the presence in the world of this mysterious God. This "glimpse of God the savior" is an expression of faith-hope in the mystery of God. To end this section, if we want quotes that capture the Archbishop Romero in whom Ellacuría saw something of himself, or that might express the archbishop's influence on Ellacuría's faith, the following words will do:

> His (Archbishop Romero's) hope rested on two pillars. It rested on an historical pillar, which was his knowledge of the people to whom he attributed an inexhaustible ability to resolve the most difficult problems. And it rested on a transcendent pillar, which was his conviction that God is finally a God of life and not of death, that the ultimate dimension of reality is good and not evil. This hope not only helped him overcome any temptation to discouragement, but it motivated him to keep working, conscious that his effort would not be in vain, no matter how short the time.[92]

*  *  *

> Archbishop Romero never tired of repeating that political processes, no matter how pure and idealistic, are not enough to bring integral liberation to human beings. He understood perfectly the saying of St. Augustine that to be human, one must be "more" than human. For him, history that would be only human, that only wanted to be human, would soon stop being human. Neither humanity nor history is sufficient unto itself. That is why he never stopped calling upon transcendence. In almost all of his homilies this subject emerges: the word of God, the action of God, breaking through the limits of what is human.[93]

## 2.4. To Walk Humbly with God

My third reflection is that it is obvious that Ellacuría's faith could not have been naïve. From the perspective of reason, there are many difficulties in accepting God today. Contemporary philosophers, with a few exceptions like Zubiri, profess agnosticism or atheism. Moreover, Ellacuría was intellectually formed during a period in which there was much talk of secularization and even the death of God.

The greater difficulty, it seems to me, comes from the scandal of the Third World. I do not believe that faith in God would be possible—for

Ellacuría or any other minimally reflective person—without some form of the question of theodicy emerging before the tragedy of that world. Why is there evil in this world, if a good and powerful God exists? The question is worse in Latin America, where Christian faith and theology confess a God of life, a God who is on the side of the victims. Consider the testimony of a priest who deals with the following thoughts and questions following the massacre of El Mozote in 1981.

> More than one thousand peasants murdered. I am not exaggerating. I saw many of the mutilated corpses rotting. For days afterwards the intolerable smell still filled the air. Homes destroyed, everyone dead. . . . In that little village, which for me was a joy, there were women and children, those children we never get to see playing in the mountains. . . . El Mozote, such a happy village with so much life. . . . When I saw the piles of corpses, the destruction, I could not stand it. How is it possible that precisely here, where I have visited so often to say that God is a God who is near to us, and who loves us, that God would remain indifferent to pain, that precisely here such an appalling massacre could occur?[94]

Not only this educated, European priest who is our example, but also the peasants ask themselves the same questions: "How many times have we said that God acts in our history. . . . But, Father, if you do act, when is this going to end? So many years of war, and so many thousands of corpses: what has happened to God?"[95]

The way each person asks him- or herself the question, the way each poses it to God, and how each one responds to the entire issue, is extremely personal. I only want to say, first, the question is nothing new. Second, these kinds of questions and demands arise clearly, without pretense, and in many forms throughout history and revelation. There is Jeremiah's protest to a God who is silent, who leaves him helpless; the painful questions of Job who must simply accept that he is a creature, not God; the skepticism of Qohelet; and the silence of God on the cross of Jesus. More for honesty rather than curiosity, I have asked myself many times which figure best captures the experience of Latin American believers who, in spite of everything, continue walking, working, and living their lives with meaning and with faith.

It seems inevitable that people like Ignacio Ellacuría would undergo some of the experiences we have mentioned, or some aspect of them. Another, more fundamental type of experience also mentioned by revelation appears there. It is that of the much-cited passage from Micah: "You have been told, Oh human, what is good, and what the Lord requires of you: to act justly, to love tenderly, and to walk humbly with your God" (6:8). As the text says in a solemn moment of revelation, whatever questions and demands human beings put to God, God's very self addresses a word that calls and invites us to make a journey in which it is possible for life and faith to find their ultimate meaning.

In my opinion, this text is a clear reflection of the lives of people like Ellacuría. It says that, though the human person may be questioning God, God is also asking something and one must respond to that question. The response may be spoken with words, but finally, if the human being does give an answer, it must be given through action. Likewise, that is where our question from God has its existential response. Revelation speaks, then, of a dialectic between questioning and being questioned. In my view, whatever his questions, Ellacuría never ceased to understand himself as one who was being questioned. His whole life, a faithful practice of justice to the end, can be interpreted as a praxis responding to the question put by God. This is something we humans must do humbly, due to the obscurity inherent in the mystery. It may also be done with clarity, because the mystery lived in justice and tenderness is not only obscurity, but also the abundance of luminosity.

Clearly, Ellacuría never ceased walking with compassion and fidelity through history, like Jesus in the Letter to the Hebrews. Thus, we can interpret Ellacuría's life as one of confidence in the ultimate good, in a God who is Father. He lived in active openness to the ultimate exigency of a Father who continues to be God. To put it in another way, one must let God be God; and it is good to let him be God. Ellacuría's journey through history was closer to Micah's, than to the object of Antonio Machado's song. It was journey toward God.[96] Machado's words, "Traveler, there is no path, the path is forged as one walks," are deep, existential, always questioning, and possibly inspiring. In the midst of the practice of liberation, they can be rephrased along the lines of Micah. This is what Pedro Casaldáliga has done:

| | |
|---|---|
| The path that is one | *Camino que uno es* |
| which one forges by walking. | *que uno hace al andar.* |
| So that others who walk | *Para que otros caminantes* |
| can find the path. | *puedan el camino hallar.* |
| So that those who are stuck | *Para que los atascados* |
| can take heart. | *se puedan reanimar.* |
| So that those who are lost | *Para que los ya perdidos* |
| can find us again. | *Nos puedan reencontrar.*[97] |

In other words, this is a decentered journey: "make the song of your people the rhythm of your march."[98] This decentered way of proceeding, which Micah demands, allows it to be understood and believed in faith, as a journey with God.

## 3. The Greater Love

Compassion for the poor and fidelity to walking humbly brought Ignacio Ellacuría to his death.[99] It can be truthfully said that they took his life. What is truer is that he gave his life freely. They took his life because it got in their way. But he gave it out of love.

I would like to end with a word about Ellacuría's martyrdom, placing it in the larger context of the martyrdom of his Jesuit companions at UCA, and of all the martyrs of El Salvador. Here, above all, I will base what I say more on personal memories than on his texts about martyrdom.

### 3.1. Why We Remember Martyrdom

We remember martyrdom, not out of routine or masochism, but because to do so is good and necessary. We remember out of gratitude, and so that it does not dehumanize us. We remember to comfort the survivors, especially family members. We remember because martyrdom sheds light on two important things.

The first is the subject of this essay: getting to know Ellacuría, his person and his faith. If it is true that the outcome gives meaning to the process, as Hegel said; if at the end we must pass a test, in the words of St. John of the Cross; and if at the end we will be judged for the last time, as Jesus says in the story of the Final Judgment; then it is good to know how Ellacuría died in order to know him better and to assess his character. We will also know whether Ellacuría's fate confirms his historical and Christian vision of things, and what type of tradition this martyrdom might produce.

It is possible and meaningful to ask this because a martyr's death is a dual reality. It is simultaneously an assassination-martyrdom, in the words that Ellacuría always used to explain the death of Archbishop Romero. As an assassination, it is darkness, the *mysterium iniquitatis*. But as martyrdom, it is luminosity, the *mysterium salutis*. It is very important to remember both, especially when they want to make us forget them.

More than that, the martyrdom of Ellacuría and the others also sheds light on what is central to the Christian faith. In effect, these martyrdoms help us better understand the fate of Jesus, his Cross and resurrection. Through these we better understand the origin of our faith and of the church. We must see their birth in the Cross of Jesus, as tradition has it, and the outpouring of the Spirit. In other words, Jesus dies on the cross with a great cry—the darkness of assassination. This cry is gathered up by God in the resurrection, and it is also gathered up by the men and women who follow Jesus. In this way, the Cross, through the luminosity of martyrdom, generates faith and lays a foundation for history.

Thus, Ellacuría and many other Latin American martyrs have died, objectively speaking, in ways that are similar to the way Jesus died. This has happened because they lived in ways similar to the way Jesus lived. If I may briefly digress to capture the significance of what we have just said, it is known that a century ago the original intent of Jesus' mission came to light: the kingdom of God, not directly the church. This rediscovery has helped us better understand not only the person and the motive of Jesus, nor even the church as servant and sacrament of the reign of God, but it has also made the following of Jesus and Christian martyrdom better understood, seen now from the perspective of the reign of God.

No doubt, many Christians in Latin America have lived as Jesus lived, announcing and initiating the reign of God, opting for, supporting, and defending the poor and the weak, denouncing and unmasking the powerful and the oppressor. This is why they have been slandered, persecuted, and assassinated as Jesus was. This is also why many have come before God, asking that the chalice be taken away, but doing God's will to the end. In the end, they have shown great love. This keeps their presence alive, as an analogy to the resurrection of Jesus, in such places as the Divine Providence Hospital where Archbishop Romero lived, the rose garden of the UCA where the Jesuits died, in the diocesan parish of El Despertar, and in many other places in El Salvador. Remembering the martyrs of today is a great aid to understanding Jesus, and to understanding the faith and the church that emerged from his Cross and resurrection.[100] It is a measure of the real harm that forgetting today's martyrs brings to the church.

In what follows, I reflect on the martyrdom of Ellacuría against the backdrop of El Salvador and what happened to Jesus. This will enable us to understand better who Ellacuría was, but also to understand the reality of our country and our faith.

### 3.2. Accepting Death

Ellacuría was very conscious of the possibility they might kill him, though he did not speak much about it. I believe there were two reasons for this. First, as already said, he was not much given to speaking of personal, much less of intimate, matters. Second, as the person in charge of a large institution being threatened, and as a natural leader, he did not want in any way to reinforce fear, much less generate panic. That is why when someone would speak of rumors about imminent dangers, he used to say that we were already immersed in "the catastrophic a priori."

Nonetheless, in those days one spoke of such things out of necessity. Fr. César Jerez, the Jesuit provincial from 1976 to 1982, used to say: "If they kidnap me, don't pay a cent." Someone else used to say: "Death is tolerable, but don't let them torture me." These conversations showed that finally everyone, each in his or her own way, was thinking of the possibility of death. As I said, Ellacuría was not given to speaking of these matters. Sometimes he would say, as if to minimize the importance of death, "the pain could only last twenty seconds." I remember another time discussing what Epicurus said about fear aroused by the thought of death. It goes, more or less, "If I am alive, I don't have to worry; and if I am dead, I can't worry."

I bring up these incidents to point out the obvious: Ellacuría was very conscious of the danger he was in, though he knew how to handle it subjectively. He did not want to spread panic. In any case, we can still recall that he was the object of persecution. This shows not only that he was not at all naïve, but that he accepted death with freedom and for love.

Oligarchs, military leaders, and government officials spoke frequently and with great virulence against Ellacuría.[101] The insults and slanders in the newspapers became proverbial.[102] From January 1976 to November 1989, bombs exploded on fifteen different occasions at UCA in critical locations like the central administration building, the computer center, the library, the office for *ECA,* and above all, the printing presses. On four occasions, the security forces searched our private residence, and four other times they planted bombs.

While these attacks were directed against all of us, they persecuted and threatened Ellacuría in a very particular way. From the beginning of the 1970s, he received personal death threats, and many times he was at the top of the lists of those to be assassinated. In 1977 he was not able to return to El Salvador after the assassination of Rutilio Grande. He said from Madrid, where he was, that he could not sleep all night after learning of the assassination.

To graphically describe the persecution against Ellacuría and the barbarity afoot in the country, it is enough to recall the events in 1980. That year they assassinated Archbishop Romero, four other priests, Cosme

Spezzotto, Manuel A. Reyes, Ernesto Abrego, and Macial Serrano; four North American missionaries, Ita, Maura, Dorothy, and Jean; and a seminarian about to be ordained, Otmaro Cáceres, just to mention religious people. They also assassinated Félix Ulloa, rector of the National University; the five directors of the Democratic Front, with its president, Enrique Alvarez Córdoba; and the hundreds of peasants massacred in the Sumpul River. At the end of that year, Ellacuría headed a list prepared by military personnel of people who were going to be assassinated. He had to leave the country under cover.

The conclusion that emerges from this brief review is that Ellacuría knew it was possible, even probable, that he would be assassinated. So if, in spite of that, he continued working in the country to the end, without changing the way of being, of speaking, and of acting, then his death demonstrates commitment, freedom, and love.

He was prudent, not suicidal, like Jesus, who, when he heard they had assassinated John the Baptist, moved to another place. He was also steady and resolute, as Jesus was. Jesus went up from Galilee to Jerusalem, where he was going to be betrayed. Ellacuría left Spain to return to El Salvador, and he decided to stay at the residence during an all-out offensive, in spite of many warnings to leave. To return to the example of Jesus, we recall that he began his mission "when John was arrested," his friend and teacher. In spite of that, and perhaps moved existentially by it, at that moment Jesus took up John's mission, although in a different way, and continued doing precisely that for which John had been arrested: prophetic denunciation. We can say this is something like what happened in El Salvador. When the prophet Rutilio Grande was murdered, the prophet Archbishop Romero emerged. When he was killed, the prophet Ignacio Ellacuría arose, though he had emerged earlier.

Ellacuría did all this naturally. During the long years of persecution, I never saw him doubt his mission or his place. He didn't seem to have to discern a lot about it either, the language of which at least is much used among religious nowadays. That was because, "the obvious is not the object of discernment."[103] Moreover, he saw something good and necessary in martyrdom. Earlier I cited his belief that, "Christians should be ready to be first and most at risk . . . even for martyrdom." Among the words he most often quoted from Archbishop Romero were the following:

> Brothers and sisters, I am happy that our church is being persecuted precisely for its preferential option for the poor, and because it tries to incarnate itself in the affairs of the poor. . . . It would be sad in a country

where people are being murdered so horribly, that we would not also count priests among the victims. They are the testimony of a church incarnated in the problems of its people.[104]

Ellacuría was convinced that persecution and martyrdom were a historical and Christian necessity, and he accepted them freely. This is how he was able to say as Jesus did, "No one takes my life from me; I give it freely" (John. 10:18). That freedom expresses love. "No one has greater love than a person who lays down his life for his friends." (John. 15:13).

### 3.3. Shouldering the Weight of Sin

Why did they kill Ellacuría? Though it is well known, and it may be clearly inferred from what has been said here, it is not a bad thing to return to this question because of the light it sheds on the martyrs and the country. As in the case of Jesus, two types of reasons were used against Ellacuría. The first were concrete and simply false. The second, more comprehensive reasons, did not justify killing Ellacuría, of course. But they were true statements. Let us examine them, comparing them with the accusations against Jesus.[105]

Regarding the first, Jesus was accused at the religious trial of blasphemy, and at the political trial of inciting the people to rebellion. None of it was true, but those were the accusations. Likewise, they accused Ellacuría of what, in our age, sounds like "blasphemy": Marxism, communism, being antipatriotic, even atheism. As the ultimate inversion and distortion of the Christian faith, they also accused him of being "liberationist." He was also accused of inciting to rebellion: supporting the FMLN and being its front man, of fomenting violence, war, terrorism, and so on.

We are not going to analyze here the false nature of these accusations. Rather, we will go to the heart of the matter. Turning to Jesus, the condemnation at the religious trial is decided based on the accusation that Jesus wants to destroy the Temple, and at the political trial based on opposition to Caesar. In this they were correct. Though Jesus did not want to physically destroy the Temple or to physically attack the emperor, he did desire, propose, work for, and struggle for a society quite different and even contrary to the one organized around the Temple and shaped by the Pax Romana. In the same way, Ellacuría proposed a society different from and even contrary to the present one, as we have seen. That was the real reason for killing Ellacuría, Archbishop Romero, and so many others.

So the murderers did say false and aberrant things about Ellacuría, but in what is fundamental, they were right.[106] Archbishop Romero used to say, "whoever gets in the way gets killed." Ellacuría interfered in a big way with the maintenance of a radically unjust, oppressive, and repressive society. He fought all his life to transform it into a just society of life and liberty. Thus, there were no good reasons to kill him, but there was a certain necessity. That necessity does not emerge from the cruelty of this or that person or group. Rather, it is structural. It is the implacable reaction of the idols. In the language of Archbishop Romero, "Woe to whoever touches the idol of wealth! It is like a high-voltage wire. You get burned!"

It is a profound conviction of the Latin American faith and theology that idols exist in this world. Ellacuría was one of those who contributed the most to theoretically conceptualizing and prophetically unmasking the idols. To summarize,[107] we can say that idols are existing historical realities that pass themselves off as divinities and display the characteristics of divinity: ultimacy, self-justification, untouchability. They offer salvation to those who adore them, though what they really do is dehumanize them, and they demand worship and orthodoxy. Their most salient characteristic is that, like the god Moloch of mythology, they demand human victims to survive.

This was Ellacuría's theory of idolatry. He also analyzed and denounced the concrete idols of El Salvador.[108] The first, the worst, and the origin of all the others is turning capital into an absolute. The second is national security, the armed forces, the security forces, and the death squads placed at the service of capital. The third idol could be called the popular organization because it absolutizes itself and creates a mysticism of violence. So, the idols do exist. The issue is how to destroy them.

Ellacuría did this concretely, above all, by analyzing and condemning the truth about reality. For this, seemingly so good and beneficial, he was persecuted unto death by the idols. That is because idols, like sin, do not only kill; they continually try to disguise themselves. Scandal and cover-up are correlative, so telling the truth also unmasks the lie. In still other words, the world in which Ellacuría lived, and in which we survivors live, is both a world of death and a world of lies. As the New Testament says, the devil is both a murderer and a liar.

Ellacuría wanted to liberate truth from the slavery imposed on it by society's oppressors; to shine light in the midst of a lie, justice in the midst of oppression, hope in the midst of despair, love in the midst of indifference, repression, and hate. That is why they killed him. That is how he shouldered the weight of our country's sin.

### 3.4. The Rose Garden

A final question remains. Ellacuría spoke so clearly of the *need* to bear the burden of sin like the servant of Yahweh, and not only to combat it from the outside. Has Ellacuría brought a *historical salvation* as well? The answer is important. We must clarify from the start that this salvation depends on us, whether or not we pick up his legacy and put it into practice.

It is well known that the martyrdom of Ellacuría and his companions, because of its magnitude and international repercussions, and the historical moment when it occurred, undoubtedly helped bring about a negotiated end to the war. In addition to this, however, we must think about the salvation Ellacuría and the martyrs leave us over time. This salvation is real. It consists, I believe, in having generated a historical and real tradition, both supremely necessary and constructive. This means that by their life and death, these martyrs have opened a track in history along which it is easier to travel. They have left a force that still acts *quasi ex opere operato* due to the power of that force, and the proximity of the events. Undoubtedly, this also implies an effort on the part of we who survive them. We are the ones who can make the track deeper, or, little by little, grade it away; making it easier, or more difficult to travel along its route.

Regarding Ellacuría, would that all that has been said in this essay become tradition. But perhaps I could highlight three things in which he was truly exemplary: his hunger and thirst for justice for the crucified people, his tireless condemnation of and analysis of the truth about their crucifixion, and the steadiness and fidelity of his praxis toward seeing them taken down from the cross. This is the legacy and the backing of a powerful tradition that he has left us.

How is this tradition doing in our country, in the church, at UCA, and in the Society of Jesus? All of this would have to be studied in detail. Nevertheless, to end, I would simply mention something important that has already become a reality. As happens with all traditions, the martyrs have already become symbols. They have given their names to communities, resettlements, centers for teaching, community-based clinics, and the like. This tradition already has its sacred sites: the Archbishop Romero Chapel where they are buried and the rose garden. They have their poets and their songwriters.[109] Just to mention one, Don Pedro Casaldáliga wrote the following about the garden of roses in March 1990:

| You are truth as a cross | *Ya sois la verdad en cruz* |
|---|---|
| and science as prophecy | *y la ciencia en profecía* |
| and the company is everything | *y es total la compañía* |
| companions of Jesus. | *compañeros de Jesús.* |
| The oath is fulfilled, | *El juramento cumplido,* |
| the UCA and this wounded people | *la UCA y el pueblo herido* |
| give the same lecture | *dictan la misma lección* |
| from the professorship of the grave | *desde las cátedras fosas* |
| and Obdulio tends the roses | *y Obdulio cuida las rosas* |
| of our liberation. | *de nuestra liberación.* |

Compassion for the poor and fidelity to walking humbly brought Ignacio Ellacuría to his death. Of him, as with so many others, it can be said that his life was taken away. What is truer is that he gave it freely. They took it because he got in the way. He gave it for love. All martyrs are different, but they all converge in what is fundamental. That is why I attribute to Ignacio Ellacuría the words he wrote about Archbishop Romero after the latter was martyred:

> This incarnation earned him the love of an oppressed people, and the hatred of their oppressor. It earned him persecution, the same persecution suffered by his people. That is how he died, and that is why they killed him. For that reason he became an exceptional example of how the force of the Gospel can become an historical force for transformation. That is why he continues to live after death . . . because many are ready to follow in his footsteps, knowing that Archbishop Romero, in the last three years of his public life, was an exemplary follower of Jesus of Nazareth.[110]

In spite of all the differences that exist between human beings, the same can be said of Ellacuría, his martyred companions at UCA, and so many others.

\*   \*   \*

To summarize, Ignacio Ellacuría was an exceptional human being and an exceptional Christian. He had an exceptional influence on our country, the church, and the Society of Jesus. I have tried to show what he was like, and why his influence was so great and so positive. Yet, as a human being, he was also limited. He had shortcomings and character flaws, and he made mistakes. The preceding pages were not intended as a eulogy. Nevertheless, it is true that he was an exceptional person, and that following his path is important and beneficial. If asked to sum up in a few words how I remember Ignacio Ellacuría as a human being and a Christian, I could only repeat what I wrote in a letter on the first anniversary of his death:

Dear Ellacu:

For years I have thought about what I would say at the Mass for your martyrdom. As in the case of Archbishop Romero, I never wanted to accept that this would come to pass. But your death was very likely, and the thought of this day has sent me in circles many times. These are the two things that most impressed me about you.

The first is that your intelligence and your creativity had a large impact on me, obviously, yet nonetheless I always thought this was not your most salient characteristic. It is true that these things were very important for you, but you did not orient your life to become a famous intellectual, or a lauded university president. To cite an example, I remember that while you were in exile in Spain you wrote a manuscript that would have made you famous in the world of philosophy. And yet you did not give it much importance, and you did not finish it when you came to El Salvador because you always had other more important things to do: from helping resolve some national problem, to attending to the personal problems of someone who asked for your help. The conclusion for me is very clear: service was more important to you than the cultivation of your intelligence and the recognition that it could bring you.

But whom to serve and why? You served at the UCA, but you did not finally serve the UCA itself. You served in the church, but you did not finally serve the church itself. You served in the Society of Jesus, but you did not finally serve the Society of Jesus itself. The more I got to know you, the more I became convinced that you served the poor of this country, and of all the Third World, and that this service is what gave finality to your life.

You were a faithful disciple of Zubiri, a liberation philosopher and theologian, and a theorist regarding community-based political movements, but you did not fight for those theories as if they were "dogmas." Rather, you changed your points of view, you the inflexible one. And when you would do that, it was always one thing that made you change your mind: the tragedy of the poor. That is why I believe that if you had any fixed "dogma," it was only this: the pain of the crucified peoples.

This brought me to the conclusion that first and foremost you were a man of compassion and mercy, and that what was deepest in you, your guts and your heart, was moved by the immense pain of this people.

This never left you in peace. It drove your creativity and your service. And your life, then, was not only service. Rather, it was the specific service of "taking crucified peoples down from the cross," very much your words, the kind of words that are invented not only with great intelligence, but with an intelligence moved by compassion.

This is the first thing I wanted to mention. The second thing I remember about you, and this is very personal, is your faith in God. I will explain what I mean. Faith in God was not made easy by your contact with modern philosophers, most of them nonbelievers, with the exception of your beloved Xavier Zubiri; or the atmosphere of secularization including even the death of God that predominated in the era when you achieved intellectual maturity; or your own critical and honest intelligence, not at all given to easy belief; or finally the great question about God posed by the unjust poverty of Latin America. I remember one day in 1969 you told me something I never forgot: that your great teacher Karl Rahner bore his doubts with great elegance. This brought you to say that faith was not something obvious for you either, but rather a victory.

Yet, nonetheless, I am convinced that you were a great believer, and to me, you certainly communicated faith. You did it one day in 1983 when, upon returning from your second exile in Spain, you spoke to us at the mass of the "Heavenly Father." And I thought to myself that if Ellacu, the thinker, the critic, the honest intellectual, used those words, then it was not just sentimentalism. If you spoke of the Heavenly Father, it was because you believed in him. You communicated faith to me many other times when you spoke or wrote of Archbishop Romero and his God, and when you spoke simply of the religiosity of the poor. And you communicated it to me through your way of speaking and writing about Jesus of Nazareth. In your writings you express your faith that what we human beings truly are has been revealed in Jesus. But there you also gratefully express your faith that Jesus displayed that "more" that surrounds everyone, that ultimate mystery and utopia, which attracts everything to itself. I don't know how much you struggled with God, like Jacob, Job, and Jesus. But I believe that God won you over, and that the Father of Jesus oriented what was deepest in your life.

Ellacu, this is what you have left us, for me at least. Your exceptional abilities can dazzle, and your limitations and defects can leave one in the dark. I believe, Ellacu, that neither has the one dazzled, nor the other obscured, the fundamental thing you have left me: that nothing is more essential than the practice of compassion for a crucified people, and that nothing is more human and humanizing than faith.

These things have come to mind over these years. Today, one year after your martyrdom, I say them with pain and with joy, but above all with gratitude. Thank you, Ellacu, for your compassion and your faith.

This essay was published in Spanish in two parts as "Ignacio Ellacuría, el hombre y el cristiano. 'Bajar de la cruz al pueblo crucificado,'" I and II, *RLT,* nos. 32 and 33 (1994) 131–61, 215–44. While the translation follows the original, it employs the continuous footnote numbering of the Spanish republication in a single article as "Ignacio Ellacuría, el hombre y el cristiano. 'Bajar de la cruz al pueblo crucificado,'" in Ignacio Ellacuría, Jon Sobrino, Rudolfo Cardenal, *Ignacio Ellacuría, el hombre, el pensador, el cristiano* (Bilbao, Spain: Ediciones EGA, 1994).

---

[1] The appreciation of Aristotle's thought, or Beethoven's music, for practical purposes does not still depend on our knowledge of them as persons. However, in the case of certain other thinkers and public personalities this is not true, especially in the following circumstances: proximity of time; public and sufficiently widespread knowledge of the person and their influence, explicitly understood, on society, especially if one adds a martyr's death. Thus, to give two examples, in order to understand the theology of Dietrich Bonhoeffer or the sermons of Archbishop Romero, it is very important to know about their personal lives and their deaths, in both cases by martyrdom.

[2] "Liberation," *Revista Latinoamericana de Teología,* no. 30 (1993) 217; periodical henceforth *RLT*. Ellacuría refers to personal sin in this text, but what he says can be applied to any human action.

[3] *Subs specie contrarii,* this can be clarified by seeing how some people cite and try to interpret Ellacuría, the *thinker,* independently of his *person*. What usually happens, then, is that they understand, or are able to understand, the *formal* content of the concepts he uses, but they do not seem to sufficiently grasp the historical *weight* of their contents.

[4] Antonio González, "Aproximacion a la obra filosófica de Ignacio Ellacuría," *ECA,* nos. 505–6 (1990) 980; see "Assessing the Philosophical Achievement of Ignacio Ellacuría," in *Love that Produces Hope,* 74. This same thing can be said even more correctly of his theology, since theological themes touched the deepest roots, the Christian roots, of his person.

[5] The truth is that the right still rejects or ignores Ellacuría. The manipulation, gross or subtle, comes perhaps more from the left at this time. Some people outside El Salvador want to use him to support ideals and even violent approaches he condemned. Others inside El Salvador now recall his work as a mediator and negotiator to justify relativizing everything prophetic and utopian on behalf of political realism, a realism that Ellacuría certainly supported, but not divorced from prophecy and utopia.

⁶ Ellacuría had outstanding qualities, but also limitations, especially in the area of character and temperament, which he himself recognized. What I would like to add is that Ellacuría, when he thought about reality and acted on it, did so *with* these limitations, but not *because of* them. In other words, his limitations were not the origin, in the sense of that which "originates," puts into motion, and gives direction to a life. That origin, even though accompanied and somehow affected by his limitations, must be sought in the positive dimensions of his person that we are going to study here.

⁷ To say this in a graphic way, I cannot imagine Ellacuría radically changing his basic manner of being, thinking, and acting, even though, for some hypothetical reason, he might have had to leave the Society of Jesus or the church.

⁸ I have used this concept of compassion in *El principio misericordia. Bajar de la cruz a los pueblos crucificados* (Santander, Spain: Editorial Sal Terrae, 1992; San Salvador, 1993), trans. as Jon Sobrino, *The Principle of Mercy: Taking the Crucified People from the Cross*, (Maryknoll, NY: Orbis, 1994). If I mention this here, it is to point out that much of what I write in this book comes from observing persons like Ellacuría and Archbishop Romero. This is why, though it is not my habit, this essay repeats the subtitle, which seems to me the best introduction to the person of Ellacuría: taking the crucified people down from the cross.

⁹ Xavier Gorostiaga, "La mediación de los cambios sociales y los cambios internacionales," in *Cambio social y pensamiento cristiano en América Latina,* J. Comblin, J. I. González Faus, J. Sobrino, eds. (1993) 131.

¹⁰ Ignacio Ellacuría, "El desafío de la mayorías populares," *ECA,* nos. 493–4 (1989) 1076. ["The Challenge of the Poor Majority" in J. Hassett and H. Lacey, eds., *Towards a Society That Serves Its People* (Washington, D.C.: Georgetown University Press, 1991) 171–6; collection henceforth *TSSP*.]

¹¹ It often happens that the type of persons mentioned are not interested in confronting reality because they do not want to be exposed, without defenses, to the questionings and demands of that reality. It could be added that some, especially intellectuals, usually think that coming close to concrete reality cannot contribute anything important to its theoretical comprehension.

¹² Ignacio Ellacuría, "Discernir el signo de los tiempos," *Diakonía* 17 (1981) 58. In my opinion, in this paragraph Ellacuría is using the concept "sign" (of the times) not only in its accepted historical-pastoral sense as something that characterizes an epoch (*GS* 4), but also in its accepted historical-theological sense as the place of the presence of God or of God's plans (*GS* 11). This is to say, theologically, this same God is present in the crucified people and, by stating this in radically theological terms, the ultimate character of the historical tragedy is also being affirmed.

¹³ Ignacio Ellacuría, "Función liberadora de la filosofía," *ECA,* nos. 435–6 (1985) 50. Ellacuría is making an allusion to the well-known question of Heidegger in *Was ist Metaphysik?*

¹⁴ Ignacio Ellacuría, "Quinto centenario de América Latina. ¿Descubrimento o encubrimiento?" *RLT,* no. 21 (1990) 278.

¹⁵ "God the Father had and/or produced many poor children. . . . This is a primary and statistically massive fact that no one who wants to talk about God can ignore," Ignacio Ellacuría, "Pobres," in *Conceptos fundamentales de Pastoral,* C. Floristán and J. J. Tamayo, eds., (Madrid, 1983) 790.

[16] Ellacuría was largely the inspiration for the section of the fourth pastoral letter by Archbishop Romero dealing with idolatry; see "Misión de la Iglesia en medio de la crisis del país," in *La voz de los sin voz,* J. Sobrino, I. Martín-Baró, R. Cardenal, eds., (San Salvador: UCA Editores, 1980) 145–9, trans. Michael J. Walsh as "The Church's Mission amid the National Crisis," Archbishop Oscar Romero, *Voice of the Voiceless* (Maryknoll, NY: Orbis, 1985) 114–61.

[17] Ignacio Ellacuría, "Aporte de la teología de la liberación a las religiones abrahámicas en la supración del individualismo y del positivismo," *RLT,* no. 10 (1987) 9.

[18] In "Liberación," 697–703, he elaborates a systemic and comprehensive concept that takes into account the personal, the social, the historical, and the theological dimensions.

[19] We do not know, of course, what Ellacuría would have done if he had been, for example, secretary general of a union, the superior of a religious order, or a parish priest or a bishop. However, I believe that his basic personal approach would have been the same: to relate any of these realities—unions, religious order, parish, diocese—to justice and liberation, and place them at the service of justice and liberation.

[20] Putting it simply, during the seventies when he was forming young Jesuits who were restless with the desire to participate in the processes of liberation and discouraged by the long years of study that seem to be an obstacle, Ellacuría, both as a consolation and a demand, used to say to them repeatedly that knowledge was indispensable for liberation, and what they had to do was study in an appropriate way, developing "a revolutionary passion for study."

[21] This is why he used to insist that the specific instrument—the weapon, if you will—for the university to influence society was the reasoned word. He also found in this an affinity with the church. This connection was clarified in an important way by the actions of Archbishop Romero in his pastoral voice.

[22] Ignacio Ellacuría, "Discurso de graduación en la Universidad de Santa Clara, 12 de junio de 1982," *Carta a las Iglesias* 22 (1982) 12, trans. as "The Task of a Christian University," in J. Sobrino, I. Ellacuría and others, *Companions of Jesus: The Jesuit Martyrs of El Salvador* (Maryknoll, NY: Orbis, 1990) 147–51, henceforth, "Discurso de graduación" [149].

[23] Ignacio Ellacuría, "Universidad y política," in *ECA,* no. 383 (1980) 813.

[24] Ibid., 816.

[25] Ellacuría, "Discurso de graduación," 11, 13 [149].

[26] Sobrino, and others, *La voz de los sin voz,* 453.

[27] Ellacuría, "Discurso de graduación," 14 [150].

[28] This is a colloquy St. Ignatius placed at the end of the meditation on sin that reads: "Imagining Christ our Lord present and placed on the Cross, let me make a colloquy, how from being the Creator He is coming to making Himself human, and from life eternal he is coming to temporal death, and so to die for my sins. Likewise a little later, looking at myself, I ask what have I done for Christ, what am I doing for Christ, what ought I to do for Christ? And so, seeing Him in this condition, and thus nailed to the Cross, to go over that which presents itself." *Ejercicios Espirituales* n. 53, trans. George Ganss as *The Spiritual Exercises of Saint Ignatius* (St. Louis: Institute of Jesuit Sources, 1992) 42.

[29] Ignacio Ellacuría, "Las iglesias latinoamericanas interpelan a la Iglesia de España," *Sal Terrae,* no. 826 (1982) 230.

[30] Ignacio Ellacuría, "Hacia una fundamentación filosófica del metodo teológico latinoamericano," *ECA,* nos. 322–3 (1975) 419.

[31] Ibid.

[32] Ignacio Ellacuría, "La teología como momento ideológico de la praxis eclesial," *Estudios Eclesiásticos* 207 (1978) 457–76.

[33] Ignacio Ellacuría, "Los pobres lugar teológico en América Latina," *Conversión de la Iglesia al reino de Dios* (San Salvador: UCA Editores, 1985) 163.

[34] *Libertatis nuntius* says, "The Gospel of Jesus Christ is a message of freedom and a force of liberation" (Introduction). "The aspiration to liberation . . . touches on a basic theme of the Old and the New Testament" (III, 4). *Libertatis conscientia* says that the Gospel "is, by its very nature, a message of freedom and of liberation" (Introduction 1). For an English translation of the two instructions see Congregation for the Doctrine of the Faith, "Instruction on Certain Aspects of the 'Theology of Liberation'" (Aug. 6, 1984) in A. Hennelly, ed., *Liberation Theology: A Documentary History* (Maryknoll, NY: Orbis, 1990) 393–414; CDF, "Instruction on Christian Freedom and Liberation" (Mar. 22, 1986) in *Liberation Theology,* 461–97.

[35] "Liberación," 213f.

[36] Ignacio Ellacuría, "Estudio teológico-pastoral de la *Instruccion sobre algunos aspectos de la teología de la liberación,*" *Revista Latinamericana de Teología,* no. 2 (1984) 150.

[37] We are not referring here to the maieutic method, but to the general disposition of his way of thinking toward exposing hidden interests and praxis, all for transforming the *polis.*

[38] This applies still more clearly to the first theologies of the Old and the New Testament. Its authors, whoever they were, were faced with reality and could not, by definition, refer to prior traditions or theologies to interpret it.

[39] Ellacuría emphasized what we have called the Socratic and pre-Socratic dimensions of the intellectual task, especially for the First World, since they are very frequently ignored there. Here where we are, with cultural and scientific shortages of every type, he especially emphasized the analytic dimension so we might gather the best and the highest number of rigorous disciplines that were to be always placed at the service of liberation.

[40] Ignacio Ellacuría, "Utopía y profetismo desde América Latina: un ensayo concreto de soteriología histórica," *RLT,* no. 17 (1989) 141–84. Also in *Mysterium Liberationis,* vol.1 (San Salvador: UCA Editores, 1993) 393–442. [Ignacio Ellacuría, "Utopia and Prophecy in Latin America," in I. Ellacuría and J. Sobrino, eds., *Mysterium Liberationis: Fundamental Concepts of Liberation Theology* (Maryknoll, NY: Orbis, 1993) 289–328, trans. James R. Brockman; collection hereafter cited as *MLT* (English translation) and *ML* (Spanish original).]

[41] Ibid., 141f. [*MLT* (1993) 289f.].

[42] Cf. Ibid., 142 [*MLT* (1993) 290].

[43] Ignacio Ellacuría, "El reino de Dios y el paro en el tercer mundo," *Concilium* 180 (1982) 593, henceforth, "El paro." [Ignacio Ellacuría, "The Kingdom of God and Unemployment in the Third World," in J. Pohier and D. Mieth, eds., *Unemployment and the Right to Work* (New York: Seabury, 1982) 91–6.]

[44] In his appearances on television, especially during his last years, he communicated all this very vigorously, and it created a tremendous impact. I remember a woman

told me after seeing him on television: "Since they killed Archbishop Romero nobody has spoken like Fr. Ellacuría."

[45] Ellacuría, "Quinto centenario de América Latina," 277.

[46] Ellacuría, "El paro," 591.

[47] The phrase is powerful and strong, but, as I remember, Ellacuría never softened it. While Ellacuría was still alive, don Pedro Casaldáliga used it in the following way. "To the phrase a 'civilization of love' perhaps should be added what the Salvadoran, Basque, Spanish, Jesuit theologian Ellacuría called, in a happy turn of phrase, a 'civilization of poverty.'" "A los quinientos años: 'descolonizar y desevangelizar,'" *RLT,* no. 16 (1989) 118. More recently, don Pedro has spoken of the civilization of "solidarity-based poverty." If I can insert a personal anecdote, in January 1990 I spoke on Spanish television about the civilization of "shared austerity." I said then that if I should frame this utopia in the words of Ellacuría, the audience might stone me.

[48] I remember at the beginning he used to talk about the "culture of poverty," but someone dissuaded him from using it due to the pejorative connotations of the term in cultural anthropology. This serves to indicate the concern that Ellacuría invested in the term.

[49] Ellacuría, "El paro," 588–96.

[50] Ignacio Ellacuría, "Misión actual de la Compañía de Jesús," *RLT,* no. 29 (1993) 115–26.

[51] Ellacuría, "El paro," 595.

[52] Ibid., 590f.

[53] Ibid., 591.

[54] Ibid., 592.

[55] Ellacuría, "Misión actual de la Compañía de Jesús," 119f.

[56] Ellacuría, "Utopía y Profetismo," 170f. [*MLT* (1993) 315–6].

[57] Ellacuría, "Las bienaventuranzas, carta fundacional de la Iglesia de los pobres," "Los pobres, 'lugar teológico,' en América Latina," in *Conversión de la Iglesia al reino de Dios,* 129–51, 153–78.

[58] Ellacuría, "El desafío de las mayorías populares," 1078.

[59] Ellacuría, "Quinto centenario de América Latina," 281f.

[60] Ellacuría, "El desafío de las mayorías populares," 1078.

[61] This can be seen clearly in his article "Teología de la liberación y marxismo," *RLT,* no. 20 (1990) 109–35, especially in the part he titles "El aporte de la teología de la liberación al marxismo," 127–35.

[62] Ibid., 119.

[63] I. Ellacuría, "El pueblo crucificado. Ensayo de soteriología historica," *RLT,* no. 18 (1989) 326 [*MLT* (1993) 597–8].

[64] "Palabras en el doctorado *honoris causa* en ciencias politicas al presidente de Costa Rica, Dr. Oscar Arias," mimeographed text, 6.

[65] As far as I remember, Ellacuría wrote two important articles on the subject of violence, one at the beginning of the seventies and another at the end of the eighties. "Violencia y cruz," in *Teología política* (San Salvador: Ediciones del Secretariado Social Interdiocesano, 1973) 95–127 [*Freedom Made Flesh,* trans. John Drury (Maryknoll, NY: Orbis, 1973) 167–231; collection henceforth *FMF* (English translation) and *TP* (Span-

ish original)] and "Trabajo no violento por la paz y violencia liberadora," *RLT,* no. 29 (1993) 189–208; originally published in *Concilium* 215 (1988) 85–94; henceforth "Trabajo no violento" [*Concilium* 195 (1988) 69–77].

⁶⁶ Jon Sobrino, "Apuntes para una espiritualidad en tiempos de violencia. Reflexiones desde la experiencia salvadoreña," *RLT,* no. 29 (1993) 189–208.

⁶⁷ Ellacuría, "Trabajo no violento," 88 [72].

⁶⁸ Ibid., 94 [77].

⁶⁹ Ellacuría, "Carácter politico de la mission de Jesús," *TP,* 30 [57].

⁷⁰ Ellacuría, "El papel de las organizaciones populares en al actual situación del país," *ECA,* nos. 372–3 (1979).

⁷¹ Ellacuría, "Historia de la salvación y salvación en la historia," *TP,* 8 [15].

⁷² Ellacuría, "Utopía y profetismo," *RLT,* no. 17 (1989) 184 [*MLT* (1993) 327–8].

⁷³ Ellacuría, "Misión actual de la Compañía de Jesús," *RLT,* no. 29 (1993) 119.

⁷⁴ Ibid., 119–20.

⁷⁵ The text of this meditation reads as follows: "to consider the discourse which Christ our Lord makes to all His servants and friends whom he sends on this expedition, recommending them to want to help all, by bringing them first to the highest spiritual poverty, and if His Divine Majesty would be served and would want to choose them, no less to actual poverty; the second is to be the object of scorn and contempt, because from these two things humility follows. So that there are to be three steps: the first, poverty as opposed to riches; the second, scorn and contempt as opposed to worldly honor; the third, humility as opposed to pride. And from these three steps let them infer all the other virtues." *Ejercicios espirituales,* no. 146 [Ignatius Loyola, *The Spiritual Exercises of Saint Ignatius,* no. 146, trans. and ed. G. Ganss (St. Louis: Institute of Jesuit Sources, 1992) 66]. On the subject of the Spiritual Exercises seen from the point of view of Latin America, Ellacuría gave a course at UCA in 1974 that we published posthumously under the title "Lectura latinoamericana de los Ejercicios Espirituales de san Ignacio," *RLT,* no. 23 (1991) 111–47; and regarding poverty, 128–33.

⁷⁶ Ellacuría, "Teología de la liberación y marxismo,"134.

⁷⁷ Ellacuría, "Liberación," *RLT,* no. 30 (1993) 219.

⁷⁸ Ibid., 224.

⁷⁹ See his essay "Monseñor Romero, un enviado de Dios para salvar a su pueblo," *RLT,* no. 19 (1990) 5–10, published originally in *Sal Terrae,* no. 811 (1980) 825–32.

⁸⁰ See his essay "Pedro Arrupe, renovador de la vida religiosa," *RLT,* no. 22 (1991) 5–23; published originally in M. Alcala, ed., *Pedro Arrupe: Así lo vieron* (Santander: Sal Terrae, 1986) 141–72.

⁸¹ "Liberación," 227.

⁸² Ibid., 228, 229–30. Ellacuría is playing here with the words *madre* [mother] and *maestra* [teacher] used to describe the church. He explains both in the article: their mutual relationship, their primary subject, and finally, the priority of creative motherhood over the regulatory magisterium.

⁸³ In 1984 he edited and wrote a prologue for a posthumous book by Xavier Zubiri, *El hombre y Dios* (Madrid: Alianza Editorial, 1984).

⁸⁴ Ellacuría, "Voluntad de fundamentalidad y voluntad de verdad; conocimiento-fe y su configuracion histórica," *RLT,* no. 8 (1988) 113–31.

[85] "Liberación," 226.

[86] To mention a single example, when he went to Chalatenango with Archbishop Rivera to negotiate the release of Duarte's daughter with the leaders of the FMLN, he especially wanted Archbishop Rivera to be able to meet with the priests of the zone, and above all, that he might be able to give religious encouragement to the people.

[87] *Carta a las Iglesias,* 245 (1991) 10.

[88] Ellacuría, "La UCA ante el doctorado concedido a Monseñor Romero," *ECA,* no. 437 (1985).

[89] To be exact, on one occasion he expressed his doubts, with respect, regarding the prudence of a decision by the archbishop. This was when, after doubt had arisen as to whether Fr. Ernesto Barrera had died fighting with a gun in his hand, the archbishop decided to preside at the funeral—"his mother will certainly be there" was his argument. Meanwhile, it seemed dangerous to Ellacuría for him to do this, because of the tremendous criticism that would fall on the archbishop from ecclesiastical authorities.

[90] Ellacuría was probably also impacted by Archbishop Romero's direct, effective, and affective closeness to the poor—something he admired in Rutilio Grande as well—perhaps because he did not live this way on the outside.

[91] I also think he felt supported by the faith of simple, suffering, committed, and hopeful people with whom he came into contact in daily life, and that he appreciated in the testimonies in *Cartas a las Iglesias,* a publication he held in great esteem precisely because of the testimonies from the people.

[92] Ellacuría, "La UCA ante el doctorado concedido a Monseñor Romero," 174.

[93] Ellacuría, "Monseñor Romero, un enviado de Dios para salvar a su pueblo," 9.

[94] María López Vigil, *Muerte y vida en Morazán. Testimonio de un sacerdote* (San Salvador: UCA Editores, 1987) 94–5. Ellacuría knew this book and the priest who gives the testimony well. He wrote a prologue for the Italian edition of the book that appeared in Spanish in *Carta a las Iglesias* nos. 168–70 (1988) 7–10, 11–3, 5–7.

[95] Maria López Vigil, *Muerte y vida en Morazán,* 119.

[96] Zubiri also helps us conceptualize access to God as a real journey to God. "The act or acts of human access to God are not formally intellective, but rather they are those actions that physically and really take us effectively to God as an absolutely absolute reality. . . . God is constitutively accessible in real things themselves. Never, not even in the supreme access of the great mystics, does one find access to God without things or outside of things: one always gains access to God in things. Real things are the personal presence of God," Zubiri, *El hombre y Dios,* 181, 186.

[97] Pedro Casaldáliga, "Camino que uno es," in *Cantares de la entera libertad* (Managua, 1984) 47.

[98] Ibid., 48.

[99] Regarding the martyrdom of Ellacuría and his companions, see what I wrote a few days after the assassination in Jon Sobrino, "Compañeros de Jesús. El asesinato-martirio de los jesuitas salvadoreños," *ECA,* nos. 493–4 (1989) 1041–74 [trans. Dinah Livingston as "Companions of Jesus," in J. Sobrino, I. Ellacuría and others, *Companions of Jesus* (Maryknoll, NY: Orbis, 1990) 3–56].

[100] In technical terms, there is a hermeneutical circularity between Jesus the martyr and the present-day martyrs of Latin America due to the horizon of the reign of

God common to both. Meanwhile, in other epochs, martyrs have been understood more from the perspective of the church than from the reign of God. Obviously, this does not imply any judgment regarding the subjective holiness of the martyrs of either the church or the reign. Neither, of course, does it relativize the preeminence of Jesus the martyr. But it does help us understand the reciprocal relation between the Cross of Jesus and the martyrs of today.

[101] Likewise, the ecclesiastical institution, some offices of the Vatican, CELAM, and certain bishops from the country questioned his orthodoxy and disapproved of his public actions.

[102] In one of his most famous appearances on television with Ray Prendes and D'Aubuisson, even though he clearly rejected the idea that Marxism and communism were the principal forces shaping his person, his thought, and his praxis; almost all the callers to the program insisted on accusing him of being a Marxist, understanding this as the worst of all evils.

[103] He was so convinced he had to run risks that when they killed Archbishop Romero, which some attributed to Romero's denunciation [of the government] the evening before on March 23, Ellacuría insisted this was the archbishop's lot. He also used to ask political leaders to return to El Salvador sometime after the end of the war.

[104] Cited in J. Sobrino, I. Martín-Baró, and R. Cardenal, *La voz de los sin voz. La palabra viva de Monsignor Romero* (San Salvador, 1981) 454.

[105] See Jon Sobrino, *Jesus the Liberator* (Maryknoll, NY: Orbis, 1993) 196–200, trans. Paul Burns and Francis McDonagh from *Jesucristo liberador* (Madrid: Editorial Trotta, S.A., 1991).

[106] The famous Rockefeller report written shortly after Medellín says that if what the bishops said there was put into practice, the interests of the United States would be threatened. This does not make much sense at a military and strategic level, but it does at the social level: Latin America endangers the values of the *American way of life*.

[107] See Sobrino, *Jesus the Liberator,* 180–92.

[108] The theoretical articulation and historicization of idolatry appear, as we have said, in the fourth pastoral letter of Archbishop Romero, inspired by Ellacuría.

[109] The complete works of Ellacuría are being published. From his philosophical and theological thought, various articles have already been published. Doctoral theses are being written, a play has been written, and a film is being made.

[110] Ellacuría, "Monseñor Romero, un enviado de Dios para salvar a su pueblo," 10.

# Chapter 2

# No One Takes My Life from Me;
# I Give It Freely*

*Gustavo Gutiérrez*

There can be no doubt that Ignacio Ellacuría has a very special place among those who, through their commitment and their thought, have desired to walk with the poor of Latin America as they strive to have their dignity as human beings and as daughters and sons of God recognized and respected. His place is special, of course, because of his terrible assassination; but also, and above all, because of his life. Furthermore, in this case, life and death are inseparable: his life led him to death.

## To Give One's Life

I vividly remember the morning I heard on a Lima radio station the unbelievable news of what had happened a few hours earlier in El Salvador, of lives cut short by hate and by the rejection of a peace based on justice that the victims had supported in the best prophetic tradition. The poor of that country had been deprived of individuals firmly committed to them. Two simple women of the Salvadoran poor were also assassinated: Julia Elba and her young daughter, Celina. Actually, they were all part, by birth or by choice, of the same people. They received the ignominious and

* Translated by James B. Nickoloff.

cruel death so many Salvadorans suffered in those years from bullets that came from the same side as those that killed Monseñor Romero. The crusts of the Jesuits' blood spilled in the garden and those found in one of the rooms of the house where a mother and daughter were assassinated were alike. On these basic levels there are no differences. The assassination revealed—if this were necessary—a transfusion of life dating back to the decision to share the sufferings of an entire people. This is what led Ignacio and his friends to death. It was the outcome of a choice for life. It is not that Ignacio sought a violent death. Martyrdom is a radical faith witness, but it cannot be sought; it is found on the path of faithfulness. Georges Bernanos reminded us of this in unforgettable terms in "Dialogue of the Carmelites." The life Ignacio chose makes us understand the scope of the death he encountered. Like Jesus, Ignacio could say, "No one takes my life from me; I give it freely" (John 10:18).

He gave it, in fact, out of love for the God of the Bible and for the people he made his own. The people compelled him to learn about the scandal of their poverty and their unending suffering. Thus he came to understand the central role that justice has in the Gospel message and that without it there is no authentic peace. His choice made him see that he couldn't follow in Jesus' footsteps without walking with the people in their aspiration to dignity, life, and liberation from all that marginalizes and oppresses them.

In the face of this difficult challenge, he did not take refuge—and this is another of the traits that give him his special place—in something he had at hand and that could have hidden the fear of solidarity and its demands from others and even from himself: namely, an intellectual life flowing quietly along in the purely academic world. This kind of life, although it might occasionally reflect what was happening to the marginalized, would in fact be far from them and their afflictions. Chances to excel in the university world were not lacking, this we know. He possessed a solid formation in philosophy and theology; he was well known as the favorite student of a great teacher, Xavier Zubiri. The academy's doors stood open to him.

But neither did he give in to another easy temptation: to leave aside his intellectual competence under the pretext of meeting the demands of commitment. There was no lack of pretexts, or even fairly serious reasons, for doing so. He only had to appeal to so many scholarly works far removed from the concrete existence of people, even in our crisis-ridden countries. He could easily have explained away the fear of slipping into this way of thinking (and of doing so unconsciously). There are dubious searches for the truth that are a lie from the very beginning and that therefore do no more than cover up fears, swell the desire for personal prestige, and contribute to library catalogues. Since they fail to sink their teeth into reality, they are sterile, they dry up, and they disappear as soon as the sun comes up. Ignacio could not help but think of this risk.

We cannot know with scientific accuracy how many tensions and perplexities, vacillations and inconsistencies, bad moods and painful impasses he experienced along the path he chose to follow. Naturally, his could be neither a tranquil nor a triumphal journey. It never is. What is certain is that he put his intelligence, his analytical acumen, and all his intellectual talent to work doing the discernment necessary for finding the correct path amid the jumble of events taking place in El Salvador and Latin America. Not only did he not forget his philosophical formation; he used it as a source of criteria for acting in a changing situation full of surprises. Thus he gave his academic formation its due and, going against one of the most subtle forms of intellectualism, made clear the role it can play in the daily life of individuals no matter how conflictual the situation in which they find themselves. One of my old professors (of physiology, to be more specific) always said, "There is nothing more practical than a good theory." Ignacio lived out this kind of theorizing with passion.

Like all of us, he learned through trial and error. Is there any other way to learn if you want to be faithful to ordinary life and from that vantage point try to make out what's coming? Or is there any other way if you forswear always having to be right when it means distancing yourself from the present and abandoning the solidarity to which the present challenges us? Ignacio did not pretend in this way to have clean hands; perhaps he was remembering what Péguy said: "They say they have clean hands but it turns out that they have no hands." Our friend did have hands, and he often plunged them into the mud of which human life is made, with all the delicacy and all the risks this implies.

## In Solidarity with a Crucified People

As various works published in this book make clear, Ignacio also put his intellectual formation at the service of his reflection on faith. History was for him a key notion in constructing an anthropology and a theology in harmony with the message of the God who became one of us. He therefore thought the persistence of a Christian vision that did not sufficiently take into account the history of salvation (a notion strongly emphasized by Vatican II and liberation theology) made it difficult if not impossible to understand what was happening in Latin America. In an unpublished work from 1987, published after his death, he took up this question once again.[1] Because he did not see history as something abstract but rather as the concrete field where human beings encounter each other and where human beings encounter God, he drew near the suffering of the poor and marginalized with such dedication and examined their suffering in the light of faith. This is what led him to call the Latin American people a "crucified people," an expression that still offends many ears but moves our hearts. With this expression we not only have the accurate rendering of a human reality analyzed using the tools of social science, but above all we also find in his words profound biblical resonances: the identification with the poor proclaimed by Jesus and the reassertion of the consequences of his death on the cross. This is why Ignacio saw in that crucified people the presence in history of Yahweh's Servant, even to the point of seeing his face disfigured, as we can behold among us everyday. To this crucified people—victim of so many kinds of violence—he consecrated his life and his thought. And with that consecration he demonstrated philosophy's relevance as a constitutive element of a liberating praxis serving the vast majority and, beyond them, every person involved in one way or another in the present situation.

With great fidelity to Ignacio, Jon Sobrino has shown us the consequence of this vision by speaking of the pressing need to "take the crucified people down from the cross." To do this we must begin by radically rejecting the unjust suffering caused by the indifference of those who pretend not to see others, or by the selfishness of those who see no further than their own interests or who seek only to protect their privileges. It is the world of the poor and the disinherited of the earth, more excluded (and expendable) with each passing day in a society that makes profit and luxury the object of its concern.

For decades we have been saying in Latin America and the Caribbean that we are not with the poor if we are not against poverty. By poverty we do not mean, as we well know, only the lack of material possessions; rather, we take into account an all-encompassing situation we describe as unjust and premature death. In this way we are pointing to the deepest meaning of poverty: physical death that results when people have no way to feed themselves or care for their health, but also cultural death caused by scorn, social insignificance, and discrimination based on race, culture, or gender. We are faced, then, with a people crucified for a variety of reasons. These people will not be taken down from the cross if we don't get to the roots of the current state of things, to their causes, as John Paul II has said again and again.

There is no structural analysis, no statistics, no matter how much they make us feel the cruelty of a situation, that can take the place of direct contact with a person who is suffering, of intimate solidarity with victims. This happens only when we look behind the data and our investigation of the present social and political moment and perceive human beings who have names and who see their most elemental rights to life and liberty being trampled. As a Christian and as a philosopher, Ignacio was an impassioned devotee of the human person, the sacrament of God in history. I say "impassioned" because he saw in poverty not only a summons to his intellect but also to his human heart, as is said of the Samaritan in Luke's famous parable. There is no other way to understand Ignacio's stubbornness in remaining—and thus risking his life—in the midst of a people able to steal his heart despite his austere frame of mind (which, as we now understand better, was more appearance than reality).

In the face of the horrors of those years, Ignacio used to say with shock and pain, "Here in El Salvador life is worthless." These words unfortunately also fit other places on our continent that is called a continent of hope, but that, at the same time, continues to be a continent of suffering where human dignity doesn't count for much. Nevertheless, we have to say that Ignacio's own testimony is the clearest refutation of his statement. The lives of those men and women must have been worth a lot if someone like him, his friends, and so many others, gave up their own lives for the lives of those who could not attain the respect of others.

In the course of every human existence lived for others, there will be uncertainties, fears, impulsive mistakes; no one is exempt from this. Such an existence is always a source of life. It nourishes thinking that in turn deepens faith and hope in the death and resurrection of Jesus. Ignacio and those with whom he died could not have evoked this more powerfully.

---

[1] Ignacio Ellacuría, "Salvación en la historia," in C. Floristán and J. J. Tomayo, eds., *Conceptos fundamentales del cristianismo* (Madrid: Trotta, 1993) 1252–74; also published as "Historia de la salvación," *RLT,* no. 28 (1993) 325.

# Chapter 3

# Assessing the Philosophical Achievement of Ignacio Ellacuría*

*Antonio González*

The subject we will discuss here will be limited in at least two respects. First, we will consider only one aspect of the copious and certainly varied intellectual activity of Ignacio Ellacuría: his philosophical work. Second, this philosophical work will not be treated from the point of view, however legitimate and important it might be, for example, of his collaboration with Xavier Zubiri. Rather, it will be treated from a perspective of special interest for those of us who work or have worked in philosophy in El Salvador: the perspective of his contribution to what, in general terms, we could call a "philosophy of liberation." In my view, his 1985 article "The Liberating Role of Philosophy"[1] appropriately defines the ultimate goal not only of his philosophical writings, but also the philosophical interests he wanted to advance at the University of Central America José Simeón Cañas (UCA) in El Salvador. This direction of his work, however, was based to such an extent on the philosophy of Zubiri that, as we will see in what follows, it can not be properly understood without reference to Zubiri.

* Translated by Robert Lassalle-Klein.

## 1. The Socratic Task as the Task of Philosophy

How should one define Ellacuría's contribution to the constitution of what we have loosely called a "philosophy of liberation"? In my opinion, it would be a mistake to begin seeking an answer to this question among his many philosophical writings,[2] to try to determine which theses are most directly linked with the liberating role that Ellacuría attributes to philosophy. One could, for example, begin by saying that his *Philosophy of Historical Reality* constitutes the point of departure for a philosophical consideration of liberating praxis. This is without doubt interesting, as we will see, but I think it is neither the first thing to deal with, nor the most radical aspect of his contribution to Latin American philosophy. In my view, the relevance of his work does not primarily reside in this, or in any specific *content* of his philosophical reflections, but rather in the *character* itself of his intellectual activity.

Indeed, strictly speaking, one must begin by saying that Ellacuría did not construct a philosophy; he did not elaborate a philosophical system as it is usually understood in the history of philosophy. Nevertheless, one can say that Ellacuría was a *philosopher* in the full sense of the word, though perhaps not in the usual sense, without fear of falling into the facile panegyric that the very character of his many intellectual endeavors was philosophical. In a well-known work on Socrates, Xavier Zubiri pointed out that the great contribution of Socrates to the history of philosophy does not consist of a specific thesis that can be attributed to him, nor even the fact that Socrates, contrary to the "naturalist" philosophers who preceded him, had proposed human life and the world of ethics as the proper objects of philosophy. Rather, his originality resides in having turned philosophy itself into a style of authentic human life, in having fashioned from theory a truly ethical form of existence.[3]

Perhaps the Socratic model of doing philosophy and of being a philosopher should be the first key for approaching the work of Ignacio Ellacuría. Paraphrasing Zubiri, we could draw a parallel to Socrates, saying that *what distinguishes the intellectual work of Ignacio Ellacuría does not consist so much in having placed the historical praxis of liberation at the center of his philosophical reflections, but in having made philosophy a constitutive element of a life dedicated to liberation.*

Analyzing this in specifics would get us into biographical considerations for which we do not have space here. Perhaps it will suffice to say that Ellacuría demonstrated with his own life (and—why not say it?— with his death as well), that the social role of philosophy is not primarily an academic function, and much less a legitimizing function for one or another power, but—at least as a possibility—a liberating function. He demonstrated that this liberating role does not primarily consist in the transmission of a specific philosophy, a specific tradition, or a few specific philosophical understandings, but rather, as was also the case with Socrates, in a *maieutic* and *critical* task.

It is maieutic not only in the usual sense of bringing to light in an "educational" sense (as derived from *e-ducere,* to bring out) what students already know on their own, but rather in a sense closer to the original Greek expression *maieuomai* (to help in the process of giving birth, to let loose). Indeed, it is a question the philosophical accompaniment of the peoples of the Third World in a difficult historical hour, preferentially situated on the side of those who are trying to thwart the triumph of death and on the side of a new idea that, in spite of all the difficulties, is striving to be born. This *historical midwifery* does not render intellectual labor useless, but rather places demands with true urgency and, if possible, for greater quality than usual; even though, of course, it marks out intellectual horizons and goals that go beyond merely professional ones.

It is also, therefore, a labor that is *critical,* because the philosophical option for life leads to confrontation with so many ideologizations—both philosophical and nonphilosophical—that present the dominion of violent oppression and death, not only in El Salvador but in the political and economic world order, as a system of freedom and democracy. Ellacuría invested his many intellectual qualities in this de-ideologizing task, his refined and mordant sense of irony, and even his excellent knowledge of the ancient weapons of the sophists, now placed not at the disposal of elite Athenians, but rather at the service of those whom he used to call the "common majorities."

We are well aware that the price for this kind of activity has to be paid to the powerful of this world. Here also our reference to Socrates becomes tragically significant; Ellacuría had written of him years ago that his philosophical activity had been a true critique "as much for his personal dissatisfaction with what he already knew, as for his constant confrontation with those who thought of themselves as the repositories of true knowledge and the true interest of the city simply because of the social or political position they occupied. The first led him to a permanent struggle with himself; the second to an uneven battle with the powerful figures of his day. He had to abandon everything, and the little that was left—the last years of his life, the ashes of his existence—was taken away from him in the name of the gods and the respectability of the city."[4]

## 2. Ellacuría's Philosophical Education

Obviously, what we have called here a philosophical life in the Socratic model of doing philosophy does not consist simply in a way of life like that of a public figure or a social critic. The philosophical life, to be truly such, has to confront the problems proper to philosophy, and not only in an occasional fashion, but rather as a radical question that determines the very character of that life. In other words, the liberating dimension of a philosophical way of life is inseparable from the philosophical question of liberation, precisely because of the character of ultimacy of all philosophy. What, then, is the contribution of Ellacuría to the philosophical formulation of this question?

Like the great majority of Catholic priests of his time, Ignacio Ellacuría was initially trained in Neo-Scholastic philosophy, particularly during his studies at the Jesuit philosophate in Cotocallao (Ecuador). However, he soon realized the limitations of the Aristotelian-Thomist tradition and, even before continuing his education in Europe, he became interested in the philosophy of Ortega y Gassett and Bergson, on whom he published a few articles. At Innsbruck (Austria) between 1958 and 1962, he came into contact with Karl Rahner, and through him with the philosophy of Heidegger and with existentialism. From the early sixties he maintained frequent contact with Xavier Zubiri, who profoundly impressed Ellacuría, and with whom he began the preparation for his doctorate. From that time on, Ellacuría became the Basque philosopher's closest collaborator.[5]

"La principialidad de la esencia en Xavier Zubiri" is the title of the doctoral dissertation he completed in 1965 that he had to defend before a committee comprised chiefly of former adversaries—Scholastic philosophers—of Zubiri. Ellacuría's thought during this period is dominated almost exclusively by new perspectives opened up by Zubiri's metaphysics, especially his *"talitativo"* [suchness-oriented] and transcendental study of the ancient philosophical problem of essence. Zubiri's book on this problem had been published a few years earlier and was regarded as the philosopher's definitive work, something that today, after Zubiri's trilogy on intelligence,[6] can no longer be maintained.

At this point, one can justifiably ask: then what does this analysis of essence, where Zubiri certainly contests the key themes of classical metaphysics, have to do with what we have called here a "philosophy of liberation"? Certainly, Ellacuría's philosophical works during this period, though still very influenced by Zubiri's thought, already give us some clues of his interests and the direction that he is going to follow in his further evolution. Above all, Ellacuría is interested in the novel approach that Zubiri develops to human *historicity*,[7] because he understands that this is precisely one of the principal themes in the dialogue with Marxist philosophy, that is, with historical materialism. Thus, given that historical materialism was grounded by Engels in dialectical materialism, the problems posed by that philosophy also attend to the philosophy of nature and even more radically to *first philosophy*.[8]

This dialogue with dialectical materialism produces Ellacuría's interest in two great themes in Zubiri's metaphysics: first, the original idea of *structure* outlined in *Sobre la esencia*, which can be especially fruitful not for a "structuralist," but rather for a structural study of social and historical realities.[9] Second, Ellacuría attempted to undo what was certainly a false image of Zubiri's philosophy, though this image was perhaps due to the fragmentary style and character of *Sobre la esencia*. He insists that Zubiri's philosophy does not provide a static image of the real, but rather one that is radically dynamic. This is why he repeatedly calls our attention[10] to Zubiri's lecture course of 1968 given the precise title, *Estructura dinámica de la realidad*, which, in spite of its importance, has remained unpublished until very recently.[11]

In my view, this study is of paramount importance, not only because it provides us an interesting approach to Zubiri's philosophy, but also, from the perspective that interests us here, because it gives us the key to understand Ellacuría's philosophical evolution. It will help us understand how Ellacuría, moving beyond a dialogue between dialectical materialism and what we could call Zubiri's "cosmovision," will end up outlining a true philosophy of liberation.

## 3. The Horizon of the Philosophy of Liberation

The question we are trying to answer—how to arrive at a philosophy of liberation by way of Zubiri's philosophy—could be formulated, in the particular case of Ellacuría's intellectual trajectory, in the following manner. Ellacuría has interpreted the philosophy of Zubiri as an "open materialist realism,"[12] a definition that emphasizes, on the one hand, Zubiri's rigorous critique of the Western idealist tradition and, on the other hand, the central role Zubiri gives to matter in his evolutional cosmovision. However, this no doubt somewhat hasty qualification could awaken the suspicion that, deep down, Zubiri continues to move within what he himself has considered the horizon of Greek philosophy, that is, the horizon of nature and movement, the horizon within which Aristotle, with his profound biological astuteness, establishes the categories of substance, act, and potency.[13] In this sense, Zubiri would appear as a corrective, no matter how original, of the ancient categories of classical philosophy, but one who finds himself situated within the same horizon of problems as the ancients: substance would now be *substantivity,* act would be *actuality,* and potency would be *dynamism.* His philosophy would certainly contribute a rejection of modern subjectivism, which turns human consciousness—as Ortega vividly described it[14]—into the container of the entire universe, but his alternative would be no more than a new type of naturalism, as is also the case with the dialectical materialism of Engels. For such a philosophy, humanity and its intelligence would constitute a mere outcome of the natural evolution of the cosmos, from which—and only from which—they will have to be understood.

Nevertheless, and in spite of having frequently emphasized the relevance of the material and the biological dimensions of human life,[15] this is not the way Ellacuría has interpreted Zubiri. From the start, Ellacuría realizes that at the core of Zubiri's philosophy there is an intimate connection between the reality of the cosmos and human intelligence.[16] This connection prevents our speaking simply of naturalism, since "reality is only a source of light with reference to an intelligence that, it is clear, is in its turn oriented toward reality."[17] Or, as Zubiri himself used to say in a concise manner that, in my view, brilliantly summarizes the ultimate meaning of his trilogy on intelligence, "an intrinsic priority of knowing over reality, or of reality over knowing is impossible. Knowledge and reality are, at their very root, strictly and rigorously of the same species."[18] Thus, human beings, who, on the one hand, are certainly the result of the evolution of the cosmos, are, on the other hand, in Zubiri's words, "the location of reality."[19] To say this means to go beyond both the naturalist Greek horizon and beyond modern subjectivism, and by doing so, Zubiri will have situated himself, according to Ellacuría, within a new horizon in which "humanity is neither the dust of the universe nor its container; it is intrinsically both at the same time."[20]

Obviously, the problem is *how* to keep "both things" at once. This is, in my view, one of the decisive questions for Zubiri's hermeneutics. It is possible, for example, to emphasize the first pole of the synthesis, that is, the primacy of reality over intelligence, which finally would be nothing but just one more of the realities of the cosmos, though certainly a privileged reality due to its transcendental openness to the unity of the real. It is also possible, based mainly on recent genetic studies of Zubiri's thought and regarding his relations with phenomenology,[21] to hold the theory of intelligence as the radical starting point of Zubiri's philosophy, allowing, of course, the *prius* of reality *in* intellection.

We are not interested here in the "intra-Zubirian" discussion, but rather in determining Ellacuría's position relative to Zubiri. We could say the following about this: at the beginning, under the influence of *Sobre la esencia*, Ellacuría tends toward a more, so to speak, "cosmological" or naturalist interpetation of Zubiri's philosophy. However, Ellacuría's interest in the constitution of a philosophy of liberation disposes him, in some of his writings, toward another type of solution that differs from those already referred to. This is where the course on *Estructura dinámica de la realidad* is especially revealing.

This course has, in principle, a very "cosmological" angle: after analyzing the dynamics of matter, life, the person, and society, Zubiri culminates his study of the dynamic structures of the real with a study of the dynamic of history. For Zubiri all these spheres of the real are "dynamically sustained" one by the other, in a constitutive respectivity. This is why when he comes to the dynamic of history, he can do nothing less than assert that all the other dynamics of the real become present in history. But these other dynamics, Zubiri says, are in turn affected by history, "which means that the world, reality as world, is constitutively historical. The dynamic of history affects reality, constituting it as reality. History is not simply an event that happens to certain poor realities the way gravitation happens to material realities. No: it is something that affects precisely the character of reality as such."[22]

This is a decisive text for understanding Ellacuría's philosophical thought. In the perspective taken here, *the location of the interweaving between reality and intelligence, between humanity and world, is precisely history*. The transcendentality of the real does not simply set itself up before an individual phenomenological consciousness, but rather in what Zubiri calls the "historical world." This is why history is precisely the place where the aforementioned third horizon of philosophy is defined. This horizon is different from both the Greek horizon and the horizon of modernity since, according to Ellacuría, with the consideration of history a new concept of ultimacy appears for philosophy. In his study "The Liberating Function of Philosophy," Ellacuría asserts that the concept of the ultimate, limited in classical philosophy to natural being, has undergone a radical change in the modern age that conceives the ultimate of reality in subjective terms. He argues, "after the eighteenth century the necessity would be seen of expanding this concept of the ultimate even further so that the reality of the historical could enter into it with full force."[23]

Obviously, the purpose here is not to replace nature or human sub-jectivity, but rather to point to the place from which these have to be understood. For that very reason one speaks of an "expansion" of other concepts toward a horizon from which one can adequately and nonreduc-tionistically approach the whole of the real. In this connection Ellacuría had already asserted in 1972 that "philosophy claims to deal with what is ultimately real, with what reality is as a whole. Therefore this totality of the real requires total concretion, and this total concretion is specified by its final realization in history and through history,"[24] which, there-fore, makes it the true object of philosophy.[25]

## 4. The Object of Liberation Philosophy

"The object of philosophy" is precisely the title of one of Ellacuría's most important philosophical works.[26] In this article, after analyzing what Hegel, Marx, and Zubiri have understood as the object of philo-sophy, Ellacuría proposes, based on their work but going beyond their ap-proaches, that *historical reality*—no longer history—should be considered the proper object of philosophy. If it is true that for both ancient and modern thinkers the object of philosophy is the totality of the real,

> what happens is that this totality has been building so that there is a qualitative increase in reality, but in such a way that the higher reality . . . is not given separately from all the previous moments of the process of reality. . . . This last stage of reality, in which all others become pres-ent, is what we call historical reality. . . . It is the whole of reality as-sumed into the social reign of freedom; it is reality exhibiting its richest manifestations and possibilities.[27]

That is why one speaks about historical reality and not simply about history, since historical reality embraces all the other forms of reality (material and biological reality, personal and social reality) upon which it is dynamically sustained. At the same time, historical reality is where the other types of reality give more of themselves and where they reach their highest degree of openness: in historical reality we are given not only the highest form of reality, but also the open-ended scope of the maximum possibilities of the real.[28] From this per-spective one well understands the title and the contents of the next book on which Ellacuría had been working since the seventies. It is about a *Philosophy of Historical Reality* understood as an analysis of the presence in history of the other forms and other dynamics of reality.

Here we also catch a glimpse of what Ellacuría understood as a possible philosophy of liberation: it would consist above all of a reflection on historical praxis, because it is precisely in history that the maximum possibilities of the real are actualized, specifically, the possibility of a progressive integral liberation of humanity.

Thus, the analysis of the different structures and dynamics that comprise historical reality (from matter to human society) should really be a study of, so to speak, the transcendental structures of all possible liberating activity. After this analysis, Ellacuría ends the book by asking himself in the last chapter for what is particular to the historical dynamic, that is, what is the formal character of history. He concludes that so-called historical reality, considered as a whole, has the character of *praxis*. By praxis he does not mean one type of human activity as opposed to other activities (for example, as opposed to theory or, as Aristotle desired, as opposed to *posiesis*), but rather "the totality of the social process as transformer of both the natural and the historical dimensions of reality."[29] Due to its transformative nature, historical praxis is the sphere where the interwovenness of humanity and world is most clearly expressed, since "in this interwovenness subject-object relations are not always unidirectional." He says this is true to such a degree that "it is preferable to speak of codeterminate respectivity."[30]

On the other hand, once such a comprehensive concept of historical praxis has been understood, it is easy to see that theory as a moment of this praxis or, more radically, human intelligence itself, is affected by historicity. Realizing this implies adequately revisiting the ancient philosophical problem of knowledge from the point of view of its historicity.[31] What is needed in order to do this, according to Ellacuría, is an

> interpretation of intelligence as historical intelligence. Historical intelligence is, first of all, a situated intelligence, that is, an intelligence that knows that it cannot go to its own foundations except in a situated manner that also tries to go to the foundation of the situation taken as a whole. In other words . . . reality is historical and . . . only a logos of history, an historical logos can explain reality. A purely natural logos would never adequately explain a reality that is more than nature.[32]

## 5. The Historization of Intelligence

In what does this historization of intelligence exactly consist? Ellacuría had already indicated in the sixties the new possibilities created by Zubiri's philosophy for analyzing the social and historical nature of intelligence.[33]

However, Ellacuría's writings in this area are rather occasional and fragmentary since it was not until Zubiri's trilogy, *Inteligencia sentiente,* was published in the eighties that more comprehensive studies of the problem became possible.

We cannot enter here into a detailed account of the multiple contributions that Zubiri's work offers to the analysis of what has classically been called the "relation between theory and praxis." In my view, Zubiri appears in this trilogy as an heir to the two great intuitions of post-Hegelian (and, in a sense, postmodern) philosophy concerning the problem of intellection. First, Nietzsche's intuition that the classic mistake—or, as he would say, the inveterate lie—of idealism has at its root the artificial split between intelligence and sentience, which we already encounter in Parmenides. From the time of the Greeks, the separation of these two cognitive faculties has corresponded with a metaphysical dualism between two spheres of the real: the sentient world and the intelligible world. Additionally, it is important to remember as regards our subject that from the time of Parmenides this duality of cognitive faculties has also grounded a sociotheoretical rather than metaphysical dichotomization between the so-called "wise," guided by the logos, and the "common people" who followed the deceptive impressions of their senses. In any case, Zubiri understands, as does Nietzsche, that the radical overcoming of Western idealism is only possible through the reaffirmation—rigorously grounded in Zubiri's case—of the intimate unity between sensing and intellection.

On the one hand, as to the senses themselves, Zubiri inherits an insight we already encounter in the critique of the young Marx of earlier versions of both idealism and materialism: sensibility is not primarily a passive and simply receptive faculty; it is constitutively active in its relation to the environment. That is why the relation of the human person with the natural and social world does not consist primarily of contemplation, but rather of transformative activity. Indeed, in virtue of the active character of human sensing, Zubiri does not speak of "sensibility," but of a *sentient process*. And, since this process, as we have seen, is radically united with intelligence, he uses the nonwhimsical term *sentient intelligence* that exactly epitomizes the two great post-Hegelian insights to which we have referred.

This is precisely what we were seeking: the historicity constitutive of human intelligence has its fundamental foundation in the praxical character of intellection or, in more rigorous terms, in the structural unity of intellection with a sensing that is, in itself, active.

Even though Ellacuría was not able to thoroughly work out these ideas, he did develop in several occasional works the general outline of what we have called, with him, "historical intelligence."[34] Ellacuría emphasizes, above all, that the evolutionary ground of the *sentient* nature of intelligence is precisely its elemental biological function: intelligence emerges in order to make the human species viable and, therefore, has in its very structure a primordial connection to life.[35] Of course this does not hinder intelligence, once it has made possible for the human person the apprehension of things as real, to be able to assume functions that go beyond the biological maintenance of the species. But the primary function of intellection determines its fundamental praxical character, with the following consequences.

First, intelligence has its origin in a concrete social and historical praxis that precisely determines the *possibilities* of all rational activity.[36] If what is specific to the historical dynamism is the appropriation of possibilities, then we can say that rational truth, even in the most abstract disciplines, has a constitutively historical nature.[37] In light of this, one also understands why Ellacuría, speaking of the phenomenon of ideologies, says that before focusing on the pejorative connotations attached to this expression (for which he reserves the term ideologization), it is necessary to understand ideology in its strict social constraint, given the historical structure of human intelligence.[38]

Second, intelligence has not only a social origin, but also a social destination. This destiny does not deny the relative autonomy of intelligence, but it determines in the form of interests the greater part of its contents and tasks. Third, and more fundamentally, the link between intelligence and history is not only a question of the origin and destination of rational activity but, as Ellacuría points out, it is a constitutive characteristic itself of intellection. Given the active nature of intelligence and the similarly dynamic nature of everything real, the reference of human knowing to praxis is the very condition of its own scientificity.[39] The development of this third thesis is where Zubiri's trilogy on intelligence can be especially fruitful for the philosophy of liberation.

In any case, the entire preceding discussion implies that any philosophy and, in general, all human knowing must be conscious of its own historicity, of its concrete connections with the social praxis from which it arises, which it serves, and in which it moves. It must do this since it is only by beginning with the consciousness of one's own situation that it is possible to seek objectivity and even universality, though it will always be a question of a situated objectivity and universality.

## 6. Conclusion: The Point of Departure
## for Liberation Philosophy

Now, all this has far-reaching significance for defining the task of a philosophy of liberation. If the horizon of this philosophy is the horizon of history, and by history we understand historical praxis in the sense mentioned above, it must be pointed out that philosophy itself, like any other form of theory, is also affected by this horizon. In other words, history as a horizon and as an object is something shared by various contemporary philosophies. But making historical praxis, and specifically liberating praxis, its precise point of departure would be what is properly distinctive about the philosophy of liberation. That is why Ellacuría says, "philosophy will only be able to exercise its critical and creative ideological role in favor of an efficacious praxis of liberation if it adequately situates itself within that liberating praxis."[40]

At this point in our reflection we can better understand our initial references to the Socratic dimension of Ellacuría's intellectual work: to make liberation a way of life is not simply an ethical or political problem; it is a philosophical question, because it touches the starting point of philosophizing itself. The historicity of intelligence does not simply determine a series of epistemological questions, but it affects the understanding that philosophy has of itself, since it discovers itself not only as a form of knowledge, but as a way of life. For that reason, not just for esoteric or critical reasons, a philosophy of liberation is not possible without a true historical link with a liberating praxis.

Here we cannot enter into a consideration of how this point of departure entails a new treatment of many classical philosophical problems through what Ellacuría called their "historization." Let us think, for example, of the historization of concepts such as property, human rights or the common good, a subject to which Ellacuría dedicated several especially interesting works on social philosophy.[41] Suffice it to say at this point that what is decisive to understand this historization does not simply consist in giving problems a historical framework, but rather that its very treatment is historical; that is to say, it begins with the fact that it is linked to a historical praxis that wants to be liberating.

This means the question of the object of philosophy, to which we have referred above, is not enough to determine what is most proper to the philosophy of liberation. Or, more fundamentally, the object of philosophy defines what is characteristic of the philosophy of liberation only if one takes to its ultimate consequences the acceptance of historical reality as that object. Because one cannot simply understand the object of philosophy as the "subject" upon which philosophy reflects with supposed neutrality, as the term "historical reality" could mistakenly suggest. Historical *praxis,* in addition to being a subject of philosophy, determines the point of departure and, therefore, the character and the contents themselves of that reflection.

That is why Aristotle held that philosophy is "the science that seeks itself," because the constitution of its object is also the constitution of itself. This is something Ellacuría began to raise in his last philosophical writings: "the complexity and richness of the historical," he said in 1985, "not only reframes the exact dimension of the ultimate and the appropriate categories used to develop it, but, as is necessary, it also reframes the relation between *thinking* and *being* in new terms that oblige us to take the problem of ideology and ideologization beyond purely sociological or psychological considerations to the very heart of metaphysical discourse."[42]

The introduction of the problem of ideologies at the very heart of metaphysics would imply the construction of a philosophy of liberation as a philosophy *of* historical praxis. And this "of" is simultaneously objective and subjective because it refers both to the object and to the starting point of the pursuit of philosophy. This approach, which Ellacuría was unable to develop, could even have led him to introduce important corrections to his *Filosofía de la realidad histórica.* That is because historical praxis, which is the culmination of that book, now becomes *also* a beginning, both in the *ordo essendi* and in the *ordo cognoscendi:* nature and humanity are affected partially, but "physically," by historical praxis, which in turn conditions human knowledge of them.

But these are subjects that go beyond the limits we have set for this approach. In any case, it is important not to forget the fact that, as Ellacuría himself used to say, "what is essential is to dedicate oneself philosophically to the most completely integral liberation . . . of our peoples and of persons; the constitution of a philosophy will then come about by addition. Here too, the cross can come to life."[43] I hope that this essay has helped to clarify and to deepen the philosophical context and content of this affirmation.

This essay was originally published in Spanish as "Aproximación a la obra filosófica de Ignacio Ellacuría," *ECA,* nos. 505–6 (1990) 979–89. It subsequently appeared in J. Gimbernat and C. Gómez, eds., *La pasión por la libertad: Homenaje a Ignacio Ellacuría* (Navarra, Spain: Editorial Verbo Divino, 1994) 307–27.

[1] Ignacio Ellacuría, "Función liberadora de la filosofía," *ECA,* nos. 435–6 (1985) 45–64.

[2] We hope that Ellacuría's book *Filosofía de la realidad histórica* (San Salvador: UCA Editores, 1990) will be published in English very soon. A more complete bibliography of his philosophical writings will be published with it.

[3] See Xavier Zubiri, *Naturaleza, historia, Dios,* 9th edition (Madrid: Editora Nacional, 1987) 251.

[4] See Ignacio Ellacuría, "Filosofía ¿para qué?" *Abra* 11 (1976) 42–8. [Ignacio Ellacuría, "What Is the Point of Philosophy?" in *Philosophy and Theology* (vol. 10, no. 1, 1998) 3–18, trans. T. Michael McNulty.]

[5] His files from this period contain the summaries that Ellacuría made of his conversations with Zubiri, which sharply reflect the rather desolate Spanish intellectual panorama of that time and Zubiri's opinions about it.

[6] See Xavier Zubiri, *Sobre la esencia* (Madrid: Gráficas Cóndor, 1962); *Inteligencia sentiente* (Madrid: Alianza Editorial, 1981); *Inteligencia y logos* (Madrid: Alianza Editorial, 1982); *Inteligencia y razón* (Madrid: Alianza Editorial, 1983).

[7] See Ignacio Ellacuría, "La historicidad del hombre en Xavier Zubiri," *Estudios de Deusto* 28 (1966) 245–86 and 523–48.

[8] Another question, which Ellacuría does not then put to himself, is whether dialectical materialism is or is not, in reality, the best expression of Marxist philosophy.

[9] See Ignacio Ellacuría, "La idea de estructura en la filosofía de Xavier Zubiri," in *Realitas I. Seminario Xavier Zubiri* (Madrid: Sociedad de Estudios y Publicaciones, Editorial Moneda y Crédito, 1974) 138.

[10] See idem, "La idea de filosofía en Xavier Zubiri," in A. Teulon, I. Ellacuría, and others, *Homenaje a Zubiri,* vol. 1 (Madrid: Editorial moneda y Crédito, 1970) 477–85.

[11] Xavier Zubiri, *Estructura dinámica de la realidad* (Madrid: Alianza Editorial, 1989).

[12] Ignacio Ellacuría, "Aproximación a la obra filosófica de Xavier Zubiri," in I. Telechea Idígoras, ed., *Zubiri 1898–1983* (Victoria: Edita Departamento de Cultura del Gobierno Vasco, 1984) 55; first published in *ECA,* nos. 421–2 (1983) 965–83.

[13] See Zubiri, *Naturaleza, historia, Dios,* 267–87.

[14] See Ortega y Gasset, "Las dos grandes metáforas" (1924), in his *Obras Completas,* vol. 2 (Madrid, 1963) 384–400.

[15] See Ignacio Ellacuría, "Fundamentación biológica de la ética," *ECA,* no. 368 (1979) 418–28.

[16] See idem, "La idea de la filosofía en Xavier Zubiri," 487–8.

[17] See idem, "Función liberadora de la filosofía," *ECA* 40, nos. 435–6 (1985) 53.

[18] See Zubiri, *Inteligencia sentiente,* 10.

[19] See Zubiri, *Sobre el hombre,* 79.

[20] See Ellacuría, "La idea de filosofía en Xavier Zubiri," 523.

[21] See A. Pinor Ramos, *Génesis y formación de la filosofía de Zubiri,* 2nd ed. (Salamanca, 1983).

[22] See Zubiri, *Estructura dinámica de la realidad,* 272.

[23] Ellacuría, "Función liberadora de la filosofía," 57.

[24] Ignacio Ellacuría, "Filosofía y política," *ECA,* no. 284 (1972) 377.

[25] Ibid.

[26] This article was first presented at a meeting of the Encuentro Latinoamericano de Filosofía and was published as "El objeto de la filosofía," *ECA*, nos. 396–7 (1981) 963–80.

[27] Ibid., 977–8.

[28] Ibid., 978.

[29] Ellacuría, "Función liberadora de la filosofía," 57.

[30] Ibid.

[31] Regarding the urgency of this study for the philosophy of liberation, see ibid., 54.

[32] Ellacuría, "Filosofía y política," 384.

[33] See Ellacuría, "La historicidad del hombre en Xavier Zubiri," 539ff.

[34] See, for example, idem, "La superación del reduccionismo idealista en Zubiri," *ECA*, no. 477 (1988) 633–50.

[35] See Ignacio Ellacuría, "Hacia una fundamentación filosófica del método teológico latinoamericano," *ECA*, nos. 322–3 (1975) 419.

[36] Ibid., 420.

[37] See Zubiri, *Inteligencia y razón*, 292–317.

[38] See Ellacuría, "Función liberadora de la filosofía," 47–9.

[39] See idem, "Hacia una fundamentación filosófica del método teológico latino-americano, 421.

[40] Idem, "Función liberadora de la filosofía," 56.

[41] See Ignacio Ellacuría, "La historización del concepto de propiedad como principio de desideologización," *ECA*, nos. 335–6 (1976) 425–50; idem, "Historización del bien común y de los derechos humanos en una sociedad dividida," in E. Tamez and S. Trinidad, eds., *Capitalismo: violencia y anti-vida*, vol. 2 (San José: EDUCA, 1978) 81–94.

[42] Ellacuría, "Función liberadora de la filosofía," 52.

[43] Ibid., 62.

# Chapter 4

# Ignacio Ellacuría's Debt to Xavier Zubiri: Critical Principles for a Latin American Philosophy and Theology of Liberation

*Robert Lassalle-Klein*

## Introduction

Ignacio Ellacuría's trenchant critique of philosophical modernity, and his powerful Christian historical realism[1] contextualize and reinterpret key themes in Western philosophy from a Latin American perspective. They also serve as "critical and creative"[2] philosophical principles for the development of a "truly Latin American philosophy"[3] and "Latin American theological method."[4] This essay will focus on how key aspects of Ellacuría's efforts to develop a truly Latin American philosophy and theology of liberation emerge from, and at points, supersede the contributions of his mentor, the Basque philosopher, Xavier Zubiri. The first section will show how Ellacuría appropriates dimensions of Zubiri's powerful reconstructive critique of the role of "reductionistic idealism" in modern phenomenology and Western philosophy. The second section will show how Ellacuría builds upon Zubiri's constructive proposals regarding "sentient intelligence," and the philosophical primacy of a formal concept of reality. The third section will highlight the originality of the philosophical and theological principles underlying Ellacuría's liberating and Christian historical realism, showing how they move beyond Zubiri's proposals in five important ways. The reader who is more interested in the originality of Ellacuría's philosophical thought and its theological implications may want to skip directly to Part III (p. 104).

## I. Reductionistic Idealism of Western Philosophy in Modernity

In 1988, the year before his assassination, Ellacuría treated Zubiri's critique of idealist reductionism, and his constructive proposals regarding intellection and reality in an article entitled, "Zubiri's Solution to Idealist Reductionism."[5] Given both the nature and the timing of the article, it constitutes perhaps the closest thing we have to an explicit synthetic statement of how Zubiri's broad-reaching thought and massive philosophical corpus shaped Ellacuría's own thought on these subjects. I will use this article in tandem with a number of other sources to show how Ellacuría's philosophical project involves both a deconstructive critique, and an original reconstructive contextualization from a Latin American liberationist (one could add postcolonial) perspective, of aspects of the Western philosophical tradition, especially the phenomenological tradition.

Ellacuría laments with Zubiri the apparent inability of modern Western philosophy, theology, and even political language to find "an adequate manner to face up to reality and to realize the weight of it."[6] He adopts Zubiri's interpretation that this shortcoming both reflects and perpetuates the fact that a good deal of "modern philosophy is laboring under the affliction of idealism."[7]

The influence of Zubiri's "post-critical"[8] and, if you will, "post-Kantian" perspective on philosophical modernity, is pervasive in Ellacuría's work. He argues that Zubiri's approach remains "'critical,' not in the Kantian sense of the term, but in the sense of having assimilated . . . the data afforded by science and philosophy on critical intellection."[9] Zubiri accordingly produces a strikingly original philosophical realism, which draws from the philosophy of science, classical and medieval philosophy, and the phenomenologies of Edmund Husserl, José Ortega y Gasset, and especially Martin Heidegger, among others. Zubiri's postmodern[10] approach to the classical problem of philosophical realism is grounded in a powerful critique of a form of idealism, which he argues has afflicted the history of Western philosophy. He writes:

> Sensing, it is said, is one thing; intellection is another. This perspective on the problem of intelligence contains, at bottom, an affirmation: intellection is posterior to sensing, and this posteriority is an opposition/dichotomy. This has been an initial thesis of philosophy since Parmenides, which has quietly loomed, with a thousand variants, over all of European philosophy.[11]

Ellacuría explains that Zubiri believes the dichotomization of sensing from intellection[12] has produced two "distortions" in Western philosophy: (a) the "logification of intelligence," and (b) the "entification of reality." Ellacuría's liberationist (and postcolonial) approach will argue that these distortions must be overcome in order to construct a truly contextualized "Latin American" philosophy and theology.[13]

## A. The Logification of Intelligence

Ellacuría asserts that, for Zubiri, the first, and most basic distortion of the Western philosophical tradition produced by idealist reductionism has been the "progressive subsuming" of the other aspects of intellection into what the mind *("nous")* as *"logos"* predicates about the object.[14] Zubiri calls this the "logification of intelligence."[15] Zubiri and Ellacuría argue that this reductionistic narrowing of intelligence impoverishes our appreciation of other aspects and sources of knowing. Most especially it reduces sense-based forms of knowledge to the status of mere sense data. Ellacuría summarizes Zubiri's analysis of how this form of idealism functions at various moments in the history of Western philosophy. In what follows, because of the massive influence of twentieth-century phenomenology on contemporary philosophy and theology, I focus on Ellacuría's reconstructive critique of the logification of intelligence in this philosophical movement.

Diego Gracia highlights the breakthrough importance of Zubiri's critique of the phenomenological tradition in the development of philosopher's thought. Gracia explains that, early in his career, Zubiri "clearly identifies himself with [Husserl],"[16] and that he is trying to find an alternative to classical realism and modern transcendental idealism through "the discovery of a philosophically viable route for the phenomenological method."[17] *On the one hand, if this is correct (and I believe it is), the philosophies of both Zubiri and Ellacuría may be at least partially situated as attempts to "correct" the phenomenological tradition "from within."*[18]

On the other hand, both clearly go beyond phenomenology. Zubiri and Ellacuría want to argue that the phenomenological description of the object ("historical reality" in the case of Ellacuría) is limited to the status of a methodological first step in the philosophical process. Thus, while philosophy will involve phenomenology, it will finally have to be more than simply phenomenology. Accordingly, Ellacuría will argue that the proper object of Latin American philosophy and theology is historical *reality,* not merely history, or the historical process. We shall see in a moment what both Ellacuría and Zubiri mean by the term "reality."

The arguments of Ellacuría and Zubiri with phenomenology are best exemplified by their critique of Husserl, the philosopher to whom Zubiri's work is most directly related, and with whom he studied. Zubiri comments widely on what he sees as the role of the idealist logification of the intelligence in the work of Kant, Husserl, Ortega y Gasset, and even Heidegger (whose advances over Husserl he considers correct), among others. However, a focus on Zubiri's critical appropriation of Husserl will help us to show what is common and what is unique in the approaches of Zubiri and Ellacuría to the phenomenological tradition.

The reader will recall that Husserl creates phenomenology, at least in part, as a way to overcome the naturalistic objectivism of modern science. Husserl believes the latter has created a crisis in Western culture by subordinating the human cultural realms of beauty, valuing, judging, knowing, and so on, to the causality of the physical world. In 1980, near the end of his life, Zubiri describes the significance of Husserl's project thus: "Philosophy was becoming a mixture of positivism, historicism and [crude] pragmatism founded in the last instance in the science of psychology."[19] Praising Husserl, he asserts, "Phenomenology was the key movement that opened an appropriate ground for philosophizing as such." For Zubiri it also represented an advance over Kant, in that "it was a philosophy about things, and not only a theory of knowledge."

Gracia notes that Zubiri's doctoral dissertation says Husserl distinguishes two aspects of all phenomena, or "objects," as they are present to consciousness: first, their "reality" or "existence"; and second, their "content."[20] Trying to recapture the vitality of humanity's prescientific life, Husserl wants phenomenology to describe the "immediate and mediate" content of experience, while withholding judgment about its existence and/or reality. For Zubiri, the essence of the phenomenological approach is that "the content of my perception remains in suspension, and, as Husserl says graphically, 'placed within parentheses [the "epoche" or "brackets"].'" Zubiri observes, "We call this correction the 'act of phenomenological neutralization or reduction.' The object as such does not lose anything of its content; it only loses its reality; and by means of this loss, the real object is reduced to a pure phenomenon."[21]

Zubiri's master's thesis concedes that this move "requires a certain violence, or rather, an intellectual asceticism."[22] However, he asserts that one is rewarded with a kind of knowledge about things as they are present to consciousness or awareness. The dissertation adds that phenomenology provides "something more fundamental and prior to all explication [scientific or otherwise]: a phenomenology of knowing about which . . . subjectivists and realists might come to agreement."[23]

However, Diego Gracia shows that a decade later, in a 1935 article, Zubiri makes a crucial move to "correct"[24] phenomenology. This move will play a crucial role in shaping Zubiri's future work, and that of his student, Ignacio Ellacuría. Here we find the key to Zubiri's efforts to "correct" the phenomenological tradition "from within," by appropriating yet simultaneously limiting the scope of its key insights.[25]

*Gracia argues that Zubiri's attempts to "correct" phenomenology by hypothesizing that the primogenital location of intellection is actually sensation itself, rather than Husserl's "pure consciousness," or even Heidegger's better formulated "understanding of being"[26] or "understanding of Dasein."[27]* Zubiri argues that, while understanding has often meant "demonstration" or "speculation," it has sometimes been used to refer to "experience." He offers the example of Aristotle's emphasis on the role of "sensation" and the sensible impression of reality in the act of knowing (though, for Aristotle, sensation is not formally part of the act of knowing).

Four implications of Zubiri's move are of particular significance for his own future work, and that of Ellacuría. First, Zubiri will argue that intelligence and sensation are unified in what he will call the "sensing" or "sentient intelligence."[28] Second, his phenomenology will take seriously the stubborn sense of being something "in its own" right *[en propio]*, or something "of its own" *[de suyo]* that characterizes the way the objects of sense are manifested by sensible apprehension.[29] Third, Zubiri will use the word "reality" to refer to this persistent phenomenological characteristic, which defines how things are manifested by sensible apprehension. Zubiri will coin the word "reity," using it interchangeably with the term "reality," in order to emphasize the "formal" nature of his approach. And he will define "reality" (or "reity") as the formality of the way the thing is actualized as an apprehension that possess the character of something "in its own" right *[en propio]*, or something "of its own" *[de suyo]*, or "as something that already is what it is before its presentation, as a 'prius,' more in a metaphysical than a temporal sense."[30] And, fourth, Zubiri, Ellacuría, and others will insist that Zubiri's position is nothing like a naïve realism. Their point is that "reality," or "reity," does not here refer directly to things as they exist in the world "outside" apprehension and independent of it.

*I would suggest that Zubiri makes a second major "correction" of phenomenology, and its development after Husserl. Zubiri more precisely limits the scope of Husserl's "epoche" or bracketing of the question about the reality or existence of the thing*. He does this primarily by reframing Husserl's distinction between objects as *"noesis"* (the "act" of consciousness in grasping the phenomenal object), and *"noema"* (the referent of noesis, or the thing as it is "intended" by consciousness). Zubiri switches this to a distinction between the aforementioned formal reality of the thing as it imposes itself in the sensible apprehension *(noesis)*, and the reality of the thing as it may exist apart from the question of its sensible apprehension *(noema)*.[31] As already stated, Zubiri believes that *noesis* consists in the "primordial apprehension" of the formal reality of the thing (as being "of its own"), and its "re-actualization" before the distancing and predicating judgments[32] of the *logos*.[33] But he also suggests that, since the formal reality of the thing is a physical actualization of the thing in the apprehension, and since that reality (or "reity") is open to every other thing (however nascently), therefore it is proper for the deepening, measuring, and searching thought of reason to develop provisional models, hypotheses, and postulates about the noema.

This move limits the role of the epoche to helping philosophy establish the formal reality of the thing as it is first manifested in the primordial apprehension of the object. In this way the epoche is limited to the status of a methodological first step in the philosophical process. Thus, Zubiri explicitly rules out ontological claims based on the epoche (for which he criticizes Heidegger[34]). But Zubiri also insists that once the question of reality has been raised using phenomenological terms and methods, philosophy has an obligation to address it. And this it will do, Zubiri asserts, through the models, hypotheses and postulates of reason. Thus, he will argue that philosophy will have to be more than simply phenomenology. This is both the implication and the substance of his second "correction" of Husserl's understanding of the phenomenological approach to philosophy.

## B. The "Entification of Reality"

This brings us, then, to what Zubiri believes are a second set of "distortions" in the Western philosophical tradition created by idealist reductionism: *the reduction of what he calls reality to a form or a subcategory of being*. Using the Spanish word *ente*[35] for "being" in the sense of "entity," Zubiri and Ellacuría call this the "entification of reality."[36] The substance of this critique can be captured in two affirmations, the first of which manifests the profound influence of Martin Heidegger on the work of Xavier Zubiri.

*First, Ellacuría argues that for Zubiri, the entification of reality means that not only being-as-an-entity* [ente], *but also the larger category of being* [ser] *itself, have improperly displaced reality in philosophy.* Zubiri himself puts the point concisely:

> Classical philosophy has addressed the problem of being from the perspective of what I have called conceiving intelligence. Intellection is "understanding"; and understanding is intellection that something "is" *[es].* This was a primary thesis for Parmenides. . . . [Later g]rounded in Parmenides, both Plato and Aristotle continued to subsume the act of intellection to the work of the logos. This was what . . . I have called a *logification of the intelligence.* But it is something else as well, for it is assumed that what has been intellected is "being" *[ser].* And this implies that reality is just a form of being, though certainly its fundamental form. Nonetheless, however, reality is merely a form of being: it is *esse reale* (real existence). In other words, reality is formally being-as-an-entity *[ente]:* reality has the character of an entity. This is what I call an *entification of reality.* And in this way, the logification of intellection, and the entification of reality intrinsically converge. The "is" of intellection consists in an affirmation, and the "is" that is conceived by intellection has the character of an entity. This convergence (between the act and the object of intellection) has largely framed the path of European philosophy.[37]

Ellacuría clarifies what is at stake by arguing that Zubiri, who studied with Heidegger and appropriated aspects of his interpretation of Husserl, both incorporates and supercedes Heidegger's relentless critique of what calls the "forgetfulness of being *[ser].*"[38] More specifically, he argues that Zubiri's notion regarding the entification of reality includes but moves beyond the reach of Heidegger's idea that "being *[ser]* has been reduced to the status of a thing *[cosa],* or to being-as-an-entity *[ente].*" Thus, it must be said that Zubiri and Heidegger overlap to some extent on this important point.

Ellacuría notes Zubiri's great appreciation for Heidegger's "fundamental and foundational . . . ontological distinction . . . between 'being-as-an-entity' *[ente]* and 'being' *[ser]*" itself, asserting that Heidegger interprets this as the distinction between the ontic versus the ontological sense of "being." He acknowledges that the German's "constant" efforts to move "from the ontic plane, to go toward the ontological" mean that "one cannot speak of an entification of reality in Heidegger." And he recognizes that both Zubiri and Heidegger appreciate the dangers of reducing being to the status of being-as-an-entity.

But Ellacuría insists that Zubiri is making a larger point. He says Zubiri is arguing that *both* "being-as-an-entity *[ente]* and being *[ser]* have displaced reality in philosophy."[39] Here we must recall that Zubiri defines "reality" (or "reity") as the formality that characterizes the way things are actualized in our sentient intelligence as apprehensions possessing the character of something "in its own" right *[en propio]*, or as something "of its own" *[de suyo]*. And it is helpful to remember that Zubiri coins the word "reity" precisely in order to emphasize the phenomenological and formal character of this approach. Thus, it will come as no surprise that Ellacuría wants us to see that Zubiri's formal definition of reality is designed to avoid what he sees as the error of philosophical approaches in which being (either as *ente* or *ser*) displaces what Zubiri calls "reality" (or "reity") as the proper object of philosophy.

Zubiri says such approaches tend to fall into one of two broad categories. On the one hand, some philosophies make "the radical error of having identified *being* and *reality*."[40] Among these he names the *"esse real"* (real being) of Scholasticism, the *"esse* is *percipi* . . . of empirical idealism," and the *"esse* is *concipi* of logical idealism." On the other hand, while at least two other philosophies "are able to distinguish being from reality,"[41] each ultimately goes wrong when "reality becomes one type of being among others."[42] Here he cites *"esse* is *poni,"* which he says "is the thesis of the transcendental idealism *(sein ist Setzung)* . . . [of] Kant." In this approach being becomes "a posture of thought"; and *"being-an-object"* (my emphasis).[43] Next, he adds Heidegger's thesis that "being itself . . . is the character with which all real things show up by letting [*'dejar-que'* or *'sein-lassen-von'*] what is present go on showing itself to itself." On the one hand, Zubiri praises Heidegger for advancing the discussion by affirming that being "is not an act of thought." On the other hand, however, he believes that Heidegger, like Kant, finally goes wrong when he "makes[s] reality a type of being."

The underlying problem, in Zubiri's view, is that what Heidegger means by "being" cannot be said to formally exist (in the phenomenological sense described earlier). Indeed, he argues that Heidegger makes a substance out of what would be better described as an *"act* of being." This position flows from Zubiri's studies of exciting pre-War breakthroughs in physics and other sciences, which convince him that "modern philosophy . . . has been riding upon . . . four incorrect substantivations: space, time, consciousness, and being."[44] He charges, "It has been thought that things are in time and space, that all are apprehended in the acts of consciousness, and that their ontic character is a moment of being." However, Zubiri believes that relativity theory and emerging studies of human perception and the brain have begun to show that, "Space, time, consciousness, being, are not four receptacles for things . . ." He argues instead that, "Real things are not in space or time, as Kant thought (following Newton), but rather real things are spatial and temporal." And "Intellection is not an act of consciousness, as Husserl thought." Rather, "there is not consciousness; there are only conscious acts." Indeed, "neither consciousness, nor 'the' unconscious, nor 'the' subconscious exist; there are only conscious, unconscious and subconscious acts."[45] It must be understood, then, that these "are not acts of consciousness, of the unconscious, or of the subconscious," because, "[c]onsciousness does not perform acts"[46] (my emphasis).

Turning then to Heidegger, Zubiri asserts, "In his own way (which he never managed to conceptualize or define), he has accomplished the substantivation of being." Like the aforementioned approaches to space, time, and consciousness, Zubiri says that, for Heidegger, "things are things in and through being; for this reason things are entities." On the positive side, this allows Heidegger to highlight what he calls the crucial "ontological difference" between the "being of things (entities)" and "being itself" mentioned above. On the negative side, however, Zubiri protests that, while there are *acts* of being, in point of fact, "real being does not exist."[47] He argues, rather, that "Only *being real* exists, or "realitas in essendo," as I would say."

Thus, echoing Husserl's earlier call to return "to the thing!" Zubiri asserts (contra Heidegger) that, for a truly phenomenologically oriented approach, "what formally characterizes the human person is not the comprehension of being, but rather the mode of our apprehension of things."[48] He asserts (contra Husserl) that the mode of our apprehension is defined by what Zubiri calls our "sentient intelligence." And he suggests that the proper beginning point for the strictly intramundane philosophy will be the formal "reality" (or "reity") that characterizes the way things are actualized by our sentient intelligence as apprehensions possessing the character of something "in its own" right *[en propio]*, or as something "of its own" *[de suyo]*.

Accordingly, Ellacuría concludes that "one can and should speak of an ontologization of reality"[49] in Heidegger. His point is that while Heidegger's approach, on the one hand, "overcomes what had been, up to that point, an entification of reality," on the other hand "it is still not sufficient, as important as it is, because it follows the path of being *[ser]* and loses its roots in reality [or "reity"]."[50]

Zubiri's great appreciation for Heidegger's achievement aside, reality or "reity" as the proper object of a phenomenologically oriented philosophy remains fundamental, and the dangers for modern thought of its displacement by being (or any other category) remain real. When this happens, for Ellacuría and Zubiri, "philosophy has ceased to be what it should be, and people, whether intellectuals or not, are led away from the exigencies of reality [or "reity"] toward the possible illusions of being *[ser]*, when being is not rooted in reality."[51]

Ellacuría's then offers five key arguments for the assertion that "rooting being in reality, and not reality in being, is one of the fundamental principles of Zubiri's philosophy."[52] One, Ellacuría's interpretation is that "what Zubiri is insisting is that only by approaching being *[ser* as *real being]* as a later actualization of reality [or "reity"] is [philosophy] safeguarded . . . from all sorts of subjectivisms and illusions."[53] He explains that Zubiri overcomes this idealism by affirming that "In the . . . [sensible] impression of reality, not only reality, but also . . . being is physically actualized." Ellacuría says that, "by doing it this way, being is removed from the process of logification [the reduction of intellection or knowing to what the mind as 'logos' predicates about the object], be it predicative or prepredicative.".

Two, Ellacuría says Husserl's key mistake in this regard is "having interpreted essence as meaning."[54] He notes Zubiri's assertion that the essence of the thing "for Husserl is, in effect, an eidetic unity of meaning, which has nothing to do with empirical realities."[55] Three, Zubiri's argument is that this position of Husserl's gives an illegitimate priority to meaning over reality, or "reity". "Thus, for Husserl, essence is an eidetic unity of meaning, and as such it rests on itself as an absolute, distinct, independent, and separate world of being from the world of empirical reality."[56] Four, Zubiri's judgment is that this aspect of Husserl's work constitutes a "logification of intelligence . . . in the form of consciousness,"[57] and an entification of reality, or "reity" in the form of a "substantification . . . of 'the' consciousness."

Five, Ellacuría's account of how Zubiri approaches this problem sets the pattern for why he will later criticize European theology for giving priority to meaning over reality.[58] He writes:

> For Zubiri, on the other hand, what happens in acts of consciousness . . . is a reactualization not of "meaning," but of a "physical" act that is also an intellectual actualization. Therefore essence is not an eidetic unity of meaning, but rather something realized as an intrinsic and formal moment of the thing, as "a structural *eidos* of things," "a structural *eidos* of reality." Thus, "each and every essence is an essence of a thing, and is by no means independent of empirical reality."[59]

Ellacuría believes the key to Zubiri's discussion of idealism is his belief that "these ways of philosophizing end by giving priority to the logical-mental structures over the structures of reality."[60] And while "'knowing' might be easier [to conceptualize] this way," it means "that knowing will have fallen away from reality,"[61] if reality, or "reity," is understood in Zubiri's formal phenomenological sense.

*Second, Ellacuría says that Zubiri is arguing that the entification of reality reverses the proper priority of reality, or "reity," over meaning in the philosophical conceptualizations of the true and the good.* In regards to the true, Ellacuría asserts that Zubiri's desire to conceptualize the philosophical requirements of the "search for truth"[62] leads him to formulate "a method through which the most reality [or "reity"], qualitatively and quantitatively understood, would actualize itself in the intelligence"[63] ("including . . . intellection in all its complexity in reality.")[64] In regards to the good, Ellacuría says there is "ethical value"[65] in Zubiri's notion that the search for truth is grounded in the actualization of reality or "reity." Thus, Ellacuría will assert that "dedicating one's life to the search for truth" makes the human person "more honest, . . . more free and . . . more useful."[66] I will return to Ellacuría's powerful appropriation of this important aspect of Zubiri's thought in the final section of the essay.

*Third, Ellacuría says giving priority to reality, or "reity," in the search for the true and the good "actualizes the transformative capacities of . . . philosophy" in three respects.*[67] One, it arms the reader with "tools"[68] and a mandate to verify or critique truth claims. Two, it demands sufficiently complex ways of thinking about the natural, personal, and historical dimensions of human reality. And three, "even though the applications . . . are not very explicit in Zubiri's own thinking . . . his contribution . . . makes it possible . . . with added effort, but without distortions, to better fulfill and realize" philosophy's transformative promise.[69] This focus on praxis emblemizes Ellacuría's own approach to Zubiri's work, which I will discuss in the final section.

These assertions, then, capture Ellacuría's appropriation of Zubiri's critical reading of the phenomenological tradition. Ellacuría writes how he learned from Zubiri that, "the return [of phenomenology] to things is not enough . . . if that turn presupposes reducing them to their being, or to their meaning."[70] Ellacuría says that what is necessary is "to return to the reality of things because, anchored in that reality, restrained by it and driven by it, one can reach both being and meaning, *as the being and meaning of reality*"[71] [or "reity"].

## II. Ellacuría's Interpretation of Zubiri's Postmodern Alternative to the Reductionistic Idealism

In this section I briefly examine Ellacuría's interpretation of key Zubirian principles regarding (a) human intellection (or sentient intelligence) and (b) the primacy of reality. In so doing, I describe their role in "overcoming reductionistic idealism,"[72] and try to show how they structure Ellacuría's liberating Christian historical realism.

It must be understood from the outset that, for both Zubiri and Ellacuría, sentient intelligence and the primacy of Zubiri's formal definition of reality (or "reity") function as reciprocal concepts. In a frequently quoted section of *Inteligencia sentiente,* Zubiri insists, "The fact is that an intrinsic priority of knowing over reality [or "reity"], or of reality [or "reity"] over knowing is impossible. Knowing and reality are, given their common roots, strictly and rigorously of the same genotype. There is no priority of one over the other."[73] Zubiri argues that, "this is . . . due to . . . the very idea [we have] of reality and knowing. Reality is the formal character—the formality—by which what is apprehended remains something 'in its own' right *[en propio],*[74] something 'of its own' *[de suyo]."*[75] Therefore, it will be important to keep in mind in what follows that, for Zubiri and Ellacuría, intellection and the formal definition of reality are formally reciprocal concepts.

### A. What Is intellection? Sentient Intelligence

Ellacuría suggests that Zubiri's analysis of human intellection as "sentient" or "sensing" intelligence constitutes the latter's positive alternative to the "logification of intelligence."[76] He says the central thesis behind the notion of sentient intelligence is captured in Zubiri's statement, "I think that intellection formally consists in apprehending the real as real, and that sensing is apprehending the real as an impression."[77] Ellacuría finds two fundamental principles in this important thesis.

*First, Ellacuría says Zubiri correctly insists on "the structural unity of intellection and sensing"*[78] as two dimensions of a single act of sentient intelligence. Zubiri writes:

> It is not only that human sensing and intellection are not in opposition. Rather, their intrinsic and formal unity constitute a single and distinct act of apprehension. As sentient, the act is an impression. As an intellection, the act is an apprehension of reality [or "reity"]. In this way, the distinct and unified act of sentient intellection is an impression of reality. Intellection is a way of sensing. And, in human persons, sensing is a mode of intellection.[79]

Ellacuría says Zubiri's point is "much more radical" than the usual for-mulation that intelligence apprehends reality by thinking about the data given by the senses. Zubiri is arguing that the "distinct and indivisible act of intellection" is not only an apprehension of reality (the intellective moment), but also an impression of reality (the sensible moment).[80] The intellection of reality, or "reity," is not simply the product of affirmative, propositional, or predicative judgments about a collection of sense data. Rather, "reality is already actualized in sensing itself, in the sensible ac-tualization itself."[81]

On the other hand, Ellacuría insists that Zubiri is not at all interested in reducing the various subsequent, or other intellective functions "in one way or another to sensing."[82] Zubiri's claim is that "intellective sens-ing, does not simply yield contents that can be subsequently gathered and interrelated, etc." Rather, "the formal dimension of reality manifests itself in these contents themselves," which is "something neither the sensualists nor the idealists understood."[83]

Ellacuría explains the distinction in terms of the difference between ani-mal stimulus/response and true human intellection. He argues that the existence of "an impression of reality implies a state of really being affected by a cause, and not simply by a stimulus."[84] It implies a state in which "the thing affecting me manifests itself with the variability of reality, and not only as an objective sign. That which is apprehended imposes itself on me with its own force, not the force of a stimulus, but with the force of a real-ity."[85] The idea is that "the sentient character of intellection is not only a source of contents, and a motor for the subsequent employment/unfolding of intellection itself."[86] Rather, sensing turns out to be the impression of the formal dimension of a reality (or "reity") itself, so that "reality will have as many ways of presenting itself as there are different ways of sensing."[87]

*Second, while the act of intellection formally consists in the unitary sentient apprehension of the real as real, it has three moments or aspects.* Here Zubiri moves beyond theses about the "intrinsic and formal unity of intellec-tion and sensing."[88] Ellacuría says Zubiri's three-volume work on the sentient intelligence, published near the end of his life, magisterially conceptualizes both "the formal character of intellection," and "the pri-mary and principle act of all intellective functions."[89]

Ellacuría summarizes the essence of Zubiri's argument in three affir-mations. *One, intellection begins with* what Zubiri calls *the sentient, primary, or primordial apprehension of something as being "of its own" [de suyo], something "in its own" right [en propio].*[90] This apprehension of something's identity-maintaining character might be called the primary sensible phenomenon of reality. Zubiri calls it "a primary apprehension of the real," or the "formality" of reality. He treats this apprehension as the actualization of a relationship that "is physical and real, because the transcendentality of the impression of reality is physical and real."[91] One of Zubiri's most important works, *Sentient Intelligence* (1980), the first volume of the trilogy on the intelligence, is dedicated to the analysis of this moment.

*Two, intellection then moves to a "second moment" to determine "what is real with respect to other real things,"*[92] *that have been apprehended. Here, Zubiri says intellection can be described as an act of the logos.* It is noteworthy that Zubiri insists that this moment of intellection remains "within" the apprehension. It involves a move, however, from what he calls "primordial apprehension" to a "dual apprehension."[93] The idea is that intellection "reactualizes"[94] the moment of "primary apprehension of the thing," and relates it to the sensible apprehension of "other real things" through affirmative, propositional, and predicative judgments[95] (for example, "this thing is a tree"). With this development, intellection has moved into the mode of the logos. Zubiri's rejection of the "logification of intelligence" is intended to critique the reduction of the entire process of intellection to this moment. *Intelligence and Logos,* the second volume of the aforementioned trilogy (1982), is a study of this moment of judgment that locates it within the larger unified act of what he calls "intellection."

*Three, intellection finally moves "beyond what can be apprehended directly, immediately, and as a unity" by relating the aforementioned apprehension of reality, or "reity," to "a worldly reality."* [96] *Here, intellection has the character of an act of reason.* Ellacuría notes that Zubiri's presentation of the first two moments of the act of sentient intelligence is based on developments within the global reality of apprehension. However, in the third moment of intellection, "reason is simply the march from a field of reality [or "reity"] to a worldly reality." Here, reason relates the global character of an apprehension of reality, or "reity," to the larger and more varied reality of the world. Ellacuría insists that, though it "is a transcendental march toward the world," the act of reason nonetheless remains "grounded in the sentient character of intelligence."[97] Here, then, intellection operates in what is usually understood as the mode of reason, developing provisional models, hypotheses, and postulates about the reality of things as they exist outside of sensible apprehension (the *"noema"*). Zubiri dedicates the third volume, *Intelligence and Reason,* to the role of sentient reason in intellection.[98]

Ellacuría concludes that, by maintaining the structural unity of intellection and sensing, and by explaining the formal character of sentient intelligence, Zubiri is simultaneously able to overcome the narrowing intellectualization of knowledge and the logification of intelligence. He claims this has far-reaching implications for disputes in academic disciplines about method and what counts as knowledge, and in politics regarding what is truly human.[99] At the very least, it helps explain why Ellacuría would argue that sentient intelligence and the primacy of reality must function as reciprocal concepts in the work of theology and philosophy, particularly for Latin American theologies and philosophies of liberation and other postcolonial approaches.

### B. What Is Reality? The Formal Concept of Reality and the Primacy of Reality

Ellacuría says that Zubiri's key argument against the "entification of reality" (its reduction to being-as-an-entity) is his formal concept of reality and his insistence on the philosophical primacy of reality. He summarizes Zubiri's position in three key sets of arguments.

*First, Ellacuría emphasizes that Zubiri answers the question, "What is reality?" in the context of his position that intellection consists in the actualization of the real as formally real.*[100] Following Zubiri, he makes three key points. One, "it is in the act of intellection and only in the act of intellection, formally considered, where the real manifests itself as real."[101] Two, reality is first actualized for intelligence as the sensible apprehension of a formal reality. As stated earlier, he means that reality is what is sensibly apprehended as being something "in its own" right *[en propio]*, as something "of its own" *[de suyo]*, or "as something that already is what it is before its presentation, as a *'prius,'* more in a metaphysical than a temporal sense."[102]

Three, the "formality of reality opens us . . . to the arena of real things as real."[103] Here Ellacuría says that Zubiri wants to emphasize that, "even if reality is a formality, real things are not a formality, but rather simply real things."[104] Ellacuría makes this distinction somewhat more explicit and empirical with the argument that "the reality of the real thing has to be measured—for there are degrees of reality—in terms of the degree to which it is 'of itself.'" For example, "a rock does not have the same degree of reality as an animal, or an animal [the same reality] as a human person."[105] The idea is that as the ecology of material, biological, sentient, and human systems evolve epigenetically, one from the other, each becomes progressively more something "of its own." This progresses "until, in human persons, their physical 'of its ownness' becomes 'their own' physicality." Thus, it is precisely the human person's awareness of his or her own formal reality (as being something "of his or her own") that finally "permits them to be reduplicatively self-possessed."[106]

*Second, Ellacuría says that Zubiri argues for the philosophical primacy of "formal reality." He states that, for Zubiri, this reality (or "reity") has a "transcendental function."*[107] Ellacuría explains that Zubiri is arguing for the primacy of reality "in the dual sense that reality is both the end and the origin [of] . . . everything else," and that "being,[108] existence, meaning, etc., sprout within and from reality."[109] He explains that, for Zubiri, the sensible apprehension of the formal reality of a thing (the quality of being something "of its own") has a transcendental function that opens the subject "to more and more reality."[110]

Ellacuría's point is that, for Zubiri, the formal reality of a thing has a "transcendental function." He describes it as a function, "through which, by being installed in real things and without abandoning or annihilating them, we physically extend and expand ourselves by means of our modest intellective sensibility toward the real as real, toward a reality which is always open."[111] Ellacuría insists that it is precisely here "where any type of reality can make itself present in one way or another, including the absolutely absolute reality that we call God."[112] Together with the aforementioned "facts of intellection," the "transcendental function" of formal reality places a claim upon the subject that underlies Zubiri's argument for its philosophical primacy (see point four below). This constitutes the substance of Zubiri's "positive" alternative[113] to the entification of reality.

It is worth adding that Ellacuría's emphasis on the philosophical primacy of "formal reality" also frames his treatment of the problem of God, and what he calls the absolute or "theologal"[114] dimension of reality (among several other themes). A fuller treatment of Ellacuría's philosophy of God (which we cannot develop here) would show how it is shaped by Zubiri's thesis regarding the "transcendental function" of the formal notion of reality.

*Third, as noted earlier, Ellacuría says it is completely erroneous to characterize Zubiri's understanding of reality as a type of naïve realism.*[115] He makes three key points. One, we are dealing here with a formal concept of reality (or "reity") as the actualization of the real as real. Two, this concept makes no claims to being absolute and must be constantly revised. Indeed, it "can never have sufficient security" regarding its reference to "what things are in their worldly reality."[116] And three, though the formal concept of reality does refer to things in their worldly reality, Ellacuría emphasizes that there is no claim that reality as formality refers to what things are "in themselves." Rather, "the reality of the world is intellectively sensed," by means of primal apprehension and the logos. Thus, it is "only by means of an intellective march . . . of reason, that one can tentatively reach it."[117]

Ellacuría then adds a *fourth* element to the, by now familiar, terms of this argument. *He says Zubiri believes that we are not only open to reality, and located in reality, but we are bound to reality.*[118] It is not just that Zubiri believes reality forcefully makes itself present, as we have seen, or simply that reality imposes its formal character as being something "of its own" *[de suyo]* on us. Rather, Ellacuría says that, for Zubiri, reality places certain claims or demands on us that we ignore to our own peril. The idea is that, "intellective sensing not only opens us to both reality and being," it also "drives us irresistibly to endlessly explore every type of reality and every form of being"[119] that we encounter. Zubiri calls this our "bondedness" *("religacion")*[120] to reality.

Zubiri argues that the 'bondedness' of the subject to reality means that the actualization of reality 'as real' creates a corresponding demand for the self-actualization of the reality of the subject.[121] The subject must decide whether and how to live by the truth of the formal reality that is actualized by their sentient intelligence. Ellacuría's point is that, through the day-by-day actualization of the real as real by the sentient intelligence, "a life is being constructed in which the force, the richness, and the power of the real intersect and intertwine with the problematic presented by reality itself."[122] The idea is that, because of the subject's fundamental and unavoidable relationship to the "power of the real," the self is faced with a steady diet of choices regarding whether and how to appropriate itself in relation to the realities, or "reities," it encounters.

Ellacuría concludes that, for Zubiri, it is "only by grasping and being grasped by more reality," that the human person "will become not just more intelligent, but, finally more real, and more human."[123] Ellacuría concludes that "giving in to reality in a will-to-truth, in a will-to-live, and in a will-to-being is a splendid way to overcome reductionistic idealism."[124] In what follows, I will briefly suggest at least five ways in which this intention guided Ellacuría's efforts to face up to the historical reality of the "crucified peoples" of Latin America and El Salvador.

## III. Originality and Significance of Ellacuría's Liberating and Christian Historical Realism: How Ellacuría Moves Beyond Zubiri

Thus far we have focused on Ellacuría's appropriation of Zubiri's critique of reductionistic idealism in philosophical modernity, and Zubiri's proposals regarding sentient intelligence and the primacy of the formal dimension of reality. I have examined writings in which Ellacuría critically summarizes and incorporates aspects of Zubiri's proposals into his work. And I have suggested these constitute the best sources to show which aspects of Zubiri's massive corpus shaped Ellacuría's powerful thought. On the other hand, it must be said that Ellacuría's work not only builds upon, but also diverges from (or moves beyond) his philosophical mentor in some important ways. I conclude, therefore, by indicating how Ellacuría's philosophical and theological work, especially his liberating and Christian historical realism, diverges from Zubiri's proposals in five important ways.

*First, Ellacuría diverges from Zubiri by explicitly grounding his life and work as a Christian philosopher and theologian in the historical reality of Latin America. Indeed, it is Ellacuría's encounter with the historical reality of Latin America's crucified majorities that calls forth the compassionate response of liberating solidarity that eventually defines his life as a human being and a Christian.* In the words of Jon Sobrino, Ellacuría's closest friend, Jesuit companion, and coworker over thirty years of shared Jesuit life, Ellacuría's "passion for service . . . was the foundation of his life, his vocation as a Jesuit, and . . . as a human being."[125] Sobrino adds, however, that, "Slowly he came to understand that it was not just any service [to which he was called], but a specific service: to take the crucified people down from the cross."[126]

While it may seem obvious, I believe this Latin American contextualization, and its grounding in the church's call to an option for the poor, are the most important sources of the striking originality of Ellacuría's thought. One can find its roots articulated in Ellacuría's most important talk on Jesuit spirituality, given at the 1969 province retreat. Virtually all the Jesuits of Central America had gathered to make the Spiritual Exercises of St. Ignatius, as they struggled with how to respond to Vatican II (1962–1965), and to the 1968 call by the Latin American Bishops at Medellín, Colombia to an "option for the poor." Ellacuría argues passionately for the historical reality of "The Third World as the Optimal Place for the Christian to Live the Exercises."[127] Though he correctly warns that the path of Medellín will lead to persecution and death, he nonetheless suggests that the historical reality of Latin America and the leadership of the Catholic Church are calling the Jesuits of Central America to an option for the poor. In an important aside, Ellacuría asserts that his thoughts should be understood as a "small" attempt to go beyond the work of his teacher, Karl Rahner, by focusing on the historical particularity of Latin America's "worldly reality and to conceive of it in theological terms."[128]

The vast majority of Ellacuría's subsequent writing follows the same pattern. Thus, much of the work summarized above is dedicated to developing the outline, the "foundations," and the substance of a truly Latin American philosophy and theology grounded in the historical reality of the Continent's "poor majorities."[129] As board member (1967–1989) and then president of the University of Central America (1979–1989), and a powerful theoretician on the nature of the Christian university,[130] Ellacuría played a leading role in formulating and implementing the school's mission in historical terms. One can hear Ellacuría's voice in the school's charter document for the 1980s when it insists, "the UCA seeks to be an institutional university response to the historical reality of the country, considered from an ethical perspective as an unjust and irrational reality that should be transformed. . . . It does this in a university manner and . . . with a Christian inspiration."[131]

Likewise, as El Salvador's leading public intellectual and an important political figure, Ellacuría came to embody the university's mandate in civil society to be a "critical and creative conscience regarding the Salvadoran reality within the Central American context."[132] His "political writings,"[133] analyzing virtually every major proposal for political and social reform between 1969–1989 in light of Catholic social teaching, fill three volumes and two thousand pages. He met endlessly with political, military, and popular leaders from all sides for over twenty years. This is how Ellacuría actualizes his commitment to a Latin American "*histori-cization* of university activity,"[134] which he hoped would "impel it to create models that historically correspond better to the Reign of God."[135]

What follows, then, will be guided by an abiding interest in how each of the remaining philosophical and theological developments reflect Ellacuría's Christian vocation, his Jesuit mission, and his human commitment to take the crucified people of Latin America down from the cross.

*Second, Ellacuría develops the outline of a liberating and Christian historical realism from the philosophy of Xavier Zubiri. He does this, in part, by making "historical reality"[136] the proper object of philosophy and theology, rather than Zubiri's more abstract "unity of intramundane reality in its process toward superior forms of reality such as . . . the human person and history."[137]*

Ellacuría explicitly accepts what he calls Zubiri's "strictly intramundane metaphysics"[138] when he grounds the argument for his *Philosophy of Historical Reality* in the thesis, "all of intramundane reality constitutes a single complex and differentiated physical unity."[139] He builds carefully on Zubiri's cosmology, analyzing matter, biological life, sentient life, and human history (in its personal and social dimensions), as subsystems of the more comprehensive reality of the cosmos. However, Ellacuría's analysis makes an important change in emphasis when he says "historical reality" is the proper object of philosophy.

He justifies this departure with the assertion that "historical reality" is understood as "the totality of reality as it is given in its highest qualitative form, the specific form of which is history."[140] Ellacuría suggests that it is precisely here "where we are given not only the highest forms of reality, but also the field of the maximum possibilities of the real." He asserts that, "historical reality . . . includes all other types of reality." And he argues that "there is no historical reality without purely material reality . . . biological reality . . . [and] personal and social reality." In the end, however, Ellacuría says "historical reality is where reality is 'more' . . . where it is both 'more its own,' and 'more open.'" It is on this point (which is derived from Zubiri) that Ellacuría will focus his most creative efforts.

This important change in emphasis explains (theoretically) why Ellacuría, unlike his mentors Zubiri and Rahner, grounds virtually his entire philosophical and theological project in a specific historical reality, that of Latin America. The earlier example highlights the significance Ellacuría attributes to the specificity and local character of historical reality. Interestingly, however, this preoccupation also allows him to treat aspects of the historical reality of Latin America as concrete universals (in Rahner's sense of the term). His ecclesiology insists powerfully on the "universal"[141] ecclesiological significance of the "reconversion of the Church to the Third World."[142] He argues eloquently that, what he calls the "crucified people"[143] of the Third World, constitute the "principle . . . sign of the times" that should orient the "universal historical mission" of the church today.

Ellacuría's emphasis on historical reality also lets him resituate praxis, a most important and controverted concept for Latin American philosophies and theologies of liberation, in a much larger philosophical context. It is a context that both includes, yet radically critiques, the contributions of Marx.[144] On the one hand, Ellacuría's fundamental move here is to redefine praxis in terms of the concept of historical reality that he derives from Zubiri. There can be little doubt this is his intention when he concludes the *Philosophy of Historical Reality* with the assertion, "finally, then, historical reality, dynamically and concretely considered, has the character of praxis. When it is joined to other criteria, it leads one to the truth about reality, and also to the truth about the interpretation of reality."[145] On the other hand, the pressing need in Latin America for critical Christian dialogue with Marx evidently influences Ellacuría's reading of Zubiri on this point as well. Elsewhere in this volume, Antonio González makes the historical claim that, "Zubiri's novel treatment of human *historicity*[146] interests Ellacuría, above all, precisely because he believes that this is one of the principal themes for the dialogue with Marxist philosophy, and specifically, with historical materialism."[147]

Accordingly, Ellacuría both explicitly engages,[148] yet radically critiques Marx through his reading of Zubiri's philosophy. Indeed, he describes the latter as an open materialist realism. In his assessment of the philosopher's "complete work,"[149] Ellacuría argues that Zubiri's "realism is materialist from the physical-metaphysical point of view, because in the intramundane order everything emerges in matter, from matter, and is dynamically sustained by matter. And his realism is materialist from the epistemological point of view, because reality is always sentiently apprehended in an impression of reality."[150] Concomitantly, however, he emphasizes that Zubiri's "materialist realism is open because, physically-metaphysically, it does not reduce everything to matter—there are strict nonreducibles—and because, epistemologically, there is a transcendental openness to reality as real."[151]

Ellacuría concludes that Zubiri's "willingness to attribute everything that is material to matter and to the material condition of humanity, without allowing this to reduce either reality or the human person to strictly closed limits, is one of the greatest achievements of Zubirian thought."[152] Ellacuría finds a rigorous philosophical framework in Zubiri that simultaneously rationalizes the Christian emphasis on human freedom, while respecting its material conditions. This is clearly in view when he identifies praxis with "the historical process itself . . . as . . . productive and transformative"[153] of "both natural and historical reality."[154] For our purposes, these moves beyond Zubiri and Marx show how Ellacuría initiates a new and promising stage in the Latin American discussion of praxis[155] by resituating its key term in the very complex, critical, and constructive philosophical discussion outlined in this article.

*Third, Ellacuría's liberating Christian historical realism develops Zubiri's principle of historicization into a contextualized truth test for the claims of theology and philosophy.* Zubiri accepts Neitzsche's intuition that the artificial encision between intelligence and sensibility is largely responsible for various forms of reductionistic idealism. He says the exclusion of sensibility from intelligence has legitimated metaphysical dualisms, and sometimes reified political divisions by opposing the sensible knowledge of the common people to the true knowledge of the elite. Zubiri's focus on sentient intelligence undermines the various forms of this dualism.

While accepting these arguments, Ellacuría extends the emphasis from sentient intelligence to historical intelligence. He accomplishes this, in part, by using historicization, a more limited term from Zubiri, as his method par excellence for the verification of truth claims.

In fact, one finds two primary uses of the term "historicization" in Ellacuría's work. First, in the *Philosophy of Historical Reality,* Ellacuría uses the term to refer to the incorporative and transformative power human praxis exerts over the historical and natural dimensions of reality. Here, "the historicization of nature consists . . . in the fact that humanity makes history from nature and with nature."[156] Praxis appropriates from historical tradition its concepts, values, practices, and other ways of being in reality, simultaneously being shaped by and transforming them. In its primary sense, "historicization" refers to this process. This usage is derived from Zubiri. However, in a 1976 article, Ellacuría suggests a second meaning: "Demonstrating the impact of certain concepts within a particular context is also . . . understood here as their historicization."[157] It is this secondary sense of the term that predominates in the great majority of Ellacuría's occasional pieces, and which is our focus here.

Ellacuría's brilliant development of historicization as a method for verifying truth claims provides methodological criteria concretizing three key themes in his work. First, historicization operationalizes Ellacuría's "Zubirian" historical realism. Concepts can be said to be historicized "when they refer to historical realities."[158] Ellacuría notes this is the opposite of being abstract, in the negative sense. Second, historicized concepts must be constructed to be verifiable, or they are not valid. Using a classic notion of counterfactual proof, Ellacuría argues that if a "hypothesis cannot be nullified by data, it is not . . . [historicized.]"[159] Indeed, he suggests, in that case "one is falling into sheer idealism, no matter how much the realist or materialist one might claim to be."[160] And third, historicization is a procedure for testing and validating truth claims associated with a concept. Ellacuría holds that the truth of a historicized concept is actualized in its "becoming reality." Thus, its "truth can be measured . . . [or verfied] in its results." [161] Here we must note that nowhere does Ellacuría say that truth is identical with, or can be reduced to, those results.

Accordingly, it is necessary to continually revise the content of a given concept in light of its historical effects, in order to maintain the "essential meaning" of that concept. The meaning of a concept is determined, at least in part, in terms of the practical effects, or the impact of a concept on historical reality. Ellacuría's use of historicization as a contextualized truth test is illustrated in the way he historicizes Zubiri's understanding of the "critical and creative" functions of philosophy (below).[162]

*Fourth, Ellacuría's liberating Christian historical realism consistently historicizes Zubiri's proposals regarding the "critical"[163] and the "grounding"[164] functions of philosophy, and, more generally, intelligence. This is seen in the de-ideologizing role he assigns philosophy and theology, and how he historicizes theology as the theoretical (or "ideological") moment of the praxis of the church.*

In a very important 1985 article, "The Liberating Function of Philosophy," Ellacuría concretizes the preceding discussion by historicizing what he calls the aforementioned "critical and creative" functions of philosophy. Ellacuría develops a programmatic sketch for "the constitution of a new philosophy . . . that is conceived [both] from within . . . and for the reality of Latin America."[165] He suggests that, to be truly Latin American, it must be a philosophy that is placed "at the service of the popular majorities who define that reality." He argues that it must have a "liberating function" in Latin America, in order to fulfill philosophy's more general mandate to be both "critical and creative."[166] He concretizes this in what he calls the role of philosophy to "de-ideologize" historical reality.[167]

Ellacuría's argument is based on the fundamental distinction he draws between "ideology" and "ideologization." Addressing ideology, Ellacuría argues that while the "entire dynamism of historical reality . . . must be understood as praxis," nonetheless praxis "has many forms" and/or "moments," each possessing "a relatively absolute" autonomy.[168] He says many of those forms "are accompanied by a theoretical moment," which happens when the "conscious character of praxis" achieves a "relatively autonomous" level. Following the general approach taken by Juan Luis Segundo, he says these "take the form of *ideology* . . . in the non-pejorative sense."[169] This simply means "praxis . . . is accompanied by a series of representations, evaluations, and justifications" that offer "a coherent, totalizing, and value laden explanation, through concepts, symbols, images, references, etc."[170]

On the other hand, while he insists that the "phenomenon of ideology is necessary and inevitable," it is also inherently "ambiguous."[171] Thus, ideology can "degrade into *ideologization*"[172] that "adds . . . visions of reality that, far from manifesting reality, mask and deform it, while appearing to be true."[173] Ellacuría says, typically "these deformations answer unconsciously to collective interests," such as "classes or social . . . ethnic, political, religious groups."[174]

What happens, then, when "[i]deologization confronts us with nothing under the appearance of reality, with falsity under the appearance of truth, with non-being under the appearance of being?"[175] Ellacuría answers that philosophy's historical commitment to "criticism" and to "the search for its grounds" *("fundamentalidad"),* makes it "a powerful weapon" for de-ideologizing the necessarily theoretical dimension of historical reality, or praxis.[176] Here we see Ellacuría moving to historicize Zubiri's critique of reductionist idealism, and his constructive proposals regarding sentient intelligence and the formal character of reality. This is clear when Ellacuría asserts that philosophy must include a "critical, systematic and creative" contextualized reflection on historical processes (praxis), or risk "degenerating into ideologization" itself.[177]

In 1978 Ellacuría takes another important step, historicizing the work of theology as a theoretical or "ideological moment of ecclesial praxis."[178] Two of the many issues addressed in this important piece are especially relevant. First, Ellacuría argues that "theology should place itself at the service of ecclesial praxis whenever that praxis is Christian, or in order that it be so."[179] Ellacuría summarizes the significance of this deeply traditional affirmation:

> Establishing theology as a moment of ecclesial praxis highlights the fact that theological production is not an autonomous theoretical undertaking, but an element within a broader structure. Ecclesial praxis is taken here in the broad sense that includes every undertaking of the church that is in some fashion historical, understanding the church as a community of humans who, in one way or another, realize the Reign of God. This latter referent is chosen in order to stress the aspect of praxis, that is, of transformative action, which the church necessarily assumes in its historical pilgrimage.[180]

This move particularizes, localizes, historicizes, and grounds the work of theology in the historical praxis of the church. On the one hand, it relativizes theology's "ancient claim to being an absolute and supreme form of knowledge that stands above the historical vicissitudes of other forms of knowledge and . . . praxis."[181] On the other hand, a crucial role emerges for theology in conceptualizing and "grounding" what Christians generally believe is, in fact, a transcendent dimension of the historical reality and praxis of the church.

Ellacuría's approach contains the elements of a fundamental eccle-siology that views the church in terms of a praxis that mediates and generates historical signs of the reign of God in history.[182] Theology generally points toward the "theologal" dimension of the experience of something "more"[183] that suffuses this history as its ground and its term. Thus, theology reminds the church not to confuse itself and its struc-tures with its role in historicizing God's presence in history. It helps the church to understand that, while its special role in "announcing and re-alizing the Reign of God in history intersects with other historical tasks," this role has "its own autonomy as a living entity."[184]

Secondly, theology has a crucial role to play in de-ideologizing ecclesial praxis. As a general principle Ellacuría asserts, "Theological production is not an end in itself, nor does it have roots in itself. But neither can it sub-ordinate itself to just any ecclesial praxis."[185] Exploiting an approach he learned from Rahner, Ellacuría argues, "while ecclesial praxis as a whole cannot fundamentally separate itself from the following of Jesus, it can do so in particular moments and in large sectors of ecclesial structure." Thus, theology is forced to ask, "which ecclesial praxis [is best]?"[186]

This is due in part to the inherent limitations of an ecclesial praxis dedicated to the realization of a reality (the reign of God) that is "both historical and transhistorical."[187] But it is also due to the more serious problem of sin. Ellacuría argues, "if historical praxis is . . . divided," and "if the Reign of God and the reign of evil [or sin] present themselves and operate in that divided praxis," then theology has a crucial role to play in helping ecclesial praxis to discern its proper place within the larger historical praxis of society. This demands that theology be more than "a pure reflection on the Reign of God."[188] It must "insert itself through ecclesial praxis into the larger totality of historical praxis." [189] In this way theology must humbly, yet authentically, take responsibility for itself as an ecclesial praxis (its theoretical moment). Thus, it can be, but is not necessarily so, a response to grace that truly participates in the historical realization of the reign of God.

In "The Liberating Function of Philosophy," Ellacuría describes the role of the Christian philosopher and theologian in terms of the "Socratic existence that continually points to the deficiencies of knowing and doing." [190] He warns, however, that if these servants of the church and society "are not allowed" to fulfill their vocation, then they "must under-take it on their own, even if it brings about their condemnation and os-tracization by society" or the church.[191] Turning to the example of Jesus, Ellacuría offers a sobering reminder of the dangers of this mission:

A Reign of God that does not enter into conflict with a history shaped by the power of sin, is not the Reign of God of Jesus, as spiritual as it might seem. Likewise, a Reign of God that does not enter into conflict with the malice and criminality of personal existence, is not the Reign of God of Jesus.[192]

For Ellacuría, the de-ideologization of historical reality, particularly the historical reality of El Salvador, would be a way of taking the poor down from their cross. Ultimately it would cost him his life.

*Fifth and finally, Ellacuría's liberating Christian historical realism transforms one of Zubiri's key epistemological principles (intellection involves the reciprocal actualization of reality and the subject) into an ethical imperative with deeply religious implications.*

As we have seen, Zubiri argues that the process of intellection of reality makes a demand on the subject. In Zubiri's words, the human person is required to "realize the weight of the reality" *[hacerse cargo de la realidad]*.[193] In a 1966 article, Ellacuría reveals this formulation is based on an 'explicit allusion' to Heidegger's notion of the thrownness of being (as Dasein).[194] Ellacuría shows that Zubiri significantly modifies Heidegger's idea, arguing rather that human "being gives itself to the thrownness of the real thing in its reality." The point is that when something "is already given as a reality, I not only have to allow it to be *[dejar que sea]*, but I am forced to realize the weight of it *[hacerse cargo de ella]* as a reality."[195] Thus, "when I intellectively face up to the thing, I am not only being in the thing, but I am being-together with reality. In this being-together, the human person can reappropriate him- or herself as a reality. . . . " As a result, the apprehension of reality requires the actualization of the subject.

Diego Gracia suggests that, "In Ellacuría, Zubiri's thesis that the human person must 'realize the weight of reality' is transformed into an ethical imperative."[196] This is seen when Ellacuría adds that the human person is also obligated "to shoulder the weight of reality" and "to take charge of the weight of reality." In a 1979 paper on the "Biological Foundation for Ethics,"[197] Ellacuría appears to confirm this interpretation, but in its more radical form. Ellacuría's thesis is that the human person, "formally constitutes himself as a moral reality" precisely "by having to open himself to reality, to what things are 'of their own,' . . . [and] by having to face up to himself and things as real."[198] But he insists that intellection's "ethical opening to reality has a very exact structure."[199]

This structure is best articulated in a now famous 1975 article, "Toward a Philosophical Foundation for Latin American Theologial Method."[200] Here Ellacuría predictably asserts, "The formal structure of intelligence and its differentiating function . . . [is] to apprehend reality and to face up to that reality."[201] However he adds, "This facing up to real things as real has a triple dimension." First, *realizing the weight of reality,* "assumes being in the reality of things—and not merely being before the idea of things or their meaning."[202] Jon Sobrino calls this the *"noetic"* moment. The idea is that sentient intelligence must be "incarnated in reality."[203] Elsewhere in this volume, Gustavo Gutiérrez eloquently articulates the biographical impact on Ellacuría of the "weight" of his encounter with the reality of the poor. He says this encounter provides the ultimate fundamental frame of reference within which to interpret the larger reality of Ellacuría's life and death. Looking backward, Gutiérrez suggests:

> The life Ignacio chose makes us understand the scope of the death he encountered. Like Jesus, Ignacio could say, "No one takes my life; I give it freely" (Jn 10:18). He gave it, in fact, out of love for the God of the Bible, and for the people he made his own. The people compelled him to learn about the scandal of their poverty and their unending suffering. Thus he came to understand the central role that justice has in the gospel message, and that without it there is no authentic peace.[204]

Gutiérrez's words capture beautifully and precisely what Ellacuría means by the assertion that realizing the weight of reality "implies being among the reality of things through their material and active mediations."[205] Here, truth, justice, and love create the conditions for more and better understanding. Each enriches and deepens the relationship that emerges from the "weight" of Ellacuría's encounter with the reality of the poor. It is truly a "noetic" moment.

Second, Ellacuría says that *"shouldering the weight of reality . . .* expresses the fundamentally ethical nature of intelligence."[206] He insists the idea is that "intelligence was not given to humanity so that it might evade its real obligations, but rather so that it might shoulder upon itself the weight of what things really are, and what they really demand."[207] Sobrino takes this to mean that "intelligence is interrogated by reality and must respond to its demand."[208] In moving words, undoubtedly drawn from his own experience, Gutiérrez shares his view of the inner conflicts of the intellectual who takes responsibility for the reality of a relationship with the poor:

His choice made him see that he couldn't follow in Jesus' footsteps without walking with the people in their aspiration to dignity, life, and liberation. [Yet, i]n the face of this difficult challenge, he did not take refuge—and this is another of the traits which give him his special place—in something he had at hand. It was something that could have hidden the fear of solidarity and its demands from others, and even from himself: namely, an intellectual life flowing quietly along in the purely academic world. This kind of life, although it might occasionally reflect what was happening to the marginalized, would in fact be far from them and their afflictions. Chances to excel in the university world were not lacking, this we know. He possessed a solid formation in philosophy and theology; he was well known as the favorite student of a great teacher, Xavier Zubiri. The academy's doors stood open to him.[209]

In fact, we know that in 1968 Zubiri formally petitioned Fr. Pedro Arrupe, S.J., superior general of the Society of Jesus, to release Ellacuría from the University of Central America, and to assign him permanently to Spain so they could collaborate.[210] However, after a period of discernment involving the highest levels of Jesuit government, it was decided that Ellacuría would return to El Salvador. He was given permission to return to Spain to work with Zubiri during summer vacations at the UCA.[211] Thus Ellacuría would never leave behind the reality of El Salvador or the poor. Sobrino[212] describes Ellacuría's path as exemplifying the type of ethical response demanded by a path of "fidelity to the real,"[213] in this case the reality of the poor of El Salvador. Sobrino's challenge, which Ellacuría embraced, was to "be faithful to that reality, regardless of where it might lead."[214]

Third, Ellacuría says *"taking charge of the weight of reality . . .* points to the praxis-oriented nature of intelligence."[215] His idea is that "intelligence only actualizes its nature, including its character of knowing reality and comprehending its meaning, when it undertakes really doing things."[216] Sobrino says this implies "carrying the weight of real tasks."[217] Gutiérrez again captures Ellacuría's point in poignant biographical terms:

> We cannot know . . . how many tensions and perplexities, vacillations and inconsistencies, bad moods, and painful impasses he experienced along the path he chose to follow. But naturally his could be neither a tranquil nor a triumphal journey. It never is. What is certain is that he put his intelligence, his analytical acumen, and all his intellectual talent to work doing the discernment necessary to find the correct path amid the jumble of events taking place in El Salvador and Latin America. Not only did he not forget his philosophical formation. He used it as a source

of criteria for acting in a changing situation full of surprises. Thus he
gave his academic formation its due, and . . . made clear the role that it
can play in the daily life of individuals, no matter how conflictual. . . .
One of my old professors . . . said, "There is nothing more practical than
a good theory." Ignacio lived out this kind of theorizing with passion.[218]

Thus, Ellacuría transforms Zubiri's epistemological theory into an
ethical imperative, which leads him to say and to do things in defense of
the crucified people of El Salvador that ultimately lead to his death.
With this move, Ellacuría articulates a powerful theoretical foundation
for historicizing the formal unity of what both he and Sobrino call the
noetic, the ethical, and the praxical dimensions of intelligence. Ellacuría
also offers a historical model for what each contributes to the practical
work of Christian theology and philosophy as the "ideological moment
of an ecclesial and historical praxis."[219]

## Conclusion

This essay, then, has outlined certain aspects of Ellacuría's Christian
historical realism, showing how each builds upon, contextualizes, and
sometimes transforms key elements of the philosophy of Xavier Zubiri. I
have argued that Ellacuría builds on Zubiri's critique of the role of "reductionistic idealism" in modern phenomenology, and Zubiri's notions
of "sentient intelligence" and the philosophical primacy of reality. I have
tried to demonstrate the originality of Ellacuría's proposals, suggesting
five areas in which this liberating and Christian historical realism diverges from or moves beyond the work of Zubiri.

In an article published four years after Zubiri's death, Ellacuría argues
that Zubiri's critical and constructive reappraisal of the "reductionistic
idealism" of the Western philosophical tradition is particularly suited to
the project of developing a truly Latin American approach to philosophy
and theology. Given the "ultra-Coperican turn" of European and Latin-
American philosophy, Ellacuría argues that Zubiri's approach is "of enor-
mous significance both for its negative (de-ideologizing) critique and in
its positive focus on problems."[220] With typical realism, Ellacuría asserts,
"in Latin America and in the Third World one achieves a brute appreciation for the seriousness of the idealist trap, transmitted above all by philosophy and traditional theologies, but also by political language."[221] He
says the Latin American context requires a rigorous philosophical approach that can handle "the obscuring and falsifying idealization of real-

ity."[222] Ellacuría says that it is precisely here that "the thought of Zubiri, without intending to do so, helps tremendously by preparing one to discover and to overcome such idealist and ideologizing distortions."[223]

In the end, the ways in which Ellacuría and others historicize the ideas discussed in this essay provide valuable clues regarding their ultimate significance. We have seen that Ellacuría develops his Christian historical realism and its critique of philosophical modernity as critical principles for the emergence of "truly Latin American" and liberating approaches to theology and philosophy. Elsewhere in this volume, Jon Sobrino encourages us to read Ellacuría's proposals against the details of his remarkable life.[224] My own essay has been explicitly guided by an interest in how the original aspects of Ellacuría's liberating Christian historical realism reflect what he sees as his Christian vocation, Jesuit mission, and human commitment to take the crucified people down from the cross. Indeed, each of the essays in this volume in some way addresses how Ellacuría's ideas are being historicized in ongoing efforts to contextualize the Christian faith in parts of Africa, Europe, Latin America, and North America.[225]

This type of approach helps us to appreciate the depth of Ellacuría's character as a human being, and a Christian, as well as the substance of his contribution as a Christian intellectual. This essay on Ellacuría's debt to Xavier Zubiri will have achieved its goal if it lends texture and substance to Ellacuría's efforts to take the crucified people down from the cross through his vocation as a Christian intellectual. As we have seen, that response cannot be separated from his attempt to historicize Zubiri's ideas regarding sentient intelligence, historical reality, and the reductionist idealism of philosophical modernity. I have suggested that Ellacuría's efforts produced a strikingly original and powerful approach that contextualizes and reinterprets key themes in Western philosophy from a Latin American, liberationist (and one could add postcolonial) perspective.

I am convinced Ellacuría's liberating Christian (and very Catholic) historical realism has much to offer as we struggle in the years ahead to adequately conceptualize the promise of what Karl Rahner calls a "world church,"[226] in a context deeply distorted by sin and oppression. Theology can and must make its contribution to the churches' efforts to forge ecclesial praxes that are truly "one, holy, catholic, and apostolic" from a human community torn by conflict, and challenged by diversity. Ellacuría and his companions gave their lives to ensure that both followers of Jesus and the world might be enriched and challenged by the profound contextualization of Christianity's *"depositum fidei"* embodied in the faith, hope, and love of the marginated peoples of Latin America. Thus, following in the footsteps of Archbishop Oscar Romero, his incandescent life and death models not only the Christian call to take "crucified peoples" of this world down from the cross through the crucial struggle for human rights. Ignacio Ellacuría also helps us believe that "love produces hope, and great love produces great hope."[227]

---

[1] The restricted scope of this essay will not allow me to argue the specifically "Catholic" nature of Ellacuría's historical realism, though it is reflected in the theological arguments alluded to in the final section of the paper. It appears quite explicitly in Ellacuría's important contributions to Ignatian spirituality, the philosophy of God, Catholic fundamental theology, ethics, and Catholic social teaching. However, Ellacuría also clearly intends to address all Christians when he makes philosophical claims with links to Christianity. For these reasons, I have chosen to emphasize the "Christian" character and roots of Ellacuría's historical realism, though it could also be characterized as a "Catholic" historical realism. In this connection, it should be noted that Ellacuría always emphasizes the "Christian" rather than the "Catholic" character of the university in his writings. This is explained, in part, both by the relatively homogenous Catholic character of El Salvador, and by Ellacuría's ecumenical concern to expand the conversation about the university beyond the somewhat narrow sectarian concerns of members of the local hierarchy.

[2] Ignacio Ellacuría, "Función liberadora de la filosofía," *Estudios Centroamericanos (ECA)* 40, no. 435 (1985) 47; henceforth, "Función liberadora."

[3] Ellacuría, "Función liberadora," 46. Ellacuría writes, "the Latin American continent has not produced its own philosophy, one that emerges from its own historical reality and which fulfills a liberating function for Latin America."

[4] Ignacio Ellacuría, "Hacia una fundamentación filosófica del método teológico Latinoamericano," *ECA,* nos. 322–3 (Agosto, Septiembre, 1975) 409–25; henceforth "Hacia una fundamentación."

[5] Ignacio Ellacuría, "La superación del reduccionismo idealista en Zubiri," *ECA,* no. 477 (1988) 633–50; henceforth "Reduccionismo."

[6] Ignacio Ellacuría, "Zubiri, cuatro años después," *Diario* 16 (21 de septiembre de 1987) 2.

[7] Ellacuría, "Reduccionismo," 633.

[8] Ignacio Ellacuría, "Introducción crítica a la antropología filosófica de Zubiri," *Realitas* 2 (1975) 137.

[9] Ibid.

[10] Diego Gracia situates Zubiri in a "postmodern philosophical horizon." Diego Gracia, *Voluntad de verdad: Para leer a Zubiri* (Barcelona: Editorial Labor, 1986) xii.

[11] Xavier Zubiri, *Inteligencia sentiente: Inteligencia y realidad,* vol. 1 (Madrid: Alianza Editorial, 1980) 11–2.

[12] Zubiri's aforementioned distinction between sensing (apprehending something by means of an impression) and "pure sensing" (the mere stimulation of the senses) is critical here. He asserts that the opposition should not be between "intellection and sensing," but between "pure sensing and intellection." But, he argues, "Classical philosophy confused sensing with 'pure sensing,' which led it to think that there was an opposition between sensing and intellection" (Zubiri, *Inteligencia sentiente,* 80).

[13] Ignacio Ellacuría, "Zubiri en El Salvador," *ECA,* nos. 361–2 (1978) 949–50, esp. 950.

[14] Ellacuría, "Reduccionismo," 634.

[15] Zubiri, *Inteligencia sentiente,* 86.

[16] Gracia, *Voluntad,* 89.

[17] Diego Gracia, "Zubiri, Xavier," in Latourelle, R. and Fisichella, R., eds., *Dictionary of Fundamental Theology* (New York: Crossroad, 1995) 1165–9, esp.1165.

[18] Gracia, *Voluntad,* 89, 90.

[19] Xavier Zubiri, "Dos etapas," *Revista de Occidente* 4:32 (1984) 47. Cited in Gracia, *Voluntad,* 33.

[20] Xavier Zubiri, *Ensayo de una teoria fenomenológica del juicio* (Madrid: Ediciones de la Revista de Archivos, bibliotecas y Museos, 1923) 46. Cited in Gracia, *Voluntad,* 49.

[21] Ibid.

[22] Xavier Zubiri, "Le Problème de l'objectivité d'après E. Husserl: I. La Logique pure" (mimeograph, Lovaina, 1921) 49. Cited in Gracia, *Voluntad,* 49.

[23] Zubiri, *Teoria fenomenológica,* 48–9.

[24] Xavier Zubiri, "Filosofía y metafísica," *Cruz y Raya* 30 (1935) 7–60, esp. 40. On Zubiri's attempts to "correct" phenomenology see Gracia, *Voluntad,* 90–4.

[25] Gracia, *Voluntad,* 89, 90.

[26] Zubiri, "Filosofía y Metafísica," 40. Cited in Gracia, *Voluntad,* 90.

[27] Xavier Zubiri, *Sobre el hombre* (Madrid: Alianza Editorial, 1986) 439–40. Cited in Gracia, *Voluntad,* 68.

[28] Recall that for Zubiri and Ellacuría, the primordial act of intellection that is "sensation . . . consists [precisely] in apprehending something by means of an impression," Zubiri, *Inteligencia sentiente,* 79. Additionally, the act of sensing "has three essential moments": the "provocation," the "modification" of a state or balance, and the response (not to be confused with a simple "reaction"), Zubiri, *Inteligencia sentiente,* 29, 30. To my way of thinking, the specificity of Zubiri's definition of sensing, and the generality of its three moments, leave plenty of room for functions like memory, imagination, and affectivity, about which Zubiri says very little, in the operations of sensing as intellection.

[29] I find this aspect of autonomy akin to what C. S. Peirce means by "secondness."

[30] Ignacio Ellacuría, "La Superacion del reduccionismo idealista en Zubiri," *ECA* (no. 477, 1988) 648. Zubiri writes, "Given the completely distinct character that the term 'reality' can have in vulgar and even in philosophical language, that of knowing reality outside of any apprehension, the term 'reidad' can serve in order to avoid confusion. I will employ the two terms indiscriminately: 'reidad' will mean here simply 'reality,' simply being 'of itself.'" Zubiri, *Inteligencia sentiente,* 57.

[31] Diego Gracia argues, "it is important to keep in mind that the word 'reality' has two meanings in Zubiri: 'reality as formality' (or reality *qua* given in apprehension) and

'reality as fundamentality' (or reality as the actualization in a sensible apprehension of the thing beyond apprehension)" (*Dictionary,* 1166). Gracia insists that the apprehension of "reality as formality" is the "elementary act of intelligence," and therefore the basic meaning of the term. However, for Zubiri, this is not "the only" act of intelligence. On the one hand, Zubiri argues that "without apprehension" of the formally real "there would be no further acts" of intellection. However, he also argues that "without further acts, we would not know what things are beyond our apprehension of them, i.e., in the reality of the world." Gracia says this is why Zubiri insists on a unity-in-distinction of "reality as formality" and "reality as fundamentality." While the first meaning of reality is primary, it has inherent reference to the second. An inspection of Zubiri's use of the distinction between "reity" and "reality" in his last and most important works confirms Gracia's analysis on this point. Zubiri writes, "Given the completely distinct character that the term reality can have in popular language and even in philosophical language, that of knowing reality outside of any apprehension, the term 'reity' can serve to avoid confusions. . . . [R]eity *[reidad]* will mean here simple reality, simply being something 'of its own' *[de suyo]*." Zubiri, *Inteligencia sentiente,* 57.

[32] Zubiri actually argues that intellection engages in three types of judgments when it assumes the posture of the logos: affirmative, propositional, and predicative. Xavier Zubiri, *Inteligencia y logos* (Madrid: Alianza Editorial, Sociedad de Estudios y Publicaciones, 1982) 152, 155–6, 161.

[33] Zubiri, *Inteligencia sentiente,* 14, 275–79; Zubiri, *Inteligencia y logos,* 52.

[34] Zubiri praises what he calls Heidegger's "theory of ontological knowledge," but critiques the ontology Heidegger derives from it. "Heidegger places the problem of 'being' in the line or order of comprehension. . . . If Heidegger were content with saying that there is a comprehension of 'being,' and with undertaking to explicate it in its irreducible originality, there would be not the least objection in principle to oppose to him. . . . What would have been reached by this route would not have been an ontology, but a theory of ontological knowledge, so to speak. Nevertheless, Heidegger is in search of an ontology. To this end, he conceives the comprehension of 'being' in a manner which is, in its own turn, ontological: he considers the comprehension of 'being,' not only as the act in which 'being' *shows* itself to itself and from itself, but as a *mode of being,* that is to say, as a mode of the very same thing which is showing itself, of 'being,'" Xavier Zubiri, *Sobre la esencia* (Madrid: Gráficas Cóndor, Sociedad de Estudios y Publicaciones, 1962, 1980) 441–2. On this point see Gracia, *Voluntad,* 66–73.

[35] I have chosen to translate this word as "being-as-an-entity." Zubiri is certainly aware, on the one hand, that the Spanish word "ente," is also the ablative form of the Latin word "ens, entis." The latter was used by Scholastic philosophy to distinguish "real being" *[ens]* from being as existence *[esse]*. Zubiri explicitly recognizes, on the other hand, that the Spanish word "ente" is closer in meaning to what several medieval philosophers meant by "esse," or "esse real" (real existence); see *Inteligencia sentiente,* 226. Thus, it appears to me that Zubiri wants to exploit the terminological ambiguity of the word "ente" to draw the Spanish reader's attention to the fact that Western philosophy has used "being" (a) to refer both to existence and to the larger category of being itself, and (b) to reify and replace what Zubiri considers the more dynamic and inclusive concept of "reality."

[36] Ellacuría, "Reduccionismo," 637. I shall argue later in this section that Zubiri's position on this point shares important elements with Martin Heidegger's criticisms in *Being and Time* of the Western philosophical tradition.

[37] Zubiri, *Inteligencia sentiente*, 224–5.

[38] Ellacuría, "Reduccionismo," 637.

[39] Ibid. NB: the following quotations are from the same source and page unless otherwise noted.

[40] Zubiri, *Sobre la esencia*, 437.

[41] Ibid., 438.

[42] Ibid., 437.

[43] Ibid., 438.

[44] Ibid., 15.

[45] Ibid., 16.

[46] Ibid.

[47] Ibid.

[48] Ibid., 451.

[49] Ellacuría, "Reduccionismo," 637.

[50] Ibid., 638–9.

[51] Ibid., 637.

[52] Ibid.; Zubiri, *Inteligencia sentiente*, 226.

[53] Ellacuría, "Reduccionismo," 637.

[54] Ibid., 639.

[55] Ibid.

[56] Zubiri, *Sobre la esencia*, 27.

[57] Ibid.

[58] Ellacuría, "Hacía una fundamentación," 420.

[59] Ellacuría, "Reduccionismo," 639; citing *Sobre la esencia*, 31–2.

[60] Ibid., 640.

[61] Ibid.

[62] Ibid., 642.

[63] Ibid.

[64] Ibid.

[65] Ibid.

[66] Ibid.

[67] Ibid.

[68] Ibid.

[69] Ibid.

[70] Ibid., 639.

[71] Ibid.

[72] Ibid., 634.

[73] Zubiri, *Inteligencia sentiente*, 10.

[74] My translation of the two terms in brackets follows Gracia, *Dictionary*, 1166; Zubiri, *Inteligencia sentiente*, 10; Ellacuría, "Reduccionismo," 643.

[75] Zubiri, *Inteligencia sentiente*, 10.

[76] Ellacuría, "Reduccionismo," 642.

[77] Zubiri, *Inteligencia sentiente,* 12. Cited in "Reduccionismo," 644.

[78] Ellacuría, "Reduccionismo," 644.

[79] Zubiri, *Inteligencia sentiente,* 13.

[80] Ellacuría, "Reduccionismo," 645.

[81] Ibid.

[82] Ibid.

[83] Ibid.

[84] Ibid.

[85] Ibid.

[86] Ibid.

[87] Ibid.

[88] Ibid.

[89] Ibid.

[90] Ibid., 646.

[91] Ibid.

[92] Ibid.

[93] Xavier Zubiri, *Inteligencia y logos,* 55, 56.

[94] Ibid., 52.

[95] Ibid., 109–10.

[96] Ellacuría, "Reduccionismo," 646.

[97] Ibid.

[98] Zubiri, *Inteligencia y razon.*

[99] Ibid., 647.

[100] Ibid., 648.

[101] Ibid., 647.

[102] Ibid., 648.

[103] Ibid., 649.

[104] Ibid.

[105] Ibid.

[106] Ibid.

[107] Ibid. Recall that Gracia says "the word 'reality' has two meanings in Zubiri: 'reality as formality' (reality *qua* given in apprehension), and 'reality as fundamentality' (reality *qua* the actualization in a sensible apprehension of the thing beyond apprehension)," Gracia, *Dictionary,* 1166.

[108] Being is understood in terms of the more inclusive Spanish word "ser," but it also includes the more specific German meaning of "Dasein."

[109] Ellacuría, "Reduccionismo," 649.

[110] Ibid.

[111] Ibid., 649–50.

[112] Ellacuría, "Reduccionismo," 650.

[113] Ibid., 642.

[114] Ignacio Ellacuría, "Voluntad de fundamentalidad y voluntad de verdad: conocimiento-fe y su configuración histórica," *RLT,* no. 8 (1986) 113.

[115] Ibid., 648.

[116] Ibid.

Jesús, José, Ignacio, nanny, and Luis Ellacuría, ca. 1931, Portugalete, Spain.

Luis, José, Ignacio, their father, Ildefonso, and Jesús Ellacuría, ca. 1931, Portugalete, Spain.

Ignacio Ellacuría as a young student at the Colegio S. Francisco Javier in Tudela (Navarra), Spain.

1947 graduation photo of
Ignacio Ellacuría, Colegio
S. Francisco Javier, Tudela
(Navarra), Spain.

Graduation from high school 1947, bottom row, second from right.

Ignacio Ellacuría with his
father Ildefonso, while
teaching at the diocesan
seminary (1955–1958),
San Salvador.

First Mass of Ignacio Ellacuría shortly after ordination on July 26, 1961, blessing his brother Jesús.

Ignacio Ellacuría, Amando López, S.J., Rodolfo Cardenal, S.J., ca. 1978–1979.

Ignacio Ellacuría (fourth from left), Oct. 14, 1979, eve of reformist coup against Gen. Carlos Romero. With UCA faculty and staff, nineteen of whom joined the government in a final attempt to avoid civil war.

Segundo Montes, S.J., Ignacio Ellacuría, Archbishop Oscar Romero at the end of 1979, months before March 24, 1980, assassination of Archbishop Romero.

José A. Morales Ehrlich, member of the second reformist junta, and Ignacio Ellacuría, 1980.

Author María López
Vigil (third from left)
and Ignacio Ellacuría
(second from right).

Ignacio Ellacuría,
honorary doctorate
from Santa Clara
University, June 12,
1982, delivering
famous speech on the
Christian university.

Ignacio Ellacuría,
delegate photo for 33rd
General Congregation of
the Society of Jesús
(Sept. 1–Oct 25, 1983).

Pope John Paul II and Ignacio Ellacuría during 33rd General Congregation in Rome, September 1983.

Archbishop Rivera Damas, Ignacio Ellacuría, March 22, 1985, UCA. Posthumous honorary doctorate for Archbishop Oscar Romero.

Ignacio Ellacuría (third from left), Archbishop Rivera Damas
(center), Jon Sobrino (right), Archbishop Oscar Romero
Chapel at the UCA, ca. 1986.

Ignacio Ellacuría,
Jon Sobrino, Archbishop
Oscar Romero Chapel,
UCA, 1986–1989.

Ignacio Martín-Baró, S.J.; papal nuncio; President Alfredo Cristiani; Ignacio Ellacuría;
Oscar Arias, President of Costa Rica, and his wife, September 1989.

Felices los que tienen hambre y sed
de justicia, porque serán saciados.

"Happy are those
who hunger and thirst
for justice, for they
shall be satisfied."
Ignacio Ellacuría,
Nov. 9, 1930–Nov. 16, 1989.

**Ignacio Ellacuría, S.J.**
9, XI, 1930 - 16 XI, 1989

November 1999,
ten-year anniversary
of the assassination
of the UCA martyrs.

[117] Ibid.

[118] Ibid., 650.

[119] Ibid., 649.

[120] Xavier Zubiri, *El Hombre y Dios* (Madrid: Alianza Editorial, Sociedad de Estudios y Publicaciones, 1984, 1985) 92–4, 139–40.

[121] Ibid., 248.

[122] Ellacuría, "Reduccionismo," 648.

[123] Ibid.

[124] Ibid., 650.

[125] Jon Sobrino, "Ignacio Ellacuría, the Human Being and the Christian: 'Taking the Crucified People down from the Cross,'" *Love That Produces Hope,* 45; henceforth "Ignacio Ellacuría, the Human and the Christian." [Trans. by Robert Lassalle-Klein from "Ignacio Ellacuría, el hombre y el cristiano: Bajar de la cruz al pueblo crucificado," *RLT,* no. 32 (1994) 134.]

[126] Ibid.

[127] Ignacio Ellacuría, "El Tercer Mundo Como Lugar Optimo de la Vivencia Cristiana de los Ejercicios," (Dia 29:1), "Runion-Ejercicios," (Mimeographed) 1–12.

[128] Ibid., 2.

[129] Ellacuría, "Función liberadora," (1985) 46. See also, "Historización del bien común y de los derechos humanos en una sociedad dividida," in E. Tamez and S. Trinidad, eds., *Capitalismo: violencia y anti-vida,* vol. 2 (San José, 1978) 81–94; *Freedom Made Flesh* (Maryknoll, NY: Orbis, 1976) 7–11, 127–63; "Hacia una fundamentación;" 409–25; "Tesis sobre la posibilidad, necesidad y sentido de una teología latinoamericana," in Vargas Machuca, A., ed., *Teología y mundo contemporáneo: homenaje a Karl Rahner en su 70 cumpleaños* (Madrid: Ediciones Cristiandad, 1975) 325–50; "La historización del concepto de propiedad como principio de desideologización," *ECA,* nos. 335–6 (1976) 425–50; "Fe y justicia," in I. Ellacuría and others, *Fe, justicia y opción por los oprimidos* (Bilbao: Editorial Desclée de Brouwer, 1980) 9–78; "El pueblo crucificado, ensayo de soteriología histórica," in I. Ellacuría and others, *Cruz y Resurrección* (Mexico City: CTR, 1978) 49–82; "Monseñor Romero, un enviado de Dios para salvar a su pueblo," *Sal Terrae: Revista de Teología Pastoral,* no. 811 (1980) 825–32; "Discernir 'El signo' de los tiempos," *Diakonia* 17 (Enero/Abril, 1981) 57–9; "Universidad, derechos humanops y mayorias populares," *ECA,* no. 406 (Agosto, 1982) 791–816; "El Reino de Dios y El Paro en El Tercer Mundo," *Concilium* 180 (Madrid: Ediciones Cristiandad, 1982) 588–96; "Historicidad de la salvación cristiana," *Revista Latinoamericana de Teología,* no. 1 (1984) 5–45 ["The Historicity of Christian Salvation" in I. Ellacuría and J. Sobrino, eds., *Mysterium Liberationis: Fundamental Concepts of Liberation Theology* (Maryknoll, NY: Orbis, 1993) 251–89; collection hereafter cited as *MLT* (English translation) and *ML* (Spanish original)]; "Aporte de la teología de la liberación a las religiones Abráhamicas en la superación del individualismo y del positivismo," *RLT,* no. 10 (1987) 3–27; "La teología de la liberación frente al cambio socio-histórico de América Latina," *RLT,* no. 12 (1987) 241–64; "Utopia y profetismo desde America Latina: un ensayo concreto de soteriologia historica," *Revista Latinoamericana de Teologia,* no. 6 (1989) 141–84 [*MLT,* 289–328].

[130] Ignacio Ellacuría, "Discurso de la Universidad Centroamericana José Simeón Cañas en la Firma del Contrato con el BID," in *Planteamiento Universitario 1989* (San

Salvador: UCA Editores, 1989) 12. Delivered by Rev. José María Gondra, s.j., 1970 [mistakenly noted as delivered by Rev. Luis Achaerandio, s.j.], and written by Ignacio Ellacuría; idem, "Diez años despues: ¿es posible una universidad distinta?" *ECA* 30, nos. 324–5 (Oct.–Nov. 1975) 605–28. [Trans. "Is a Different Kind of University Possible?" in John Hasset and Hugh Lacey, eds., *Towards a Society That Serves Its People* (Washington, D.C.: Georgetown University Press, 1991) 177-207]; idem, "La inspiración Cristiana de la UCA en la docencia," *Planteamiento Universitario 1989* (San Salvador, El Salvador: Universidad Centroamericana José Simeón Cañas, Febrero, 1989) 195–200. Delivered Sept. 30, 1988, University of Central America; idem, "The Task of a Christian University" (address given at the University of Santa Clara) in I. Ellacuría and J. Sobrino, *Companions of Jesus* (Maryknoll, NY: Orbis, 1990) 147–51.

[131] Ellacuría, "Las funciones fundamentales de la universiadad y su operativizacion," in *Planteamiento Universitario 1989* (San Salvador: UCA Editores, 1989) 47. First published May 1979.

[132] Ellacuría, "Discurso de la Universidad Centroamericana José Simeón Cañas," 12.

[133] Ignacio Ellacuría, *Veinte años de historia en El Salvador (1969–1989): Escritos políticos* (San Salvador: UCA Editores, 1991).

[134] Ellacuría, "Funciones fundamentales," 47–8.

[135] Ibid., 53.

[136] Ignacio Ellacuría, "El objeto de la filosofía," in  *Filosofía de la realidad histórica* (San Salvador: UCA Editores, 1990) 42; originally published in *ECA,* no. 396–7, 1981, 963–80.

[137] Ibid., 30, 25.

[138] Ibid., 26.

[139] Ibid., 31.

[140] Ibid., 43–4.

[141] I. Ellacuría, *Freedom Made Flesh: The Mission of Christ and His Church* (Maryknoll, NY: Orbis, 1976) 145, 146. Originally published as *Teología política* (San Salvador: Ediciones del Secretaridado Social Interdiocesano, 1973) [*TP,* 80].

[142] Ibid., 145 [*TP,* 80].

[143] Ellacuría, "Discernir 'El signo' de los tiempos," 58, 59.

[144] Ellacuría, *Filosofía de la realidad histórica,* 591–6.

[145] Ibid., 599.

[146] See "La historicidad del hombre en Xavier Zubiri," *Estudios de Deusto* 28 (1996) 245–86 and 523–48.

[147] Antonio González, "Assessing the Philosophical Achievement of Ignacío Ellacuria," in *Love That Produces Hope,* 73–87. [Trans. Robert Lassalle-Klein from "Aproximación a la obra filosófica de Ignacio Ellacuría," *ECA,* nos. 505–6 (1990) 981; originally in *ECA,* nos. 435–6 (1985) 45–64.]

[148] See Ellacuría, *Filosofía de la realidad histórica,* 18–30.

[149] Ignacio Ellacuría, "Aproximación a la obra completa de Xavier Zubiri." *ECA,* nos. 421–2 (1983) 965–83.

[150] Ibid., 975.

[151] Ibid., 975–6.

[152] Ibid., 976.

[153] Ellacuría, *Filosofía de la realidad histórica,* 595.

[154] Ellacuría, "Función liberadora," 57.

[155] Antonio González appears to support this conclusion in his prologue to *Philosophy of Historical Reality*. He asserts that Ellacuría's faithful, yet original appropriation of Zubiri's philosophy provided him "the possibility of a profound and creative dialogue with Marxism," (10) something dangerous, yet urgently needed in Latin America. And Diego Gracia, director of the Xavier Zubiri Foundation and a longtime colleague of Ellacuría, catches something of this in highlighting the originality of Ellacuría's own thought vis-à-vis Zubiri. Gracia writes, "the philosophy of history has been debated for centuries in a sterile struggle between idealists and materialists. [Yet] Ellacuría tries to overcome this dichotomy, taking as his point of departure certain fundamental concepts of Zubiri. For Ellacuría it is possible to engage, yet criticize, both extremes from a more realist position," Central America Province News, 1993; quoted in Letter from Dean Brackley to Charlie Beirne, Sept. 2, 1993.

[156] Ellacuría, *Filosofía de la realidad histórica,* 169.

[157] Ignacio Ellacuría, "The Historicization of the Concept of Property," in Hassett and Lacey, *Towards A Society That Serves Its People,* 109; trans. from "La historizacion del concepto de propiedad como principio de desideologizacion," *ECA* 31, nos. 335–6 (1976) 425–50.

[158] Ibid., 427.

[159] Ibid.

[160] Ibid.

[161] Ibid., 428.

[162] I have argued elsewhere that Ellacuría's use of historicization as a truth test exhibits important parallels with the "pragmatic maxim" of Charles Sanders Peirce, founder of philosophical pragmatism. Robert Lassalle-Klein, "The Body of Christ: The Claim of the Crucified People on North American Theology and Ethics," *Journal of Hispanic-Latino Theology* 5, no. 4 (May 1998) 68–74.

[163] I refer here to Zubiri's criticisms of the "logification of intelligence" and the "entefication of reality" as examples of "reductionistic idealism" that are outlined above.

[164] This refers to Zubiri's constructive proposals regarding the "sentient intelligence," and the philosophical primacy of "formal reality," also outlined above. For the meaning and importance he attributes to what he calls the "will-to-fundamentality," see Zubiri, *El Hombre y Dios,* 204, 286–7.

[165] Ellacuría, "Función liberadora,"46.

[166] Ibid., 47.

[167] Ibid., 63.

[168] Ibid.

[169] Ibid.

[170] Ibid., 49.

[171] Ibid., 63.

[172] Ibid.

[173] Ibid., 49.

[174] Ibid.

[175] Ibid., 50.

[176] Ibid.

[177] Ibid., 63.

[178] Ignacio Ellacuría, "La teología como momento ideológico de la praxis eclesial," *Estudios Eclesiasticos,* no. 207 (1978) 457–6; henceforth, "Teología como praxis."

[179] Ibid., 466.

[180] Ibid., 460–1.

[181] Ibid., 457.

[182] On this point see the essay by Roger Haight, "Ecclesiology from Below: Principles from Ignacio Ellacuría," in *Love That Produces Hope,* 183–200. Also see Kevin Burke, s.j., *The Ground Beneath the Cross: The Theology of Ignacio Ellacuría* (Washington, D.C.: Georgetown University Press, 2000) 138.

[183] Ellacuría, "Teología como momento ideologico," 462.

[184] Ibid., 462.

[185] Ibid., 466.

[186] Ibid., 466, ff.

[187] Ibid., 470.

[188] Ibid.

[189] Ibid.

[190] Ellacuría, "Función liberadora," 59.

[191] Ibid.

[192] Ellacuría, "Teología como praxis," 472.

[193] Zubiri, *Sobre la esencia,* 447.

[194] Ellacuría, "La historicidad del hombre in Zavier Zubiri," 526.

[195] Ibid.

[196] "Diego Gracia," Central America Province News, 1993; quoted in letter from Dean Brackley, s.j., to Charles Beirne, s.j., Sept. 2, 1993. Gracia's book on Zubiri, however, explicitly recognizes the moral dimension implicit in Zubiri's concept of "religación." Quoting from Zubiri as he explains this concept, Gracia writes, "the 'power of imposition' is not only actualized in the human person as a 'bondedness,' (the basis for all religiosity), but also as an 'obligation' (the ground of all morality)." (Gracia, *Voluntad,* 214.)

[197] Ignacio Ellacuría, "Fundamentación biológica de la ética," *ECA,* no. 368 (1979) 419–28.

[198] Ibid., 422.

[199] Ibid.

[200] Ellacuría, "Hacia una fundamentación," 409–25.

[201] Ibid., 419.

[202] Ibid.

[203] Sobrino, "Ignacio Ellacuría, the Human Being and the Christian," in *Love That Produces Hope,* 18.

[204] Gustavo Gutiérrez, "No One Takes My Life from Me; I Give It Freely," trans. by James Nickoloff, in *Love That Produces Hope,* 69; henceforth, "No One Takes My Life."

[205] Ellacuría, "Hacia una fundamentación," 419.

[206] Ibid.

[207] Ibid.

[208] Sobrino, "Ignacio Ellacuría, the Human Being and the Christian," in *Love That Produces Hope,* 19.

[209] Gutiérrez, "No One Takes My Life from Me; I Give It Freely," in *Love That Produces Hope,* 69.

[210] Letter from Ignacio Ellacuría to Xavier Zubiri, April 30, 1968. Cited in Teresa Whitfield, *Paying the Price: Ignacio Ellacuria and the Murdered Jesuits of El Salvador* (Philadelphia: Temple University Press, 1994) 42.

[211] Letter from Paolo Dezza to Segundo Azcue, April 23, 1968. Cited in Whitfield, *Paying the Price,* 42.

[212] Sobrino writes, "I could highlight three things in which he was truly exemplary: his hunger and thirst for justice for the crucified people, his tireless condemnation of and analysis of the truth about their crucifixion, and the steadfastness and fidelity of his praxis toward seeing them taken down from the cross." Sobrino, "Ignacio Ellacuría," in *Love That Produces Hope,* 56.

[213] Jon Sobrino, s.j., *Spirituality of Liberation* (Maryknoll, NY: Orbis, 1988) 14, 17, trans. Robert R. Barr from *Liberacion con espiritu* (San Salvador: UCA Editores, 1985).

[214] Sobrino, "Spirituality of Liberation," 17.

[215] Ellacuría, "Hacia una fundamentación," 419.

[216] Ibid.

[217] Sobrino, "Ignacio Ellacuría, the Human Being and the Christian," in *Love That Produces Hope,* 19.

[218] Gutiérrez, "No One Takes My Life from Me; I Give It Freely," in *Love That Produces Hope,* 70.

[219] Ellacuría, "Teología como praxis," 457–76.

[220] Ellacuría, "Zubiri, cuatro años después" (1987) 2.

[221] Ibid.

[222] Ibid.

[223] Ibid.

[224] Sobrino, "Ignacio Ellacuría, the Human Being and the Christian," in *Love That Produces Hope,* 1–4.

[225] Ellacuría is being read in Asia and Oceana as well, however the editors were unable to secure contributions from these regions.

[226] Karl Rahner, "Basic Theological Interpretation of the Second Vatican Council," *Concern for the Church, Theological Investigations,* XX (New York: Crossroad, 1981) 85.

[227] Jon Sobrino, "El asesinato-martirio de los jesuitas salvadoreños," *RLT,* no. 18 (1989) 304 ["Companions of Jesus," trans. Dinah Livingstone, in Jon Sobrino, Ignacio Ellacuría, and others, *Companions of Jesus: The Jesuit Martyrs of El Salvador* (Maryknoll, New York: Orbis, 1990) 56].

# Chapter 5

# Karl Rahner:
# The Teacher of Ignacio Ellacuría*

*Martin Maier, S.J.*

There is no doubt that Karl Rahner is the theologian who had the most impact on the thought of Ignacio Ellacuría.[1] From 1958 to 1962, Ellacuría studied theology in Innsbruck, Austria. During those years, Rahner was on the theological faculty of the University of Innsbruck as professor of dogmatic theology. He had already reached the peak of his theological creativity and enjoyed international renown. During that time, he also actively participated in the preparation for the Second Vatican Council that Pope John XXIII had called on January 25, 1959. In October of 1961, Rahner became private conciliar advisor to Cardinal Franz König of Vienna. Despite suspicions raised against him in conservative circles, Rahner was officially appointed *peritus* of the council in February of 1963, and even his adversaries had to concede that Rahner was "'the most powerful man' at the Council."[2]

Victor Codina, Ellacuría's classmate during those same years, remembers him in these words:

> Ellacuría stood out because of his strong athletic build, his typically Basque features, and above all his great intelligence. His innate leadership skills already manifested themselves in those early years. He was always

* Translated by Anna Bonta and Kevin Burke, S.J.

somewhat distant, serious, and occasionally ironic, with an acute sense of strength and security. Colleagues and friends surrounded him. One began to jokingly call him the Sun King, alluding to his brilliance and dominance. Some considered him neither outgoing nor easily accessible.[3]

In Rahner, Ellacuría had as his teacher one of the central theological actors of the council, and one can imagine that Rahner shared his thoughts on the preparation for that new theological and ecclesial openness with his class. There is no doubt that the young Ellacuría attentively followed the preparation for this new theological and ecclesial openness.

## The Coherence of Theology and Life

Karl Rahner's influence on the theological thought of Ignacio Ellacuría is not simply limited to the four years of direct contact. Rather, Rahner's way of doing theology had a permanent influence on Ellacuría. It should be said up front that for both Rahner and Ellacuría the theological task presupposes what we can call, in the words of Johann Baptist Metz, a "theological and existential biography."[4] Metz characterizes the theological work of Rahner, his teacher and friend, in this way. Furthermore, he affirms that Rahner's life and work cannot be separated. As such, Rahner's theology surpasses the way of doing theology in his time, for "Catholic theology of the modern age seems to be characterized by a profound schism between theological system and religious experience, doxology and biography, dogmatics and mysticism."[5] From this perspective, Rahner represents a theological model that overcomes this schism by developing itself within a "kind of theological and existential biography. . . . Such theology should be called a mystical biography of religious experience, of personal history that stands before the veiled face of God."[6] Rahner himself, when asked at the end of his life about what inspired his way of doing theology, responds in this way: "I would say that I have always done theology with a view to kerygma, preaching, pastoral care."[7] Rahner's skill consisted in making theology confront the questions posed by life itself.

Following Metz's lead, Ignacio Ellacuría presents a special case of a "theological and existential biography." This theologian was even assassinated for defending in his historical life what inspired his theology. Along with this fundamental similarity of the coherence between theology and the biographical and existential dimension, there exist other formal similarities. One of these is the emphasis on the necessary intellectual rigor of theology. In the prologue to his *Foundations of Christian Faith*, Rahner says he wrote this book for readers with a certain intellectual formation "who are not afraid to 'wrestle with an idea,'"[8] and it is true. Similarly, Ellacuría insisted on the intellectual nature of the theological task, "which should not be confused with mere preaching, prophecy or a voluntary and passionate morality that rejects the necessary intellectual elaboration of the Christian faith."[9] On the undeniable role of the intellectual he says that "intellectuals can present a danger, but just the same they do not cease to be necessary in the Church as well."[10]

Finally, it should be observed that both Rahner and Ellacuría wrote few systematic books. They let the themes they would address be dictated by their historical situation or by people who asked them for papers and articles on current topics. As a result, the twenty-two volumes of Rahner's *Theological Investigations* are largely a compilation of conference talks or occasional articles. In the same way, Ellacuría's theological work primarily responds—and perhaps with greater urgency—to the demands and challenges of historical reality.

## Two Different Contexts

Despite the similarities mentioned, it is clear that Rahner and Ellacuría represent two different theological paradigms. They both surpass the Neo-Scholastic theology of the time, but each in a different way. In Metz's terminology, Rahner's theology represents a transcendental-idealist model.[11] Rahner's fundamental concern, in effect, is to create a new theological discourse that confronts the challenges of modernity with its denial of knowledge or even the existence of God. His principle interlocutor is the European who has been strongly influenced by the Enlightenment and by modern science.

Ellacuría, for his part, represents a post-idealist theology that responds to the challenges of oppression and injustice in the Latin American context. If, according to Bonhoeffer, the principal question that European theology raises is "how to make God believable in a world of unbelief," Latin American theology, according to Gustavo Gutiérrez, takes as the central question "how to speak about God in a world of suffering and injustice." Hence, their perspectives differ. But we have to fully understand what this means. When in the following comparative analysis we propose that Ellacuría surpasses Rahner in certain respects, we must recognize that we cannot expect Rahner to answer questions that arise in another context. At the same time, we must maintain the importance of the Latin American context for Western or European theology.

Having seen these similarities and differences, we now analyze how Rahner's theology is the most important source of *theological* inspiration for Ellacuría's theology. This analysis encounters a serious difficulty, namely, Ellacuría's writings contain few explicit references to Rahner. Nevertheless, we suggest applying to his entire theology what he says at the beginning of his essay "Theses on the Possibility, Necessity and Meaning of a Latin American Theology," published in honor of Rahner's seventieth birthday: "Although the essay makes no explicit reference to Rahner's theological work, it is clear that it is very present in many ways."[12]

My goal in this essay is to clarify the presence of Rahner's theological work in Ellacuría. My approach is comparative in the following way: I first briefly present central themes in Rahner's theology, then analyze his influence on Ellacuría's and the extent to which and how Ellacuría modifies and surpasses him. As for the selection of texts, in Rahner's case I concentrate on those written before 1962. We can then be certain that Ellacuría would have been familiar with them, for he would have analyzed them during his theological studies at Innsbruck. Naturally, this does not exclude the fact that Rahner would have dealt with topics in his classes on which he would later publish, and that Ellacuría would have read Rahner's work published after 1962. In the case of Ellacuría, we consider the whole of his theological writings along with some philosophical works.

## The Theological Roots of Rahner and Ellacuría: Ignatian Spirituality

In an interview I was privileged to conduct with Rahner in 1981, I asked how he would advise me to acquaint myself with his theology. Rahner began by relativizing what I called "his theology," and began by speaking not of his properly theological works, but rather of his spiritual writings, although in their own distinct way, those works contained as much theology as his explicitly theological works. Specifically, he advised me to read his book *The Need and the Blessing of Prayer*.[13]

It suffices to glance at Rahner's bibliography to recognize the importance of the spiritual writings in his immense corpus. In Rahner there is, therefore, a continuity between his theology and his spirituality: the primary object of his theological effort is to make us conscious of the openness of every human being to the inexhaustible and absolute mystery of God. In his transcendental theology, Rahner wants to ontologically and anthropologically explore and analyze the conditions for the possibility of experiencing in the most intimate part of human existence the dynamic openness to God as mystery. At the same time, on the logical level the fundamental presupposition of his transcendental method is the actual experience of God. Rahner explains it in this way: "In my theology a true and original experience of God and the Spirit is foundational. This precedes theological reflection and verbalization logically (not necessarily chronologically) and it can never be adequately reached by that reflection."[14] When asked concretely about the most profound roots of his thought, Rahner responded, "the spirituality of Ignatius, which we receive through the practice of prayer and religious formation, has been undoubtedly more important to me than all the specialized philosophy and theology both within and outside the Society."[15]

On both the existential and methodological levels, the fundamental presupposition of theology for Rahner is the personal experience of God, of God as mystery who freely communicates Godself. Therefore, what precedes theological reflection is the experience of God, and the experience of God is the foundation and starting point of theological reflection. There is here a clear parallel to the method of liberation theology, which, according to Gustavo Gutiérrez, understands itself as a second act that follows upon spiritual experience and praxis.[16] Ignacio Ellacuría expresses himself in the same way when he writes on the method of liberation theology. "The following is none other than the reflection of believers on a lived reality."[17] He also expresses the primacy of experience over reflection in his well-known definition of theology as the ideological moment of ecclesial and historical praxis.[18] In a similar vein, referring to Monseñor Romero, Ellacuría writes, "Monsignor Romero's historical judgments arose from a profound personal experience of God, such as has been revealed in Jesus Christ and such as is made present to us through his Spirit."[19]

In the area of spirituality, Ellacuría strongly emphasized history and historicization. He understands spirituality to signify the adequate historicization of the most true and vital elements of the Gospel. History and historical action must mediate every encounter with God. This does not mean just any action, but rather the action of justice. This way of historicizing spirituality results in the discernment of spirits at the personal level and, at the historical level, in the discernment of the signs of the times. Regarding the former, Ellacuría explicitly refers to a key theological concept that Rahner drew from the Ignatian exercises.[20] With the phrase "the logic of existential knowledge," Rahner refers to specific knowledge of the will of God through the process of election. This will can be reduced neither to revelation that has already occurred nor to universal ethical principles.[21] By adopting this idea, Ellacuría affirms that the Spiritual Exercises historicize the word of God "insofar as they are a way to find the will of God which cannot be deduced from universal principles." This presupposes that "there is something essential in one's life about which God has not yet spoken and which emerges as something new and future-oriented."[22] As we shall see, this intuition is fundamental to the systematic integration of the signs of the times in theology.

One of Ellacuría's most important contributions to the theology of the spiritual life is the relation he establishes between the self-communication of God and the preferential option for the poor. God does not communicate Godself in the same way in all situations, but rather does so in a preferential way to and through the poor. Similarly, the self-communication of God comes to the poor in a preferential way. The poor are, then, the most appropriate place to find God in history. They are the continuation of the crucified Christ in history. They are the most important sign of the times.[23]

Another of Rahner's fundamental themes that penetrated Ellacuría's thought is the concept of mystery. In his classic text "On the Concept of Mystery in Catholic Theology," Rahner conceives mystery not as something merely provisional that has not yet been penetrated by the *ratio,* "but as the primordial and permanent."[24] Even in the beatific vision God continues to be incomprehensible. The human being appears as the "being who is oriented to the mystery as such, this orientation being a constitutive element of his being both in his natural state and in his supernatural elevation."[25] The human being, in the most profound aspect of his or her existence, is a being that pertains to mystery.

Ellacuría incorporates the understanding of God as a God of mystery, but—once again—historicizes it. Thus, in his essay "Pedro Arrupe, Renewer of Religious Life," he characterizes Fr. Arrupe's God as

> a God who is greater than human beings; a God who is greater than the Constitutions and historical structures of the Society of Jesus; a God who is greater than the Church and all its hierarchies; a *Deus semper maior et semper novus,* who continues to be the same, but who never repeats himself; who needs to be expressed in dogmatic formulas, but who is never exhausted by them. A God, in short, who is unpredictable on the one hand, but unmanipulable on the other.[26]

In another place, Ellacuría insists on the scandalous character of the Christian God. "The God of Jesus, let us not forget, is an absolutely scandalous God, unacceptable for both Jew and Greek, for both the religious and the intellectual."[27] Ellacuría overcomes the somewhat abstract character of Rahner's concept of mystery by making it more concrete and historical as the mystery of God present in the historical reality of the poor.

## Philosophical Foundation of Theology

In all their theological work, both Rahner and Ellacuría placed great importance on the philosophical foundations of theology. On the one hand, both insist on the autonomy of philosophy from theology, but, on the other hand, they consider philosophy as an irreplaceable moment in theology. Rahner's philosophical thought has as its principal objective the reconciliation between the subjectivism of modernity and the experience of faith. Against Kant's delimitation of speculative thought to the sphere of the sensible, Rahner has shown in his works, "Spirit in the World"[28] and "Hearers of the Word,"[29] that the human person as spirit is radically open to a transcendental horizon and can experience this openness through knowledge of the sensible world. The role of philosophy is to show that the human being in his or her ontological structure, in his or her *potentia oboedientialis,* is open to divine revelation.

Ellacuría criticizes the philosophical model that grounds European theology in idealism and reduces theology to a mere *interpretation* of reality. A philosophy that grounds Latin American theology should take Latin American reality as its starting point—a reality of injustice and oppression—and it should contribute to the *transformation* of this reality. "Philosophical concepts must be historical and total, effective and real."[30]

Ellacuría outlines such a philosophical model in an essay entitled "The Liberating Function of Philosophy."[31] In the first place, he insists that the critical function of philosophy is to unmask the false ideologies that ground and justify unjust and oppressive social orders. But the liberating function of philosophy is not limited to this ideological criticism. Rather, a creative function also appears in the elaboration of a liberating philosophy. Ellacuría enumerates five themes in this philosophy: (1) a theory of human intelligence and knowledge; (2) a general theory of reality which would function analogously to metaphysics in classical philosophy; (3) an open and critical theory of the human person, society, and history; (4) a theory that rationally grounds an adequate assessment of the human person and his or her world; (5) a philosophical reflection on ultimacy and the transcendent.[32]

In summary, we can say that, for Rahner, the principle of unity between philosophy and theology lies in the transcendental analysis of the a priori structures of human knowledge and action. For Ellacuría, however, the point of convergence between philosophy and theology lies in the active commitment to the realization of the kingdom of God in history. Thus, at the end of his article on the liberating function of philosophy he writes: "If it makes sense to speak of a Christian philosophy or a philosophy somehow inspired by Christianity, it is because a philosophy done from the perspective of the poor and oppressed that works toward their integral and universal liberation can place itself in its autonomy on the same path as those who work for the kingdom of God prefigured by the historical Jesus."[33]

## Toward a Theology of the Signs of the Times

As we have already seen, the presupposition of the Rahnerian theology of the *Spiritual Exercises* is that God can communicate God's will to a person making the *Exercises,* but in such a way that this will can be deduced neither from a revelation that occurred previously nor from universal ethical principles. God tells the individual something new and undeducible. In the same way, Rahner presupposes that God can communicate something new to the church that has not yet been said or recognized as such. With this, the conditions are given to comprehend the signs of the times as manifestations of the presence and action of God in history and in the world. On this basis, Ellacuría would come to speak of a "history of revelation." We also find this insight in the discourse with which Pope John XXIII inaugurated the council.

In this discourse, John XXIII opened a new horizon not only for the church but also for theology. In his profound, faith-driven optimism the pope trusted that God had not only communicated Godself in the past, but that God was continuing to become manifest today in the signs of the times. After disagreeing with the "prophets of gloom" who "can see nothing but calamities and ruin in these modern times," John XXIII broaches the topic of the diverse ways of transmitting sacred doctrine. While remaining always faithful to the fundamental doctrine and tradition of the church, the Pope hopes the council will "lead toward a doctrinal penetration and formation of consciences in faithful and perfect conformity to the authentic doctrine. This doctrine, however, should be studied and taught through the methods of research and the literary forms of modern thought."[34] In this way, John XXIII invited theologians to be attentive to the signs of the times and to appraise their value systematically. The Pope of the council broke with a form of revelatory deism that held, first, that God spoke only in the past and, second, that the task of the church consisted solely in guarding the treasure of revelation. Both Rahner and Ellacuría will use this insight of John XXIII to build theological foundations for affirming the possibility of the evolution of dogma and the progressive history of revelation in the signs of the times.

In an essay written in 1954 entitled "The Development of Dogma,"[35] Rahner affirms that the dogmatic explanation of the faith develops. In a certain manner, we find here an application of the *logic of existential knowing* to dogmatic theology: God can communicate something new, something that has not previously been spoken or recognized as such, not only to an individual but also to the church. In this way a true progress of revelation can occur.

Ellacuría incorporates this Rahnerian thesis and makes it the starting point of his historical hermeneutic of the word of God. His presupposition is that the word is actualized in historical events. That is, the word of God "contains real possibilities that can only be actualized according to the various new necessities of historical events."[36] The word of God reveals its true contents through historical reality. In this way, the word of God is alive and creative, and it is capable of saying new things in new historical situations.

The key elements in this hermeneutical dialogue between revelation and history are "the signs of the times." Theology brings about the "leap forward"[37] demanded by John XXIII precisely in the systematic integration of the signs of the times. The novelty of this theologal acceptance of the signs of the times appears in the fact that they are taken seriously as a theological place.[38] Ellacuría writes, "the revelation of God in history happens in the most commonplace signs of the times."[39] To decipher the signs of the times means, therefore, to put the revelation of God in relationship with real history. In so doing, this theology does not displace the Gospel as the most important source of all theological knowledge, nor does it depreciate the tradition and the ecclesial magisterium. But it does try to relate the signs of the times to the *depositum fidei,* to place them in dialogue, to interpret them in light of the Gospel.

In this context, Ellacuría introduces a fundamental distinction between the place and sources of theology. The sources would correspond to the *depositum fidei,* and the place would be where theology is done. Ellacuría describes the interaction between them in the following way:

> The distinction is not strict nor, even less, is it exclusive, because in a way,
> the place is a source insofar as the place makes it possible for the source to

present one thing or other, so that, thanks to the place and by virtue of it, certain specific contents are actualized and made really present.[40]

In other words, what the sources themselves offer depends on the place. And Ellacuría proposes that the most appropriate place to "read" the sources—from the specifically Latin American context—is the world of the poor. In this way, the option for the poor also has a fundamental hermeneutical function.[41]

## The Unity of Nature and Grace

In modern theology Karl Rahner is perhaps the most important theologian with respect to what has been called the anthropological turn. The theological foundation of this anthropological turn in Rahner's theology is a new conception of the relationship between nature and grace, which he elaborates in his writings on the *supernatural existential*. This new conception is also necessary to understand the relationship between world history and salvation history and the relationship between love of God and neighbor. Ellacuría incorporates and surpasses all of these in his understanding of historical transcendence.

Rahner made an important contribution to the famous controversy between nature and grace that developed in the fifties. Henri de Lubac summarized the underlying question in the following way: "We are creatures and we shall see God. The desire to see God is within each of us, but it will only be granted through pure gift."[42] Rahner, in his transcendental method, asks about the conditions of possibility in the human for receiving this free gift of divine grace. The fundamental capacity of the human person to receive a possible self-communication of God is what Rahner calls *potentia oboedientialis*. "The natural openness of the human makes her, by virtue of her transcendence (obediential potency), a possible addressee of the free self-communication of God Godself in grace and in the intuited vision of God."[43]

We have also highlighted that, in Rahner's theology, the self-communication of God already received is a fundamental presupposition, both on the existential and the methodological level. From this fact, the *potentia oboedientialis* is always already actualized. To designate this actualization of the *potentia oboedientialis,* Rahner uses his famous concept of the "supernatural existential." The human, in the most profound depths of his or her existence, is ordered toward the self-communication of God as a pure gift of God's grace. Grace is nothing other than the radicalization of the essence of the human person, and it does not constitute an additional level that is superimposed upon human nature. In this way, Rahner surpasses every dualism and extrinsicism between nature and grace.

Once again, Ignacio Ellacuría adopts this Rahnerian conception of the supernatural existential, but he surpasses it by appropriately historicizing it. In his essay dedicated to Rahner, "Theses on the Possibility, Necessity and Meaning of a Latin American Theology," he writes: "The classical thesis that the plenitude of the concrete human person requires historically the communication of God and that the plenitude of the communication of God leads to the plenitude of the historical human person is a basic hypothesis of Latin American theology."[44] However, in refining this thesis Ellacuría goes further than Rahner. Only in the *historical* experience of Christianity are the plenitude of the human person and the plenitude of God known, for these are not idealistic and ahistorical plenitudes. These plenitudes "pass" through struggle and death, and lead from oppression to liberation. In the same way Ellacuría insists on the social and historical dimension of the event of the self-giving of God—dimensions that are not sufficiently present in Rahner's thought.[45]

In his late, untranslated essay *"Historia de la salvación,"* Ellacuría directly mentions Rahner. "This openness which in every person is the transcendental openness that is elevated from a 'supernatural existential' (Rahner), is in the totality of history the transcendental openness that is elevated from a gratuitous historicity."[46] Therefore, Ellacuría transposes to the level of historical reality what for Rahner is the supernatural existential on the subjective human level. This is how he transcends Rahner's transcendental subjectivism and moves toward the objectivity and the reality of history. In a way analogous to how the human spirit is open to the gratuitous revelation of God, history is open to being gratuitously elevated to God. In the same way, he overcomes extrinsicism in the conception of the salvific elevation of history to God: "History is in itself transcendentally open and in that transcendentality it is already in the presence, at least inchoate, of God."[47]

Ellacuría situates the nature-grace discussion in the field of history, and—through this—also criticizes the usual way of distinguishing the natural and the supernatural. The framework inherent in the nature/supernature dualism is superceded by the framework inherent in the distinction between history-of-salvation/salvation-in-history, a distinction that conforms itself much more to the idea and experience of God held by the people of Israel and the Bible. Hence, Ellacuría supplants a naturalist conception of reality with a historical conception, and an individualist conception of the human person with a sociohistorical conception. The emphasis on the historical dimension of faith and Christian salvation also has important consequences for the conception of theology. If theology was once seen as a "pure, theoretical knowledge about unchanging realities which, as a result, has little to do with history,"[48] now it is understood in its historical contextuality and density.

Although Ellacuría vigorously underlines the interrelation between history and salvation, this does not mean that he neglects the reality of sin. The one history of salvation appears as a history of grace and a history of sin. Actions that attempt to destroy life are from the reign of sin, and actions that favor life are from the reign of grace. In this sense, Christian praxis must contribute to a change of history in terms of justice and liberation. Here, Ellacuría—explicitly this time—adopts another important insight from Rahner. "In the final analysis, those who work in the world for the new future of history, if they live by the Christian promise and hope, work for the definitive appearance of God as the absolute future of the human (Rahner)."[49] However, Ellacuría later shows in what way the Rahnerian idea of God as the absolute future of the human has to be superceded. God should not only be affirmed as the absolute of individual experience, but also as the absolute of historical experience: "the hiddenness of God can be recognized through the course of history."[50]

The upshot of these reflections is that the theological works of Rahner and Ellacuría manifest important similarities. For both, theology is a faith-driven theology, a committed theology that makes "honesty with reality" its foundation, a theology whose finality resides not in itself but in the service of faith and justice. In the final analysis, it is a theology that tastes like Good News, a theology that generates and transmits hope. Ellacuría's affirmation that Rahner's theology is, in a variety of ways, very present in his own thought is thus prefectorially confirmed. Yet this is true not in the form of mere repetition, but rather as creative reception. Schematically speaking, there is in Ellacuría a superceding of Rahner's theology that moves from the ontological to the historical, from the individual to the sociopolitical, from the transcendental-idealist paradigm to a praxical-historico paradigm. In this sense, Karl Rahner, by means of his theological innovations, prepared the way for liberation theology as the first theology born outside of the Western-European context.

## Karl Rahner and Liberation Theology

With this last statement we are not saying that Rahner was a liberation theologian, but with his unerring instincts he sensed something exceedingly positive and promising that was born here. With the openness of the Second Vatican Council to the universal world, Rahner recognized the necessity of the openness of theology to other cultures. He frequently spoke of a "legitimate pluralism in theology." In an interview he made the following observation regarding liberation theology: "If in Latin America a theology is born that arises more from the experience of the community, from the foundation of the Church, from the socio-political undertakings of the Church, then I can only be joyful."[51] In a similar way, he declared: "Liberation theology has opened our eyes to structural injustice. Previously that wasn't in our moral books, and it is very important."[52]

Rahner was deeply affected by the martyrdom of Monseñor Romero and he spoke many times of his witness given in blood. "But if Oscar Romero preaches in such a way that in the end he is killed, such a bishop should be praised and honored more than in fact has been done." In one of his final essays, Rahner proposes an extension of the traditional concept of martyrdom. Whoever dies "actively fighting for the Christian faith and its moral demands, including with respect to society,"[53] should also be considered a martyr in this sense. Rahner takes as a concrete example the martyr's death of Monseñor Romero. "But why, for example, should a Monseñor Romero not be a martyr: he fell in the struggle for justice in society, in a struggle that he undertook because of his most profound Christian convictions?"[54]

Rahner defended liberation theology when it came under suspicion and was attacked in Latin America and by Rome. A few days before his death he wrote a letter to Cardinal Juan Landázuri Ricketts, of Lima, in which he defended the orthodoxy of the theology of Gustavo Gutiérrez and the fundamental principles of liberation theology. What Rahner says of Gutiérrez can be easily applied to Ellacuría:

> I am convinced of the orthodoxy of the theological work of Gustavo Gutiérrez. The theology of liberation that he represents is orthodox in its entirety. He is conscious of its limited meaning within the globality of Catholic theology. Moreover, he is conscious—and with good reason in my opinion—that the voice of the poor should be heard in theology in the context of the Latin American Church.[55]

---

[1] In this essay I have revised and condensed an earlier, two-part article entitled "La Influencia de Karl Rahner en la Teología de Ignacio Ellacuría," *RLT*, no. 39 (1996)

233–55; *RLT,* no. 44 (1998) 163–87. The revised essay has also been published as "Karl Rahner, el maestro," in J. Sobrino and R. Alvarado, eds., *Ignacio Ellacuría, "Aquella libertad esclarecida"* (San Salvador: UCA Editores, 1999) 171–93.

[2] Herbert Vorgrimler, *Understanding Karl Rahner: An Introduction to His Life and Thought* (New York: Crossroad, 1986) 99.

[3] Victor Codina, "Ignacio Ellacuría, teólogo y mártir," *RLT,* no. 21 (1990) 263.

[4] See Johann Baptist Metz, *Faith in History and Society,* trans. David Smith (London: Burns and Oates, 1980) 219–27.

[5] Ibid., 219, trans. from the Spanish by A. Bonta and K. Burke.

[6] Ibid., 220.

[7] P. Imhof and H. Biallowons, *Karl Rahner in Dialogue: Conversations and Interviews 1965–1982,* trans. Harvey Egan (New York: Crossroad, 1986) 256.

[8] Karl Rahner, *Foundations of Christian Faith,* trans. William Dych (New York: Seabury Press, 1978) xi.

[9] Ignacio Ellacuría, "Recuperación del Reino de Dios," in *Conversión de la Iglesia al Reino de Dios* (Santander, Spain: Sal Terrae, 1984) 16; collection hereafter cited as *CIRD.*

[10] Ibid., 168.

[11] See Johann Baptist Metz, "Teología europea y teología de la liberación," in J. Comblin, J. I. González-Faus, J. Sobrino, eds., *Cambio social y pensamiento cristiano en América Latina* (Madrid, 1993) 263.

[12] Ignacio Ellacuría, "Tesis sobre posibilidad, necesidad, y sentido de una teología latinoamericana," in A. Vargas Machuca, ed., *Teología y mundo contemporáneo: homenaje a Karl Rahner* (Madrid: Ediciones Cristiandad, 1975) 325; hereafter cited as "Tesis sobre teología."

[13] Karl Rahner, *The Need and the Blessing of Prayer,* trans. Bruce W. Gillette (Collegeville: Liturgical Press, 1997).

[14] P. Imhof and H. Biallowons, *Rahner in Dialogue,* 257.

[15] Ibid., 251.

[16] Gustavo Gutiérrez, *On Job: God-Talk and the Suffering of the Innocent* (Maryknoll, NY: Orbis, 1987) 17; see also Jon Sobrino, "Lo fundamental de la teología de la liberación," *Proyección,* no. 138 (1985) 176.

[17] Ignacio Ellacuría, "Los pobres, lugar teológico en América Latina," *CIRD,* 153; first published in *Misión Abierta,* nos. 4–5 (1981) 225–40; hereafter cited as "Lugar teológico."

[18] Ibid., 168; see also "La teología como momento ideológico de la praxis eclesial," *Estudios Eclesiasticos,* no. 207 (1978) 457–76; hereafter cited as "Teología como praxis."

[19] Ignacio Ellacuría, "El verdadero pueblo de Dios, según Monseñor Romero," *CIRD,* 101; first published in *ECA,* no. 392 (1981) 529–54.

[20] See Karl Rahner, *The Dynamic Element in the Church,* trans. W. J. O'Hara (London: Burns and Oates, 1964).

[21] See Martin Maier, "La Théologie des Exercices de Karl Rahner," *Recherches de Science Religieuse,* no. 79 (1991) 535–60.

[22] Ignacio Ellacuría, "Lectura Latinoamericana de los Ejercicios Espirituales de san Ignacio," *RLT,* no. 23 (1991) 113.

[23] Ignacio Ellacuría, "Discernir el signo de los tiempos," *Diakonía,* no. 18 (1981) 58.

[24] Karl Rahner, "The Concept of Mystery in Catholic Theology," *Theological Investigations,* vol. IV (Baltimore: Helicon Press, 1966) 41.

[25] Ibid., 49.

[26] Ignacio Ellacuría, "Pedro Arrupe, renovador de la vida religiosa," *RLT,* no. 22 (1991) 12.

[27] "Lugar teológico," *CIRD,* 164.

[28] Karl Rahner, *Spirit in the World,* trans. William Dych (New York: Herder and Herder, 1968).

[29] Karl Rahner, *Hearers of the Word,* trans. Michael Richards (New York: Herder and Herder, 1969).

[30] Ignacio Ellacuría, "Historia de la salvación y salvación en la historia," *Teología política* (San Salvador: Ediciones del Secretariado Social Interdiocesano, 1973) 4, trans. John Drury [*FMF* (1976) 8].

[31] Ignacio Ellacuría, "Función liberadora de la filosofía," *ECA,* no. 40 (1985) 45–64.

[32] See ibid., 54–5.

[33] Ibid., 64.

[34] *The Teachings of the Second Vatican Council: Complete Texts of the Constitutions, Decrees, and Declarations* (Westminster, MD: Newman Press, 1966) 4, 7.

[35] Karl Rahner, "The Development of Doctrine," in *Theological Investigations,* vol. I (Baltimore: Helicon Press, 1961) 39–77.

[36] Ignacio Ellacuría, "Predicación, palabra, comunidad," *CIRD,* 266; first published as "La predicación ha de poner en contacto vivificante la palabra y la comunidad," *Sal Terrae,* no. 778 (1978) 167–76; henceforth "Predicación."

[37] The original Italian text speaks of a "balzo innanzi." On the alterations that appeared in the official Latin text in comparison to the original Italian, see L. Kaufmann and N. Klein, *Johannes XXIII: Prophetie im Vermächtnis* (Fribourg/Brig, 1990) 74ff.

[38] See Jon Sobrino, "Los 'signos de los tiempos' en la teología de la liberación," in J. M. Lera, ed., *Fides quae per caritatem operatur: Homenaje al P. Juan Alfaro S.J. en sus 75 años* (Bilbao, 1989) 249–69; Martin Maier, "Teología de la liberación en Latinoamérica," *Razón y Fe,* no. 236 (1997) 281–96.

[39] Ignacio Ellacuría, "Anuncio del Reino y credibilidad de la Iglesia," *CIRD,* 233; first published as "El anuncio del Evangelio y la misión de la Iglesia," in *Teología política* (San Salvador: Ediciones del Secretariado Social Interdiocesano, 1973) 44–69; hereafter cited as "Anuncio del Reino" [*FMF* (1976) 82–126].

[40] "Predicación," 268.

[41] See also, Juan Luis Segundo, "La opción por los pobres como clave hermenéutica para entender el Evangelio," *Sal Terrae,* no. 74 (1986) 473–82.

[42] Henri de Lubac, "Le mystère du surnaturel," *Recherches de Science Religieuse,* no. 36 (1949) 11.

[43] K. Rahner and H. Vorgrimler, *Diccionario Teológico* (Barcelona, 1970) 475. [Idem, *Theological Dictionary,* trans. Richard Strachan (New York: Herder and Herder, 1965) 367.]

[44] "Tesis sobre teología," Tesis 9.6.

[45] Johann B. Metz criticizes his teacher Rahner in this way; see Metz, *Faith in History and Society,* 164–77.

[46] Ellacuría, "Historia de la salvación," *RLT,* no. 28 (1993) 8.

⁴⁷ Ibid.

⁴⁸ "Teología como praxis," 458.

⁴⁹ "Anuncio del Reino," *CIRD,* 245 [*FMF* (1976) 108].

⁵⁰ Ibid., 245 [109].

⁵¹ Vorgrimler, *Understanding Karl Rahner,* 180.

⁵² K. Rahner, *Faith in a Wintry Season: Interviews and Conversations with Karl Rahner in the Last Years of His Life, 1982–1984,* ed. H. Biallowons, P. Imhof and H. Egan (New York: Crossroad, 1990) 64.

⁵³ Rahner, "Dimensiones del martirio," *Concilium,* no. 181 (1983) 322.

⁵⁴ Ibid., 323.

⁵⁵ *Misión Abierta,* no. 77 (1984) 497.

# Chapter 6

# Contemplation in the Action of Justice: Ignacio Ellacuría and Ignatian Spirituality

*J. Matthew Ashley*

Other essays in this book treat the important contributions that Ignacio Ellacuría made as a philosopher, theologian, university administrator, and political mediator. However, he was also a Jesuit who knew the spirituality of his order intimately and comprehensively.[1] The briefest look at his biography makes it clear that Ignacio Ellacuría was a man passionately committed to Ignatian spirituality, who sought to put it at the service of the church in Latin America. The thesis of this essay is that he did this in large measure by seeking philosophical and theological language and arguments to articulate the encounter with Christ that is structured by Ignatius Loyola's *Spiritual Exercises*. While he had the particular dilemma of the Latin American church in mind, his contribution has much to say for the rest of the church as well. Thus, he deserves a place among such Jesuit theologians as Karl Rahner, Henri de Lubac, and Pierre Teilhard de Chardin who have sought to elaborate the conceptual presuppositions and implications of Ignatian spirituality for late modernity.[2]

The first task is to give some indication of what Ignatian spirituality meant for Ellacuría. For this, we have his own lecture notes for a course that he conducted on the *Spiritual Exercises*.[3] While much can and should be said about his novel interpretation of Ignatius's masterwork, here I limit myself to discussing the implications of Ellacuría's use of the philosophical term "historicization" to identify and deploy what he took to be the central dynamism of the *Spiritual Exercises*.[4] In a second stage, I demonstrate the power of appropriating Ignatian spirituality in terms of this dynamism by showing the difference it makes for a particular theme that is important for Ignatian spirituality, but extends far beyond it: contemplation in action.[5] This notion has surely been an important achievement for a modern spirituality that is at home in the world. However, it has not been without its own pitfalls, particularly in our modern milieu that privatizes spirituality and converts it into a set of techniques for making one's peace with an increasingly alienated culture, rather than seeking to evangelize it. Ellacuría's contribution, I contend, lies in his perception of this ambiguity, and in a creative response that drew on the novel way he lived and interpreted Ignatian spirituality.

## Ellacuría and the Spiritual Exercises

It might not be too much to say that Ignacio Ellacuría was a man obsessed with the transformative power of Ignatius of Loyola's *Spiritual Exercises*. Juan Hernández Pico suggests that Ellacuría's career could be summed up in terms of his work to actualize (or historicize, as Ellacuría would say) this power in successively broader social contexts.

> Although he did not formulate it programmatically in these words, what Ignacio Ellacuría did in his apostolic life as a mature Jesuit was first and foremost to bring the Central American Province [of the Society of Jesus] to undergo the spirit of the Spiritual Exercises, especially in the structures through which it formed young Jesuits, and then to do the same for the University of Central America "José Simeon Cañas" (UCA). Then, and building on this, he wanted to make the national reality of El Salvador undergo this same experience.[6]

What was it about the *Spiritual Exercises* that made them so important to him? A comparison with his theological mentor, Karl Rahner, provides an answer. Rahner was convinced that conveying the experience of God made possible and structured by the *Spiritual Exercises* should be the center of any Jesuit's work, including as an intellectual.[7] For theologians this demands finding conceptual resources to mine and communicate the resources of the *Exercises*. Specifically, in his analysis of the experience of spiritual consolation or desolation treated in the *Spiritual Exercises*, Rahner asserted that what is at issue for the theologian is

whether or not he already has at his disposal in his theology the means
really to bring explicitly before the mind the concrete experience in question, to make it more exactly comprehensible and to justify it. Or the fact
is revealed that his theology would first have to be developed through
contact with these works and what they say, and allow itself to be cor-
rected by them.[8]

In this essay, Rahner was particularly concerned with the Ignatian rules
for discernment, especially as they revolved around the experience of
"consolation without prior cause." For Rahner, this experience and these
rules provided Christians with a way of finding God and God's will in an
increasingly secularized and pluralistic world. Consequently, their theological articulation, defense, and elaboration constituted for Rahner an
important *ecclesial* service on the part of the theologian.

For Ellacuría theology is also defined as ecclesial service and, like
Rahner, Ignacio Ellacuría, the Jesuit, turned to the *Spiritual Exercises* to
render this service. This is the reason why Ellacuría begins his lectures on
the *Exercises* not by talking about individual spiritual development, but
by defining the most pressing need of *the church* in Latin America. "The
fundamental problem that confronts both Latin American theology and
pastoral practice is that of comprehending and realizing the history of
salvation in the specifically Latin American situation."[9] This was, in fact,
the challenge that the Latin American Church had set itself at Medellín:
to read the signs of the times in the light of the Gospel in its own specific
reality and to respond adequately to them. Ellacuría notes that this difficult task can be accomplished neither by simply applying universal norms
worked out in Rome, Europe, or North America, nor by the use of social-
scientific tools alone. The first trivializes the problem and the second
secularizes it.[10] The problem then is this: Where can the church find a
vantage point, a "place" from which to carry out this necessary task?

Ellacuría's claim is that the *Spiritual Exercises* provides such a place. After
stating the problem of making theology and pastoral practice Latin American, Ellacuría entitles the next section "The *Exercises* of Saint Ignatius as a
Theological Place for Historicization."[11] Now, to "historicize" a concept or a
set of concepts (including one's understanding of theological concepts
such as "salvation history" or "God's will") means to understand it as a
part of an ongoing historical process, to grasp how its usage interacts with,
resists, or transforms the various dynamisms that constitute one's own
specific historical situation; and finally, to hold oneself accountable to the
way that this understanding leads one to act (or fail to act) in that situation. This term is worked out in great detail in Ellacuría's philosophy, and

its development constitutes one of the major ways in which he both built on and moved beyond his philosophical mentor, Xavier Zubiri.[12] Its appearance here, as the cornerstone of Ellacuría's interpretation of the *Exercises,* suggests that the term serves to disclose and deploy what Ellacuría took to be the central import of the *Exercises* for the church. Further, it suggests that a full understanding of what historicization means for Ellacuría needs to attend not only to its intricate philosophical background, but also its (in Ellacuría's eyes at least) exemplary instantiation in the "place" constituted by the *Spiritual Exercises* for the church. In terms of my comparison with Rahner, by working out a philosophy and theology focused on historicization (and its important correlative, "historical reality"), Ellacuría was forging conceptual tools to make the resources of a spiritual tradition available to the church in Latin America.

What was Ellacuría trying to disclose about the *Spiritual Exercises* in using this term? He tells us that the *Exercises* "historicize the word of God insofar as they turn to historical, personal and situational signs so that that word might be discovered in the concrete."[13] He then elaborates on this point with the claim that they "make the historical into the essential part of the structure of the Christian encounter with God."[14] This is nowhere more evident, on his reading, than in the "Second Week" of the *Exercises* that "contains those texts most original to Saint Ignatius."[15] The Second Week is the point at which the retreatant makes the "election," a life-determining choice (for instance, to enter religious life). Making this choice in conformity with God's will is the purpose of the *Exercises*. To that end, the Second Week weaves a complex fabric of contemplations of the mysteries of Jesus' life, that is, prayerful engagements with the life of Jesus, taken primarily from the synoptic gospels, in which one participates imaginatively in the drama that the stories recount, so that one will come to know and love Christ and, as a consequence, to imitate him more closely. These contemplations are given a backdrop of metahistorical reflections, such as a comparison between the call of Christ and the call of an earthly king, discursive conceptual considerations like the different degrees of humility, the indifference to which a Christian is called, or the applications of different "rules for discernment." The goal is always to take charge of one's own history, to make a choice in conformity with the saving will of God who has acted and continues to act in history.

In applying the term "historicization" here, Ellacuría is highlighting the way the *Exercises* interweave one's own individual history with the broader world history in which it is embedded, and finally with the history of God's salvific work in the world, with its definitive manifestation in Jesus' history. The goal, as Ellacuría stresses, is not simply knowledge of God and God's will, but a decision to incarnate that will in one's life.[16] The goal is the praxis of discipleship. In terms of the threefold definition of historicization suggested above, through the *Exercises* one grasps God's will as a part of a historical process, with its high point in Jesus of Nazareth, but continuing through those whom Jesus sends out into the world under his "standard."[17] One strives to understand how that historically specified will applies in one's own historical situation and, finally, one labors to develop the dispositions and be open to the graces that will bring one to act out of the understanding thus gained. The result is that one comes to follow Jesus more closely. This is not a matter of imitating an ahistorical ideal, but effecting a historical continuation—Ellacuría named it a "progressive historicization"—governed by "the spirit of Christ who animates those who follow him."[18] He was convinced the *Exercises* could do this not only for individuals, but corporately, if only the adequate philosophical and theological structures could be formulated to unleash their power.[19] We conclude, then, that the *Spiritual Exercises* were so important for Ellacuría not only because he was a Jesuit, but because they provided him with a crucial resource for meeting the needs of the Latin American church.

To be sure, Ellacuría has not been the only one to notice Ignatius's focus on the historical as the locus for prayer and action. The historian of mysticism Ewert Cousins places Ignatius in a tradition he calls the "mysticism of the historical event," reaching back to Francis of Assisi.[20] What unifies this tradition, Cousins argues, is a devotion to the humanity of Christ, exemplified in Francis's erection of a crèche for midnight Mass at Greccio in 1223. This focus on the historical embodiment of Jesus began a tradition that, Cousins contends, offers a real alternative to the Neoplatonic mystical tradition, with its penchant for the risen, glorified Christ, and its tendency to find in historical events allegories propelling the mystic out of history and into the timeless.[21] Cousins describes this alternative as follows:

> I believe that it [this new form of prayer] is rooted in the very historicity of human existence and that it activates that level of the psyche whereby we draw out the spiritual energy of a past event. I have called this elsewhere "the mysticism of the historical event." By that I mean that it constitutes a distinct category of mystical consciousness. . . . Just as in nature mysticism we feel united to the material world, so in this form of mysticism we feel part of the historical event—as if we were there, as eyewitnesses, participating in the action, absorbing its energy.[22]

Cousins goes on to describe the work of Franciscan theology, led by Bonaventure, as that of integrating this new spirituality into the classical Christian theological traditions, which had developed primarily in the Neoplatonic stream.[23] This integration not only gave conceptual articulation to Francis's spirituality, but also effected a fundamental shift, "Franciscanizing" the foundations of the Neoplatonic theological structure. Cousins concludes by wondering whether Ignatius has had a "Bonaventure" of his own to integrate his spiritual vision into the broader stream of Christian spirituality, and to situate it within a comprehensive theological vision.[24]

The gist of my argument thus far has been to propose Ellacuría as a prime candidate. While never using these terms, Ellacuría understood very well the "mysticism of the historical event" that lies at the heart of Ignatian spirituality, and he strove to work out a philosophy that could highlight that spirituality and deploy its resources. He chose tools from Zubiri, but also from Marx and others, "Ignatianizing" these resources in the process. Thus, not only does his philosophical work shed light on his understanding of Ignatian spirituality, but knowledge of Ignatian spirituality also helps us understand his philosophical agenda.[25] The extent of his appropriation of this depth structure of Ignatian spirituality, and the difference it makes, can be displayed by considering his understanding of that quintessentially Ignatian theme, "contemplation in action."

## Contemplation in Action for Justice: Ellacuría's Contribution to the History of a Concept

Books have been written on the history of attempts to interrelate contemplation and action, and it is not my intention here even to summarize this history. I choose figures that will help illuminate what is at stake theologically in an understanding of the relationship between contemplation and action, and that will help understand better how Ellacuría's theological and philosophical positions integrate with his spirituality.[26] In its origins, Christian reflection on the theme of contemplation and action was determined terminologically by the patristic incorporation of the Greek debate over the relationship between theory and praxis, and scripturally by the biblical pairs of Leah and Rachel, Peter and John, and Martha and Mary. Origen was probably the first to associate Martha with a life of *praxis* and Mary with a life of *theoria*. In so doing, he largely accepted the superior evaluation of *theoria* by philosophers of antiquity, as well as the arguments they used to establish this superiority.[27] These arguments, particularly in late antiquity, relied on a Neoplatonic scheme that portrayed temporal involvement in general and the life of politics in particular, more and more negatively. Two of these arguments are important for our story. First, it was argued that *praxis*—which for antiquity meant primarily political life—involves one in temporal affairs that disperse one's energies. *Theoria,* on the other hand, as contemplation of what is eternal, removes one from the dispersal of temporal existence. To prefer *theoria* over *praxis* is to prefer the One over the many. Second, it was noted that the full and fulfilling realization of *praxis* depends on the vagaries of historical circumstances and on the cooperation of others. *Theoria,* on the other hand, did not depend as much on one's social setting. It could be realized in isolation, or in the modest but more structured context of the philosophical school. It was more self-sufficient. To prefer *theoria* over *praxis,* then, is to be realistic about what sorts of ideals one chooses around which to structure one's life. As the *polis,* in both its Greek and Roman forms, degenerated in late antiquity, this realism increasingly meant the dismissal of *praxis* as a possible arena for human fulfillment.[28]

One can aptly characterize the millennium subsequent to the adoption of these categories by the Christian apologists as a long labor to overcome the philosophical limitations of the Greek terms to more adequately express the complexity of the life of discipleship portrayed in the New Testament. Augustine of Hippo is an important figure because he was largely responsible for transmitting this debate into Latin Christianity, and because he developed some crucial theological strategies for reconfiguring the logic of *praxis* and *theoria*. One of his enduring contributions was to render explicit the necessary shift in social context: from *polis* to *ecclesia,* from the human city to the city of God. He also grasped the need for a christological point of reference for relating *praxis* and *theoria,* action and contemplation.[29] Finally, Augustine took up the evaluation of temporality, which was a crucial background for the evaluations of the two lives. Let us examine these contributions in a bit more detail, beginning with the second.

In his homilies on Luke 10:38-42, Augustine places the unifying context for Martha and Mary in their relationship to Jesus. Martha fed Jesus in the flesh, while Mary was fed by Jesus in the spirit.[30] We continue to feed Christ incarnate in the needy (Augustine cites Matt 25). Christ, the Word of God, feeds us primarily in the liturgy. This opens the way to understanding the unity of the two ways by means of the Chalcedonian logic that applies to the two natures of the hypostatic union—without confusion, without change, without division, without separation. Augustine further molds this christological focus eschatologically. "The kind [of life] Martha was leading, that's what we are; the kind Mary was leading, that's what we are hoping for; let us lead this one well, in order to have that one to the full."[31] Martha's life of service to the needs of others is both fully possible and obligatory for us now. Mary's life of absorption in the Word is *not* fully possible now; it is only inchoately present, particularly, Augustine suggests, in the liturgy.[32] Thus, Augustine interprets Jesus' reproach in Luke 10:41f. as follows:

> So the Lord did not find fault with work, but made a distinction between functions. "You are busy," he said, "about many things; for all that, there is one thing necessary." Mary has already chosen this for herself; the multiplicity of toil passes away, the single unity of charity remains. So what she has chosen shall not be taken from her. What you have chosen though . . . will be taken away from you. But it will be taken away for your benefit, so that the better part may be given you.[33]

Augustine both exploited and transformed the logic by which *theoria* was placed above *praxis*. He accepted the Neoplatonic preference for the One over the many, the integrating focus of contemplation over the dissipating exteriority of service. On the other hand, he rejected the prudential choice of *theoria* as the best candidate for a fully realized human life. The demands of charity exclude such a choice and the ephemerality of contemplative union in this life negates the underlying rationale. We may *desire* the contemplative life more now, but we must live in the knowledge that it will only be achieved beyond this life, and that we are required to live this one giving priority to the life of loving service that *praxis* represents, enjoying along the way those brief foretastes of our final goal that are available, however fleetingly, in the life of *theoria*.

These insights were expressed in ecclesiological focus in *The City of God*, where Augustine speaks of the "mixed way" *[vita mixta]*.[34] The active and contemplative lives are coordinated in terms of love: the active life answers to the *necessitas caritatis*—the necessity of love to respond to the needs of others. The contemplative life is associated with the *suavitas ex caritate*—the peace and restfulness of the love of God. The eschatological framework laid out above is again evident. Indeed, while initially presented alongside the *vita activa* and the *vita contemplativa,* the context makes it clear that the *vita mixta* represents the only way the other two are available to us in a church *in statu viae*. It is the *one* way open to Christians under the eschatological conditions of our present state of following Christ.[35]

Augustine's contributions to the understanding of the contemplative and active lives, then, lie first in making relationship to Christ, expressed in terms of love, the standard by which both lives are judged and interrelated. This is an important modification of the Greek model of *praxis* and *theoria*. Second, Augustine placed the two lives in the context of the church, the city of God. Finally, because he works out his ecclesiology in an eschatological key, Augustine forecloses any simple choice of one life over the other. It must be noted, though, that however much Augustine shows the necessity of the active life, in the final analysis action is only extrinsically related to that union with God that is our final end, because union with God is defined in terms of contemplative vision, perfect in the next life, and available inchoately and ephemerally in this life.

Meister Eckhart's importance for the history of this issue strikes one immediately upon reading his remarkable sermons on Martha and Mary. Here *Martha* and not Mary is the mature Christian, the one who has reached the end of the mystical itinerary, as far as this is possible in this life.[36] In Sermon 2, which, tellingly, deals only with Martha, Eckhart tells us that Martha is "virgin and wife."[37] That soul is a virgin that "is free of all alien images." The soul is a wife insofar as she brings forth fruit; in her, God is fruitful.[38] Remarkably, Eckhart contends that "wife," here connoting the active life, is a nobler title for the soul than "virgin" because it entails fruitfulness.[39] Best of all is the soul that is a virgin *and* a wife, who combines the detachment of the virgin with the fruitfulness of the wife:

> This virgin who is a wife brings this fruit and this birth about, and every day she produces fruit, a hundred or a thousand times, yes, more than can be counted, giving birth and becoming fruitful from the noblest ground of all—or, to put it better, from that same ground where the Father is bearing his eternal Word, from that ground is she fruitfully bearing with him. For Jesus, the light and the reflection of the Fatherly heart . . . this Jesus is united with her and she with him, and she shines and glows with him as one in the oneness and as a pure bright light in the Fatherly heart.[40]

When a person is rooted in this "ground," then he or she enjoys a union with God as profound as that union which is the goal of contemplation or *theoria*. Eckhart writes, "here a work done in time is as valuable as any joining of self to God, for *this work joins us as closely as the most sublime thing that can happen to us,* except for seeing God in his pure nature."[41] We can leave aside for the moment Eckhart's reference to seeing God in God's pure nature that was generally reserved for the next life and of dubious possibility. We are left with Eckhart's extraordinary reversal of the tradition grounded in his claim that action, when the fruit of a soul properly disposed, unites one *as fully* with God as anything that can happen to us in this life, including (the context makes clear) contemplative rapture, represented by Mary. Since this kind of "grounded action" can be sustained continually (whereas Eckhart followed the tradition in holding that contemplative rapture cannot), it is superior to contemplation. For this reason, Eckhart makes Mary the beginner, and Martha the adept; the better part that Mary has chosen is in fact *Martha's* part.[42] Martha's worry, he suggests, is that Mary has become so absorbed in the pleasure of contemplation, that she will not leave it behind for the deeper union of the person whose soul is a "virgin and wife."[43]

Eckhart deployed a complex theological metaphysics to buttress his proposal that the participation in the life of God *[theiosis]* that is our salvation can be understood not only in terms of the union of knower and known in speculative vision—which was the ruling metaphor taken over with the Greek concept of *theoria,* and underlies the scholastic notion of beatific vision—but in terms of a union in and with the divine action that God *is.* For Eckhart, God is characterized by the inner-trinitarian "boiling" *[bullitio]* of the eternal begetting of the Son by the Father, in the union of the Spirit. This trinitarian life "boils over" *[ebullitio],* in the eternal act of creation and the historical act of incarnation, in which the event of inner-trinitarian begetting stamps creation. For Eckhart this inner-trinitarian event can be consciously recapitulated within the soul that is a virgin and wife when one "breaks through" to the soul's ground in God, a ground on which the soul and God are one.[44] Action becomes itself the locus for a form of union with God that is neither merely a preparation for a union with God in contemplative vision, nor a fruit (however necessary) that ensues upon it. This form of union is not so much an "experience" we have, but a mode of being we partake in. As Dietmar Mieth puts it, "for Eckhart, the *'unio mystica'* of the birth of God consists not in an experience, but rather in the ontological integration of the person into the divine work of salvation, which proceeds from God and returns to God."[45]

Eckhart's contribution, then, is to overcome, or at least supplement, the "ocular" imagery that dominated the understanding of mystical union, and that made it so difficult to envision action as a place where mystical union might occur. Modern Christianity is heir to Eckhart's conception of a "mysticism of everyday life." It deserves affirmation insofar as it has broken down an elitist division of labor in the church. In that paradigm, prayer, particularly mystical prayer, has been reserved for those who "leave the world" for monastic or eremitic life. The laity, and even priests and religious outside the monastery, are left with the work of evangelization and Christian service—worthy tasks, but necessarily exclusive of the life of silent withdrawal contemplative prayer requires.

Eckhart's approach has a darker side, however, that has been exploited in the cultural landscape of late modern capitalist societies. As Princeton sociologist of religion Robert Wuthnow warns, spirituality in America has not so much been integrated with everyday life, as swallowed up by it. It is in danger of becoming a palliative, a new haven in a heartless world.[46] Appeals to "contemplation in action" in this context threaten to become a halo we paste onto any activity whatsoever to convince ourselves that we have not lost our way, particularly our way to the sacred, in the late modern labyrinth we have constructed.

Moreover, spirituality has become a marketable commodity. "Spirituality has become big business," Wuthnow notes, "and big business finds many of its best markets by putting things in small, easy-to-consume packages."[47] "Contemplation in action" is a highly saleable commodity indeed, since it can be marketed to anyone in any occupation who feels overwhelmed and/or alienated by his or her work. Yet, in the process of simplification and commodification, important nuances are lost and critical questions begged. Can *any* action be the basis for "contemplation in action"? Can the wisdom of this tradition and the practices it recommends be abstracted and then inserted into any institutional context for action? A growing genre of books plunder the world's mystical traditions and give an implicit yes to these questions. For example, in a burgeoning literature of "spirituality of business," mystical practices are presented as ideal techniques by which executives can manage stress, increase corporate esprit de corps, and get a greater sense of fulfillment from their work, without ever considering the wider social impact of corporate practices.[48] Is Wuthnow right when he worries that the spiritual traditions of Christianity are being packaged, even by well-meaning teachers and spiritual directors, as little more than techniques that help us fit in and adapt to our increasingly transient and complex world? Can the ideal of contemplation in action be reconfigured to give a more central place to the prophetic challenge of this world, in solidarity with its victims?

Ignacio Ellacuría's contribution lies precisely in the depth and fidelity of his reconfiguration of this tradition. He proposed a union of contemplation and action that is a "contemplation in the action of justice." In so doing, Ellacuría took up not only the elements in Loyola's spirituality in continuity with Eckhart, but he brought to bear the historical depth-structure of Ignatian spirituality, which he understood under the category of "historicization," as we saw above. In this, he integrated important elements of Augustine's synthesis, transposed by a profoundly modern sensitivity to human historicity. In what follows I take up first the continuity with Eckhart, and then the christological and ecclesiological configuration of Ellacuría's synthesis that overcome some of the weaknesses, particularly on late modern terrain, of the model of contemplation in action.

First, then, Ellacuría takes over Eckhart's insight that the *unio mystica* should not be conceived exclusively in terms of vision, but can be understood as an "acting-with" that recapitulates both the eternal generation of the Word within the Trinity and the temporal creation and redemption of the world *ad extra*. Consider, for example, Ellacuría's discussion of the Ignatian motto of "finding God in all things," and the notion of contemplation in action implicit to it. Although the phrase is not contained there, the traditional locus for discussing it has been the "Contemplation to Attain Love" that concludes Ignatius's *Spiritual Exercises*.[49] As Ellacuría presents it, this contemplation shows "the real possibility of encountering God in creation and the possibility of recovering creation as the presence of God."[50] "What is involved" he continues, "is a contemplation of God in things that gives way to contemplation in action with things," in which "God becomes present to the person at work, and the person makes God present and becomes present to a God at work."[51] The crucial point to be made about this statement is that these three events or processes—God becoming present, the person making God present, and the person becoming present to a God at work—are strictly correlative and simultaneous.[52] We find God in all things by laboring in the midst of all things.

In his Latin works Eckhart brought to bear all the complexity and nuances of Scholastic method to undergird the insights about contemplation in action made in his vernacular sermons. Likewise, we have seen how Ellacuría strove to construct a philosophical framework that would disclose and deploy the insights he gleaned from his engagement with Ignatian spirituality. A third important convergence is their common appeal to trinitarian ontology. This is clear in Ellacuría's article on "The Historicity of Christian Salvation." There, as he builds toward his statement of the ideal of contemplation in action, he insists that creation be understood as "the *[plasmación] ad extra* of the very life of the Trinity, giving-form that is freely willed, yet still of the trinitarian life itself."[53] This ongoing and constitutive presence of the triune God to creation is what Ellacuría connotes with references to the "theologal dimension" of reality.[54] This dimension gives rise to a profoundly dynamic and self-donative character in reality. It becomes most fully present and actualized in human praxis, and the history it constitutes. We saw that for Eckhart work can be a participation in the creative work of God. Similarly, praxis for Ellacuría can be a participation in the creative and redemptive presence of God at the very roots of reality, and is as such the most adequate form of the "unitive way" toward intimacy with God.

Thus, the "things" in which we find God are not just statically "out there," for passive observation and manipulation. An adequate knowing of things as elements of historical reality must go far beyond an observation and description of realities from the outside. Rather, such knowing must include "a being in the midst of the reality of things . . . which, in its active character of existing, is anything but static and inert"[55] At the theological level, it means to become present to a trinitarian God who is at work in things, as Ignatius makes so clear in the "Contemplation to Attain Love."[56] To "be in the midst of the reality of things" is to encounter in the profoundest way possible a trinitarian God at work for us, precisely by placing oneself with and in that work.

Mining this theological-philosophical background, so necessary for Ellacuría's reconfiguration of the model of contemplation in action, required his profound, sustained, and implacable resistance to the depreciation of history and temporality. This depreciation, as we saw above in considering the Neoplatonic foundations of *praxis* and *theoria,* made it almost impossible to articulate a value for *praxis* except as a preparation for or outflow of *theoria.* To be sure, there are "philosophical" reasons to oppose this bias (which Ellacuría certainly knew and adduced). There are also, however, important "spiritual" reasons insofar as this bias makes it impossible to fully unleash the power of the concept and practice of contemplation in action, both generally speaking, and in its specifically Ignatian form. It is not too much to say that *the* objective of Ellacuría's "philosophy of historical reality" was to overcome this bias, so pervasive to the philosophical tradition. Not even Augustine was able to escape it, and Eckhart's solution valorized temporal involvement in a way that is dangerously abstract, as we shall see.

The crucial *discontinuities* with Eckhart can be discussed in terms of the Augustinian perspective offered earlier. Augustine understood that the Greek model of *praxis* and *theoria* had to be organized around a christological center of gravity and coordinated in terms of the primacy of love. In Eckhart's thought, this is done by focusing on the multiply instantiated birth of God (the Son) and the fruitfulness that attends it. In bearing fruit in the world, the contemplative in action is actualizing the union of the eternal inner-trinitarian generation of the second person of the Trinity with the birth of God in the soul. What is underdeveloped (at best) in Eckhart's scheme is the third instantiation of God's relation to the world through the Son: the historical incarnation of the Son in Jesus of Nazareth, which continues historically in the church through the power of the Spirit. Because it is thus cut loose from its historical moorings, the "fruitfulness" that characterizes the contemplative in action becomes precariously abstract. It is this abstractness that allows the model to be privatized and applied indiscriminately to almost any action that is not overtly immoral. What is lacking are concrete criteria, or a method for discerning *which* forms of work in the world are open to contemplation in action.

Ellacuría's approach also played on the trinitarian "form" of God's being and, consequently, of God's relation to the world and to humans in the world. Yet he adds to this the emphasis on *history,* trying to disclose its role as the key feature of Ignatius's *Spiritual Exercises,* and put it at the service of the church. Ellacuría focuses relentlessly on the "mystical" (in the sense of a "mysticism of the historical event") encounter with the historical Jesus that the *Exercises* make available. Thus, for Ellacuría, "fruitfulness" depends primarily on a person recapitulating in his or her own life the history of Jesus of Nazareth. "It is in the historical following of the historical life of Jesus that the true Christian contemplation in action is going to occur."[57] This leads to a critical emendation of the ideal of "finding God in all things."

> It is not so much a matter of finding God in all things, as if God were present in the same form in all things or in the same manner; clearly God is not in the Athenian Parthenon and in Jesus of Nazareth in the same way, and God is not in domination in the same way as in oppression . . . Scripture shows us that the true God and the true encounter with God are two different things; it is not enough to "acknowledge" the former in order for the latter to happen. Consequently, contemplation— that is, the moment of faith—will not be true unless it is realized within that action that is really demanded by the historical following of the historical Jesus.[58]

The essential christological inflection of the model of contemplation and action is not achieved by a breakthrough to the ground of the soul/God in which the eternal generation of the Son is occurring, to which both the incarnation in history and one's own historical response are related a posteriori and extrinsically. Rather, this christological inflection comes from a correlation of one's own history with the history of Jesus' life, work, and fate. Thus, we come back to the focal point of the *Spiritual Exercises*, as Ellacuría interpreted it. Put somewhat differently, in Ellacuría's view the thoroughly incarnational wisdom of the *Exercises* is that "a human presence and an historical action are always necessary to make God present."[59] This applies even to God's becoming present to the individual in prayer, and a fortiori to the union of contemplation and action. The encounter with God is not first or even primarily actualized and expressed in images or words, not even the exalted words of dogma and theology. Its primary actualization comes by being enfleshed in a historically realized human life, a life lived with spirit, as Ellacuría liked to say.[60]

For Ellacuría as for Eckhart, then, the *unio mystica* is grounded in the trinitarian relations of God to the world, and entails "an integration of the person into the divine work of salvation." The crucial difference is that this only happens insofar as the person forms his or her own life in discipleship. This means in turn that it is not just any action that can present the material within which such an integration can occur. Beyond the test of moral rectitude or ecclesial legality, such action must answer the criteria of discipleship, which includes the others but goes beyond them. Ellacuría thus recovers the Augustinian insight that it is only in relationship to Jesus Christ that action and contemplation can be authentically and fruitfully integrated, as well as the tradition's later insight into the importance of "fruitfulness" for understanding that relationship. Ellacuría also shows how feeding Christ who continues to take flesh in the poor is the essential active matrix within which one is fed by Christ in the Spirit.

As for Augustine, Ellacuría's synthesis has a strong ecclesiological dimension as well. We saw above that in Augustine's view the *vita mixta* is configured according to the specific conditions of the church as an eschatological community, a people *in statu viae*. This is true for Ellacuría, too, but for him the journey through history is inextricably tied to an engagement with history. "[The church's] praxis fundamentally consists in realizing the Kingdom of God in history, in activity that leads to the Kingdom of God being realized in history."[61] It is in carrying out this never-completed task that the church fulfills its vocation to be "the people of God who continue in history that which was definitively marked out in Jesus as God's presence among men and women."[62] This historical continuation is precisely the sort of "progressive historicization" that Ellacuría identified as the locus for "contemplation in action." Thus, being a contemplative in action means being integrated into this people of God and its never-ending task of planting in history "a small seed that little by little can become a great tree sheltering all people."[63] Contemplation in action cannot be realized in isolation, but only in a community.[64]

Since the kingdom always comes by taking away the sin of the world, by opposing those social and historical forces that dehumanize men and women, its coming is best described from the Third World in terms of liberation. In every age the Church must "read the signs of the times" in order to see the specific form in which this praxis is obligatory to it, and the place where that praxis must be focused. In our own age, Ellacuría insists, this form is the struggle for justice and the place is the poor. The church, consequently, must not only struggle for the poor, it must—as Medellín and Puebla insisted—find its place there, take flesh there, with them. This "taking flesh" does not mean that the physical embodiment of the church in its institutions and membership will only be found in the geographical place where the poor are. It does, however, require that this enfleshment extend to and modify substantially even (especially!) those ecclesial institutions and structures which are not geographically located with the poor.[65]

Here we have an answer to the modern tendency to commodify spirituality and sell it to modern men and women. The synthesis of contemplation and action cannot be privatized on Ellacuría's view because it demands that one be a part of a people, the people of God, who take as their task continuing Jesus' presence in history. Too much of modern "spiritual writing" abstracts the model of contemplation in action from the focal reality of discipleship and the social context of the church. Ellacuría showed how and why this fundamentally distorts the model. His criticism does not rule out a "spirituality of business" or a "spirituality of university work," that would deploy the formidable and laudable resources offered by a "mysticism of the everyday." It does, however, subject these spiritualities to the criteria of discipleship, derived and applied within a concrete methodology (that of the *Spiritual Exercises*). Furthermore, it holds them accountable to a people who have taken as their work making the kingdom of God real in history.[66]

Responding to these two challenges is no easy thing; it demands a strict spiritual ascesis. Indeed, Ellacuría believed that it required nothing less than the sort of regimen that Ignatius laid out in the *Spiritual Exercises,* now enacted on a social-historical scale. Something like the rules for discernment of spirits would be necessary, open to the intellectual resources made available by the social sciences, but also contextualized within a profound desire to know, love, and imitate Jesus and to make the love of God concretized in his life a reality for ours as well. Contemplation in the action of justice is no easy spiritual tint that can be applied to any and all our actions, but its power for animating lives of discipleship that bring life to cultures and histories of death, is evident in the lives of the Salvadoran martyrs, who followed its difficult but christomorphic logic to the end.

## Conclusion

Much more could be said about Ellacuría's appropriation of Ignatian spirituality, and about his contribution to a Christian integration of contemplation and action. I have been able to do justice neither to the philosophical ground on which they were built, nor to the richness of the christology and ecclesiology that give them depth and made them so densely Christian. This shows, if nothing else, how Ellacuría's lived engagement with Ignatian spirituality shaped a philosophy and theology that, in turn, enriched that spirituality. I have tried here to demonstrate the importance of Ignatian spirituality for Ellacuría's philosophical and theological production, and to highlight the difference this made for his very Ignatian articulation of the ideal of contemplation in action. That integration preserves the gains make by Eckhart's "democratization" of the *unio mystica*. But it overcomes the dangerous abstractness of Echkart's approach that makes it vulnerable to the privatization and commodification of spirituality, so pervasive in late modern capitalist societies.

The preceding analysis suggests a final point. Ellacuría's focus on *praxis* and on the centrality of the struggle for justice for Christian faith, practice, and theology, have led some to accuse him (and virtually all liberation theologians) of being Marxist, of surrendering the substance of faith to a foreign intellectual conceptuality. The foregoing should remind us, however, that Marx was a relative latecomer to a debate on the relationship between *praxis* and *theoria* that had been going on for millennia, albeit under different terms (the relationship between the *vita contemplativa* and the *vita activa*). Ellacuría took up this debate in large measure because he *lived it* in the spirituality that defined who he was, how he thought, how he lived, and, ultimately, how he died. I believe that Ellacuría's opus (with liberation theology as a whole) will continue to grow in stature as a classic and a source for future theologies. This is precisely because he takes up crucial strands in the Christian tradition like this one, faithfully and creatively integrating intellectual tools into the discussion wherever they are to be found. In Ellacuría's hands, they become new and life giving for the Church today as it struggles to be faithful to its nature and mission.

This essay was written in English for *Love That Produces Hope,* and the original appears here. However, it was subsequently translated into Spanish and appeared as "La contemplación en la acción de la justicia: La contribución de Ignacio Ellacuría a la espiritualidad cristiana," *RLT,* no. 51 (2000) 211–32.

---

[1] He was, for example, director of formation for four years (1970–1974), albeit not without controversy! Furthermore, when the Central American Jesuits came to choose a delegate for the Jesuits' Thirty-Third General Congregation of 1983, they elected Ellacuría, a strong indication of their judgment about his appropriation and mastery of Jesuit spirituality.

[2] For some reflections on this theme, see the essays by Avery Dulles: "Saint Ignatius and the Jesuit Theological Tradition," *Studies in the Spirituality of Jesuits* 14 (March 1982); "Jesuits and Theology: Yesterday and Today," *Theological Studies* 52 (1991) 524–38; "The Ignatian Charism and Contemporary Theology," *America* 176 (April 26, 1997) 14–22.

[3] See Ignacio Ellacuría, "Lectura Latinoamericana de los *Ejercicios Espirituales* de San Ignacio," *Revista Latinoamericana de Teología,* no. 23 (1991) 111–47; henceforth, "Lectura." All translations are my own.

[4] For a more detailed discussion of Ellacuría's intellectual engagement with the *Spiritual Exercises,* see J. Matthew Ashley, "Ignacio Ellacuría and the *Spiritual Exercises* of Ignatius Loyola," *Theological Studies* 61 (2000) 16–39.

[5] Ellacuría's elaboration of this theme is contained in his essay, "Fe y Justicia," which was published in two parts in *Christus* (August 1977) 26–33 and *Christus* (October 1977) 19–34. Of particular interest is the fifth part of this essay, entitled "La contemplación en la acción de la justicia." The whole essay has recently been published as a book: Ignacio Ellacuría, Jon Sobrino, *Fe y Justicia* (Bilbao, Spain: Desclée, 1999). I cite from this text, giving my own translations. Another important articulation of his understanding of contemplation and action is found in "The Historicity of Christian Salvation," in I. Ellacuría and J. Sobrino, eds., *Mysterium Liberationis: Fundamental Concepts of Liberation Theology* (Maryknoll, NY: Orbis, 1993) 251–89, esp. 283–7; trans. by Margaret Wilde from "Historicidad de la salvación cristiana" (1984); collection hereafter cited as *MLT* (English translation) and *ML* (Spanish original) [*ML* 1 (1993) 323–72].

[6] See Juan Hernández Pico, s.j., "Ellacuría, Ignaciano," in J. Sobrino and R. Alvarado, eds., *Ignacio Ellacuría, "Aquella libertad esclarecida"* (San Salvador: UCA Editores, 1999) 305; translation mine.

[7] See Karl Rahner, "Rede des Ignatius von Loyola an einen Jesuiten von Heute," *Schriften zur Theologie XV: Wissenschaft und christlicher Glaube* (Zürich: Benziger, 1984) 373–408, esp. 379–80.

[8] Karl Rahner, "The Logic of Concrete Individual Knowledge in Ignatius Loyola," in *The Dynamic Element in the Church* (London: Burns and Oates, 1964) 109. Rahner concludes that the "theology of the schools" is not up to this task.

[9] Ellacuría, "Lectura," 112. The title for this subsection is "The *Exercises* as a Theologal Experience and Pastoral Principle in the *Ecclesial* Reality of Latin America," 111; emphasis added.

[10] Ibid., 111.

[11] Ibid., 113. This is the title of the second part (of two) of his introductory lecture.

[12] See Robert Lassalle-Klein, "Ignacio Ellacuría's Debt to Xavier Zubiri: Principles for a Latin American Reading of Western Philosophy," above, p. 88 in this volume.

[13] Ellacuría, "Lectura," 113.

[14] Ibid., 115.

[15] Ibid., 124.

[16] Ibid., 113f.

[17] See the "Contemplation on the Kingdom of Christ and the Meditation" and the "Meditation on the Two Standards," in *Ignatius of Loyola, The Spiritual Exercises of St. Ignatius,* translated with introduction and commentary by George E. Ganss, s.j. (St. Louis: Institute of Jesuit Sources, 1992) 53–5, 65–7.

[18] Ellacuría, "Lectura," 127.

[19] I contend that he learned this during his novitiate years under the remarkable Miguel Elizondo, and that he first attempted to put it into practice in giving the *Spiritual Exercises* corporately to the Central American Jesuits in 1969. On his novitiate and the important role Elizondo gave to the *Exercises* for inculturating his charges, see Teresa Whitfield, *Paying the Price: Ignacio Ellacuría and the Murdered Jesuits of El Salvador* (Philadelphia: Temple University, 1995) 15–24. On the 1969 corporate retreat, see Juan Hernández Pico, "Ellacuría, Ignaciano," 305–26; Robert Lassalle-Klein, "The Jesuit Martyrs of the University of Central America: An American Christian University and the Historical Reality of the Reign of God" (Ph.D. dissertation, Graduate Theological Union, 1995) 51–6, and Charles Beirne, s.j., *Jesuit Education and Social Change in El Salvador* (New York: Garland, 1996) 84–7.

[20] The relevant texts are Ewert Cousins, "Franciscan Roots of Ignatian Meditation," in *Ignatian Spirituality in a Secular Age,* ed. George Schner, s.j. (Waterloo, Ont.: Wilfrid Laurier University, 1984) 51–64; idem, "The Humanity and Passion of Christ," in *Christian Spirituality II: High Middle Ages and Reformation,* ed. Jill Raitt (New York: Crossroad, 1989) 375–91; idem, "Francis of Assisi: Christian Mysticism at the Crossroads," in *Mysticism and Religious Traditions,* ed. Steven Katz (New York: Oxford University, 1983) 163–91.

[21] See Cousins, "The Humanity and Passion of Christ," 376–80.

[22] Cousins, "Franciscan Roots of Ignatian Meditation," 60. He cites "Francis of Assisi: Christian Mysticism at the Crossroads."

[23] Cousins, "Francis of Assisi," 175.

[24] Cousins, "Franciscan Roots," 63. He suggests Bonaventure might do this work still for Ignatius, or a modern-day theologian strongly influenced by Bonaventure: Karl Rahner.

[25] For a somewhat fuller demonstration of this claim, see Ashley, "Ignacio Ellacuría and the Spiritual Exercises," 30–7.

[26] For a fuller history of this theme up to the late Middle Ages, see Dietmar Mieth, *Die Einheit von Vita activa und Vita contemplativa in den deutschen Predigten und Traktaten Meister Eckharts und bei Johannes Tauler* (Regensburg, Germany: Friedrich Pustet, 1969). For a history of reflection on Martha and Mary, through the Reformation, see Giles Constable, "The Interpretation of Martha and Mary," in *Three Studies in Medieval Religious and Social Thought* (Cambridge: Cambridge University Press, 1995) 1–141.

[27] For an overview of these arguments, see Nicholas Lobkowicz, *Theory and Practice: History of a Concept from Aristotle to Marx* (New York: University Press of America, 1967) 3–57.

[28] Ibid., 53–7.

[29] On Augustine's understanding of the relationship between the active and contemplative lives, see Mieth, *Einheit,* 84–96.

[30] Augustine, Sermon 103.1, in *The Works of Saint Augustine: A Translation for the 21st Century* (New York: New City Press, 1990), vol. III, part 5:76f. Cf. Sermon 104.3 in *Works,* 82.

[31] Sermon 104.4, in *Works,* 83f.

[32] Ibid., 84.

[33] Sermon 104.3, 83.

[34] Bk. XIX.19, in *The City of God,* trans. Marcus Dods, with an introduction by Thomas Merton, The Modern Library (New York: Random House, 1950) 697f.

[35] See Mieth, *Einheit,* 93–5.

[36] See Sermon 2, in *Meister Eckhart: The Essential Sermons, Commentaries, Treatises and Defenses,* translations and introductions by Edmund College and Bernard McGinn (New York: Paulist, 1981) 177–81; and Sermon 86, in *Meister Eckhart: Teacher and Preacher,* ed. Bernard McGinn (New York: Paulist, 1986) 338–45.

[37] Sermon 2, *Meister Eckhart: The Essential Sermons,* 177. Eckhart takes liberty in translating from the Latin to the vernacular, translating *mulier* in Luke 10:38 as virgin and wife!

[38] Ibid., 178. Reversing the tradition's tendency, he asserts here that "'Wife' is the noblest word one can apply to the soul, much nobler than 'virgin.'"

[39] This theme had already been adumbrated in the tradition, particularly when the pair of Leah and Rachel was used to limn the relationship. With this pair, Leah is fruitful but "bleary-eyed," whereas Rachel does not (at first) bring forth fruit, but is clear-eyed and beautiful. The fruitfulness of love was central to so-called bridal mysticism, and may well have been conveyed to Eckhart by Beguine mystics like Hadewijch and Mechthild of Magdeburg, who represent a high point in the development of this theme.

[40] Sermon 2, *Meister Eckhart: The Essential Sermons,* 179.

[41] Sermon 86, *Meister Eckhart: Preacher and Teacher,* 341f.; emphasis added.

[42] "Martha knew Mary better than Mary Martha, for Martha had lived long and well; and living gives the most valuable kind of knowledge" (Sermon 86, p. 338). Thus, Eckhart reverses another evaluation, according to which the contemplative knows better the active because the active life is a prelude to the contemplative.

[43] Ibid., 339, 343f. In essence, Jesus tells Martha to let him worry about Mary, that she will indeed not be denied the better part (Martha's life) which she has chosen, even though at present she is only on the first steps of the road that leads to it: "He

responded by giving her [Martha] the comforting message that it would turn out for Mary as she desired" (339).

⁴⁴ For an overview of this issue that also argues persuasively for the importance of explicitly theological issues in Eckhart's mystical vision, see Bernard McGinn, "The God Beyond God: Theology and Mysticism in the Thought of Meister Eckhart," *Journal of Religion* 61 (1981) 1–19. On Eckhart's trinitarian theology in particular (and the notions of *bullitio* and *ebullitio*) see pp. 12–5.

⁴⁵ Mieth, *Einheit,* 215; trans. mine.

⁴⁶ Wuthnow writes of spirituality in the United States: "Our spirituality is often little more than a therapeutic device. A relationship to God is a way of making ourselves feel better. . . . We pray for comfort but do not expect to be challenged. We have domesticated the sacred by stripping it of authoritative wisdom and by looking to it only to make us happy"; see Robert Wuthnow, *God and Mammon in America* (New York: Free Press, 1994) 5f.

⁴⁷ Wuthnow, *After Heaven: Spirituality in America Since the 1950s* (Berkeley: University of California Press, 1998) 132.

⁴⁸ See, for example, Gay Hendricks and Kate Ludeman, *The Corporate Mystic* (New York: Bantam, 1997).

⁴⁹ *Spiritual Exercises,* nos. 234–7, 94f.

⁵⁰ Ellacuría, "Lectura," 143.

⁵¹ Ibid., 146.

⁵² Some of the force of Ellacuría's assertion escapes translation, as the verbs translated "become present," "make present" and "at work" are all forms of the same verb, *hacer* (*se hace presente, hace presente a,* and *haciendo,* respectively).

⁵³ Ellacuría, "The Historicity of Christian Salvation," 276; translation emended [357].

⁵⁴ Ibid., 277. Ellacuría attributes this philosophical insight to Zubiri. It is worth noting, however, that it also corresponds to the profoundly trinitarian character of Ignatian spirituality. This centrality had been persuasively presented by Pedro Arrupe (for whom Ellacuría had immense respect as *the* "historicization" of Ignatian spirituality for our time) in an address given four years prior to the composition of this article (Pedro Arrupe, "The Trinitarian Inspiration of the Ignatian Charism," 1980). Here we find another provocative interweaving of spirituality (Ignatian, as interpreted by Arrupe), philosophy (Zubiri's), and theology (Ellacuría's).

⁵⁵ See Ellacuría's sketch of a fundamental philosophical grounding of liberation theology, in "Hacia una fundamentación del método teológico latinoamericano," in E. Ruiz Maldonado, ed., *Liberación y Cuativerio: Debates in Torno al Método de la teología en America Latina* (Mexico City, 1975) 609–35. The quoted passage is on p. 626. I follow Kevin Burke's translation in *The Ground Beneath the Cross: The Theology of Ignacio Ellacuría* (Washington, D.C.: Georgetown University Press, 2000) 100. For a more extensive reconstruction of the philosophy that Ellacuría was attempting to develop, and its implications for theological method, see chapters 2–5 of this book, as well as the essay above by Robert Lassalle-Klein, pp. 88–124.

⁵⁶ See the three introductory points to the contemplation that emphasize the ways God is present as giver of gifts, as sustainer of all created things, and as laboring and working for us. See *Spiritual Exercises,* nos. 234–7, 94f.

[57] Ellacuría, "Lectura," 146.

[58] Ellacuría and Sobrino, *Fe y Justicia,* 210. Compare with Ellacuría, "Historicity," 285f.

[59] Ellacuría, "Lectura," 125.

[60] Ibid. On the significance for theological work of actualizing Jesus' life in today's circumstances, see I. Ellacuría, *Freedom Made Flesh: The Mission of Christ and His Church* (Maryknoll, NY: Orbis Books, 1976) 24–7.

[61] See Ellacuría, "La Iglesia de los pobres; Sacramento historico de liberación" [*ML* 2 (1993) 134]. Translations are mine, but see "The Church of the Poor: Historical Sacrament of Liberation," trans. Margaret Wilde in *MLT,* 543–64. In his interpretation of the *Spiritual Exercises,* Ellacuría put it this way: "The followers of the historical Jesus, as a people of God, prepare the definitive arrival of the reign of God in their historical following," "Lectura," 127.

[62] Ibid., 127 [*MLT,* 543].

[63] Ibid., 151f. [*MLT,* 561].

[64] Exploring the roots of Ellacuría's insight in the "ecclesiology" of Ignatian spirituality exceeds the limits of this essay. In his magisterial account of the first Jesuits, however, John O'Malley argues that they understood the church according to what was absolutely central to their identity: mission. He asserts that they viewed the church as "'the Lord's vineyard' in which they were called to imitate the apostles and disciples of Jesus in the exercise of their *consueta ministeria*" (John W. O'Malley, *The First Jesuits* [Cambridge, MA: Harvard University Press, 1993 301]). The church was for them the essential place within which to serve under the banner of Christ, in which they were schooled by the *Exercises.*

[65] Ellacuría attended most forcefully to this issue in his reflections on a Christian university: "Is a Different Kind of University Possible?" in *Towards a Society That Serves Its People: The Intellectual Contribution of El Salvador's Murdered Jesuits* (Washington, D.C.: Georgetown University Press, 1991) 177–207, trans. by Phillip Berryman from "Diez años después: ¿es posible una universidad distinta?" *ECA* 30, nos. 324–5 (1975) 605–28. See also Jon Sobrino's reflections on the "place" of Christian faith and theology in *The Principle of Mercy, Taking the Crucified People from the Cross* (Maryknoll, NY: Orbis, 1994) 30–6.

[66] And, it might be added that a "spirituality of ministerial priesthood" is equally subject to these requirements, something not always evident today. For an attempt to respond to these criteria, see Jon Sobrino, "Toward a Determination of the Nature of Priesthood: Service to God's Salvific Approach to Human Beings," in *The Principle of Mercy,* 105–43.

# Part Two

# Reception of Ellacuría's Thought

# Chapter 7

# Christian Salvation and the Disposition of Transcendence: Ignacio Ellacuría's Historical Soteriology

*Kevin F. Burke,* S.J.

From the beginning of the church until today, Christian thinkers have wrestled with the question of how to construe the disposition of transcendence toward human reality. How can theology speak coherently and convincingly about the relationship between the realm of God and the human world? Framed in terms of cosmology, the issue concerns the relationship of heaven and earth. It also appears in the christological controversies regarding the two natures of Jesus Christ and in the Reformation disputes concerning grace and freedom. Neo-Scholastic theology engages the problem when it devises a philosophical distinction of planes between the supernatural and the natural. Following the meeting of the Latin American Bishops' Conference that took place at Medellín, Colombia, in 1968, Latin American theologians began confronting this question in soteriological categories, above all in the language of salvation and liberation. Ignacio Ellacuría represents an important voice in this more recent chorus. In a key text dealing with soteriology and ecclesiology, he defines liberation theology in terms of the effort to articulate the link between the divine and the human.

> The theology of liberation understands itself as a reflection from faith on the historical reality and action of the people of God, who follow the

169

work of Jesus in announcing and fulfilling the Kingdom. It understands itself as an action by the people of God in following the work of Jesus and, as Jesus did, it tries to establish *a living connection between the world of God and the human world*.[1]

Ellacuría's special concern with soteriology appears in his first published collection of theological essays, *Freedom Made Flesh*.[2] Here, too, he frames the question of salvation in terms that evoke the structure of the divine-human relationship: salvation history is a salvation in and of history. This formula might seem simplistic, but Ellacuría uses it to invest the Christian vision with a profound, historically conscious, philosophical realism. The first term, "salvation history," refers to the great salvific acts of God that break into the history of Israel and the movement begun by Jesus. But Ellacuría insists that "[t]here is not only a salvation history, but salvation must be historical."[3] Hence, theology does not discharge its responsibility by simply reciting salvation history or analyzing its transcendent logic in systematic concepts. Theology itself must *be* salvific. It does not conceive a merely notional connection between the realm of God and the human world, but embodies a real, living connection. It cannot simply point to a salvation that occurred once and for all. Rather, as the ideological moment of ecclesial praxis,[4] it must embrace and practically mediate a salvation that is longed for and desperately needed right now. Nor can soteriology focus exclusively on a salvation that occurs "after" or "beyond" this life. It must seek to render a concrete account of Christian hope (1 Pet 3:15) that relates the eschatological fullness of salvation to its actualization in particular historical situations. In short, Ellacuría insists, "[s]alvation should not be understood univocally nor should it be understood as if the human being were a spirit without history, without incarnation in the world, nor as if salvation in the hereafter were not supposed to be signified, to be made into a sign, in the here and now."[5]

Behind Ellacuría's insistence that salvation radically involve history lurks a concern. When theology fails to adequately account for its historical element, it tends to produce an abstract theoretical *notion* of salvation that corresponds to an empty theological *ethic* and a distorted, potentially destructive ecclesial *praxis*. In the extreme, ahistorical theologies of salvation seem either mythological and incredible or boring and irrelevant. More seriously, they not only misrepresent what salvation involves, they actively thwart and oppose God's salvific will by imprisoning the truth in injustice and covertly participating in the corresponding oppression of the children of God (Rom 1:18). This way of putting the problem is characteristic of Ellacuría's theological vision. These three considerations—notion, ethics, and praxis—correspond to the practical imperatives that orient humans in reality and account for the threefold structure of theological method: theology as *reflection* on, as *option* for, and as *active response* to the reign of God revealed in and through history.[6] A few words about this threefold method are in order.

Ellacuría maintains that human intellection entails more than the accumulation of facts or the interpretation of meaning. It involves facing reality and allowing oneself to be confronted by the burdens and demands of reality. In his view, theological method mirrors the encounter with historical reality. First, prior to conceptualizing what they know, humans grasp realities simply and primordially through the exercise of their "sentient intelligence" that functions in the first place on behalf of biological survival.[7] The awareness of reality is not generated by mere sentience, nor does it occur through the meditation of a detached or "pure" reason. Rather, it follows from the activity of the human's grounded, embodied intelligence and issues in an engaged and active knowing. Second, the encounter with historical reality involves a primary option regarding the specific place where one locates oneself so as to most adequately apprehend reality. The element of place clearly has spatial-temporal vertices, but it also involves historical, cultural, social, political, and economic aspects. Thus, as a dimension of theological method, the option of place involves finding the most advantageous social-historical location from which to do theology. Third, just as knowing includes opting for an adequate place from which to know, the option only becomes actual as praxis. The encounter with reality is conditioned by historical reality and, in its turn, it shapes and reshapes that reality. Similarly, theology is a praxis. It achieves its end not in an abstract search for the truth about reality, but in an active commitment to foster the full realization of reality.[8]

Ellacuría emphasizes that the three levels of the encounter with reality do not unfold in a temporal sequence. They occur mutually and simultaneously. Hence, theology does not first conceptualize a faith content, then take up an ethical stance on the basis of that conceptualization and, as a final step, adopt a pastoral praxis in response to these first two. Nor does it invert this schema—as some superficial explanations of liberation theology would have it—and begin with praxis, move to an ethical stance, and from there conceptualize the faith. Rather, Ellacuría's method starts from the integral human encounter with historical reality. When confronting the problems of living in and among realities, the three dimensions of human intellection—intelligent apprehension, ethical stance, and praxis—operate in dynamic tension. Likewise, every act of theological reflection and production is simultaneously a noetic exercise, a deployment of one's fundamental ethical stance, and a historically real praxis. Conceiving theological method in this contextually embedded, praxis-oriented way allows Ellacuría to align the universal character of theological assertions with the critical exigence generated by historical consciousness.

The concrete operation of Ellacuría's method appears most clearly in the critical-constructive process that he calls the *historicization* of concepts:

> The prevailing tendency today of measuring the truth by the way it functions, rather than making it more difficult to recognize the theoretical validity of theology, reminds theology to elaborate anew the meaning of Christianity in terms of historical validity. With this there appears a principle of theological historicization which compels theology to refer to historical reality as the place of verification.[9]

Historicization does not primarily seek to articulate the history of a concept. In theology, for example, it aims first at uncovering the connections between theological affirmations and the historical realities that initially gave rise to them, whether these represent the original medium of a divine revelation or the elaboration of that revelation in scripture, liturgy, dogma, and so on. Its critical function guards against idealized interpretations of the media of revelation and faith transmission, and overly literal views of how those instruments transcribe God's presence. Constructively, it discovers the logic at work in the human experiences that gave rise to the faith tradition to foster new encounters with that faith as living and real. But the task of historicization is not simply that of historical research. Ellacuría uses this process to analyze the way theological affirmations continue to operate in current historical situations. He is aware that every interpretation of divine reality has concrete implications in this world. As the conquest of the Americas dramatically illustrates, these implications can include theologically justified plunder, slavery, and the dismemberment of other religious traditions. As the present world economic order demonstrates, far too many Christians and Christian churches live comfortably ignorant of the realities of impoverishment, political disenfranchizement, and cultural marginalization that make their comfort possible. In its critical moment, historicization unmasks these distortions and the damage they have caused. As a constructive operation, it helps the ecclesial community discern and respond to the signs of God's active reign in the present moment. In a word, it helps Christians be Christian.

In this essay, I examine how Ellacuría historicizes the Christian understanding of salvation in order to produce what he calls a historical soteriology, a credible, morally challenging, and efficacious account of how the salvation mediated by Jesus Christ continues to take flesh in history. I divide my analysis into three sections that bear a broad correspondence to the threefold structure of his method. Beginning with the ethical character of theology, I analyze Ellacuría's option to do theology from the place of the victims of history whom he names *the crucified peoples*. In particular, I examine the salvation theory he develops in conjunction with this privileged place. Second, turning to theological praxis, I sketch the ongoing incarnation of Christian salvation in the church's historical efforts on behalf of the crucified peoples. For Ellacuría, the actions that rescue history's victims from oppression and violence serve as *historical sacraments* of a liberating, eschatological salvation that corresponds to the advent of the reign of God. Third, I return to the disposition of transcendence and examine how Ellacuría's historical soteriology corresponds to a theory of *Christian historical transcendence*. I conclude with an assessment of his historical-theologal approach to the divine-human relationship.[10]

## 1. The Crucified Peoples

Ellacuría observes that in both the direct encounter with historical reality and the subsequent reflection on the faith dimension of that encounter, human individuals and communities stand in a particular place. In the dynamic interplay with reality, they continually move from place to place, presumably seeking those places that augment their human flourishing. Similarly, the element of place—both as physical-geographical and social-historical location—proves crucial for the life of faith and theological reflection on that faith. From Abraham and Moses to the disciples of Jesus, the stories of faith include pointed references to the places where God is encountered. Likewise, these narratives highlight the divine invitation to change one's place, to go on a journey, to enter a new land, to follow as a disciple, to be sent on a mission. In all these stories, faith is intrinsically conditioned by the places where faith is experienced and expressed, and believers are attracted to holy places where God draws near to them.

Alluding to this revelatory logic, Ellacuría maintains that theological reflection exists in dialectical relation to the place where that reflection occurs. As the theologian's primary stance within historical reality structures her encounter with reality, her option for a particular *theological place* structures that primary ethical stance. What one encounters and who one becomes both depend on where one places oneself within historical reality. At the same time, Ellacuría reserves room for the suspicion that not every place serves equally well as a place for divine manifestation or theological reflection. This is so because the historical praxis that continues redefining historical reality has been sundered by sin and remains marked by sin's conflict with grace.

> If historical praxis is a divided praxis, if in this divided historical praxis the Reign of God and the reign of evil become present and operative, if the ecclesial praxis cannot be neutral with respect to this division and this operative presence, if the theological task receives its truth, its verification, from its incarnation in the true ecclesial praxis, in a truly Christian ecclesial praxis, then it must be asked, in what form of ecclesial praxis should its ideological moment of theological production incarnate itself? Appealing to the Reign of God is not quite enough. Rather, it is necessary to determine the place in which the truth of the Reign of God is most accessible.[11]

The question arises inexorably. Where in this world riven by sin is the truth of the reign of God most accessible? The words of Jesus in the Gospel of St. Luke provide a clue. "Blessed are you who are poor, for the reign of God is yours" (Luke 6:20). Speaking from the historical context of Latin America, Ellacuría expands on this response. "The poor of Latin America are theological place insofar as they constitute the maximum and scandalous, prophetic and apocalyptic presence of the Christian God and, consequently, the privileged place of Christian praxis and reflection."[12] Drawing on the meditation at the foot of the cross from the *Spiritual Exercises* of St. Ignatius Loyola, Ellacuría intensifies this insight with a dramatic and compact image. We find access to the God of Jesus among *the crucified peoples,* "that collective body, which as the majority of humankind owes its situation of crucifixion to the way society is organized and maintained by a minority that exercises its dominion through a series of factors, which taken together and given their concrete impact within history, must be regarded as sin."[13]

In the first week of the *Spiritual Exercises,* Ignatius instructs the person making the retreat to kneel before the cross of Jesus and ask, "What have I done for Christ? What am I doing for Christ? What ought I to do for Christ?"[14] In his adaptation of this exercise, Ellacuría calls upon Christians to focus their "eyes and hearts upon these peoples who are suffering so much, some from misery and hunger, others from oppression and repression, and then, before this people thus crucified, to make the colloquy . . . by asking, what have I done to crucify them? What am I doing in order to uncrucify them? What ought I to do so that this people will be raised?"[15]

Ellacuría does not risk this scandalous allusion merely to coin a clever metaphor. Nor does he intend the image of crucified people to refer to human suffering in general. Rather, in an effort to historicize the Christian intuition regarding the real presence of the suffering Christ, he examines the death of Jesus from the perspective of those whose historically inflicted torments are tantamount to crucifixion. At the same time, he probes the oppression of such peoples from the perspective of the Cross of Jesus. Accordingly, both the critical and constructive moments of his method are activated in this mutual identification. On the one hand, the crosses of the crucified peoples represent historical realities. They are the fruit of historical choices. Thus, Ellacuría uses the language of crucified people to uncover and condemn historical mortal sins such as poverty, persecution, and violence against innocent peoples. On the other hand, this language evokes a powerful, constructive theological insight: these crosses also represent places where salvific grace irrupts into history. "What Christian faith adds to the historical confirmation of the oppressed people is the suspicion which asks whether, besides being the principle addressee of the salvific effort, this people not also be in its crucified situation a principle of salvation for the entire world."[16]

In the light of this suspicion, Ellacuría develops one line of soteriological interpretation. He draws upon the figure of the Servant of Yahweh (Second Isaiah) whom the Christian tradition has long associated with Jesus. This central identification does not preclude the association of other historical persons or groups with the Servant, although from a Christian perspective it does specify concrete criteria for making such an association. The figure of the Servant embraces all who participate in the Servant's mission, including "anyone unjustly crucified for the sins of humans, because all the crucified form a single unit, one sole reality, even though this reality has a head and members with different functions in the unity of expiation."[17] The logic of salvation revealed in the Servant unfolds as follows. The Servant is persecuted, ostensibly for remaining faithful to Yahweh. The sufferings inflicted upon him crush him. Those who witness his tragedy assume that God has rejected him and, in line with their own theological presuppositions, they conclude that he was a sinner and bury him among sinners. But the inspired author intuits that the sins for which he was punished were not his own sins. He shoulders the sins of others. Because he did this willingly and for the sake of others, the Servant achieves a victory that could not have been imagined or predicted, a victory only God could have produced.

> Because of his affliction
>    he shall see the light in fullness of days;
> Through his suffering, my servant shall justify many,
>    and their guilt he shall bear.
> Therefore I will give him his portion among the great,
>    and he shall divide the spoils with the mighty,
> Because he surrendered himself to death
>    and was counted among the wicked;
> And he shall take away the sins of many,
>    and win pardon for their offenses. (Isa 53:11-12)

In this text, the victory of the Servant involves the justification of the guilty and the forgiveness of their sins. In a word, the victory is salvation, and the medium of salvation is the victim of the sin. Ellacuría simply extends the line running from the Servant of Yahweh as the one who bears the sin of the world, through the crucified Christ as savior, to the crucified people. Based on the similarity between the passion of Jesus and the passion of the crucified peoples, Ellacuría develops the intuition that the latter appear not only as victim of the sin of the world, but as the world's judge and savior. They represent the judge in history insofar as their "judgment is salvation, insofar as it unveils the sin of the world by opposing it, insofar as it makes possible the redoing of what has been done badly, and insofar as it proposes a new exigency as the unavoidable way to achieve salvation."[18] They represent the Savior in history because they epitomize the crucified Body of Christ that bears the sins of the world in order to save the world.

The option to do theology from the place of the crucified peoples unmasks all attempts to interpret the crucifixion of Jesus in a way that spiritualizes or justifies it. However, this critical, christocentric historicization of the Servant does not allow us to render as final or exclusive just any correlation between a particular suffering people and the Servant-savior. Nor does it short-circuit the Christian community's responsibility for careful, prayerful discernment regarding who, at any given moment, embodies Christian salvation in history. Nevertheless, this identification between historical victims and the crucified Christ is important, for it indicates that certain peoples are called in their sufferings to the Servant's vocation. Moreover, by educing criteria for ongoing discernment from the traits of the Servant found in Jesus, the Christian community can approximate what the Servant figure will look like in our day.[19] Ellacuría emphasizes that the designation, crucified peoples, must remain imprecise so as not to inappropriately impose itself on any given situation. However, it is sufficiently precise to avoid confusing it with what clearly does *not* represent the crucified peoples, above all, those who are in fact crucifiers.

## 2. The Historical Sacrament of a Liberating, Eschatological Salvation

Ellacuría's historical soteriology unfolds from the theological place of the crucified people and as a theological option to be in solidarity with them. This allows the faith community to reflect on the passion of Jesus while remaining in direct contact with those who continue his suffering in history. However, as noted above, Ellacuría not only interprets the death of Jesus through the crucified people; he interprets the peoples and their sufferings from the crucifixion of Jesus. In this way, he guards against a tendency to romanticize the poor or exaggerate the salvific function of suffering.

> The focus on the death of Jesus and the crucifixion of the people, the fact that they refer back and forth to each other, makes both take on a new light. The crucifixion of the people avoids the danger of mystifying the death of Jesus and the death of Jesus avoids the danger of extolling salvifically the mere fact of the crucifixion of the people, as though the brute fact of being crucified of itself were to bring about resurrection and life.[20]

From the Servant of Yahweh to Jesus, to the crucified people of our day, God's saving presence becomes historically actual in and through the active bearing of the sin of the world. Nevertheless, *bearing* the sin of the world does not exhaust the positive content of God's salvation. Preceding the death of Jesus, the life of Jesus manifests its own salvific logic and content, refracted above all through the image of the reign of God that Jesus preached and inaugurated. Salvation appears as the *coming* of the reign of God and its *overcoming* the reign of sin. Following the death of Jesus, his disciples encounter him alive, resurrected, and exalted, and themselves as forgiven and commissioned. They begin to share their faith through an evangelical praxis that also manifests a salvific logic and content. Under the impact of resurrection faith, salvation appears as the *conquering* of death and the *forgiving* of sins. Moreover, their life of faith, empowered by the Spirit that raised Jesus from the dead, gives rise to the historical reality of the church. Thus, while the death of Jesus encompasses one crucial aspect of the salvation he brings, his life in service of the reign of God, his resurrection from death, and his presence in the church through the Spirit provide others.[21]

In his analysis and historicization of salvation, Ellacuría assumes the logic of this more encompassing approach to the question of how Jesus saves us. As the crucified people bear the death of Jesus in their suffering and so participate in the salvation he brings, the church, in its faith, bears witness to his resurrection. Likewise, in its ecclesial praxis, above all, in its praxis of "bringing the crucified peoples down from their crosses," the church continues what he began: the realization of God's reign in history. Hence, the place of the crucified people in the unfolding of God's salvific plan does not displace or render secondary the salvific vocation of the church. On the contrary, it powerfully underscores the necessity of the church, and does so precisely in and for a secularized culture that has all but discarded the church as irrelevant to faith or a hindrance to authentic spirituality.

Approaching ecclesiology from the perspective of historical soteriology, Ellacuría explores several christological images traditionally employed to explain the reality of the church. In particular, he links the New Testament image of the "Body of Christ" to the image of the church as the "sacrament of salvation." Characteristically, he historicizes both of these images, as he historicizes the reality that connects them, God's merciful love for the crucified peoples. The church is called to be *the Body of Christ in history*. It does this by following the historical footsteps and taking up the historical mission of Jesus. Above all, this means that the church becomes the historical Body of Christ (1) by devoting itself entirely to the reign of God that Jesus proclaimed, and (2) by choosing to be "neighbor to the robbers' victim" (Luke 10.36), that is, by entering into profound historical solidarity with the crucified peoples. The sacramental realization of this mission and this solidarity leads Ellacuría to view the church as *the historical sacrament of liberation*. Consequently, the church fulfills its sacramental vocation to mediate salvation to history when it makes concrete both the critical and constructive demands of the reign of God in each historical situation. The church fulfills the critical demand of God's reign when it prophetically denounces the crucifying powers of this world. It takes up its constructive task when—in deed even more than word—it announces that the reign of God draws near as salvation/liberation of the poor in relation to their terrible situation of captivity and death.

Ellacuría insists that this sacramentality of the church flows from the original sacramentality of Jesus. A parallel logic appears. As Jesus' Body becomes the sacramental symbol of the salvation he mediates, so too the church's bodiliness enables it to continue making that salvation present in history. As christology needs to approach the whole mystery of Jesus Christ by beginning from his historical corporeality, ecclesiology needs to approach the salvific sacramentality of the church from its historical corporeality. "Seen theologically, *being embodied* corresponds to the Word, which *took flesh* so that it could be seen and touched, so that it could intervene in a fully historical way in the action of humanity."[22] For the church to be the Body of Christ in history, it must be present to history through particular historical actions that continue and correspond to the life of Jesus. The center of gravity in all the church's sacramental activity, which includes but is not restricted to its liturgies and sacramental celebrations, must parallel the concern that gave focus to the ministry of Jesus: the advent of the reign of God. "The church realizes its historical, salvific sacramentality by announcing and realizing the Reign of God in history. Its fundamental praxis consists in the realization of the Reign of God in history, in action that leads to the Reign of God being realized in history."[23]

How does the church first discover and then align itself with the reign of God that Jesus preached? Ellacuría maintains that although the scholarly quest for the historical Jesus is important, by itself it does not suffice. The theological encounter with Jesus, if it is to correspond to Jesus, needs to occur in the place of the poor, the place where Jesus first preached the Good News. If it is to enable the church to continue embodying the salvation borne by Jesus, it must take effect as praxis, the praxis of a discipleship that practices what it preaches: the coming of God's reign as life, hope, and justice, both now and forever. Following Ellacuría's theological method, therefore, the church appears as the historical sacrament of a liberating, eschatological salvation. As a sacrament, "what the church contributes to the salvation of history is the constitutive sign of the history of salvation. The church belongs intrinsically to this history of salvation and carries within it the visible part that reveals and makes effective the whole of salvation."[24] Hence, the historicization of the church as sacrament does not reduce the mission of the church to working for changes in this world's social, economic, and political structures alone, just as Ellacuría's salvation in history does not reduce salvation to merely historical liberation. However, it does confront the church with what Dietrich Bonhoeffer accurately named "the cost of discipleship." It means the church cannot fulfill its vocation with its back turned to the crucified peoples of our world. On the contrary, it must seek them out, live in solidarity with them, announce God's Good News to them, and reflect to them the truth that they are God's beloved ones. At the same time, the church cannot back down in the face of this world's crucifiers. Rather, it must have the courage to approach them, evangelize them, unmask them, and when necessary denounce them prophetically from the heart of its eschatological vision.

## 3. Christian Historical Transcendence

I return now to the problem with which I introduced this essay: How can theology best conceive the disposition of transcendence toward and in relation to human reality? The theological method at work in Ellacuría's historical soteriology provides an approach to this problem. In his method, the place and praxis of historical reality provide the arena for the revelation of God's gift of salvation and subsequent theological reflection on the implications of that gift. As we have noted, he probes the content of salvation from the place of the crucified peoples whose tragic historical situation cries out for liberation. He does so as part of the praxis of an ecclesial community called to proclaim and realize the reign of God. Thus, in a real way, even prior to conceptualizing how the realm of God connects to the human world, Ellacuría has anticipated a response to the question through the dynamics of his theological method. Still, the question calls for conceptual formulation as well. What do the proclamation and realization of the reign of God have to do with historical liberation? What does historical liberation have to do with proclaiming and realizing the reign of God? These questions drive liberation theology. Not surprisingly, they also provoke the most serious criticism of this movement, namely, that it results in the practical negation of the transcendent *as reality*. I briefly touch on Ellacuría's response to this charge as a way of introducing the *historical-theologal structure* of reality, the consideration with which I conclude these reflections on his historical soteriology.

The concern that liberation theology reduces transcendence to history appears, for example, in the "Instruction on Certain Aspects of the 'Theology of Liberation'" issued in 1984 by the Vatican Congregation for the Doctrine of the Faith. While addressing a variety of complaints, including the use of Marxist forms of social analysis by liberation theologians, the Instruction focuses its central theological concern on the disposition of transcendence. "The different theologies of liberation are situated between the preferential option for the poor forcefully reaffirmed without ambiguity after Medellín at the conference of Puebla on the one hand, and the temptation *to reduce the gospel to an earthly gospel* on the other."[25] Ellacuría appreciates that this temptation represents a real danger and acknowledges the legitimacy in principle of the Vatican's critique. After summarizing the description of liberation theology criticized in the Instruction, he observes:

> This description of a hypothetical theology of liberation rejects affirmations which ought to be rejected. These include: (1) identifying—in such a way that they are taken as one and the same thing—the unfolding of the Reign of God with movements of human liberation from earthly enslavements; (2) the even more serious identification of God and history, such that they would be one and the same thing; (3) the total subordination of the affirmations of faith or theology to purely political criteria; (4) abandoning the idea of sin; (5) reducing sin to social sin; (6) abandoning evangelization and focusing completely on earthly liberation. No one would have any problem rejecting as unchristian and as objectively incompatible with the faith each and every one of these affirmations, as long as this did not presume to reject the necessary connection of the Reign of God with human liberation, of God with history, of affirmations of faith and theology with significant political affirmations, of sin in relation to God with sin in relation to humans, of personal sin with social sin, of evangelization with liberation.[26]

In this text, Ellacuría stakes out parameters for approaching the issue of the disposition of transcendence. He sees the very concept of transcendence as "something that calls attention to a contextual structural difference without implying a duality, something that enables us to speak of an intrinsic unity without implying a strict identity."[27] Hence, on the one hand, he clearly seeks to avoid the reductionism criticized by the Vatican Instruction, a type of monism that collapses transcendence into history. But on the other hand, he guards against the opposite tendency, a pernicious dualism that severs the sacred from the profane and conceives transcendence in an ahistorical and idealistic fashion.[28] This second extreme runs through the history of theology. It often cloaks itself in piety and promotes its perspectives in the name of orthodoxy. However, it contradicts the biblical framework for understanding how God acts in history and how history represents the essential arena for apprehending God. It takes the position that "the transcendent must be outside or beyond what is immediately apprehended as real, so that the transcendent must always be other, different and separated, whether in time, in space or in its essence."[29] While emphasizing the distance between the realm of God and the human world, it stresses the otherworldly disposition of transcendence and the miraculous character of its interventions in history. It attempts, in this way, to safeguard the reality and value of transcendence. Nevertheless, its very logic backfires. By trying to separate and identify which actions represent merely human actions and which come from God, it intrinsically identifies God as one actor among many—albeit the main actor—and thus assumes a rough parity between divine and human actions. As a result, it *confuses* transcendence and history and results in the very reductionism it is trying to prevent.[30]

The mutilation of transcendence in the name of transcendence produces a collateral casualty. It undermines the reality and value of history along with the multilayered dynamism of the human freedom that crafts history. "To be committed only to the religious aspect of the Reign [of God], without concern for its essential reference to the world and history, would be a clear betrayal of God's history; it would leave the field of history to the enemies of God."[31] Recognizing this, and in the name of a truly Christian view of the disposition of transcendence, Ellacuría staunchly defends the value of the human world, the centrality of human freedom, and the necessity of human liberation. To this end, he develops a trinitarian model of historical transcendence which assumes that the human world—historical reality—is a *theologal*-historical reality.

> The *theologal* dimension of the created world, which should not be confused with the *theological* dimension, would reside in that presence of the trinitarian life, which is intrinsic to all things, but which in human beings can be apprehended as reality and as the principle of personality. There is a strict experience of this theologal dimension and through it there is a strict personal, social, and historical experience of God. This experience has different degrees and forms; but when it is a true experience of the real theologal dimension of human beings, of society, of history, and in a different measure, of purely material things, it is an experience and physical probing of the triune life itself, however mediated, incarnated, and historicized.[32]

This understanding of the human world as a theologal-historical reality corresponds to an understanding of creation as "the molding *ad extra* of the trinitarian life itself . . . an act of communication and self-giving by the divine life itself."[33] In this view, every thing by its very nature represents a limited way of being God. "It would not simply be that God is in all things, as essence, presence and potential, depending on the character of those things; it would be that all things, each in its own mode, have been molded according to the triune life and refer essentially to that life."[34]

In summary, Ellacuría construes the disposition of transcendence as something "that transcends *in* and not as something that transcends *away from;* as something that physically impels to *more* but not by taking *out of;* as something that pushes *forward,* but at the same time *retains."*[35] He utilizes both the critical and constructive impulses of his method to maintain the delicate balance between the absolute "otherness" of the God who transcends history and the absolute "nearness" of the God who transcends in history. Based on the biblical witness, he argues that the transcendence of God does not simply involve distance and separation; it also involves nearness and the radical unity of God's history. More specifically, the utterly transcendent God draws near to the crucified peoples after hearing their cries of distress. The transcendent God becomes involved in their historical struggle for liberation, their historical need for healing, for restoration, for salvation. In this, the essential logic of historical soteriology appears. First, this interpretation of the disposition of transcendence, with its emphasis on a transcendent God who draws near to suffering humanity, has been revealed *by God.* Second, God draws near to *suffering* humanity, the crucified people. God draws near, above all, through the life, death, and resurrection of the crucified Jesus, who manifests in his own historical reality the reality and gratuity of God's reign. Third, by drawing near to the crucified people, the transcendent God *saves* them. Moreover, this drawing near reveals the way to salvation for all: the way of Jesus and the way of the reign of God. Therefore, the essential and primary disposition of transcendence appears in the salvation of creation. It appears *as* salvation-in-history, that is, a historical salvation that brings the crucified peoples down from their crosses and an eschatological salvation that reveals in history the end of history-as-crucifixion.

---

[1] Ignacio Ellacuría, "La Iglesia de los pobres, sacramento histórico de liberación," *Mysterium Liberationis* 2 (San Salvador: UCA Editores, 1993) 127; emphasis mine. Originally published in *ECA,* nos. 348–9 (1977) 707–22; collection hereafter cited as *ML* (Spanish original) and *MLT* (English translation); essay hereafter cited as "Sacramento histórico" (1977). All citations of Ellacuría's writings are to the Spanish; translations are my own unless otherwise indicated. Works that have appeared in English translation are cited in brackets [*MLT* (1994) 543].

[2] Ignacio Ellacuría, *Teología política* (San Salvador: Ediciones del Secretariado Social Interdiocesano, 1973), trans. by John Drury as *Freedom Made Flesh: The Mission of*

*Christ and His Church* (Maryknoll, NY: Orbis , 1976); original collection hereafter cited as *TP,* English translation as *FMF.*

³ Ignacio Ellacuría, "Liberación: misión y carisma de la iglesia latinoamericana" (1971) *TP,* 74, hereafter cited as "Liberación: misión y carisma" [*FMF* (1976) 134].

⁴ See Ignacio Ellacuría, "La teología como momento ideológico de la praxis eclesial," *Estudios Eclesiásticos,* no. 207 (1978) 457–6, hereafter cited as "Teología como praxis" (1978).

⁵ "Liberación: misión y carisma" (1971) *TP,* 74 [*FMF* (1976) 134–5].

⁶ Ellacuría weaves these three considerations together in a passage remarkable for its compact wordplay and depth. The "act of confronting ourselves with real things in their reality" involves the noetic dimension of intelligence, "realizing the weight of reality" *[el hacerse cargo de la realidad],* the ethical dimension, "shouldering the weight of reality" *[el cargar con la realidad],* and the praxis-oriented dimension, "taking charge of the weight of reality" *[el encargarse de la realidad];* see Ignacio Ellacuría, "Hacia una fundamentación filosófica del método teológico latinoamericano," in E. Ruiz Maldonado, ed., *Liberación y cautiverio: debates en torno al metodo de la teología en América Latina* (Mexico City, August 11–15, 1975) 626, hereafter cited as "Hacia una fundamentación." For an exegesis of this dense passage and a fuller treatment of the foundations and operations of Ellacuría's threefold theological method, see my book, *The Ground Beneath the Cross: The Theology of Ignacio Ellacuría* (Washington, D.C.: Georgetown University Press, 2000) 99–149.

⁷ See "Hacia una fundamentación" (1975) 624–9. Ellacuría takes his understanding of sentient intelligence from his philosophical mentor, Xavier Zubiri. He also helped Zubiri publish an important three-volume work on this theme. For an overview of Ellacuría's relationship with Zubiri, see *The Ground Beneath the Cross,* 26–33; for a brief analysis of this distinctive theory of knowledge, see ibid., 43–53.

⁸ This claim resonates with Marx's famous eleventh thesis on Feuerbach: "The philosophers have only interpreted the world, in various ways; the point, however, is to change it." Karl Marx, "Theses on Feuerbach," in R. Tucker, ed., *The Marx-Engels Reader,* 2nd ed. (New York: W. W. Norton, 1978) 145. However, Ellacuría does not simply rework Marx. His view of praxis reflects his own conviction that reality has priority over meaning. "Precisely because of this priority of reality over meaning, no real change of meaning occurs without a real change of reality; to attempt the first without intending the second is to falsify the intelligence and its primary function, even in the purely cognitive order," "Hacia una fundamentación," (1975) 626. It should be noted that Ellacuría imputes a precise, technical meaning to the phrase "the realization of reality" which corresponds to his conviction that reality is essentially dynamic; see Ignacio Ellacuría, "El objeto de la filosofía" (1981), in *Filosofía de la realidad histórica* (San Salvador: UCA Editores, 1990) 33–5, 38–41.

⁹ Ignacio Ellacuría, "Tesis sobre la posibilidad, necesidad y sentido de una teología latinoamericana," thesis no. 2.5, in A. Vargas Machuca, ed., *Teología y mundo contemporáneo: homenaje a Karl Rahner en su 70 cumpleaños* (Madrid: Ediciones Cristiandad, 1975) 326.

¹⁰ The *theologal* is "the dimension in which the person, because he is connected to reality, is more than himself, even while, at every minute, he is a pilgrim utterly awed

by the power of the real. . . . There is a theologal dimension of things and from this dimension a religious encounter with God is possible, a theological as well as a philosophical encounter." Ignacio Ellacuría, "Zubiri, filósofo teologal," *Vida Nueva,* no. 1249 (1980) 45, author's emphasis.

[11] Ellacuría, "Teología como praxis" (1978) 473.

[12] Ignacio Ellacuría, "Los pobres, 'lugar teológico' en América Latina," *Conversión de la Iglesia al Reino de Dios. Para anunciarlo y realizarlo en la historia* (Santander: Editorial Sal Terrae, 1984) 163; first published in *Misión Abierta,* nos. 4–5 (1981) 225–40.

[13] Ignacio Ellacuría, "El pueblo crucificado, ensayo de soteriología histórica," *ML,* vol. 2, 201, trans. Berryman and Barr; first published in I. Ellacuría, and others, *Cruz y resurrección: anuncio de una Iglesia nueva* (Mexico City: CTR, 1978) 49–82, hereafter cited as "El pueblo crucificado" (1978) [*MLT* (1994) 590].

[14] Ignatius Loyola, *The Spiritual Exercises of Saint Ignatius,* no. 53, trans. and ed. by G. Ganss (St. Louis: Institute of Jesuit Sources, 1992) 42.

[15] Ignacio Ellacuría, "Las Iglesias latinoamericanas interpelan a la Iglesia de España," *Sal Terrae,* no. 826 (1982) 230.

[16] Ellacuría, "El pueblo crucificado" (1978) *ML,* vol. 2, 202 [*MLT* (1994) 591].

[17] Ibid., 210 [598].

[18] Ibid., 215 [603].

[19] "The most basic is that it be accepted as the Servant by God; that acceptance, however, cannot be established except through its 'likeness' to what happened to the Jesus who was crucified in history. Therefore, it will have to be crucified for the sins of the world, it will have to have become what the worldly have cast out, and its appearance will not be human precisely because it has been dehumanized; it will have to have a high degree of universality, since it will have to be a figure that redeems the whole world; it will have to suffer this utter dehumanization, not for its sins but because it bears the sins of others; it will have to be cast out and despised precisely as savior of the world, in such a way that this world does not accept it as its savior, but on the contrary judges it as the most complete expression of what must be avoided and even condemned; and finally, there must be a connection between its passion and the working out of the Reign of God," ibid., 213–4, trans. Berryman and Barr [601–2].

[20] Ibid., 203–4, trans. Berryman and Barr [592].

[21] This approach does not require that one agree with Pannenberg's view of history and his distinctive way of arguing that the resurrection is a "historical" event; see Wolfhart Pannenberg, *Jesus—God and Man,* trans. Lewis Wilkins and Duane Priebe (Philadelphia: Westminster Press, 1968). Nor does it contradict the approach of other contemporary theologians (Schillebeeckx, Haight, Sobrino) who insist that the resurrection is best viewed as a *transhistorical* event or—to use Ellacuría's phrase—as a *theologal* reality. The focus here is on the manifestation of the resurrection to human consciousness, its being grasped in human hope. The faith-hope grasp of the resurrection occurs in historical reality, even thought the content of that "grasp" cannot be historically verified or disconfirmed.

[22] Ellacuría, "Sacramento histórico" (1977) *ML,* vol. 2, 130, trans. Wilde; author's emphasis [*MLT* (1994) 545]. Ellacuría adds: "One can say that the true historical body of Christ, and therefore the preeminent locus of his embodiment and his incorporation,

is not only the church, but the poor and the oppressed of the world, so that the church alone is not the historical body of Christ, and it is possible to speak of a true body of Christ outside the church," ibid., 184, trans. Wilde [546].

²³ Ibid., 134 [548].

²⁴ Ibid., 141 [554].

²⁵ Congregation for the Doctrine of the Faith, "Instruction on Certain Aspects of the 'Theology of Liberation,'" Vatican City, Aug. 6, 1984, section VI, no. 5; reprinted in A. Hennelly, ed., *Liberation Theology: A Documentary History* (Maryknoll, NY: Orbis, 1990) 400; emphasis mine.

²⁶ Ignacio Ellacuría, "Estudio teológico-pastoral de la 'Instrucción sobre algunos aspectos de la teología de la liberación,'" *RLT*, no. 2 (1984) 155–6. As this text insinuates, Ellacuría argues that the positions identified with liberation theology in the Instruction in fact represent a caricature of that theology. The limits of the present essay do not permit a detailed examination of this important point.

²⁷ Ignacio Ellacuría, "Historicidad de la salvación cristiana" *ML*, vol. 1, 327, trans. Wilde; first published in *RLT*, no. 1 (1984) 5–45 [*MLT* (1994) 254].

²⁸ In fact, Ellacuría implies that at least some of the misreadings of liberation theology manifest an "idealistic reductionism" that issues in an uncritical understanding of transcendence corresponding to this second extreme; see Ignacio Ellacuría, "La superación del reduccionismo idealista en Zubiri," *ECA*, no. 477 (1988) 633–50; Burke, *The Ground Beneath the Cross*, 44–6.

²⁹ Ellacuría, "Historicidad de la salvación cristiana" (1984) *ML*, vol. 1, 328, trans. Wilde [*MLT* (1994) 254].

³⁰ Ibid., 354 [274].

³¹ Ibid., 353 [273].

³² Ibid., 358, trans. Wilde; emphasis Wilde [277].

³³ Ibid., 358 [276].

³⁴ Ibid., 358 [277].

³⁵ Ibid., 328, trans. Wilde; author's/translator's emphasis [254].

# Chapter 8

# Ecclesiology from Below:
# Principles from Ignacio Ellacuría

*Roger Haight, S.J.*

Few readers of theology would fail to recognize the phrase "christology from below." Since Karl Rahner's essay a few decades ago entitled "The Two Basic Types of Christology," which described and contrasted christology from below and christology from above, these phrases have become part of the working vocabulary of Catholic theologians.[1] This is not the case with respect to the phrase "ecclesiology from below." Although ecclesiology from below has been going forward in the Catholic Church since the Second Vatican Council, this designation, by analogy with christology from below, has not taken hold. This essay rests on the presupposition that "ecclesiology from below" clarifies some alternatives in the method and content of ecclesiology and is therefore useful for ecclesiological reflection. Let me briefly explain how I understand the category "ecclesiology from below" as distinct from "ecclesiology from above" on an abstract and formal level as a point of departure for this discussion. The essay will then begin to provide material content to the distinction.

I understand ecclesiology from below in terms of a set of principles and a method that guide reflection on the church. "Ecclesiology from below," therefore, points primarily to the method by which the discipline of ecclesiology or study of the church unfolds. It is thus primarily a heuristic and an epistemological category as distinct from an ontological category. This may be illustrated by the analogy with christology. Christology

187

is an academic discipline, and christology from below or from above indicates the epistemological premises, the starting point, and the axioms
of theological method that govern one's understanding of Jesus Christ.
As such "from below" or "from above" do not refer to the ontic dimensions of Jesus Christ, his humanity and the divine initiative in his life,
but to the "from" where and how one begins to understand Jesus Christ.
Analogously, ecclesiology from below will refer to a heuristic framework
for understanding the church, to a set of presuppositions that govern the
reflection, a point of departure, all of which contribute to a method by
which an understanding of the church is generated. Finally, the character of such a method will achieve a certain clarity by its contrast to an ecclesiology from above.

Ecclesiology from below received stimulus and incentive in the Catholic Church from Vatican II's Pastoral Constitution on the Church in the
Modern World. Shortly thereafter, Latin American liberation theology,
with special attention to ecclesiology and the mission of the church, became a focused and influential vehicle for disseminating in the church
at large an approach to understanding the church I am calling ecclesiology from below. It follows that liberation theologians generally, insofar
as they take up the nature and mission of the church, would be good
subjects for an analysis of an ecclesiology from below. The writings of
Ignacio Ellacuría thus provide a fitting subject matter for illustrating
several aspects of the character of an ecclesiology from below. The goal
of this essay, however, is not to develop an integral account of the method
of ecclesiology beginning from below. It is rather to draw forward and to
generalize certain principles of an ecclesiology from below as they are
represented in the theology of Ignacio Ellacuría.

My investigation will proceed in two stages. In the first part, I enu-
merate a series of principles exemplified in Ellacuría's theology and ecclesiology. In the second, I briefly indicate that there are still other principles
for an ecclesiology from below that need to be formulated. I then summarize those principles found in the theology of Ellacuría by generalizing
them and reducing them to six. In order to show the relevance of this, I
will contrast them with what goes on in an ecclesiology from above.

## 1. Ellacuría's Ecclesiology from Below

The theology of Ignacio Ellacuría contains a number of principles and
conceptions typical of an ecclesiology from below. With this overview, I
do not intend an integral account of Ellacuría's ecclesiology. My goal is

rather quite focused; it is to gather together certain aspects of his theology which are typical of an ecclesiology from below. Despite this principle of selectivity, one will be able to recognize the broad lines of Ellacuría's ecclesiology in the series of perspectives on the church that follow.

*A Liberationist Conception of Method in Theology.* One of the most important elements of Ellacuría's ecclesiology from below is lodged in his conception of the discipline of theology, one shared with other liberation theologians. Liberation theology is "reflection from faith on the historical reality and action of the people of God, who follow the work of Jesus in announcing and fulfilling the Kingdom."[2] Theological reflection has as its objective focus or medium the concrete faith praxis of the community. This object is less the formulas of belief or the history of Christian symbols, although these are not excluded. Rather, theology envisages the living faith of the community as it unfolds in its historical life. Thus, theology is an action itself. It aims at establishing a connection between the sphere of God and human history. Moreover, it leads to historical action. Informed by faith, it has no room for faith without works, but seeks to encourage people to engage God's presence in history.

Theology is an act of reflection, in itself an ecclesial praxis, placed in a wider context of the church's role in history and in service of the church's historical praxis. Because theology is a historical action, it is historically measured and defined as occurring in a particular place at a particular time. However, most important in the definition is the logic of doing theology: it aims at ecclesial praxis and it is oriented by ecclesial praxis.[3] Theology is a privileged element of ecclesial praxis, its ideological dimension. An "ideological dimension" simply means the conscious and reflective element of the ecclesial praxis itself.[4]

*The Problem Addressed by Theology: Salvation.* The problem to which theology must respond is not the problem of God, but the problem of human existence. This problem is experienced in history as the religious question of salvation in negative experiences of contrast. The question of salvation, then, is historical, and the response to it must be historicized. These statements get close to the heart of Ellacuría's theology, and I want to briefly draw out their significance for ecclesiology from below.

Almost in passing, Ellacuría alludes to the fact that the religious question is not focused on God but on the seeming absence of God to human affairs. "The church knows that what is involved in the problem of humanity is not the problem of God as God, but the problem of God in history; it also knows that what is involved in the problem of God in history is the problem of humanity."[5] The religious question itself is historicized; viewed from below, from the immersion of human existence in history and society, this is no purely speculative problem. This theological comment, as it were, opens up to an all-encompassing perspective on religious issues.

The basic religious question, for Ellacuría, is the question of salvation. No theological subject occupies him more, and it can be found beneath the many topics he engages. The question of salvation is a human dilemma that is experienced in history. It is experienced most keenly in forces of negativity that seem to negate the meaning and purpose of life, when they do not extinguish life itself. The dialectic between negativity and positivity, between sin and salvation, is described by Ellacuría in terms of prophecy and utopia. Utopia in the Christian vision is the salvation symbolized by the kingdom of God; and the method of theology within the horizon of God's kingdom is prophecy, that is, a revelation and critique of sinful historical situations, "the critical contrasting of the proclamation of the fullness of the Kingdom of God with a definite historical situation."[6] Salvation is a way of reaching beyond the present evil to a future more in line with the kingdom of God.

The kingdom of God is a utopia; paradoxically, it is also a vision that must be concretized. Ellacuría insists that "the concretion of utopia is what historicizes the Kingdom of God, both in the hearts of human beings and in the structures without which that heart cannot live."[7] Prophecy and utopia are to be efficacious in history, even though utopia is not fully realizable in history. To actualize the kingdom of God means to give a present reality to what is formally a historical possibility not an impossibility. Because this possibility can be taken or left behind, read one way or another way, it thus lies within the grasp of human freedom.[8]

The historical concretization of utopia, of the kingdom of God, correlates with a major theme in Ellacuría's theology, a conception of the history of salvation as a salvation in and of history itself.[9] Contrasting this with an ahistorical view of salvation reveals the tendency typical in an ecclesiology from above. This would conceive human existence in individualistic terms, so that a person appears complete in himself or herself independently of the particularities of the world and history. The world and history are extrinsic to or outside the human person. God is conceived as extrinsic to worldly existence as well. God is outside time and history and the human person, so that the problem of salvation consists in getting God and human existence together.[10]

In contrast to such an ahistorical view of salvation—a salvation from history or out of history into a religious sphere apart from history—

Ellacuría understands salvation as historical. The adjective "historical" indicates that salvation occurs in history and that it has a historical character. A number of elements accompany this conception. It involves viewing salvation over against the negativity of sin. But sin is not merely individual, personal, and interior. Concrete, historical, social situations of the oppression of human liberty constitute sin.[11] Ellacuría is explicit in his insistence that this objective, social conception of sin includes the personal and individual dimension of sin; his thought is not reductionist. Nevertheless, his historical view of salvation involves viewing the liberation from sin in concrete historical terms. "If salvation is historical, then two things follow: 1) It will differ according to the time and place in which it is fleshed out; 2) it must be realized and brought about in the historical reality of human beings, in their total concrete reality."[12] With these two points a third appears: the salvation that comes from God's initiative and power should not be conceived as occurring without human agents. It is not a mythical or magical occurrence. Rather, Ellacuría implicitly enlists a theology of cooperative grace in which the saving initiative of God occurs *within* the exercise of human freedom, in its effecting liberating structures *within* history and society. Historical action is proposed as essential and intrinsic to historical salvation: it is a condition for God's action in history, a preparing the way of the Lord:

> Action in and on history, the salvation of social man in history, is the real pathway whereby God will ultimately deify man. It is not just that salvation history entails salvation in history as a corollary. Rather, the salvation of man in history is the one and only way in which salvation history can reach its culmination.[13]

This is an abbreviated account of a theme in Ellacuría that is developed at length and with deep philosophical and theological underpinning. It sets up a comprehensive framework and a synthetic viewpoint ensuring that any understanding of the church, which functions in history as a medium of God's salvation, must be envisioned "from below" in the sense of "in concrete historical terms."

*A Turn to the Jesus of History.* Another major element of an ecclesiology from below is a turn to Jesus of Nazareth, that is, the concrete person of history.[14] This return to Scripture and to Jesus in particular performs a number of key functions in Ellacuría's theology. First, it provides a foundational meaning of salvation in history in the prototypical narratives of the Jewish tradition, for example, in Moses and Exodus. Second, the turn to Jesus provides the paradigmatic example for Christians of a historical mediation of salvation. Third, with Jesus as the central historical mediation of God to Christian faith, the church appears historically as the continuation of Jesus' ministry. And on this basis, fourth, the turn to Jesus provides the defining norm and criterion of ecclesiology: the task, mission, and purpose of the church. Let me briefly comment on each of these points.

First, one of the messages of the Jewish Scriptures, illustrated well in the story of Moses, is that the very nature of God is revealed as the one who acts in history. History is open, and God is the principle of a "more" in history, the source of novelty and creativity, of the production of a better future.[15] God acts through people, and a case in point is Moses. Relative to the liberation from the Egyptians, the Scripture accounts tell us that "God is the principal author of these deeds, but they also report it as evident that Moses is the arm of Yahweh and that his historical action is simply a salvific action."[16] A religious interpretation of secular events, a religious experience of them, perceives God as a power and force within the dramas of human liberation. "Therefore, it is meaningless to ask what is sacred and what is profane in the Exodus narrative."[17]

Second, the logic underlying Jewish religiosity is transferred to Christianity, and Christians define God's action for salvation through Jesus. The most direct path to a unitary and comprehensive notion of salvation consists in an appeal to Jesus of Nazareth. One focuses on what is most fundamental about the historical Jesus, his historical mediation of salvation. This Jesus and the call to follow him together become the criterion and norm of historical ecclesial praxis. The Christian experiences transcendence and grace within the historical life and actions of Jesus. Although one can distinguish between the sacred and the profane, these are not separable spheres but are aspects of one history; there are not two different levels of history, natural and supernatural, but one history. Instead of speaking of a secular and a profane history, one has a "fundamental distinction between grace and sin, between the history of salvation and the history of perdition."[18] The fundamental division in history is between being for and against Jesus which, when generalized, means being for or against the kingdom of God, the project simultaneously of human existence and of God. This elementary either/or is portrayed in the historical ministry of Jesus.

Third, the historical approach to Jesus allows one to grasp the connection between the historical genesis of the church and the ministry of Jesus:

Jesus was the historical body of God, the full actualization of God among humanity, and the church must be the historical body of Christ, just as Christ was of God the Father. The continuation of the life and mission of Jesus in history, which is the task of the church, animated and unified by the Spirit of Christ, makes the church his body, his visible and operative presence.[19]

Ellacuría has a concrete sense of what the church is to accomplish in history, a view that is very much a function of a Latin American society. However, it is also nuanced. "Like the mission of Jesus, the mission of the church is not the immediate fulfillment of a political order, but the fulfillment of the kingdom of God, and, as a part of that fulfillment, the salvation of any existing political order."[20] I say more about the engagement of the church in the public order further on.

Fourth, the historical ministry of Jesus assumes the role of the criterion and norm for the church in its course through history. Theology is bound to ecclesial praxis, but it is not reflection on any and every ecclesial practice. The basic ecclesial praxis is oriented to the reign of God, and the fundamental object of doing theology and hence of theology itself is the realization of the kingdom of God in history.[21] Because the reign of God is by definition in conflict with sin, any ecclesial praxis or theology not in conflict with the power of sin is not the reign of God as preached by Jesus, no matter how spiritual it might appear. We have in Jesus' preaching of the reign of God a solid criterion that is historically verifiable, much surer and more profound than conformity with theoretical formulas.[22]

Jesus, in sum, is understood in a way that recognizes the central role he should have in ecclesiology. This aspect of an ecclesiology from below is firmly supported culturally by an increased historical consciousness and theologically by the influence of research into the historical Jesus.

*Historical Realism in Ecclesiology.* Ellacuría's historical realism relative to salvation spontaneously makes demands upon the church. The historicization of salvation requires that the church, conceived as the sign and sacrament of the salvation mediated by Jesus Christ, display that salvation in a public, historical manner. "As the bearer of salvation, the Church must be the sign that makes salvation present and effective in a historical way. The sign leads us beyond itself, but without the sign there is no beyond for us. The sign both is and is not what it signifies."[23] Ellacuría sees this worldly sign as involving liberationist activity, a concern for the structures of the political community, and for social justice. He appeals to the continuation of the historical ministry of Jesus. The point is that worldly or historical activity on the part of the church and Christians is meant to be a sign that implements what has been revealed in Jesus Christ. The sign, to be a sign, has to be a public and socially visible state of affairs. The rationale for church action in society, therefore, is that it is a sign or medium that carries in a public and visible way the concern of God for the historicized salvation of the biblical witness generally and more particularly as found in Jesus' ministry.

*The Sociological Base of the Church.* Up to this point, I have indicated Ellacuría's vision of a church in history that is self-consciously liberationist after the pattern of the biblical community and the ministry of Jesus; it presents itself as the sacrament of a historicized salvation. I now shift to the manner in which this conception affects church organization. How does Ellacuría's ecclesiology from below depict the institutional church? I read Ellacuría on two levels at this point: the basis of the church as institution is first the poor who are organized in base communities; in a more general way, however, one can speak of the people in the Spirit as the basis of the church.

Ellacuría comments on Rahner's suggestion that the church of the future will be made up of small intentional communities; it will be less and less a social and cultural phenomenon. The churches of the future will be built up from below through base communities of free initiative and membership.[24] "Supposedly, the force of the Spirit will be more active and alive in these communities, so that their initiatives will flow up freely from the base to the head, thus avoiding the excess weight of the ecclesial structures, which can suffocate both personal initiative and Christian inspiration."[25] This leads to a certain tension between base communities and institutional structures.

Liberation theology poses the issue in somewhat different terms. First, the church is the church of the poor. The place of the poor in the church is justified by Jesus' ministry. The massive weight of Jesus' dedication to the poor confirms the option for the poor as something that corresponds with the intention and will of Jesus, and thus the meaning of the kingdom of God. Where people are victims of social oppression and sin, the church must struggle to overcome this sin from the world. "This is the only possible polestar of the historically constituted mission of the church, its primordial purpose."[26] "In other words, the church is the historical body of Christ insofar as it is the church of the poor; and it is a sacrament of liberation insofar as it is the church of the poor."[27] Given the status of the poor in the church as the ground or foundation of the church, the poor also form the elementary social unit of the church. Base communities are the basis of the church because they are the primary units and original cells of the ecclesial organism. These base communities are communities of the poor. If a church is a church of the poor and for the poor, there will be no conflict between institution and base communities. The problem is not between base and institution, but between base and failure to be dedicated to those most in need.[28]

This formulation of the basis of church institution is representative of liberation theology and corresponds well with the church in Latin America. Without subverting that structure, I want to call attention to another vein in Ellacuría's ecclesiology, more in line with Rahner, where he speaks of the people of the Spirit as the basis of the church. It should be noted that for Ellacuría these are the same people, the poor. Moreover, what is said here of the people of the Spirit in no way conflicts with the position of the poor. However, the more general language allows one to see the basis of the church within another framework, or at least a different focus of attention, than the tensive dialectic between rich and poor, namely, the tension between community and institution.

The basis of the church, Ellacuría says, is "the people with Spirit," that is, the divine Spirit. There is no real and vital church not born of the Spirit, identified as the Spirit of Jesus. The term "Spirit" corresponds with the symbol used in the New Testament, which did not refer to the Third Person of the Trinity, but simply to God as Spirit as the principle that animated Jesus, revealed itself in Jesus, and was experienced as operative in the Christian communities formed in the wake of the Jesus movement. The symbol of the Spirit refers to the presence of God. It follows that together with Jesus, but as an internal principle, the Spirit is the basis and vital power of the church. The "people" in question are the people insofar as they give birth to a church as a community of followers of Jesus who seek to announce and actualize the reign of God in history. The church, to be self-constituted as church with its specific consciousness and organization, is necessarily born of the Spirit.[29]

The Spirit was not only the driving force at the origin of the church but is the continual basis of the church, and continually gives birth to the church. Those who follow Jesus Christ do so in the power of the Spirit. This vital principle should not be understood mystically, Ellacuría says. It is a real and creative presence of God, and a proof that Jesus continues to live in history actualizing the mission he began during his earthly life. The power of the Spirit manifests itself in the church's concern for the poor. When the Spirit of God, who is the Spirit of Jesus, takes flesh in the church, one has the fullness of the church of Christ that is the church of the poor. By contrast, from the Christian point of view, one cannot have a church of Jesus Christ, and one cannot have historical salvation, without the primary subject of this church being the people who are most in need, and who are reborn to a new life through the presence of God as Spirit. This people, reborn, will contribute in a special manner to the historical liberation of individuals and whole peoples.[30]

*The Church's Role in Society.* With this topic of the church in the world and the role of the church in society, the discussion turns back to the theme of the historicization of salvation and liberation but in more concrete and practical terms. Given the mission of the church to be the extension of God's mission as revealed in Jesus for the salvific liberation of the poor and all who suffer, how should one conceive the role of the church in society in practical terms? This requires a response in any ecclesiology, from above or from below, but it appears a particularly pressing question in a secularized world. Ellacuría addresses this issue from two points of view: in terms of the church as institution and in terms of the spirituality of the members of the church. I deal with the first here and the second in the next section.

Ellacuría understands the fact of secularization and the politicization of human existence as positive aspects of present-day culture. He calls politicization the historical form in which secularization is occurring today. Politicization refers to the eruption of freedom out of nature, and to a realignment of reality based on human freedom and action. Politicization "implies the transition from being-as-nature to being-as-history in the constitution of social man."[31] In such a world, in such a historically conscious culture, the church is called by God to play a historical role, to take its place in society, and to exercise a prophetic voice. However, it is to do so precisely as church or in the distinctive manner of church. The church as an institution is not autonomous and isolated from the world; it is part of the greater reality of the historical praxis that constitutes social and political existence. The force and direction of history is not controlled by the church. The church does not possess the material power or force to be the agency that drives history. This is the case neither by accident nor by a negative development, something not always recognized by people in the church; this corresponds to the essential nature of the church. The praxis of the church has as its center the reign of God, and it is dedicated to the actualization of the reign of God. It acts in society as a leaven that stimulates the reign of God from within society, recognizing the autonomy of various phases of society.[32] "Thus, what the church contributes to the salvation of history is the fundamental sign of the history of salvation. The church belongs intrinsically to this history of salvation and carries within it the visible part that reveals and makes effective the whole of salvation in us."[33]

*Ecclesial Spirituality.* Another approach to the church's role in society, to the historicization of sin and grace and the church's role in liberation-salvation, moves through spirituality. I briefly touched upon the way in which the experience of sin in history in a negative experience of contrast evokes a reaction against it, which in turn becomes a foundation for the positive task in history of salvation and liberation. This experience, within the framework of faith in God mediated by Jesus Christ, is also the foundation of Christian spirituality. In this context, Ellacuría comments on the efficacy of the sacraments, a basic element in Catholic ecclesial spirituality, and more generally on a spirituality of contemplation in action.

Ellacuría represents a theology of sacraments from below in this respect: the sacraments are not autonomous media for a Christian contact with transcendent reality. They are rather functions of the church. Ellacuría reminds us that "the primary sacramentality of the church does not derive from the effectiveness of what we call sacraments, but that on the contrary, the sacraments are effective insofar as they participate in the sacramentality of the church."[34] Christian sacraments were generated in function of the developing church. Since Vatican II, the conception of the church as sign and sacrament has effectively characterized the nature of the church as a whole and its role in the world. Based on the standard definition of a sacrament that points to its visibility and effectiveness, then, Ellacuría applies these two qualities to the whole church. "Sacramentality has been presented with the double mark of mediational visibility and effectiveness. Therefore when we refer to the sacramentality of the church, we are expecting the church to give visibility and effectiveness to the salvation it announces."[35] The church is mediational; it lies between God and the world, Christ and human beings, the kingdom of God and history. Not an end in itself, it must resist the temptation to self-centeredness. The mission of the church is to mediate in a historically visible and effective way the salvation it receives from God through Jesus Christ.[36]

Given this sacramentality of the church as a whole, when one views the individual sacraments as functions of this church and its mission, their efficacy takes on a historical character. This means the grace or divine influence that they mediate should be understood in such a way that they impel a definite style of Christian life in history. It is important to say that the church makes divine life present and communicates it sacramentally. But in terms of the prophecy and utopia addressed earlier,

Ellacuría points to the need of a renewal of the effectiveness of the prophetic Word and the following of that Word in the people who hear it. One cannot limit the effectiveness of the sacraments to an interior transformation; they impel action in history. "To confuse the mystery, which is the sacrament, with a process given in the interiority of the person is to devalue the mysteriousness of the sacraments's efficacy through an unverifiable and ineffective pure affirmation."[37]

Correlative to this understanding of sacramental efficacy as a dynamic force in the praxis of the whole community, Ellacuría speaks of the Christian life as a spirituality of contemplation in action. This theme has Jesuit roots in Ignatius Loyola's *Spiritual Exercises;* it is especially appropriate to the active view of the Christian life that characterizes liberation theology. It combines in an integral unity the active use of freedom in the world of the Christian who participates in history and society with a deep religious sense of God's presence and the potential ability of finding God in secular life. Ellacuría puts it this way: "The action represents the objective element and contemplation the subjective; only when contemplation is achieved in action are we truly on the way to realizing and assuming Christian historical transcendence."[38] In another place, he adds: "Action without contemplation is empty and destructive, while contemplation without action is paralyzing and concealing."[39]

Such is a sketch of some of the elements of Ellacuría's ecclesiology from below.

## 2. The Relevance of Ellacuria's Ecclesiology from Below

In this briefer, second part of the essay I synthesize and generalize what Ellacuría represents for ecclesiology and comment on its relevance. As a preface to this summary, I want to point to a number of issues that would be essential to an integral ecclesiology from below that are not developed in Ellacuría's ecclesiology. By depicting his views on the church as an ecclesiology from below, I have sought to highlight the bearing of an important and representative liberation theologian on the formal discipline of ecclesiology. It is also important to keep in mind that Ellacuría was not an ecclesiologist by trade.

Some themes integral to an ecclesiology from below and that have not been developed in this account of Ellacuría are the following. First, a treatment of the development of the church during the first century. Ellacuría properly emphasizes that Jesus is the origin and foundation of the church. It is also clear among historians that Jesus did not intentionally found a church. A careful historical and theological analysis and interpretation of how the church developed is essential to an ecclesiology from below. Second, an ecclesiology from below would also have to analyze historically and theologically the nature and function of the church as institution and the various structures that make it up. Ellacuría rightly stresses the "corporeal" and institutional character of the church, and how this relates generally to the church of the poor and the people of Spirit. But this relationship requires careful historical, sociological, and theological analysis that includes an account of the genesis of church institutions and the authority they enjoy in the church. Third, two other current issues need to be discussed within the framework of an ecclesiology from below, namely, the relation of the churches in a historically conscious ecumenical age and the relation of Christianity or the Christian church at large with other religions. In the context of the liberation theology of Latin America, these problems do not have the same immediate practical relevance for the people who make up these local churches as they do for Christians in other parts of the world. Nevertheless, increasingly the questions of inculturation and pluralism within one Christian church and the place of Christianity in a religiously pluralistic world simply are becoming everyone's problems. The ecclesial self-understanding generated in this new globalized context will have bearing on local churches everywhere.

Once it is clear that ecclesiology from below is a method and movement of thought not fully represented in any particular theologian, one is freed to depict in broader strokes the significance of the ecclesiology from below implied in Ellacuría's theology. How would one characterize an ecclesiology from below in a holistic and generalized way based on the thinking of Ellacuría? Let me respond to this question in six points.

First, Ellacuría's ecclesiology is "from below" because it proceeds from a deep historical consciousness or sense of historicity. A sense of historical realism colors every aspect of his theology. Theology should never bypass an understanding of things historically, developmentally, sociologically, and politically. A theology of the church begins with and always moves forward based on reflection on the historical reality of the church and the people who make it up. Historically, the church emerges out of people's praxis and is socially constructed. This ecclesiology, as seen in Ellacuría, can never be satisfied with any theological image that is not also descriptive of the actual, concrete church.

Second, Ellacuría represents an ecclesiology from below with his turn to the historical Jesus. The church, as a historical phenomenon, can only be understood in terms of its historical origins, and Jesus is the historical origin of the church. Jesus is also the theological foundation of the church, Ellacuría tells us, because it is defined as a community that keeps Jesus' salvific words, deeds, and mission alive in history. Research on the historical Jesus will have an impact on an ecclesiology from below, for such an ecclesiology demands a historically credible conception of the relation between Jesus and the church. Knowledge about Jesus is also essential for Jesus' central normative role in forming theological judgments concerning church praxis.

Third, an ecclesiology from below will follow Ellacuría in accentuating the role of God as Spirit in the historical community. All ecclesiology must appeal to the two symbols, Jesus as the Christ and the Spirit, for they are the two theological foundations of the church. An ecclesiology from above tends to appeal to a heavenly Christ as readily as to the Jesus of history. By contrast, Ellacuría points to the people in the Spirit as the basis of the church. His ecclesiology from below thus complements the historical work of Jesus with the immanent presence of God as Spirit in the life of the community. Although one should not think of the alternatives here in sharp exclusive ways but as matters of emphasis, still the different emphases can lead to considerably different ways of understanding the church. An ecclesiology from below is in some respects pneumatocentric, and this means that the Spirit of God as revealed in Jesus dynamically animates the church as a community and authorizes movements and developments from within.[40]

Fourth, that which the church mediates in an ecclesiology from below is a salvation in and for life in history. This is always to be understood as entailing eschatological finality and eternal life; in Ellacuría this emphasis is distinctive and emphatic but not excluding or reductive. It is a function of his historical consciousness, his attentiveness to the concrete negative experiences of history, and his practical concern that the church mediate God's salvation to actual people in their actual situations. This foundational framework of historically conscious reflection provides the theological grounding for a practical, dynamic, active, and engaged spirituality. Ellacuría's church of the poor is not a passive church; it is a church of people authorized by God in Jesus and empowered by God as Spirit to assume salvific responsibility for their lives in history.

Fifth, an ecclesiology from below is perhaps most typically characterized by an understanding of ecclesial organization and office, of "hierarchy," as emerging out of the community and as in service of the community and its mission. Although Ellacuría did not trace this theme

in the historical development of the church, he suggests it in his characterization of the church as the church of the poor and of the people of
Spirit, and in his characterization of the sacraments. In keeping with a
historical and sociological consciousness, and incorporating the themes
of a historically relevant salvation and the working of God as Spirit in
the community, Ellacuría offers a holistic framework or pattern of thinking: the groundwork of the church consists of people of faith animated
by God as Spirit. This is the church. Superstructure is always at the same
time integral to, derivative from, and functional in relation to ecclesial
community. Such a church is open to change because its very genesis
and growth consisted in responding to new historical situations in the
power of the Spirit.

Sixth, Ellacuría's ecclesiology from below entails an ecclesial spirituality because the very mission of the church is to extend Jesus' ministry
into history. The calling of the Christian and the broad lines of ecclesially
formed life in the world are built into the structure of understanding the
church because it is shaped by a historically conscious mode of thinking.

## Conclusion

This collection of essays shows that Ignacio Ellacuría has contributed
invaluable insights to a liberationist understanding of Jesus Christ and
the church in Latin America. Nevertheless, his thought has universal
relevance. One area where this is unmistakably clear is his ecclesiology
from below.

Comparing Ellacuría's ecclesiology from below with an ecclesiology
from above, as that is represented by the ecclesiology prior to Vatican II,
for example,[41] will yield sharp contrasts on almost every significant issue:
on methodological suppositions; on Jesus and the way Jesus and the earliest church are related; on the nature of the church; on the mission of
the church; on how God's will is reflected in church institutions; on the
character of the salvation mediated by the church; on the grounds and
the exercise of the authority of officials in the church; on the meaning of
Christian life and spirituality. However, more generally and more importantly, Ellacuría demonstrates how anthropological suppositions and
theological method are fundamental to making these shifts. The two
methods of ecclesiology account for the different responses to the variety
of problems the church faces today: to the ecumenical problem, to inculturation, to the nature and limits of ecclesial pluralism, to interreligious
dialogue, to the fundamental conception of the role of the Christian

church in history, to the role of the church in society. By adapting a historically conscious and realist anthropology and by approaching the church from the perspective of the concrete problems it faces in Latin America, Ellacuría has helped fashion a general paradigm for an ecclesiology from below that is universally relevant.

[1] Karl Rahner, "The Two Basic Types of Christology," in *Theological Investigations* 13 (New York: Seabury, 1975) 213–23.

[2] Ignacio Ellacuría, "The Church of the Poor, Historical Sacrament of Liberation," in I. Ellacuría and J. Sobrino, eds., *Mysterium Liberationis: Fundamental Concepts of Liberation Theology* (Maryknoll, NY: Orbis, 1994) 543, trans. by Margaret D. Wilde from "La Iglesia de los pobres, sacramento histórico de liberación" (1977); essay hereafter cited as "The Church of the Poor" (1994); collection hereafter cited as *MLT* (English translation) and *ML* (Spanish original) [*ML* 2 (1977) 127].

[3] Ignacio Ellacuría, "La teología como momento ideológico de la praxis eclesial," *Estudios Eclesiásticos,* no. 207 (1978) 461; translation mine; hereafter cited as "Teología como praxis" (1978). By "praxis" Ellacuría means action that transforms society and a type of such action that is proper to the church in its journey through history. The church in this conception is understood concretely and historically as a community of people who in one manner or another actualize in themselves the reign of God.

[4] Ibid., 464.

[5] Ellacuría, "The Church of the Poor" (1994) *MLT,* 554 [*ML* 2 (1977) 141].

[6] Ignacio Ellacuría, "Utopia and Prophecy in Latin America," (1991) *MLT,* 292, trans. by James Brockman from "Utopía y profetismo desde America Latina: un ensayo concreto de soteriología histórica" (1989); hereafter cited as "Utopia and Prophecy" (1991). Compare Ellacuría's description of the dialectic of prophecy and utopia with Edward Schillebeeckx's description of a negative experience of contrast in *Church: The Human Story of God* (New York: Crossroad, 1990) 5–6 [*ML* 1 (1989) 396].

[7] Ellacuría, "Utopia and Prophecy," (1991) *MLT,* 291 [*ML* 1 (1989) 395].

[8] Ibid., 293 [398].

[9] This theme, which undergirds the whole of Ellacuría's theology, is the principal thesis of his collection of essays, *Freedom Made Flesh: The Mission of Christ and His Church* (Maryknoll, NY: Orbis, 1976), trans. by John Drury from *Teología política* (San Salvador: Ediciones del Secretariado Social Interdiocesano, 1973); original collection hereafter cited as *TP,* English translation as *FMF.* See especially "Salvation History and Salvation in History," 3–19, trans. from "Historia de la salvación y salvación en la historia" (1973) [*TP* (1973) 1–10]; "The Church's Mission: Signs of Its Credibility," 87–126, trans. from "El anuncio del evangelio y la misión de la Iglesia" (1973) [*TP* (1973) 44–69]; and "Liberation: Mission and Charism of the Latin American Church," 127–63, trans. from "Liberación: misión y carisma de la Iglesia latinoamerica" (1971) [*TP* (1971) 70–90].

[10] Ellacuría, "Salvation History and Salvation in History" (1976) *FMF,* 12 [*TP* (1973) 6].

<sup></sup> 11 "In the concrete, anything that positively and unjustly stands in the way of human liberty is sin. It is sin because it prevents a human being from being a human being, depriving him or her of the liberty that properly belongs to a child of God. Sin is the formal exercise of an act of radical injustice. . . . By considering oppression from the standpoint of sin, the Christian radicalizes and absolutizes his or her condemnation. Sin is seen as the absolute negation and denial of the absolute in reality." "The Church's Mission: Signs of Its Credibility" (1976) *FMF,* 105 [*TP* (1971) 57].

12 Ellacuría, "Salvation History and Salvation in History" (1976) *FMF,* 15 [*TP* (1973) 8].

13 Ibid., 18 [10].

14 Ellacuría makes a distinction between Jesus, the concrete person of history, and the academic historical reconstruction of him in "The Church of the Poor" (1994) *MLT,* 551 [*ML* 2 (1977) 138]. However, the relevance of this distinction in the context of these reflections is not clear, since the person Jesus cannot be known apart from historical reconstruction.

15 Ignacio Ellacuría, "The Historicity of Christian Salvation," *MLT,* 258–9, trans. by Margaret D. Wilde from "Historicidad de la salvación cristiana" (1984) [*ML* 1 (1984) 333–4].

16 Ibid., 262 [338].

17 Ibid.

18 Ellacuría, "The Church of the Poor" (1994) *MLT,* 551–2 [*ML* 2 (1977) 138–9].

19 Ibid., 546 [131].

20 Ibid., 553 [140]. "By political order we mean here the global institutionalization of social relations, the institutional objectification of human actions, which comprises the public venue of their personal and interpersonal actions."

21 Ellacuría, "Teología como praxis" (1978) 467.

22 Ibid., 472.

23 Ellacuría, "Liberation: Mission and Charism of the Latin American Church" (1976) *FMF,* 140 [*TP* (1971) 77].

24 Karl Rahner's reflections on the future of the church are found in his "The Present Situation of Christians: A Theological Interpretation of the Position of Christians in the Modern World," in *The Christian Commitment: Essays in Pastoral Theology* (New York: Sheed and Ward, 1963) 3–37. Also, Karl Rahner, *The Shape of the Church to Come* (London: SPCK, 1974) 19–34.

25 Ellacuría, "The Church of the Poor" (1994) *MLT,* 557 [*ML* 2 (1977) 145].

26 Ibid., 558 [147].

27 Ibid., 559 [148].

28 Ibid., 557 [146].

29 Ignacio Ellacuría, "La iglesia que nace del pueblo por el Espíritu," *Conversión de la iglesia al reino de Dios: para anunciarlo y realizarlo en la historia* (Santander, Spain: Sal Terrae, 1984) 71–3; trans. mine; originally published in *Misión Abierta,* no. 1 (1978) 150–8. "It is clear, therefore, that it is this Spirit of Jesus that is the necessary factor that enables the people . . . to give birth to the church; that enables the people to become converted into an instrument of salvation and, consequently, an instrument of liberation."

30 Ibid., 75–8.

[31] Ellacuría, "Salvation History and Salvation in History" (1976) *FMF,* 10 [*TP* (1973) 5].

[32] Ellacuría, "Teología como praxis" (1978) 463.

[33] Ellacuría, "The Church of the Poor" (1994) *MLT,* 554 [*ML* 2 (1977) 141]. The church "is not equipped, as Jesus was not, to become a power in this world, which takes pleasure in having the power to subdue its subjects."

[34] Ibid., 547 [133].

[35] Ibid., 548 [133].

[36] "The church makes real its historic, salvific sacramentality by announcing and fulfilling the Kingdom of God in history. Its fundamental praxis consists in the fulfillment of the Kingdom of God in history, in action that leads to the fulfillment of the Kingdom of God in history." Ibid., 549 [134].

[37] Ellacuría, "Utopia and Prophecy" (1994) *MLT,* 326 [*ML* 1 (1989) 440].

[38] Ellacuría, "The Historicity of Christian Salvation" (1994) *MLT,* 283 [*ML* 1 (1984) 367].

[39] Ellacuría, "Utopia and Prophecy" (1994) *MLT,* 313 [*ML* 1 (1989) 423].

[40] The difference in these two modes of thinking can be quite dramatically illustrated by two different conceptions of leadership and priesthood in the church produced by them. In a christocentric ecclesiology from above, the authorization of the leader-priest has been conceived as being received from Christ in an absolute way, that is, independently of a particular community or congregation served by the minister. In an ecclesiology from below this leadership is authorized through the Spirit-filled community. See, for example, Edward Schillebeeckx's historical analysis of these developments in *Ministry: Leadership in the Community of Jesus Christ* (New York: Crossroad, 1981).

[41] This comparison is not entirely illicit, because in several respects the reforms initiated by Vatican II have not been carried forward in ways that have kept pace with culture.

# The People of God
# in the Struggle for Justice*

*María Pilar Aquino*

The powerful elites who govern this world sentenced Ignacio Ellacuría to death, destroying his flesh and bone in a brutal massacre. Ellacuría called them "oppressors,"[1] "the powers of this world"[2] or the creators of the "world of oppression."[3] But they have not exercised any real power over his prolific life, his life-giving spirit, his incorruptible body, or his liberating vision. They ordered him to be murdered more out of fear than hatred. Blinded by fear, they believed that bullets would destroy *the life* and *the truth* produced by the way his body, his mind, his words, and his actions served to bring about redemption. However, from the point of view of the Christian vision of history, the judgment of these powerful groups was mistaken, because the life and the truth of Ellacuría's way of being were the same as those embodied in that of Jesus Christ, who incarnated *the life* and *the truth of God*.

Over the course of history, persecution, torture, and death have never finally defeated either Jesus Christ or the vision of justice embodied by the true church in its struggles for change. The real impossibility of eternal death for such people lies in the mysterious reality that their being and their voices constitute just one knot in the great net which is the true people of

* Translated by Robert Lassalle-Klein.

God. The physical death of such people is finally overcome. Its ultimate un-
reality is historically and theologically emblematized by the vitality of the
people of God, who time and again arise in history as a subject and a means
of liberation from the world of oppression. The ties that bind the true people
of God together are incarnated in historical forces that move history in a direction, forces which, as historical, entail universality, changeability, openness to possibilities, and transcendence.[4] The path this people walk toward
true liberation cannot be blocked by the powers of this world. This is why I
say that they murdered Ellacuría more out of fear than hatred.

In this paper I offer some reflections on the persecution and martyrdom lived by the true people of God as a reality that manifests the complete truth of our faith. I seek to show the radical demands of Christian
faith when it is lived in a world of sin. Such reflection is needed to pay
homage to Ellacuría who actualized the vision, the way, and the destiny
of the people of God in his own life. But it is also demanded to demonstrate the possible impact of our Christian commitment on the realities
we are living today.

## The Radical Roots of the People of God

For Ellacuría, the true people of God are made up of those who seek
to fulfill the work begun by Jesus Christ. This work involves the struggle
to sow the seeds of justice in the world of today, so dominated by the sin
of injustice.[5] The true people of God, or the true church, is made up of
those who (a) "bear the sins of the world without having committed
them,"[6] proclaiming and struggling for the realization of the reign of
God on earth; and (b) all those dispossessed or abandoned groups who
struggle both for their liberation, and to convert this sinful world into a
new creation, a new reality where all humanity lives with dignity. It is
made of up of those (c) who historically incarnate the struggles of whole
peoples for justice and liberation, creating a path toward lasting peace
and true reconciliation; and (d) who support struggles for justice incarnating the fundamental values of the Christian vision. Those values include compassion and mercy, grounded in true love, for the anguish of
our peoples. They include faith in the scandalizing power of impoverished groups, a faith that finds in the oppressed the privileged place for
the manifestation of God. They include a type of hope grounded in the
intolerable character of present, the construction of a historical future
with a better quality of life for all, and the certain promise of a personal
future open to the glorious resurrection.

The true people of God, or the true church, is also constituted of those who (e) live in a constant process of conversion to God and to the oppressed that enables them to discover Christian principles of action. What is good for these peoples is good for the church. The people pre-date, and are more valuable than any bureaucratic organization or insti-tution. Indeed, the church can and must encourage the people to seek solutions to their problems on their own.[7] Finally, the distinctive character-istic of the true people of God is rooted in the fact that they are persecuted because the powers of this sinful world cannot tolerate their existence. For Ellacuría,

> The true people of God in a world dominated by sin cannot but be perse-cuted. First of all there is the persecution of the people, a persecution that at heart is that of structural oppression and then becomes repres-sion when the people have become conscious and have organized struggles for liberation. Then comes the persecution of the people of God which seeks to bring salvation history into the history of the people and to inte-grate the history of the people into salvation history.[8]

In a world imprisoned by injustice, the true people of God incarnates the true church precisely in their struggles against multiple forms of injus-tice for a new earth and a new humanity, liberated from individual ego-tism and the sin of injustice. In the context of a world permeated by sin, the fundamental task of the church is to actively participate in the world in order to open it to the saving grace of God who is already at work in the faith of the people.[9] According to Ellacuría, the struggle for justice not only substantially defines the identity and the task of the church, but it also gives the church *credibility* and *authenticity*. He writes, "The Church in itself, and before the world, must be the most pure and effec-tive sign of the salvation it proclaims."[10] From the perspective of Chris-tian faith, the people who are the true church are those who reveal the rule of God's truth over the world and who bring salvation to this world imprisoned by sin.

If the ultimate purpose of divine revelation is the salvation of the world, the authentic revelation of the Christian God does not appear among those who oppress the world with their injustice, but among those who seek to save the world from this injustice. He argues, "The presence of God in the people, in their suffering and joy, in their defeats and victo-ries, cannot but benefit the people, if it is a liberating God who presses toward a better future, in which everything will be new: the heavens, the earth, and human beings themselves."[11] Ellacuría says that if only for this

reason alone, though intolerable for the powerful of this world, the existence of the true people of God is both necessary and indispensable "not
only so that the truth of the plenitude of the gospel might shine forth, but
also so that oppressed people might achieve their integral liberation."[12]

But, if what fundamentally defines the people of God is their historization of the salvation of the world through a full harvest of justice and
integral liberation, how is it that this people can be murdered? I have
argued historically and theologically that one cannot bring about the
eternal death of a people like this. For us, the physical death of those
who have given their lives in the struggle for justice is finally overcome,
like the death of Jesus Christ himself. Ellacuría firmly reminds us of
this aspect:

> It must not be forgotten that if the life of Jesus had definitively ended on
> the cross, we would be in the same darkness that his death produced
> among his disciples. The fact that his life could not end on the cross
> shows retroactively the plenitude hidden in that life. And it empowers
> the believing community to actualize its real possibilities.[13]

For Christian faith, Jesus fully incarnates God's presence in the
world, and his exemplary life is the way humanity comes to God. This
way of life, doing good and bringing justice, brought him to the cross.
But it also showed the possibility of a new life through a resurrected
existence. This is why giving up one's life in the struggle for justice does
not reveal the futility of that struggle. Nor does it demonstrate the failure
of an entire life dedicated to the anticipation of a new life. Rather, it only
exposes the wickedness of the powerful and reveals the historical possibilities of the vision of a new earth and a new humanity. The words of
Archbishop Romero, like the faith and hope that characterized Ellacuría's
Christian commitment, forcefully express this vision of the final destiny
of the true people of God:

> I must tell you that as a Christian I do not believe in death without res-
> urrection. If they kill me, I will rise in the Salvadoran people. May my
> death, if it is accepted by God, be for the liberation of my people and as a
> witness of hope in the future. Better, of course, that they realize that they
> will be wasting their time. A bishop will die, but God's church, which is
> the people, will never perish.[14]

At the dawn of the third millennium, the church in Central America
continues to be a martyred church. The reality of martyrdom and the systematic persecution suffered by this church are due to its deliberate com-

mitment to the struggles of the poor and oppressed, not because it is deliberately seeking death. For Ellacuría, persecution and martyrdom have marked the church not so much for defending its dogmas or its institutional privileges; "rather it has been persecuted for heroically incarnating Christian virtues and especially for standing with the poor and the persecuted."[15] The commitment of the church to the common people, and to their organizations working for greater justice and human dignity, has led to inevitable confrontations with certain powerful groups. These confrontations are the direct result of the evangelical efficacy with which the church carries out its mission. The words and actions of the church have been efficacious because they communicate the Gospel message together with the theoretical and practical means to assist common people in actualizing their intrinsic human dignity. Ellacuría made it clear that in contexts of structural injustice, public pressure plays an important role in determining the efficacy of the church's work:

> When this public pressure is placed at the service of the common majorities and community-based movements, the ensuing clashes with certain dominant classes and structures leave little doubt that one is entering into a conflict. But this is not a conflict that has been sought out through attacking anyone in particular. Rather it is the result of taking the side of the oppressed majority of the common people.[16]

Surely the powers of this world do not want to change a sociocultural system that has benefitted them for centuries, and continues to benefit them precisely because it is based on injustice. In their sinful world, powerful groups choose to reproduce an unjust system, even though this implies "the ongoing death of the immense majority of oppressed humanity."[17] The various components of the overall system interact at the intersections of social power to bring about increased suffering for oppressed humanity and ecobiological destruction. But the work of the true people of God is precisely opposed to any system that "dehumanizes and dechristianizes" the whole of creation.[18]

Many times, in many ways, and before many audiences, Ellacuría declared that the inevitable consequences of the church's commitment to groups struggling for justice have, in fact, included murder, massacres, torture, and the crucifixion of entire communities. In saying this, I want to put an end to the myth invented by some theological groups in the First World that Latin American liberation theology "exalts suffering" when it does not allow the voices of martyrs to be silenced. For these groups, Latin American theological reflection on martyrdom only perpetuates a sacrificial theology that alienates people from taking charge of their lives and destinies. On the contrary, as the extensive theological work of Ellacuría (who in my opinion offers one of the *most critical and rigorous* articulations of liberation theology) surely shows, this theology tries to bring out the theological meaning of martyrdom from the perspective of faith, understood as a *principle of liberation*.[19] More fundamentally, Latin American liberation theology has sought to nourish the vision of hope that accompanies communities of faith in their daily struggles to defend real lives, and to establish justice in the world. The Christian vision of hope, of life, and of justice takes on greater saving power when it is lived in the context of a reality where persecution and physical death appear to be the inevitable and undesirable consequences of a radical Christian commitment.

## Faith Lived in the Kingdom of Hell

At the present time, the Latin American martyrology continues today to grow. There are no real signs to indicate that it will end in the near future.[20] If the true people of God continue living the Christian faith efficaciously, the only path for actualizing salvation is to continue struggling for justice. For Ellacuría, it is clear that people can attain salvation without an explicit confession of faith. It is likewise clear they cannot be saved without doing justice. He writes:

> Without being confused, faith and justice are inseparable, at least when both appear in a world of sin. The Christian faith in its fullness is not only the commitment to God, the acceptance of his revealing communication and the unleashing of a supernatural power. Rather, it is also a new form of life that necessarily includes doing justice. Likewise, doing justice is a way of knowing God. It is clearer that there is no faith without justice, than that there is justice without faith.[21]

For me, the consequence of a radically lived faith can be seen in specific human faces. In the past two years I have had the opportunity to accompany various Christian communities in Guatemala, sharing with them feminist experience and theological reflection. On several occasions of mutual sharing, I was able to relive with them experiences of the most intense and dramatic kind, which have forever marked my life and my theological commitments.[22] On the one hand, I had the opportunity to hear the testimony of several indigenous communities of Mayan peoples regarding the terror and violence they lived during the last twenty-five years, most intensely during the decade of the eighties. In a special way, I was able to share the suffering and tears that still accompany the memory of the events lived by a group of women in the village of Chimaltenango. These indigenous women speak with sorrow of how they saw the murder, the kidnapping, and the torture of their families, their mothers, their fathers, their communities, and how they barely escaped with their lives.[23]

On the other hand, I was able to relive with them the memory of my own friends who died as victims of violence and repression during the decade of the seventies and early eighties when we participated from Mexico City in the solidarity committees with El Salvador, Guatemala, and Nicaragua. Their faces and their voices took on new life in the faces and voices of today's communities. My mind raged with feelings of *anger* and *helplessness* in the face of the incredible impunity with which the powers of this world continue their injustice. Nonetheless, through the testimony of these women and other communities who received me with such kindness, I was able to rekindle the *passion for greater justice,* for true reconciliation, and for a new creation that has been a part of my life since before I began to do theology. What theology has done in my life is to give a salvific meaning to this anger and this passion. It is my contact with persecuted communities that keeps them alive.

The traumatic magnitude of the experiences lived by these Guatemalan communities has been heightened still more by impact on their lives of the massacres of Mayan people in Chiapas, Mexico in December of 1997, and especially the murder of Bishop Juan José Gerardi in Guatemala City on April 26, 1998. Bishop Gerardi, now known as Martyr for the Truth, was director of the Project to Recover Historical Memory (REMI Project). Its central purpose was to recover the *right to a voice* as a debt still owed to this persecuted people. In the introduction, the REMI Project's final report says the following:

> In addition to the individual and collective impact of violence and terror, political repression robbed the people of their right to a voice. For many years they could not share their experiences, make known what had happened, or name the responsible parties. For many of the victims and the survivors, who testified, this was the first time they had spoken about what had happened to them. The testimonies collected have the weight of that voice of the victims. One can read [this report] like a book, one can hear it as a history, but above all one can learn from this collective memory, which vindicates the dignity of the victims and the hopes for change of the survivors.[24]

The work done by the REMI Project was published in April of 1998 under the title *Guatemala: Never Again!* The report documents the grave human rights violations committed against the poorest groups in Guatemala. These groups, constituting the majority of the indigenous people of Guatemala, have been deliberately dispossessed of their basic right to a dignified and dignifying life. With this report, the REMI Project sought not only "to dignify the memory of the dead and restore self-esteem to their relatives,"[25] but also to denounce the events that had occurred, expose the sin of the world, and to bring to the collective consciousness the experiences of an oppressed portion of humanity so that those events might NEVER AGAIN be repeated.

According to the report, historical memory is necessary because this memory "not only looks at the facts of the past, but also pursues the demands for truth, respect, justice and reparation which should form part of the process of *social reconstruction*."[26] What this report did was to show how an entire people rises to reconstruct their history from the death imposed on them. The report prepared by the REMI Project testifies to what happens to those who dare to speak the truth about things in the world of sin. Bishop Gerardi, much like the persecuted people of God, Ellacuría, those who died with him, and Archbishop Romero, was brutally assassinated only forty-eight hours after the report was presented to the public at the cathedral in Guatemala City. This event confirmed yet again what Ellacuría had earlier proclaimed:

> The crucified people has a twofold thrust: it is the victim of the sin of the world, and it is also bearer of the world's salvation. A stage focused on the resurrection of the people should indicate how the one crucified for the sins of the world can, by rising, contribute to the world's salvation. Salvation does not come through the mere fact of crucifixion and death. Only a people that lives because it has risen from the death inflicted on it can save the world. *The world of oppression is not willing to tolerate this.*[27]

In this section, then, I have been describing a recent experience of the people of God in Guatemala in order to highlight its continuity, with clearly paschal implications, to the experience of the people of God in El Salvador. For me, this experience touches the deepest fibers of my being, and makes me see that persecution and martyrdom are not realities of the past.

There are several factors that explain my sensitivity to such realities. First, during the nine years that I lived, studied, and worked in Mexico City (1974–83), I maintained close contact with activities in solidarity with the Salvadoran people during the bloody decade of the seventies. My participation grew especially after the murder of Archbishop Romero in 1980, mainly through the Oscar Arnulfo Romero Christian Secretariat for Solidarity in Mexico City.

Second, together with other religious communities of women, and as a member of the religious order Society of the Helpers myself, I lived in a neighborhood located in "the misery belt" of this megacity. From these neighborhoods we learned the meaning of solidarity and hope through sharing on a daily basis the tragedies affecting marginalized people. It was an experience of the Church of the Poor. From within this reality, we better understood the new insights of the theology of liberation we were learning in a formal academic environment. Virtually all of the Christian communities shared both our commitment to the promotion of justice, given the limits of each one's situation, and our communion with the people of God in Central America. The awareness that we are part of what Ellacuría calls an "oppressed humanity" that is struggling for justice sustained a strong bond of solidarity among the communities. Having had this experience, I wrote my licentiate thesis in theology on the subject of martyrdom in the Apocalypse of John, and I dedicated my thesis to Archbishop Romero and Bishop Sergio Méndez Arceo, who encouraged my theological studies.[28]

Third, I had a brief opportunity to get to know Ellacuría while I was doing my doctoral studies at the Universidad Pontificia in Salamanca, Spain (1988–91). I learned from Ellacuría the centrality of hope in struggles for justice through the talk he gave on *"Utopía y Profecía en América Latina"*[29] during the VIII Theological Congress organized by the Association of Spaniard Theologians John XXIII held in Madrid, September 1988.

The following year Ellacuría participated in the inauguration of the Xavier Zubiri Foundation in Madrid, established in honor of the Basque philosopher. Ellacuría had been Zubiri's most important collaborator. And this event initiated my interest in studying Ellacuría's philosophical works. His philosophical work gives original structure and body to the *Latin American philosophy of liberation,* to which he made a critical, coherent, and rigorous contribution. From that time on, I have believed that, in fact, the philosophical foundations of the theology of liberation *cannot* be adequately understood without a knowledge of the critical philosophical work of Ellacuría.[30]

A few months after this event, the news of his assassination shocked the international theological community. Under the impact of this premeditated crime, bearing in mind the image of so many faces un-justly torn from the people of God, I understood the truth of the painful words of Archbishop Romero:

> It falls to me to go about retrieving the abused and corpses. I will not tire of denouncing the outrage of random kidnappings, of disappearances, of torture. The organized sector of our people is still being massacred sim-ply for going to the street in an organized manner to ask for justice and liberty. Violence, assassination, and torture, with so many killed, butchered with machetes and thrown in the sea, people discarded: *all this is the reign of hell.*[31]

It is more than twenty-five years since Archbishop Romero denounced the necrophilia of society, but this pattern is still as alive today as it was then. The *reign of hell* is still causing havoc in Guatemala, in Mexico, in other countries of the Two-Thirds World, and in mounting violence that affects marginalized groups in the wealthy Northern Hemisphere. The re-ality of violence is so great in the United States that the Catholic Bishops have called the Christian community to join forces to efficaciously con-front the culture of violence that surrounds us.[32] This reality is particularly serious at the border between the United States and Mexico, where the persecution and tragic deaths of poor migrant workers continues to grow.

The increased militarization of the U.S.-Mexico border not only has pushed the migrant population into the most unsafe and danger-ous areas along the 3,152 km (1,958 miles) border, but it has also fos-tered among various U.S. groups an anti-immigrant sentiment and ethnic prejudice against migrant workers, stereotyping them as "illegal aliens" and "criminals."[33] In the past eleven years, there has been over thirty-six hundred (3,600) tragic deaths of migrant workers in their painful journey crossing the border,[34] among whom is a growing num-ber of women and children. The majority of these deaths have taken place in Arizona, California, and Texas. From October 2004 through Sep-tember 2005, a record number of four hundred sixty-four (464) deaths of migrant workers have been recorded by the U.S. Border Patrol,[35] but the number of deaths is expected to increase by the end of the year. Ac-cording to L. Berenstein, this large number of tragic deaths "makes 2005 the deadliest year ever long the border,"[36] while it also shows that the U.S. federal government's border policies to stop undocumented migra-tion through militarization is not working. The most common initiatives against migrant workers that have had fatal results are known as "Op-eration Guardian" and the vigilante groups that include armed or unarmed civilian patrols such as the dangerous "Minutemen." R. G. Suárez Rivero reports that "through 'Operation Guardian' in San Diego/Tijuana, extremely large groups of migratory workers have been trapped by the 'Migra' at this border in an environment of constant violations of human rights and excessive use of force."[37] In October 1994 "Operation Guardian" began working through the border patrol, with the support to the U.S. Army, to contain the migratory flow from Mexico to the United States. But in view of the current situation, the question at this border zone, which is powerfully militarized against a people in search of work and minimum conditions for their human dignity, is not whether there will be more deaths, but when and how many more lives will have to be sacrificed in the name of protecting the United States.

I would say, then, that we have *the reign of hell* here at the border as well. Only in this context can we understand why, when Christian faith is lived in situations of violence and injustice against "oppressed humanity," that it can and should be understood as a dynamic force for historical liberation through the struggle for justice. With Ellacuría, I believe that these realities enable us to see the gravity and the magnitude of the sin of the world. However, they also enable us to see more clearly what the true mission of the church is. For Ellacuría, injustice should be defined as "the sin of the world." The mission of the church should be understood as a commitment that seeks "to remove the sin of the world" to communicate salvation by establishing justice.[38]

The struggle for justice, understood as action that seeks to remove the sin of the world, is the supreme expression of Christian love for God, humanity, and the whole of creation.[39] The faith lived by the people of God in the context of *the reign of hell,* can only operate as a *principle of liberation*. According to Ellacuría the primary objective of liberation is justice.[40] This principle, then, defines the deliberate choice by theology and the church to contribute efficaciously to the journey of the true people of God, presently forced to undertake "an all-out struggle against injustice and the intense promotion of justice."[41]

## Conclusion: Toward a More Just World

Ellacuria helps us see, on the one hand, that Christian faith does not achieve its full truth if it does not counter the work of injustice in a world of sin. On the other hand, he argues that Christian faith, grounded in the message of the Gospel, can manifest its full truth only to the extent that each believer contributes to the elimination of the injustice that pervades all the areas of human and eco-biological relations. In the context of a sinful world, the most coherent way of living the Christian faith necessarily includes the struggle for justice.

For Ellacuría, justice can be defined as a way of living in common where each person

> would be, have, and be given not only what is presumed to be theirs because they possess it, but what is owed to them because they are a human person, a partner in a given community, and ultimately a member of the same species, a psycho-organic unity with the responsibility to conduct right relations between its members and with the surrounding natural world.[42]

This life in common must be organized to both guarantee and demand of each person justice towards themselves, humanity, and the surrounding natural world. Elsewhere, Ellacuría says that justice "consists in giving to the people what belongs to the people, in struggling to put aside injustice and exploitation in order to create a new earth." It consists, "in the construction of a new order in which the causes of social exploitation and individual oppression would largely disappear."[43]

These two definitions of justice suggest the Christian vision of a New Humanity can only be realized in the context of a new social order, a new earth grounded in integral justice. And Ellacuría argues that an attitude of faith-filled realism—an attitude that recognizes the historical realism of the Gospel message—enables us to discern different ways of realizing this new earth in the historical circumstances of each community. In this vein, then, I want to briefly highlight five aspects of Ellacuría's thought that shed light upon how to implement our Christian commitment to a more just world.

(1) *The importance of a faith-filled realism for the true people of God.* Ellacuría believes that an attitude of faith-filled realism demands that the people of God recognize that injustice is a historical necessity in a world of sin. The unequal and exclusive character of the present socioeconomic paradigm is the result of human actions, most especially the deliberate choices of powerful elites who control the reins of the social order. Given that the historical actions of these elites do grave harm to the intrinsic dignity of human persons, their spiritual well-being, and their socioeconomic situations, these choices and actions constitute a social sin. This is true inasmuch as the major portion of humanity is oppressed as a direct result of historical actions that can and should be changed. In the words

of Ellacuría, "the oppression of the crucified peoples derives from a necessity in history: the necessity that many suffer, so a few may enjoy, that many be dispossessed, so that a few may possess."[44] In this context, then, the identity of the true people of God is primarily defined by their struggle against the sin of the world, that is, by their struggle for justice.

(2) *The true people of God must overcome naïve attitudes.* For Ellacuría, an attitude of faith-filled realism also helps the Christian community recognize that "the Gospel message is not sufficient" to carry out its commitment to historicize salvation, "because it does not have the appropriate weapons either to discern the causes of oppression, and specific plans for liberation, or to carry them out."[45] This requires a community that is overcoming its naïve attitudes, and searching for adequate theoretical and practical tools to critically understand the reality it is living. It presupposes that the community is in the process of analytically interpreting its present situation in order to reorient the world and its life itself toward greater justice for the entire human community.

(3) *The true people of God must denounce the evils of the present neoliberal capitalist paradigm.* The attitude of believing realism demands that the people of God recognize the sin and the evil of the present capitalist neoliberal paradigm that dominates the globe today. Ellacuría suggests many times that it is the world's various historicizations of capitalism which are primarily responsible "for the situation in which the majority of the population lives today."[46] Capitalism is a socioeconomic system created in Western Europe and perfected in the United States that has permitted the capitalist countries of the North to massively exploit and dominate the impoverished countries of the South. For Ellacuría, capitalism is not only grounded in injustice, in the rule of the powerful, but its greatest sin is that it universalizes injustice by deepening the poverty of the world population, and by forcing human life to submit to the laws of the global market. He argues, however, that

> Its intrinsic malice has been observed in all its magnitude only beyond the boundaries of the rich countries, which in numerous ways export the evils of capitalism to the exploited periphery. The problem is not just that of the foreign debt, or the exploitation of raw materials, or the search for third world sites to dispose of the wastes of all sorts that the more developed countries produce. More than that, it is an almost irresistible pull toward a profound dehumanization as an intrinsic part of the real dynamics of the capitalist system. . . . Predatory ferocity becomes the fundamental dynamic, and generous solidarity remains reduced to

curing, incidentally and superficially, the wounds of the poor caused by their plunder.[47]

He believes the people of God are failing in their mission if they do not raise their voices to denounce the evils of the present capitalist system. At the same time, however, the people of God can and should put the power of the church at the service of a worldwide solidarity to create ways to historically actualize salvation through justice. For Christian faith, the creative activity of women and men in the promotion of greater justice is an expression of the creative activity of God in the world.

(4) *The true people of God must participate in the creation of a new socioeconomic paradigm.* The attitude of faith-filled realism demands that the people of God recognize that the current socioeconomic paradigm is incapable of sustaining the basic levels of life compatible with the dignity of each person. This recognition requires an honest estimation of the present face of the world: poverty and misery, hunger and repression, social and domestic violence, want and growing unemployment, fear and insecurity, cultural degradation and interior emptiness, egotism and greed. Moreover, this realization presumes that the people of God in fact deliberately choose to involve themselves in the construction of a new way of life.

According to Ellacuría, the individual enjoyment of wealth is the key principle of "humanization" in the capitalist millieu of today. He says that, for the people of God, however, "the fundamental principle on which to base the new order remains 'that all might have life and have it more abundantly' (John 10:10). . . . That life must be expanded and completed by internal growth and in relation to the life of others, always in search of more life and better life."[48] This principle of a better life, of a fuller life for all of creation, does not refer to "life" as an abstract entity, or something yet to come. It refers to the elevation of the actual *quality of life* of all people. That is, it refers to the improvement of the real conditions lived by common people in their everyday lives. Thus, universal access to a full life constitutes a central principle for humanization in this new social paradigm.

(5) *The true people of God anticipate and help to bring about a New Humanity.* Finally, an attitude of faith-filled realism helps the people of God to see the outline of a New Humanity in each group dedicated to the promotion of justice. The model of humanity offered to women, to nonwhite races, and to indigenous non-European cultures by the Christian West has put us on a "death train." It has not been able to respect the liberty, the autonomy, and the dignity of our makeup as persons and peoples.

This model has been constructed to conform to the attributes of the white male: educated, well established socially, and prepared to rule.

The kyiarchal, colonizing, racist, and alienating characteristics of the Western "human" model have been copiously commented on by feminist liberation theology. However, as a criticism and an alternative to that model, I want to end by paraphrasing Ellacuría on the characteristics of the New Humanity that we see emerging in the lives of those who work for justice.[49] We see men and women of all races, ages, and cultures living in *solidarity with the struggles of "oppressed humanity,"* people who have become part of this privileged location for humanization and Christian divinization. We see women and men engaged in an unending *struggle against violence,* protesting and struggling to overcome systemic social injustice. They consider the dominant structures that create and reproduce unjust social relations, promote violence against women and other groups, and keep the majority of the world population in poverty, as evil and sinful. We see men and women who are guided and inspired by *mercy and justice* in their struggles for justice. They do not allow egotism, envy, or revenge a place in their hearts. They do not seek to dominate or use other people, but dedicate their lives as Christian disciples to doing good, and to the historical salvation of the crucified people. And we see *hope and joy* in women and men working to construct a more just world as their way of participating in the divine life. They know that their commitment to the cause of justice is not grounded in a self-sacrificial faith, but in faith as a force of liberation. Even though the night of injustice is long, these men and women live with hope and joy. For they see that God has given them the gift of the vocation to create paths for justice leading to that final sunrise when God will be all in all.

[1] Ignacio Ellacuría, "El Pueblo Crucificado," in *Conversión de la Iglesia al Reino de Dios: Para anunciarlo y realizarlo en la historia* (Santander, Spain: Sal Terrae, 1984) 45; collection hereafter cited as *CIRD*. Originally published as "El pueblo crucificado, ensayo de soteriología histórica," in I. Ellacuría and others, *Cruz y resurrección: anuncio de una Iglesia nueva* (Mexico City: CTR, 1978) 49–82 [*MLT*, 580–603].

[2] Ignacio Ellacuría, "Anuncio del Reino y credibilidad de la Iglesia," in *CIRD*, 231; hereafter cited as "Anuncio del Reino." Originally published as "El anuncio del Evangelio y la misión de la Iglesia," *Teología Política* (San Salvador: Ediciones del Secretariado Social Interdiocesano, 1973) 44–69 [*FMF*, 82–126].

[3] Ellacuría, "The Crucified People," *MLT*, 603 [*ML*, vol. 2, 215].

⁴ See the vision of Ignacio Ellacuría regarding the dynamic structure of history in *Filosofía de la realidad histórica* (Madrid: Trotta, 1991) 446–72.

⁵ In his "Anuncio del Reino y credibilidad de la Iglesia," Ellacuría presents theological reasons demonstrating how the sociohistorical liberation from sin, the absolute demand that we work for justice, and Christian love expressed in the liberation from injustice, are *the signs* of the credibility of the church's identity and mission. See *CIRD*, 223–61 [*FMF*, 82–126].

⁶ Ignacio Ellacuría, "Función de las teorías económicas en la discusión teológico-teórica: Teoría de la dependencia," in *La Teología de la Liberación*, Juan José Tamayo-Acosta, ed. (Madrid: Ediciones de Cultura Hispánica, 1990) 98. Selection from an essay originally published as "Teorías económicas y relación entre cristianismo y socialismo," *Concilium*, no. 125 (1977) 282–90 ["The Function of Economic Theories in Theological-Theoretical Discussion on the Relationship between Christianity and Socialism," in J. Metz and J. Jossua, eds., *Christianity and Socialism* (New York: Seabury, 1977) 125–31].

⁷ A detailed treatment of these characteristics can be found in Ignacio Ellacuría, "El verdadero pueblo de Dios, según monseñor Romero," *CIRD*, 81–125; originally published in *ECA*, no. 392 (1981) 529–54.

⁸ Ignacio Ellacuría, "Persecution for the Sake of the Reign of God" in Jon Sobrino, Ignacio Ellacuría and others, *Companions of Jesus: The Jesuit Martyrs of El Salvador* (Maryknoll, NY: Orbis 1990) 64, 68. Translation of the conclusion to "El verdadero pueblo de Dios según Monseñor Romero," *CIRD*, 81–125.

⁹ "No special discernment is needed to identify objective sin in the situation that the people of Latin America are living. The perception of a world submerged in ambition, hatred, and domination is nourished by faith and by the Christian sense of those who live their faith simply. It is a way of seeing the sin of the world, sin Christ came to redeem, and Christians must work to make it disappear from the world," Ignacio Ellacuría, "The Historicity of Christian Salvation," in *MLT*, 276 [*ML*, vol. 1, 357].

¹⁰ Ellacuría, "Anuncio del Reino," 231 [*FMF*, 95].

¹¹ Ellacuría, "Persecution for the Sake of the Reign of God," 75 [*CIRD*, 125].

¹² Ignacio Ellacuría, "La Iglesia que nace del pueblo por el Espíritu," *CIRD*, 78; originally published in *Misión Abierta*, no. 1 (1978) 150–8.

¹³ Ignacio Ellacuría, "Porqué muere Jesús y porqué le matan?" in *Desafíos Cristianos. Misión Abierta*, José María González Ruíz, coordinator (Salamanca, Spain: Lóguez Ediciones, 1988) 40; originally published in *Misión Abierta*, no. 2 (1977) 17–26.

¹⁴ Monseñor Oscar A. Romero, cited by Ellacuría, "Persecution for the Sake of the Reign of God," 65 [*CIRD*, 114].

¹⁵ Ibid., 66–7 [*CIRD*, 116].

¹⁶ Ignacio Ellacuría, "La teología de la liberación ante el cambio sociohistórico Latinoamericano," in *La teología de la liberación*, Juan José Tamayo-Acosta, ed. (Madrid: Ediciones de Cultura Hispánica, 1990) 85; hereafter cited as "Cambio sociohistórico"; originally published as "La teología de la liberación frente al cambio socio-histórico de América Latina" *RLT*, no. 12 (1987) 241–64 [*TSSP*, 19–43].

¹⁷ Ellacuría, "El Pueblo Crucificado," *CIRD*, 62 [*MLT*, 603].

¹⁸ Ignacio Ellacuría, "Diez Afirmaciones sobre 'Utopía' y 'Profetismo,'" *Sal Terrae* 12 (Dec. 1989) 891.

[19] Ignacio Ellacuría, "The Church of the Poor, Historical Sacrament of Liberation" *MLT*, 560; translated by Margaret D. Wilde from "La Iglesia de los pobres, sacramento histórico de la liberación," *ECA*, nos. 348–9 (1977) 707–22 [*ML*, vol. 2, 149].

[20] See Martirologio Latinoamericano in: http://servicioskoinonia.org/martirologio/.

[21] Ignacio Ellacuría, "Liberación," in *Conceptos Fundamentales del Cristianismo*, C. Floristán and J. Tamayo, eds. (Madrid: Trotta, 1993) 697; originally published as "En torno al concepto y la idea de liberación," in I. Ellacuría and others, *Implicaciones sociales y política de la teología de la liberación* (Madrid: Escuela de Estudios Hispanoamericanos y Instituto de Filosofía, Consejo Superior de Investigaciones Científicas, 1989) 91–109.

[22] In 1998 I was invited by the "Women and Theology" Group from the Department of Theology at the Catholic University of Central America, Rafael Landívar, in Guatemala City. In 1999 I was invited by the Women's Commission of the Conference of Religious of Guatemala, CONFREGUA (Conferencia de Religiosos de Guatemala). Both organizations offered a week of reflection focused on the theme of Latin American Feminist Theology of Liberation. The participation of the Guatemalan church communities in these events was massive, with more than five hundred persons coming from all parts of the country. It was also ecumenical, including numerous Catholic and Protestant communities.

[23] This group is formed by more than fifteen women from Mayan villages and it works with the Evangelical Center of Pastoral Studies of Central America, CEDEPCA. In association with the Evangelical Center, this group develops various activities to educate its families, to develop means of subsistence, and to nourish their faith with the message of the Gospel.

[24] Archdiocese of Guatemala, *Guatemala: Nunca Más. Informe del Proyecto Interdiocesano Recuperación de la Memoria Histórica*, Versión Resumida (Guatemala, CA: Oficina de Derechos Humanos del Arzobispado de Guatemala, 1998) 3 [*Guatemala: Never Again!* (Maryknoll, NY: Orbis, 1999) xxxiii].

[25] Monsignor Próspero Penados del Barrio, Archbishop Primate of Guatemala, "A 40 días del execrable asesinato contra Monseñor Juan Gerardi," in *Guatemala: Nunca Más*, 64 [*Guatemala: Never Again*, 70].

[26] *Guatemala: Nunca Más*, 3; emphasis mine [*Guatemala: Never Again!* xxxiii].

[27] Ellacuría, "The Crucified People," *MLT*, 603; emphasis mine [*ML*, vol. 2, 215].

[28] María Pilar Aquino, *Martirio-Testimonio en el Apocalipsis de Juan*, thesis submitted for the Licentiate in Theology, Catholic Pontifical University of Do Río Grande du Sul, Brasil, e Instituto Teológico de Estudios Superiores (ITES), Mexico, D. F., July 12, 1984.

[29] Ignacio Ellacuría, "Diez Afirmaciones sobre 'Utopía' y 'Profetismo,'" 889–93; see the fuller article, "Utopia and Prophecy in Latin America" in *MLT*, 289–328, trans. by James Brockman from "Utopía y profetismo desde América Latina: un ensayo concreto de soteriología histórica," *RLT*, no. 17 (1989) 141–84 [*ML*, vol. 1, 393–442].

[30] Ellacuría's work that is most relevant to the Latin American philosophy of liberation is *Filosofía de la realidad histórica* (Madrid: Trotta, 1991).

[31] Monseñor Oscar A. Romero, cited by Jon Sobrino, *Oscar Romero: Profeta y Mártir de la Liberación* (Lima, Peru: Centro de Estudios y Publicaciones CEP, 1981) 21; emphasis

mine [Sobrino, *Archibishop Romero: Memories and Reflections* (Maryknoll, NY: Orbis, 1990) 110–1].

[32] United States Catholic Conference, *Confronting a Culture of Violence: A Catholic Framework for Action* (Washington, D.C.: United States Catholic Conference, 1995).

[33] María Pilar Aquino, "La Humanidad Peregrina Viviente: Migración y Experiencia Religiosa," in *Migration, Religious Experience, and Globalization,* Gioacchino Campese & Pietro Ciallella, ed. (Staten Island, N.Y.: Center for Migration Studies, 2003) 103–42.

[34] Leslie Berestein, "Posters on fence tell of 3,600 found dead in 11 years," *The San Diego Union Tribune,* October 1, 2005, available from SingOnSanDiego.com. http://www .signonsandiego.com/news/mexico/tijunana/20051001-9999-1n1border.html; Internet (accessed Sunday, October 16, 2005).

[35] Reuters Foundation, "US says migrant deaths at record on Mexico border," available from Reuters AlertNet, October 3, 2005, http://www.alertnet.org/thenews/ newsdesk/N03594921.htm; Internet (accessed Sunday, October 16, 2005).

[36] Leslie Berestein, "Record number have died trying to cross border. Majority found in Ariz. deserts," *The San Diego Union Tribune,* September 4, 2005; available from SignOnSanDiego.com.   http://www.signonsandiego.com/uniontrib/20050904/ news_1n4border.html; Internet (accessed Sunday, October 16, 2005).

[37] Ruy G. Suárez Rivero, "Teología en la Frontera: Límite y Encuentro de Dos Mundos" in *Theology: Expanding the Borders*, María Pilar Aquino and Roberto S. Goizueta, eds. (Mystic, CT: Twenty-Third Publications, 1998) 50.

[38] Ellacuría, "Anuncio del Reino," *CIRD*, 248–9 [*FMF*, 111–2].

[39] Ibid., 258 [*FMF*, 121].

[40] Ellacuría, "Liberación," 702.

[41] Ellacuría, "Anuncio del Reino," 250 [*FMF*, 113].

[42] Ellacuría, "Liberación," 702.

[43] Ellacuría, "El verdadero pueblo de Dios, según Monseñor Romero," *CIRD*, 121–2.

[44] Ellacuría, "The Crucified People," *MLT*, 591 [*ML*, vol. 2, 203].

[45] Ellacuría, "Cambio sociohistórico," 81 [*TSSP*, 25].

[46] Ibid.

[47] Ellacuría, "Utopia and Prophecy," *MLT*, 298 [ML, vol. 1, 405].

[48] Ibid., 306 [*ML*, vol. 1, 415].

[49] This paragraph is a paraphrase of Ellacuría, "Diez Afirmaciones sobre 'Utopía' y 'Profetismo,'" 892–3.

# Chapter 10

# Ignacio Ellacuría:
# From Medellín to Martyrdom

*Gregory Baum*

## Prophets and Martyrs

Rutilo Grande, a Jesuit priest dedicated to the poor in El Salvador, was brutally murdered on March 12, 1977, by the defenders of an unjust sociopolitical order. This violent deed had a deep effect on Bishop Oscar Romero: it opened his eyes to the reality of El Salvador and made him rethink the meaning of the Christian message in his historical situation. He became increasingly convinced of the Gospel's liberating power. The sermons he preached began to change. He now denounced the structures of injustice and expressed his solidarity with the poor, the majority of the population, until he too was gunned down by the same evil forces.

Ignacio Ellacuría was also moved by the murder of Rutilo Grande. Reflecting on his violent death, Ellacuría called him a prophet and martyr of the church.[1] The Jesuit theologian wanted to show that Grande had not been killed simply because he entertained radical political ideas and worked in solidarity with local communities of the poor. Grande was not simply a political figure who threatened the power of the privileged elites. Grande was killed, Ellacuría argued, because he gave witness to the person and message of Jesus Christ in the historical circumstances of El Salvador. Grande was a prophet because he proclaimed both God's judgment on and God's promises for the society to which he belonged. He was a martyr because his fidelity to Jesus Christ provoked the anger of the powerful and persuaded them to do away with him. Ellacuría establishes these claims by referring to the testimony of the people with whom and for whom Grande worked:

> I think Rutilo has fulfilled his priestly mission. . . . He understood the Christian commitment that God wants all people to carry out. He made this commitment by serving others; he related to the humble people in the countryside and in the city, teaching them the true way of Christianity that we must show others. . . . He began to develop a line, putting it into practice with the delegates of the word, and later he began opening a Christian way, committing himself to the people, until one day we saw him killed by the murderous bullets of the enemy, who did not want him to go on working with his people . . . taking them on the way that Christ wanted to show us.[2]

Twelve years later, on November 16, 1989, Ignacio Ellacuría himself was murdered, together with five fellow Jesuits and two women, Julia Elba, the cook, and her daughter, Celina. Was Ellacuría shot to death as a politically inconvenient figure who happened to be Catholic? One way to answer these questions would be to ask the people in El Salvador who worked with the Jesuits and knew them well. This was the approach adopted by Ellacuría himself to show that his friend, Rutilo Grande, was a martyr for his faith. Another approach would be to ask whether the message preached by Ellacuría, including its political implications, truly represents the social teaching of the Catholic Church in Latin America. This is the approach I take in this essay. I argue that Ellacuría's theology of pastoral practice authentically enfleshed the church's official teaching, especially as this was articulated by the Latin American episcopal conferences at Medellín (1968) and Puebla (1979).[3] I evaluate several key themes in Ellacuría's theology in the light of the old method of "see, judge and act" associated with the Catholic action movement.[4] It immediately becomes apparent that Ellacuría offers an analysis of the Latin American reality, then judges it in the light of the Christian Gospel, and finally sets forth how the church should respond both in its pastoral policy and through the practical engagement of Salvadoran Christians. Again utilizing the same "see, judge and act" methodology, I reread the ecclesiastical documents of Medellín and Puebla and report how these two episcopal conferences understood the mission of the church on the Latin American continent.

## "Seeing" the Latin American Reality

The Latin American bishops believed that toward the end of the sixties their continent had entered a *kairos,* a special moment in time when a radical reconstruction of society had become a historical possibility. Even Pope Paul VI agreed. Addressing the Medellín Conference in 1968, he had this to say:

> We are in a moment of total deliberation. The future calls for effort, daring and sacrifice, which introduces a deep anxiety in the Church. What enters into us, like an overwhelming wave, is the restlessness characteristic of our time, and particularly in these countries, straining toward their complete development and troubled by the awareness of their economic, social, political and moral desequilibrium.[5]

The bishops gathered at Medellín were also convinced that their time was a special historical moment:

> Latin America is under the sign of transformation and development; a transformation that is taking place with extraordinary speed and influences every level of human activity, from the economic to the religious. We are on the threshold of a new epoch in the history of our continent. It appears to be a time full of zeal for full emancipation, a time of liberation from every servitude, of personal maturity and of collective integration. In these signs we perceive the first indications of the painful birth of a new civilization.[6]

The utopian expectation that inspired liberation theology was shared by the Medellín Conference. Still, the principal focus of the conference's perception of Latin America was the misery experienced by the majority of the population. "The misery, as a collective fact, expresses itself as an injustice that cries to heaven."[7] Pope Paul VI had used this expression in his encyclical *Populorum Progressio.*[8] Injustice that cries to heaven is a biblical image suggesting that the sufferings inflicted upon the people are such that God will certainly intervene. In 1979 the Bishop's Conference meeting at Puebla, Mexico, reinforced his perception of Latin America:

> From the depth of the countries that make up Latin America a cry is rising to heaven, growing louder and more alarming all the time. It is the cry of a suffering people who demand justice, freedom, and respect for the basic rights of human beings. A little more than ten years ago, the Medellín Conference observed: "A muted cry wells up from millions of human beings, pleading with their pastors for a liberation that is nowhere

to be found." This cry might well have seemed muted back then. Today it is loud and clear, increasing in volume and intensity, and at times full of menace.[9]

What has produced this misery? "Seeing" the Latin American reality calls for an analysis of the causes responsible for the death-dealing poverty spreading throughout the continent. According to Medellín, these causes are both material and spiritual.[10] The Medellín document speaks of "internal colonialism," referring to "the bi-classism" that divides society between the "few who have much (culture, wealth, power, prestige)" and "the majority that has very little." The document also speaks of "external neo-colonialism," referring to the economic and political consequences of "our countries' dependency upon the center of economic power." This is the reason that "our nations frequently do not own their resources nor have a say regarding the economic decisions that affect them." What follows, according to the bishops, is a growing distortion of international commerce, the rapid flight of economic and human capital, tax evasion by foreign and national companies, the investment at the economic center of the profits made in Latin American countries, and the ever-increasing public debt:

> We wish to emphasize that the principal guilt for the economic dependency of our countries rests with powers, inspired by uncontrolled desire for gain, which leads to economic dictatorship and the "international imperialism of money," condemned by Pope Pius XI in "Quadragesimo Anno" and Pope Paul VI in "Populorum Progressio." We here denounce the imperialism of any ideological bias that is exercised in Latin America, either indirectly or through direct intervention.[11]

While these statements are very brief, they do reflect ideas taken from the so-called dependency theory that was widely held in Latin America and used in liberation theology. Latin American dependency theory had Marxist roots. Yet this did not bother the ecclesiastical magisterium. Even Paul VI, in his *Octogesima Adveniens,* recognized that a Marxist social analysis has its usefulness, even if not free of certain risks, seeing its close link with the philosophical and political aspects of Marxism.[12] Medellín also refers to the spiritual causes of the great misery that affect the greater part of the population. The bishops lament the lack of social solidarity, which is ultimately a sinful failure of love. "The lack of solidarity on the individual and social levels leads to the committing of serious sins, as is evident in the unjust structures that characterize the Latin American situation."[13] Unjust structures are an objectification of human sins. This absence of solidarity is accompanied, the bishops think, by a lack of political consciousness.[14] People on all levels of society fail to realize their political responsibility: they do not seek conscientious participation in the building of society, "the practice of charity in its most noble and meaningful sense." The elites, we are told, remain attached to their privileges. The present situation also reveals a lack of imagination. Many people believe that the only available choice is between liberal capitalism and Marxism, both at odds with Christian values, while what is needed is an imaginative alternative that allows for a more active participation of people in their communities. At Puebla, the bishops added that "the fear of Marxism keeps many people from facing up to the oppressive reality of liberal capitalism."[15]

How do the bishops "see" the Catholic Church in Latin America? The answer is implicit in their call to the church to become poor: as an organization and, in particular, in its ministers, the church must become the church of the poor. It must glory in modesty and simplicity. In this call, Medellín admits that the church of the past had tended to be identified with the affluent elites. Eleven years later, Puebla is more outspoken. Here the bishops express their remorse over the alliance of the church with the rich and powerful:

> For all our faults and limitations, we, your pastors, ask pardon of God, of our brothers and sisters in the faith, and of humanity. We want not only to help others to self-conversion but also be converted along with them, so that our dioceses, parishes, institutions, communities, and religious congregations will provide an incentive for living the Gospel, rather than being an obstacle to it.[16]

The bishops at Puebla also recognize that the new solidarity with the poor has introduced great tensions within the church.[17] Conflicts over social justice create divisions in the Catholic community. The political opposition between what the bishops call "the masses" and "the elites" creates conflicts even in the church. Although this point is totally absent from traditional ecclesiology, it receives attention from Ellacuría. Likewise, he draws extensively on the notion of the church of the poor, as we shall see below.

## "Judging" the Latin American Reality

Latin America is a continent imprisoned in sinfully unjust structures and their social consequences. This was the judgment of Medellín.

Puebla's final document contained moving pages describing the harsh inequalities and oppressive conditions produced by the existing economic order, including the description of saddened faces: the faces of young children, of youths, of indigenous people, of peasants, of laborers, of the unemployed, of marginalized urban dwellers and of old people.[18] The situation is "a scandal and a contradiction to Christian existence."[19] These conditions of injustice can be traced ultimately to the sin of idolatry, the idolatry of wealth and power.

> The cruel contrast between luxurious wealth and extreme poverty, which is so visible on our continent and which is further aggravated by the corruption that invades public and professional life, shows the great extent to which our nations are dominated by the idol of wealth.[20]

Liberation theology has used the concept of idolatry in its evaluation of Latin American society, an idea that was absent from traditional Catholic social teaching. After Puebla acknowledged that Latin American society was under the sway of a false religion, the worship of idols, Pope John Paul II himself adopted this concept in 1987 in his own evaluation of the world situation.[21]

What is taking place in Latin America, Medellín and Puebla insist, is at odds with humanity's divinely appointed destiny, which is liberation. Since divine redemption heals and elevates God's creation marred by human sin, the Good News promises to rescue people from the powers of destruction and enables them to overcome the obstacles that impede their self-realization. The bishops argue that this liberation, which they call "integral," differs from the purely economic notion of liberation found both in liberal development theories and, in a different fashion, in Marxist philosophy. Integral liberation has several dimensions:

> The first is the liberation *from* all the forms of bondage, from personal and social sin, and from everything that tears apart the human individual and society; all this finds its source to be in egotism, in the mystery of iniquity. The second element is liberation *for* progressive growth in being through communion with God and other human beings; this reaches its culmination in the perfect communion of heaven, where God is all in all and weeping forever ceases.[22]

The church fully supports human liberation:

> We mutilate liberation in an unpardonable way if we do not achieve liberation from sin and all its seductions and idolatry, and if we do not help

to make concrete the liberation that Christ won on the cross. We do the same thing if we forget the crux of liberative evangelization, which is to transform human beings into active subjects of their own individual and communitarian development.[23]

Medellín and Puebla provide many beautiful texts on integral liberation that envisage the release of people from all forms of bondage through structural and personal transformation. Yet these texts do not all have the same weight. Some of them may be called "strong." They indicate that liberation demands radical structural transformation in a certain discontinuity with the past and that personal, spiritual transformation must be understood as serving this radical reconstruction. Other texts may be called "weak." They express the hope that the spread of personal, spiritual transformation will eventually lead to the needed reform of structures. The strong texts name the oppressive powers, call for mobilization against them, and see the spiritual life—the relation to God and neighbor—as supporting this historical struggle. The weak texts, by contrast, do not name the oppressor. They call for the spiritual conversion on all levels of society and hope that this will result in greater love and a personal commitment to justice, all in the service of institutional reform.[24]

When liberation theologians in Latin America focused on the weak ecclesiastical texts on liberation, they were critical of the church's social teaching. They argued that the official church was still pleading with the rich and powerful to recognize Christ's call for love and justice, and to cooperate in the reform of society. Yet Medellín and Puebla also provided strong texts. In these, they denounce the scandal of the existing society and accuse it of having succumbed to idolatry. They also name the oppressive system that produces poverty and social disintegration. We shall see further on that the ecclesiastical documents support the mobilization of the poor in a joint struggle to transform the material conditions of their lives.

The Medellín Conference also offers ethical reflections on violence in Latin America. It acknowledges first that, in many instances, Latin America finds itself faced with a situation of injustice that can be called "institutional violence." Here, oppressive economic, political, and social forces deprive whole communities of the necessities of life and prevent them from exercising their human right to improve the material and social conditions of their existence. "This situation demands all-embracing, courageous, urgent and profoundly renovating transformations. We should not be surprised, therefore, that 'the temptation of violence' is surfacing in Latin America."[25] Yet in the name of the Gospel, Medellín pleads for a

nonviolent struggle for the reconstruction of society. Even so, there may
be exceptions to this pacifist position in unusual circumstances. Using
quotations from Paul VI, Medellín produced this complex sentence:

> If it is true that revolutionary insurrection can be legitimate in the case
> of evident and prolonged "tyranny that seriously works against funda-
> mental human rights and damages the common good of the country,"
> whether it proceeds from one person or from clearly unjust structures; it
> is also certain that violence or "armed revolution" generally "generates
> new injustices, introduces new imbalances and causes new disasters;
> one cannot combat a real evil at the price of a greater evil."[26]

On these issues, Ellacuría stands as an authentic representative of the
church. He recognized the institutional violence in El Salvador, he understood the counterviolence of the rebelling communities, and he coura-
geously wrestled for mediation and the invention of a peaceful solution.
In his theological writings, Ellacuría always referred to the "reality" or
"historical reality" of Latin America. This terminology was intended to
make two important points. First, to engage in theological reflection it is
necessary to look at, evaluate, and respond to the concrete historical conditions of people's existence. This point emphasizes the materialist dimension of theological reflection. Secondly, this concrete history is the
"one reality" in which is taking place the divine-human drama of creation, sin and redemption, revealed in Jesus Christ. The supernatural is not
a world apart, nor an alternative reality. It is, instead, incarnate in human
history as a gratuitous part of the one, concrete reality to which we belong. Therefore, spirituality is not a journey into a hidden land of untrou-
bled peace, nor a withdrawal from the world as preparation for the eternal
reward, nor in any other way an escape from historical responsibility. Instead, spirituality refers to communion with God present in history, the
God who calls persons and peoples, judges their sins, empowers them to
act in new ways, and fulfills the divine promise of rescue and liberation.
Emphasis on the "one reality" does not intend to deny that final liberation will take place only beyond history. The emphasis suggests, rather,
that the only way to prepare for the world's consummation in God is to
become responsible subjects in history through faith in God's promises.

Puebla adopted the terminology of the one reality. Thus, the title of
Part I of the final document is "Pastoral Overview of the Reality That Is
Latin America."[27] This Latin American reality includes the works of
God's creation, the personal and structural sins that have marred the
history of the continent, including that of the church, and God's creative

and redemptive presence to this history, made manifest in the personal and communal expressions of people's faith, hope, and love and the consequent renewal of the church. The Latin American reality, despite the scandal of social disorder, and despite its surrender to idolatry, includes the divine Spirit at work in people's hearts, making them yearn for and act on behalf of their collective liberation. This is the one reality where the people of Latin America find their God.

## "Acting" in the Latin American Reality

We now turn to the political and pastoral practice called for by Medellín and Puebla. While this theme is quite large, we shall only look briefly at the following topics: the preferential option for the poor, the pastoral task of consciousness-raising, the self-evangelization of the church, and the political mission of priests and bishops.

Medellín gave witness to the church's solidarity with the poor and called for a new practice, namely "the pastoral option for the poor." This option demands that a diocese, a parish, and every other ecclesiastical institution use its material resources and its personnel in the first place to serve the people who are marginalized and to support their social initiatives. Medellín's commitment to the poor was reaffirmed by Puebla and expanded into "the preferential option for the poor." This option expresses the double commitment to look at society from the perspective of the poor and to give public witness of solidarity with their struggle for justice:

> With renewed hope in the vivifying power of the Spirit we take up again the position of . . . Medellín, which adopted a clear and prophetic option expressing preference for, and solidarity with, the poor. We do this despite the distortions and interpretations of some, which vitiate the spirit of Medellín, and despite the disregard and even hostility of others. We affirm the need for conversion on the part of the whole Church to a preferential option for the poor, and option aimed at integral liberation.[28]

This commitment is, first, a new way of perceiving reality or, better, a transformation of consciousness. Looking at society from the perspective of its victims reveals to us the cultural and religious ideologies that tend to disguise and make invisible the oppressive features of the existing order. This conversion is demanded of people belonging to the upper sector of society who entertain an organic or hierarchical image of society where social inequality and traditional authority are the guarantee of public order. Yet this conversion is also demanded of many of the poor, since they have assimilated a false self-understanding mediated through the distorted perception of their oppressors. The church itself, as we shall see, is called upon to think about itself and act in a new manner. The preferential option for the poor implies, at the same time, a new way of acting. Solidarity with the poor means giving public witness in support of their struggle for justice. Fidelity to Jesus Christ implies compassionate identification with the victims of society. Following this option, the church becomes the prophet in society, the voice of the voiceless and the ally of the oppressed and underprivileged.

The Medellín Conference had already insisted that the church's pastoral ministry included *concientización* or the raising of political consciousness among the people.[29] To detect the structures of sin, people must be made aware of the economic, political, and social obstacles that prevent them from assuming responsibility for their personal and social lives. The church's preaching must address the politicization of the Christian communities. The bishops themselves, we are told, must become more socially conscious and more aware of the forces that perpetrate injustice. They must learn to listen to the poor and enter into dialogue with groups of critical intellectuals. If priests are to raise people's consciousness through their ministry, they will have to receive an appropriate training. The national episcopal conferences are asked to set up teaching institutes and organize courses where priests and laypeople can be initiated into critical thinking and learn to analyze their society from the perspective of the excluded and marginalized.

The most daring imperative of the Puebla Conference is addressed to the church itself. The church, we are told, must be converted to the option for the poor, becoming a poor church, the church of the poor, a church no longer identified with the powerful elites. It must become a church that reveals its fidelity to Christ in the modesty and simplicity of its institutional presence. It must manifest its solidarity with the poor by supporting their struggle for justice. In keeping with this option, the church must reexamine its structures and operations.[30] Since the church is not yet the church that it is called upon to be, it must avoid a false, triumphalistic discourse and attitude.[31]

Puebla calls this critical process "the self-evangelization of the Church."[32] This is a bold idea. Traditional Catholic ecclesiology never engaged in critical theological reflection on the church's self-organization and its institutional practices. Yet the idea of self-evangelization has emerged in many parts of the world. This can be seen as early as 1971 in the document issued by the World Synod of Bishops. "The Church, ready to give witness to justice, recognizes that anyone who ventures to speak to people about justice must first be just in their eyes. Hence we must undertake an examination of the modes of acting and of the possessions and life style found within the Church itself."[33]

Action constituted by the preferential option for the poor, the raising of people's political consciousness, and the self-evangelization of the church will have an important political impact. Puebla recognizes that responsible human life has a political dimension, namely, the participation in the building of society. Therefore, to be authentic, Christian faith, hope, and charity must find an appropriate political expression. Christians, their communities, and their church, have a prophetic mission to denounce evil practices, proclaim the rule of justice, and extend their solidarity to the powerless and marginalized. The Gospel must be preached as a liberating message.

To clarify the church's political mission, Puebla distinguishes between two notions of politics and political involvement.[34] Political engagement "in the broad sense" is the exercise of political responsibility. In this sense, the entire church, its people and its ordained members, must be politically engaged in accordance with its prophetic mission. They must apply the liberating Gospel to the concrete conditions in which they live. Here the bishops must assume a certain leadership since, thanks to their position, they can speak for the powerless, for those whose voice cannot be heard. "The Church helps to foster the values that should inspire politics. In every nation it interprets the aspirations of the people, especially the yearnings of those that society tends to marginalize. And it does this with its testimony, its teaching, and its varied forms of pastoral activity."[35]

Political engagement in "the strict sense" is the exercise of political power in a government and of leadership responsibility in a political party. Puebla designates this entire field as "party politics" and follows the ruling of the Vatican prohibiting priests and bishops from becoming involved in politics in the strict sense. This is a relatively recent ruling. For many centuries, popes and bishops exercised the governing power of secular princes, and even in the twentieth century, priests were occasionally members of governments and leaders of political parties. In these situations, it was assumed—perhaps too uncritically—that Catholics were fully united behind these priest politicians. The bishops of the Puebla Conference argue that in their situations Catholics are deeply divided in their political loyalties and that, therefore, in the service of ecclesial unity, priests must stay out of party politics. However, bishops and priests must be politically engaged in the broad sense. They must sustain justice and strive for peace as prophets, teachers, pastors, and public personalities, but they must not be directly involved in party politics.

## Conclusion

In this article, I have reread the documents of Medellín and Puebla to show that Ignacio Ellacuría, in his bold theology and his courageous political involvement, was an authentic representative of the Latin American Church. Ellacuría's profound convictions that Latin America was experiencing a *kairos* are confirmed by the call of these episcopal conferences. This special moment is characterized by the misery inflicted upon the masses, an injustice "that cried to heaven." Moreover, these oppressive conditions in places such as El Salvador were caused by economic and political elites in conjunction with the economic and political policies of the center of power. In line with Medellín and Puebla, Ellacuría judged that Salvadoran society was a scandal and that the defenders of these injustices were captives of idolatry. His interpretation of human liberation was in keeping with what I have called the strong texts of Medellín and Puebla. These texts, as we saw, claimed that liberation demands radical structural transformation that stands to some extent in discontinuity with the past. Likewise, personal spiritual transformation must be understood as serving this radical reconstruction. At the same time, Ellacuría never reduced liberation to the economic and political dimension. For him, liberation was integral. He did not disguise the mystical core of his prophetic involvement. His strong emphasis on the "one reality" to which we belong, the one history in which the drama of sin and redemption is acted out, received support from the ecclesiastical documents. We also saw that his reaction to the violence in El Salvador was in keeping with Medellín. While he understood the violence of the rebels as a response to institutional violence, he worked hard for a peaceful solution through a negotiated settlement.

Ellacuría's pastoral and political involvement corresponded to the teaching of his church. The preferential option for the poor was the perspective from which he read the Scriptures, developed his thought, interpreted his society, and planned his pastoral involvement. He tried to raise the political consciousness of the people. His urgent and controversial demand that the church become "the Church of the poor" was confirmed by the episcopal call for the self-evangelization of the church. Moreover, his political involvement was in perfect accord with the church's official teaching. He acted as a prophet and teacher in solidarity with the poor, but he held no office in a political organization. He was in fact the courageous embodiment of the ideal pastor as laid down in the documents of Medellín and Puebla. He represented the Latin American church as it wanted to be, not as it was, but as it understood its divine vocation. Like Rutilo Grande and Oscar Romero, Ignacio Ellacuría and his companions were killed because they gave witness to Jesus Christ as mediated by the Scriptures and by the church's teaching.

------

[1] Ignacio Ellacuría, "The Church of the Poor, Historical Sacrament of Liberation," in I. Ellacuría and J. Sobrino, eds., *Mysterium Liberationis: Fundamental Concepts of Liberation Theology* (Maryknoll, NY: Orbis, 1994) 543–64, trans. by Margaret D. Wilde from "La Iglesia de los pobres, sacramento histórico de liberación" (1977); collection hereafter cited as *MLT* (English translation) and *ML* (Spanish original). All citations of Ellacuría's writings are to the English; works in their original Spanish are cited in brackets [*ML,* vol. 2 (1977) 127–54].

[2] Ibid., 562 [152].

[3] The Medellín Conference represented an astounding breakthrough. For an evaluation of its impact on the evolution of papal teaching and the teaching of other episcopal conferences, see Gregory Baum, "Faith and Liberation: Development Since Vatican II," in Gregory Baum, *Theology and Society* (New York: Paulist Press, 1987) 3–31.

[4] I will draw in particular on four articles by Ellacuría: "The Historicity of Christian Salvation" (1994) *MLT,* 251–89, trans. by Margaret D. Wilde from "Historicidad de la salvación cristiana" (1984) [*ML,* vol. 1 (1984) 323–72]; "Utopia and Prophecy in Latin America" (1994) *MLT,* 289–328, trans. by James Brockman from "Utopía y profetismo desde America Latina: un ensayo concreto de soteriología histórica" (1989) [*ML,* vol. 1 (1989) 393–442]; "The Church of the Poor, Historical Sacrament of Liberation" (1994), *MLT,* 543–64 [*ML,* vol. 2 (1977) 127–54]; "The Crucified People," (1994) *MLT,* 580–603, trans. by Phillip Berryman from "El pueblo crucificado: ensayo de soteriología histórica" (1978) [*ML,* vol. 2 (1978) 189–216].

[5] For the Medellín document, see CELAM, Second General Conference of Latin American Bishops in Medellín, Colombia, 1968, *The Church in the Present-Day Transformation of Latin America in the Light of the Council,* 2 vols. (Washington, D.C.: United States Catholic Conference, 1970); hereafter cited as *Medellín.* For the quotation of Paul VI, see *Medellín,* 9.

[6] "Presence of the Church in Present-Day Latin America," no. 4 *Medellín,* 35.

[7] "Justice," no. 1 *Medellín,* 40.

[8] Paul VI, *Populorum Progressio* (1967) no. 30, in D. O'Brien and T. Shannon, eds., *Catholic Social Thought: The Documentary Heritage* (Maryknoll, NY: Orbis, 1992) 247.

[9] For the texts from the Puebla Conference, see J. Eagleson and P. Scharper, eds., *Puebla and Beyond* (Maryknoll, NY: Orbis, 1979); hereafter cited as *Puebla.* For the text of "The Cry Rising to Heaven," see *Puebla,* nos. 87–8, 134.

[10] "Peace," nos. 2–9 *Medellín,* 54–7.

[11] Ibid., no. 9e *Medellín,* 57. See Pius XI, *Quadragesimo Anno* (1931) no. 109, *Catholic Social Thought,* 66; Paul VI, *Populorum Progressio* (1967) no. 26, *Catholic Social Thought,* 246.

[12] Paul VI, *Octogesima Adveniens* (1971) no. 33, *Catholic Social Thought,* 277.

[13] "Justice," no. 2 *Medellín,* 41.

[14] Ibid., no. 16 *Medellín,* 48.

[15] *Puebla,* no. 92, 135.

[16] "Message to the People of Latin America," *Puebla,* no. 2, 117.

[17] *Puebla,* no. 90, 135.

[18] Ibid., nos. 31–9, 128–9.

[19] Ibid., no. 28, 128.

[20] Ibid., no. 494, 193.

[21] John Paul II, *Sollicitudo Rei Socialis* (1987), *Catholic Social Thought,* 393–436.

[22] *Puebla,* no. 82, 190–1; emphasis mine.

[23] Ibid., no. 485, 191.

[24] The same ambiguity, I might add, is found in the papal texts on integral liberation: they can be read as support for radical institutional change or a gradual reform of structures. In the article cited in note 3, I introduced the same distinction referring to the "hard" and the "soft" concept of liberation; see "Faith and Liberation: Development Since Vatican II," *Theology and Society,* 8–9.

[25] "Peace," no. 16 *Medellín,* 61.

[26] Ibid., no. 19 *Medellín,* 63; Paul VI, *Populorum Progressio* (1967) no. 31, *Catholic Social Thought,* 247.

[27] *Puebla,* 123.

[28] Ibid., no. 1134, 264.

[29] "Justice," no. 17 *Medellín,* 48. For a further treatment of consciousness-raising, see *Puebla,* no. 77, 133 and no. 1220, 274.

[30] *Puebla,* no. 1157, 267.

[31] Ibid., no. 231, 153.

[32] Ibid., no. 228, 152.

[33] World Synod of Bishops, "Justice in the World" (1971) ch. 3, *Catholic Social Thought,* 295.

[34] *Puebla,* no. 521, 196.

[35] Ibid., no. 522, 196.

# Chapter 11

# What San Salvador Says to Nairobi: The Liberation Ethics of Ignacio Ellacuría

*Aquiline Tarimo, S.J., and William O'Neill, S.J.*

"The radical problem of human rights is that of the struggle of life against death." So wrote Ignacio Ellacuría in May 1989, the year of his own death in the struggle of "the oppressed people" and "popular majority" of El Salvador.[1] Ellacuría's remarks on human rights, the common good, and property testify to the rich ethical implications of his more systematic reflections on "salvation in history."[2] In this essay, we follow Ellacuría in reconstructing the moral-epistemological, ethical, and political aspects of Christian historical praxis in light of our own solidarity with small Christian communities in eastern Africa.[3] Part 1 sets the stage for our inquiry by situating Ellacuría's critique against the differing interpretations of human rights and the common good in liberal and communitarian political philosophy. Part 2 is devoted to an analysis of "historicization" as it figures in Ellacuría's interpretation of these themes. Our final section, part 3, illustrates the enduring significance of Ellacuría's ethical critique by applying it to the African church's contemporary "struggle of life against death."

## 1. The Problematic

In the course of a "prodigiously creative" life, Ellacuría regularly took soundings of his adopted country's historical reality.[4] As editor, political analyst, and most notably, rector of the Universidad Centro-americana José Simeón Cañas (UCA), Ellacuría played the role of Gramsci's organic intellectual.[5] "For the intellectual, to be 'for' human rights," writes Edward Said, "in effect means to be willing to venture interpretations of those rights in the same place and with the same language employed by the dominant power, to dispute its hierarchy and methods, to elucidate what it has hidden, to pronounce what it has silenced or rendered unpronounceable."[6]

In political philosophy, the locus of venturing such an interpretation—its place and language—is broadly defined by contending liberal and communitarian schools of interpretation: Our sense of justice is parsed in rival rhetorics of abstract, individual rights beholden to Kantian Morality *(Moralität)* or ethically diverse narrative traditions of Hegelian provenance *(Sittlichkeit)*.[7] Ellacuría's ethics bids us to unravel the hidden prejudice of such rhetorics, that is, the underlying antinomy of abstract universality and narrative history, if only to reweave these disparate strands into a historicized account of "integral liberation."[8]

For heirs of the regnant liberal philosophic tradition, the *epistemological validity* of claim-rights to civil-political liberties rests in a procedural abstraction from historical and social contingency, for example, our differing, even incommensurable conceptions of the good. In John Rawls' contractarian account of justice as fairness, for instance, mutually disinterested agents select lexically ordered principles of justice under the heuristic device of a "veil of ignorance."[9] Deprived of knowledge of their particular interests, desires, ideals, social roles, religious beliefs, or cultural heritage, Rawls' rational contractors regard their self-interested choice as tantamount to fairness or impartiality once the veil is lifted. In a similar vein, Jürgen Habermas argues that only a formal, proceduralist justification aspiring to the conditions of an ideal "unlimited communication community (unlimited, that is, in social space and historical time)" suffices to redeem the moral rights' claims of citizens in modern, complex societies.[10]

Communitarian critics as diverse as Charles Taylor, Alasdair MacIntyre, Richard Rorty, and Michael Walzer object that any coherent account of justice must, in Walzer's words, be "properly circumstantial."[11] Recurring to the Hegelian critique of the "empty formalism" of Kantian morality, communitarian rhetoric—whether of a traditionalist or postmodern stripe—envisions the self as "constructed" in the ensemble of social relations, the distinctive mores of our narrative traditions.[12] So it is, Rorty offers a "thick" description of Rawls' "thin" theory, for to the "thoroughly enlightened" postmodernist citizen, the "natural" rights of the sovereign Individual are but a supreme fiction.[13] In Rorty's demystified world, "no trace of divinity" remains, "either in the form of a divinized world or divinized self," that is, a subject endowed with "objective moral values" or "human rights."[14]

The *epistemological* antinomy of liberal theory's thin proceduralist justification and communitarian theory's thick circumstantial justification gives rise, in turn, to rival *ethical* programs of what Michael Sandel terms "the politics of [human] rights" and "the politics of the common good."[15] Rawls and Habermas invoke the critical rhetoric of abstract, universal rights to transcend the very "local and ethnocentric" customs from which Rorty derives the ethical substance of tradition.[16] For Rorty, as for modern feminist critics such as Seyla Benhabib, the putative impartiality of such abstract rights, ascribed to a "Generalized Other," is belied by the generalized bias of "bourgeois individuals in a disenchanted universe."[17]

At the level of *application,* legal rights, for example, to private property, may thus merely enshrine prevailing social bias, which the "politics of rights" mystifies with a spurious moral legitimacy. Yet for Rorty's radical historicism, the demystification of ideology is finally no less mystified. If for Rawls, privileging the (moral and epistemic) perspective of the dominated—the oppressed peoples and poor majorities—is finally irrational (as contrary to pure, procedural fairness), for Rorty, such partiality is no *more* rational than any local or ethnocentric "politics of the common good." Here, too, the Catholic Church's position is curiously ambivalent, for in embracing human rights' rhetoric in interpreting the common good, the church's modern social teaching joins what liberal and communitarian theories have sundered. One wonders, then, if the church has read the signs of the times aright or if its belated rapprochement with the traces of divinity in modernity is, in Rorty's words, merely "quaint."[18]

## 2. Historicization

The preceding analysis serves as a prelude to the three questions Ellacuría poses in his essay *"Historización de los derechos humanos":* the *epistemological* question of whether the validity of moral claims can be understood independently of their historical application; the *ethical* question of whether the thin rhetoric of human rights must be opposed to the thick rhetoric of the common good; and the *political* question of whether the politics of "human rights" and/or the "common good" can serve as a sufficient principle of ideological demystification. In response to each of these questions, Ellacuría's interpretation of "historicization" provides the crucial, mediating link.[19]

In his analysis of Ellacuría's seminal *Philosophy of Historical Reality,* Robert Lassalle-Klein concludes that "historicization," in its most fundamental sense, signifies "the incorporative and transformative power which human praxis exerts over the historical and natural dimensions of reality."[20] In the realm of ethics, Ellacuría observes that the truth of "historical concepts" is thus "found in their becoming reality," that is, in the "results" of their application so that *"[d]emonstrating the impact of certain concepts within a particular context is what is understood here as their historicization."*[21]

More precisely, we might say that human rights' claims, for example, to private property, exhibit both logical (with respect to their validity) and semantical (with respect to their full sense or meaning) dependence upon the historical context of their genesis and application.[22] If, for instance,

> it is claimed that property ownership promotes initiative, personal freedom and so forth, but in fact causes the opposite within the whole of a particular social body, the property under consideration is not the kind needed by that social body. Indeed, property is its antithesis if it is causing contrary effects.[23]

Claims, whose meaning *as* rights derives originally from historical resistance to repression, are thus belied by the totality of their effects, for example, if prevailing property rights undermine the initiative and personal freedom of the majority.

Rather than depicting rights abstractly as discrete properties of disembedded or disembodied Individuals, or as of merely "local and ethnocentric" origin, Ellacuría conceives human rights as a complex set of interrelated claims deriving from the exigencies of historical praxis. Human rights, that is, comprise "concretely universal"[24] claims legitimated by "the indispensable minimal conditions" of exercising historical agency—conditions that must be satisfied if our rights' rhetoric "is to have real meaning."[25] Where, conversely, the legal protection of property rights becomes "a mask to conceal the fundamental violation of the most basic human rights," for example, the nutritional rights of "over 200 million children in developing countries under the age of five [who] are malnourished,"[26] every "possible ethical defense of human rights crumbles at its base." For "[o]nly the consistent affirmation of the right to life, including the right of freedom, can be the crucial test of what the real understanding of human rights is, as opposed to its self-interested mystification."[27]

The consistent and historically effective "affirmation of the right to life" becomes, in turn, the touchstone of emancipatory Christian praxis; for the divine reign, incarnate in Jesus, reveals a divine transcendence *in,* and not "outside or beyond" history.[28] Just as for "the oppressed believers in Latin America, injustice and whatever brings death and denies dignity to the children of God are not merely historical effects, nor even a legal failing; they are sin in a formal sense," so, too, the historicized affirmation of life in "lifting up the lowly" (Luke 1:52), becomes a real symbol of "salvation in history." From the perspective of moral epistemology, Christian historical praxis thus finds its *ultimate* vindication in the incarnate reign of God, even as the church's historicization of human rights draws upon biblical narrative for its *proximate* (morally relevant) interpretation of praxis, for example, Ellacuría's critical hermeneutic of the "crucified people."[29]

The epistemological richness of Ellacuría's conception of historicization is hardly exhausted by these brief remarks, but suffice for the moment to observe that the historicization of human rights' claims, understood analogically in terms of the effective history of their genesis and validity, establishes both their relative priority and affinity with the ethical ideal of the common good.[30] *Ethically,* the lexical ordering or hierarchy of rights corresponds to the graduated urgency of the claims they embody, for to defend some human rights that are not fundamental and radical or to defend fundamental ones without concern for the real conditions that make them possible is to mystify the whole problem of human rights and the common good.[31]

Basic or "fundamental rights" to security, subsistence, and participative liberties, that is, the "rights of the poor," assume a moral (and political) priority over less exigent claims, for example, private property rights. Indeed, such basic rights, "negative" *and* "positive," are mutually implicatory, inasmuch as their enjoyment must be presumed for the exercise of any other claim-right (including, a fortiori, any other basic right).[32] The biblical "option for the poor"—far, then, from being a fideistic suspension of justice as fairness—is legitimated in the ethical priority accorded the rights of the poor; for the *equal* respect to which every moral agent is entitled justifies *preferential* regard for those whose most basic rights are systemically imperiled.

Neither are the duties correlative to such fundamental rights merely "negative" obligations of forebearance, as in classical liberal thought; for as Ellacuría argues, rights' rhetoric is reduced to an "abstract, mystifying formality," if we fail to secure the real structural "conditions which make them possible."[33] Such conditions will vary historically, yet the

structural realization of basic human rights, as the sine qua non of equi-
table and sustainable development, remains a fundamental social *telos,*
that is, a *common good* that extends analogically to national, subnational,
and supranational communities.[34] So conceived, the common good, as a
vital social *telos* or finality, is neither the mere aggregate of individual
goods (as in philosophical liberalism), nor the good of a suprapersonal
"total organism" (as adumbrated in German Romanticism). Rather, the
common good "is basically a union of structural conditions" that preserves and protects "the personal good and thus . . . the rights of the
person."[35] The ideal of the common good, that is, is conceived distribu-
tively, as a good all share in common, yet not *en masse.*

> What is proposed, then, is a common good which transcends each one of
> the individuals, but without being extrinsic to them. It is a common
> good, moreover, which surpasses each one considered individually, but in
> the same way that each one surpasses himself or herself in his or her
> *communitarian and social* dimension.[36]

Far from being "quaint," then, the church's understanding of the
*politics* of rights in terms of the *politics* of the common good (analogically conceived) serves as a critical principle of demystification or "de-
ideologization."[37] In a "divided society," rent by historical injustices, the
ideal of the common good becomes a dialectical "leaven in the world's
transformation,"[38] disputing the hierarchy and methods of the prevailing
order, elucidating what they have hidden, pronouncing what they have silenced or rendered unpronounceable. In short, the common good is properly historicized inasmuch as it inscribes the moral and epistemic privilege
of the poor in our narrative "communitarian" traditions. For "[i]t is proper
to the human condition that a vital universality can be attained only on
the basis of a very concrete incarnation." Yet what is incarnated *in concreto*
are the "fundamental rights of the person" which "as the supreme value"
must, pace Rorty, take precedence over the positive "legal and political restrictions" of tradition.[39] Moreover, it is here, through the praxis of its base
communities, notes Ellacuría, that the church fulfills its historicizing role
as a principal mediating institution of civil society.[40]

## 3. Small Christian Communities as Agents of Historicization in Africa

Any appreciation of Ellacuría's work would be remiss were it to neglect the application of his historicized interpretation of human rights

and the common good to our own historical context. The "struggle for life against death" of the church in Africa is a case in point.[41] Reports of human rights abuse in Africa are rampant: torture, kidnappings and disappearances, state-sponsored violence, child labor, detention without trial, and so on. Global financial institutions, for example, the International Monetary Fund (IMF), impose structural adjustment programs in the name of individual liberties, while African leaders such as Mobutu Sese Seko, former president of Zaire (Democratic Republic of Congo), appeal in a communitarian vein to the "traditional" common good. Yet such rhetoric is disproved by its fruits as liberal privatization severely restricts the "initiative" and "personal freedom" of the majority, while "custom" becomes a "mask to conceal" *modern* despotism.

Historicization demands rather the "establishment of those real conditions without which there can be no effective realization of the common good and of human rights."[42] Consistent with the primacy of participatory rights, such historical praxis privileges "local knowledge." Elochukwu E. Uzukwu argues that African appropriation of human rights' rhetoric must be "guided by the African relational notion" of the person.

> African anthropology (the doctrine of the human person) parts company with . . . modern Western [individualism] to insist that communicability is of the very essence of the person. The autonomy and rights of the individual subject are enjoyed in relationship, in communication. Indeed the "freedom" of the individual is "for" the construction of a better community.[43]

To a limited degree, the Banjul Charter on Human and Peoples Rights, adopted by the Organization of African Unity (OAU) on June 27, 1981, reflects such a historicized interpretation. H.O.W. Okoth-Ogendo, concludes that charter's raison d'être rested not only in the need of an effective structure "at the regional level for the institutional coordination, supervision, or implementation of efforts" directed toward "the promotion and protection of human rights," but even more in "the need to develop a scheme of human rights norms and principles founded on the historical traditions and values of African civilizations rather than simply reproduce and try to administer the norms and principles derived from the historical experiences of Europe and the Americas."[44] As recent African history attests, however, the charter itself will be nugatory unless its aims are effectively historicized in both the political and civil realm.[45]

Indeed, the suppression or relative weakness of mediating institutions in African civil society, due in part to the legacy of colonial rule and the undemocratic monopolization of state power, looms as a major stumbling block to the protection and promotion of human rights.[46] The mere accession of a new head of state, as in the Congo, does little to ameliorate underlying structural inequities. In such "limit situations," the churches inherit a prophetic role inasmuch as they prove themselves to be credible sources of social critique and faith-filled resistance.[47] Yet the church discards its prophetic mantle if it is quiescent in the face of systemic injustice, as in pre-genocidal Rwanda,[48] or if the "teaching Church" remains aloof from the "learning Church."[49]

As the bishops of Africa and Madagascar (SECAM) have themselves declared, the church's social teaching must be nourished by vibrant small Christian communities:

> It is the clear task of these communities rooted and integrated as they are in the life of their peoples, to search deeper into the gospel, to set the priorities of pastoral planning and activity, to take the initiative called for by the mission of the church, to discern, in a spirit of faith where there can be continuity between culture and Christian life and where cleavage is necessary in all aspects of life that hinder the Gospel.[50]

"[R]ooted in the soil," small Christian communities, in Jean-Marc Éla's words, hold forth the prospect of historicizing human rights in African civil society:

> The poor and oppressed are reclaiming the Word of God and changing the structures of a world that is incompatible with God's plan. Working through *historical dynamics,* the poor are called by the gospel to ask hard questions and to become participants with the power to change their own living conditions. . . . Solidarity is now the business of the poor themselves, as they learn to be together in a village or a slum and work to solve their own problems and to share their life and their struggles— everything that comprises their essence and their deepest hopes.[51]

In the "ferment of small communities committed to the poor and the downtrodden," the "rights of the poor" would then be interpreted and defended by the "poor majorities" themselves—interrupting the discourse of elites.[52]

To be sure, the challenges facing such small Christian communities are formidable. Not only must they overcome internal differences of ethnicity, gender, and class that beset society as a whole, but they must find effective means of what Ellacuría terms "social collaboration" with other churches and religious groups.[53] Such collaboration, moreover, must extend to other formal and informal associations of civil society, for example, indigenous NGOs (nongovernmental organizations).[54] As we noted above, the historicization of rights in the small Christian communities presumes the effective inculturation of rights' rhetoric,[55] for example, in the traditional "palaver" of social life.[56] Above all, in Éla's words, "loud voices" must "announce the gospel with boldness"; for as Ellacuría taught us, it is only by such costly grace that "salvation in history" is born.[57]

## Conclusions

Time permits no more than a reconstructive sketch of the moral-epistemological, ethical, and political aspects of Ellacuría's remarkable oeuvre. Our brief reflections fail to do justice to a man whose life "justiced," as the poet Hopkins says.[58] Yet the fruit of historicization can finally be no more than the effective history of a life. Jon Sobrino reminds us that in a sometimes vile and violent world, it is not death that makes the martyr, but martyrdom that reveals "the truth about our lives." Ellacuría "found God hidden in the suffering face of the poor" and "crucified in the crucified people":[59] A martyred love for a martyred God. There is no greater tribute.

---

[1] Ignacio Ellacuría, "Historización de los derechos humanos desde los pueblos oprimidos y las mayorías populares," *Estudios Centroamericanos* 502 (1990) 593; first published in J. Aguirre and X. Insausti, eds., *Pensamiento crítico, ética y absoluto: Homenaje a José Manzana* (Victoria: Editorial ESET, 1990) 147–58; essay hereafter cited as "Derechos humanos" (1990) and periodical hereafter cited as *ECA*.

[2] See Ignacio Ellacuría, *Freedom Made Flesh: The Mission of Christ and His Church,* (Maryknoll, NY: Orbis, 1976) trans. by John Drury from *Teología política* (San Salvador: Ediciones del Secretariado Social Interdiocesano, 1973); and "The Historicity of Christian Salvation," in I. Ellacuría and J. Sobrino, eds., *Mysterium Liberationis: Fundamental Concepts of Liberation Theology* (Maryknoll, NY: Orbis, 1993) 251–89, trans. by Margaret D. Wilde from "Historicidad de la salvación cristiana," *Revista Latinoamericana de Teología (RLT)*, no. 1 (1984); collection hereafter cited as *MLT* (English translation) and *ML* (Spanish original); works in the original Spanish are cited in brackets [*ML*, vol. 1, 323–72].

[3] Ellacuría, "Derechos humanos," 590. Ellacuría writes, "hay que plantearlo en un triple plano: en lo que tiene de verdadero ye de falso—problema epistemológico—en lo que tiene de justo e injusto—problema ético—ye en lo que tiene de ajustado o desajustado—problema práxico o político."

[4] Jon Sobrino, "Companions of Jesus," in J. Sobrino, I. Ellacuría, and others, *Companions of Jesus: The Jesuit Martyrs of El Salvador* (Maryknoll, NY: Orbis, 1990) 9.

[5] See Antonio Gramsci, *The Modern Prince and Other Writings*, trans. Louis Marks (New York: International Publishers, 1957). Ellacuría served as editor of *Estudios Centroamericanos (ECA), Revista Latinoamericana de Teología (RLT)*, and *Proceso*.

[6] Edward W. Said, "Nationalism, Human Rights, and Interpretation," *Raritan* 12:3 (Winter 1993) 45–6.

[7] See Jean-François Lyotard, *The Postmodern Condition: A Report on Knowledge*, trans. G. Bennington and B. Massouri (Minneapolis: University of Minnesota Press, 1984) 27.

[8] Ignacio Ellacuría, "Liberation Theology and Socio-Historical Change in Latin America," in J. Hassett and H. Lacey, eds., *Towards a Society That Serves Its People* (Washington, D.C.: Georgetown University Press, 1991) 22, trans. by James R. Brockman from "La teología de la liberación frente al cambio socio-histórico de América Latina" in *RLT* (1987) 241–64; essay hereafter cited as "Liberation Theology and Socio-Historical Change" (1991); collection hereafter cited as *TSSP;* works in the original Spanish are cited [in brackets]. See Hans-Georg Gadamer's interpretation of "historically affected consciousness" *(Wirkungsgeschichtliches Bewußtsein), Truth and Method,* 2nd. rev. ed., trans. Joel Weinsheimer and Donald Marshall (New York: Crossroad, 1991) 300–7.

[9] See John Rawls, *A Theory of Justice* (Cambridge, MA: The Belknap Press of Harvard University Press, 1971); *Political Liberalism* (New York: Columbia University Press, 1993).

[10] Sharply distinguishing the discourse of moral justification from that of application, Habermas's discourse ethics reflects a "deontological viewpoint" in which "moral deliberations must be kept completely free from goal-directed reflections." Jürgen Habermas, *Justification and Application: Remarks on Discourse Ethics,* trans. Ciaran P. Cronin (Cambridge, MA: MIT Press, 1993) 63; see also, *Moral Consciousness and Communicative Action* (Cambridge, MA: MIT Press, 1990).

[11] Michael Walzer, *On Toleration* (New Haven, CT: Yale University Press, 1997) 3.

[12] G. W. F. Hegel, *Hegel's Philosophy of Right,* trans. T. M. Knox (Oxford: Oxford University Press, 1952) par. 135.

[13] See Richard Rorty, "The Priority of Democracy to Philosophy," in Merrill D. Peterson and Robert C. Vaughan, eds., *The Virginia Statute for Religious Freedom: Its Evolution and Consequences in American History* (New York/Cambridge: Cambridge University Press, 1988) 257–82.

[14] Richard Rorty, *Contingency, Irony, and Solidarity* (Cambridge: Cambridge University Press, 1989) 45.

[15] Michael Sandel, "Introduction," in *Liberalism and Its Critics,* ed. Michael Sandel (New York: New York University Press, 1984) 4, 6, 10.

[16] Rorty, "The Priority of Democracy to Philosophy," 259.

[17] Seyla Benhabib, "The Generalized and the Concrete Other: The Kohlberg-Gilligan Controversy and Feminist Theory," in *Feminism as Critique,* ed. Benhabib and Drucilla Cornell (Minneapolis: University of Minnesota Press, 1987) 83.

[18] Within modern Catholic social teaching, one observes a shift from the perfectionist teleology of *Mater et Magistra*, no. 65, which depicts the common good as "the sum total of those conditions of social living, whereby [we] are enabled more fully

and more readily to achieve [our] own perfection," to an invocation of dignity and rights in *Pacem in Terris,* no. 60; see *Gaudium et Spes,* no. 26, and *Dignitatis Humanae,* no. 6.

[19] Ellacuría, "Derechos humanos," 590–6. For a different, yet complementary approach, see Enrique Dussel, "The Architectonic of the Ethics of Liberation: On Material Ethics and Formal Moralities," in *Liberation Theologies, Postmodernity, and the Americas,* ed. D. Batstone and others (London: Routledge, 1997) 273–304.

[20] Robert Lassalle-Klein, "The Body of Christ: The Claim of the Crucified People on U.S. Theology and Ethics," *Journal of Hispanic/Latino Theology* 5:4 (May 1998) 68. See Ignacio Ellacuría, *Filosofía de la realidad histórica* (San Salvador: UCA Editores, 1990).

[21] Ignacio Ellacuría, "The Historicization of the Concept of Property," in *TSSP,* 108–9, trans. by Phillip Berryman from "La historización del concepto de propriedad como principio de desideologización" in *ECA* 31, 335–6 (1976) 425–50.

[22] Ellacuría, "Derechos humanos," 591–3.

[23] Ellacuría, "The Historicization of the Concept of Property," 108–9. See also, "Utopia and Prophecy in Latin America," in *TSSP,* 65–7, trans. by James R. Brockman from "Utopía y profetismo desde América Latina: Un ensayo concreto de soteriología historíca" in *RLT,* no. 17 (1989) 141–84.

[24] See John P. Reeder's interpretation of the Hegelian understanding of "concrete universality" in "Foundations without Foundationalism," in *Prospects for a Common Morality,* ed. Gene Outka and John P. Reeder Jr. (Princeton, NJ: Princeton University Press, 1993) 191–214.

[25] Ignacio Ellacuría, "Human Rights in a Divided Society," in A. Hennelly and J. Langan, eds., *Human Rights in the Americas: The Struggle for Consensus* (Washington, D.C.: Georgetown University Press, 1982) 59, trans. by Alfred Hennelly from "Historización del bien común y de los derechos humanos en una sociedad dividida," in E. Tamez and S. Trinidad, eds., *Capitalismo: violencia y anti-vida,* vol. 2 (San José, 1978) 81–94 [88].

[26] Kofi A. Annan, "Foreword," UNICEF, *The State of the World's Children: 1998* (Oxford: Oxford University Press, 1998) 6.

[27] Ellacuría, "Human Rights in a Divided Society," 58–9 [87–8].

[28] Ellacuría, "The Historicity of Christian Salvation," *MLT* (1994) 254 [327].

[29] While such an understanding of the universality of rights is consonant with the "autonomy school" of moral theology, the hermeneutic function of Christian narrative in the historicization of rights (which are never mere abstract verities) reflects the theology of the *Glaubensethik* (faith ethics). Ellacuría's historicized interpretation thus offers a critical *via media* between the rival schools of Western moral theology. See also Vincent MacNamara, *Faith and Ethics: Recent Roman Catholicism* (Washington, D.C.: Georgetown University Press, 1985).

[30] Ellacuría, "The Historicization of the Concept of Property," *TSSP,* 108. See also David Hollenbach, "The Common Good Revisited," *Theological Studies* 50 (1989) 85–7.

[31] Ellacuría, "Human Rights in a Divided Society," 59 [88]; see also Ellacuría, "Derechos humanos," 594–6.

[32] Ellacuría, "Fundamental Human Rights and the Legal and Political Restrictions Placed on Them," *TSSP,* 93, 101–3, trans. Phillip Berryman from "Los derechos humanos fundamentales y su limitación legal y política," *ECA,* nos. 254–5 (1969) 435–49;

henceforth "Rights and Restrictions." See also Henry Shue, *Basic Rights: Subsistence, Affluence, and U.S. Foreign Policy* (Princeton, NJ: Princeton University Press, 1980).

[33] Ellacuría, "Human Rights in a Divided Society," 59 [88].

[34] It is thus that Ellacuría develops his criticism of the prevailing international political economy: "If the behavior and even the ideal of a few cannot become the behavior and the reality of the greater part of humanity, that behavior and that ideal cannot be said to be moral or even human, all the more so if the enjoyment of a few is at the cost of depriving the rest." Idem, "Utopia and Prophecy in Latin America," in I. Ellacuría and J. Sobrino, eds. *Mysterium Liberationis: Fundamental Concepts of Liberation Theology* (Maryknoll, NY: Orbis, 1994) 299–300, trans. by James R. Brockman from "Utopía y profetismo desde América Latina: un ensayo concreto de soteriologia historia," *RLT*, no. 17 (1989) 141–84.

[35] Ellacuría, "Human Rights in a Divided Society," 56 [85].

[36] Ibid., 57 (emphasis added) [86].

[37] Ibid., 64 [93]; see also Ignacio Ellacuría, "The Historicization of the Concept of Property," *TSSP,* 106–9.

[38] Ignacio Ellacuría, "Liberation Theology and Socio-historical Change," 26. See also, "Human Rights in a Divided Society," 64 [93] and idem, "Derechos humanos," 591–2.

[39] Ellacuría, "Rights and Restrictions," *TSSP,* 101.

[40] For Ellacuría's assessment of the role of base communities in historicizing human rights in Latin America, see "The Church of the Poor, Historical Sacrament of Liberation," *MLT,* 543–64, trans. Margaret D. Wilde from "La Iglesia de los pobres, sacramento histórico de la liberación," *ML,* vol. 2 (1993) 127–54; "The Crucified People," *MLT,* 580–603, trans. Phillip Berryman and Robert R. Barr from "El pueblo crucificado, ensayo de soteriología histórico," *ML,* vol. 2 (1993) 189–216. For his understanding of the role of the church in civil society, see "Liberation Theology and Socio-Historical Change," 29–33.

[41] For an extended treatment of the themes addressed in this section, see Aquiline Tarimo, "Human Rights and Communal Solidarity: Beyond the Banjul Charter" (STD dissertation, Jesuit School of Theology at Berkeley, 1998).

[42] Ellacuría, "Human Rights in a Divided Society," 59 [88].

[43] Elochukwu E. Uzukwu, *A Listening Church: Autonomy and Communion in African Churches* (Maryknoll, NY: Orbis, 1996) 41, 44.

[44] H.W.O. Okoth-Ogendo, "Human and Peoples' Rights: What Point Is Africa Trying to Make?" in R. Cohen, G. Hyden, and W. P. Nagan, eds., *Human Rights and Governance in Africa* (Miami: Florida University Press, 1993) 76.

[45] The phrase "civil society" figures prominently in debates regarding pluralism and democracy. Although differing on details, most critics envision civil society as an arena of friendships, clubs, churches, unions, cooperatives, business associations, and other voluntary associations that mediate between family and state. This associational sphere is seen as the place where citizens learn habits of free assembly, participation, and empowerment of grassroots communities and local institutions, dialogue, and social initiative. See Robert Putnam, *Making Democracy Work: Civic Traditions in Modern Italy* (Princeton, NJ: Princeton University Press, 1993).

[46] See Tade Akin Aina, "State and Civil Society: Politics, Government, and Social Organization," in C. Rekodi, ed., *The Urban Challenge in Africa* (New York: The United Nations University Press, 1997) 432–4; Julius O. Ihonvbere, *Economic Crisis, Civil Society, and Democratization: The Case of Zambia* (Asmara: Africa World Press, 1996) 270–91; and P. Chabal, ed., *Political Domination in Africa: Reflections on the Limits of Power* (Cambridge: Cambridge University Press, 1986) 9–42.

[47] See Ellacuría, "Rights and Restrictions," 96–9.

[48] See David Hollenbach, "Report from Rwanda: An Interview with Augustin Karekezi," *America* (December 7, 1996) 13–7.

[49] See *Lumen Gentium*, no. 37 and *Gaudium et Spes*, no. 62, in *Vatican Council II: The Conciliar and Post Conciliar Documents,* ed. A. Flannery (Northport, NY: Costello Publishing Company, 1987) 394–6 and 966–8.

[50] Symposium of Episcopal Conferences of Africa and Madagascar, *Acts of the Fourth Plenary Assembly of SECAM* (Accra: SECAM Secretariat, 1975) 73. Similar declarations appear in the proceedings of the African Synod, see *The African Synod: Documents, Reflections, Perspectives,* ed. Africa Faith and Justice Network under the direction of Maura Browne (Maryknoll, NY: Orbis, 1996).

[51] Jean-Marc Éla, *My Faith as an African,* trans. John Pairman Brown and Susan Perry (Maryknoll, NY: Orbis, 1988) 91; emphasis added.

[52] Ibid., 91–2; cf. Patrick Kalilombe, "From Outstations to Small Christian Communities," *Spearhead* 82 (1984) 54–5; and Julio Labayen, "Basic Christian Communities," *AFER* 30:3 (February 1998) 136.

[53] Ellacuría, "Liberation Theology and Socio-historical Change," (1991) 29–33.

[54] In conjunction with the Justice and Peace Department of the Catholic Secretariat, Peter Henriot's Jesuit Centre for Theological Reflection in Lusaka, Zambia, for instance, draws upon the "local knowledge" of small Christian communities in critically assessing the effects of IMF structural adjustment programs.

[55] For a methodological analysis, see William O'Neill, "Ethics and Inculturation: The Scope and Limits of Rights' Discourse," *The Annual of the Society of Christian Ethics* (1993) 72–92. See also Joseph A. Payeur, "Inculturation Through Small Christian Communities," *AFER* 35:1 (February 1993) 37–53; Gabby-Lio Kagiso Afagbegee, "Inculturation and Small Christian Communities," *AFER* 26 (December 1984) 369–71; Terese Josephine Zemale, *Christian Witness Through Small Christian Communities* (Eldoret: AMECEA Gaba Publications, 1992); Alphonce Timisa, "Basic Christian Communities in Africa and Brazil," *AFER* 27:6 (December 1985) 375–85; and Laurenti Magesa, "Basic Communities and Apostolic Succession," *AFER* 26:6 (December 1984) 338–56.

[56] See also Éla, *My Faith as an African,* 160–82; Kwame Bediako, *Christianity in Africa: The Renewal of a Non-Western Religion* (Maryknoll, NY: Orbis, 1995).

[57] Éla, *My Faith as an African,* 177.

[58] Gerard Manley Hopkins, "As Kingfishers Catch Fire," in *The Poems of Gerard Manley Hopkins,* 4th ed., W. H. Gardner and N. H. MacKenzie, eds. (London: Oxford University Press, 1970) 90.

[59] Jon Sobrino, "Companions of Jesus," 37, 16.

# Chapter 12

# Toward a Christianity of Political Compassion*

*Johann Baptist Metz*

The biblical traditions for speaking about God, as well as the New Testament stories about Jesus, know of a form of universalism that is beyond dispute, a universal responsibility. To be sure, on closer analysis it becomes clear that the universal character of this responsibility is not primarily oriented by the universalism of sin, but rather by the universalism of suffering in the world. Jesus did not look in the first instance on others' sins, but rather on others' suffering. In this way Christianity had its beginnings as a community of memory and narration in following a Jesus whose gaze was directed first at others' suffering. This sensitivity to others' suffering was a defining feature of Jesus' "new way of life." In my view, it is the strongest expression of the love that he had in mind when he spoke—completely in line with his own Jewish heritage, by the way—about the indivisible unity of love of God and love of neighbor.

There are certain parables with which Jesus has found a place narratively in humankind's memory. The image of the "Good Samaritan" belongs first and foremost among these, with its critique of the priest and the Levite, both of whom passed by the one fallen among robbers "for the sake of a higher concern." Whoever says "God" in Jesus' sense is very

---

* Translated by J. Matthew Ashley.

much aware of the way that preconceived religious certainties are shattered by others' misfortune. To speak of Jesus' God means that one will not fail to give voice to others' suffering, and to lament the ways that responsibility has been shirked and solidarity evaded. In the images and metaphors of an archaic provincial society—and, of course, without having to worry about the structural problems of late modern societies—this parable guides us into God-talk's sensitivity to suffering. What this means is that this sensitivity to others' suffering is not the moral consequence of biblical talk about God, but rather its imaginative presupposition.

Very early on Christianity had great difficulties with the elementary sensitivity to suffering of its message that we are talking about here. All too quickly Christianity talked its way around the disturbing question about justice for those who suffer innocently. The question was turned into the question of the redemption of the guilty. The question of suffering fell under a soteriological spell; soteriology silenced the theodicy question. From a religion that was sensitive first and foremost to suffering, Christianity was transformed into one primarily sensitive to sin. It was no longer the creature's suffering, but the creature's guilt that took center stage. This crippled the elementary sensitivity for others' suffering and occluded the biblical vision of that comprehensive justice of God, which, after all, according to Jesus ought to be the object of all our hunger and thirst.

Again and again I have tried to find a convincing German word for the elementary sensitivity to suffering that belongs to the Christian message. "Sympathy" *[Mitleid]* takes us too much into a purely emotional realm, and "empathy" *[Empathie]* sounds too unpolitical to me. So I have stayed with the word that I have used more or less successfully with non-German speakers: compassion. Compassion is the key word for a global program for Christianity. Compassion. In my view this is the biblical gift to the European spirit, just as theoretical curiosity is the Greek gift, and the concept of rights the Roman gift to Europe.

Falling back on this compassion, on this political empathy, is in no way a sign of resignation or evasion; it does not have anything to do with a religiously motivated narcissism. It is anything but a matter of pure feelings. Rather, it points toward a comprehensive justice, but one achieved precisely by means of compassion for and with those who suffer unjustly and innocently! This compassion sends us to the front lines of social and cultural conflicts in today's world. For perceiving and articulating others' suffering is the unconditional prerequisite of any future politics of peace, of every new form of social solidarity in the face of the

widening gap between rich and poor, and of every promising inter-
change between different cultural and religious worlds. To give a few examples from the recent history of Europe: What would have happened
in Yugoslavia if the ethnic groups there, whether Christian or Muslim,
had acted according to this imperative of compassion? If they remembered not only their own suffering, but the suffering of others, the suffering of those who had heretofore been their enemies? How much
unspeakable suffering would have been avoided? How would the civil
wars in Northern Ireland or Lebanon have turned out if Christians had
not again and again betrayed this compassion—just as they have down
through the centuries? And only if we here in Central Europe also embrace a political culture inspired by this compassion will it be more likely
that Europe will become a blooming rather than burning multicultural
landscape, a landscape of peace rather than a landscape of imploding
violence, which is to say, a landscape of escalating civil wars.

Now, certainly, one might ask how politically viable such compassion
can be with democratic structures. This compassion protests against a
pragmatism of democratic freedom which has cut itself free from the re-
membrance of suffering, and has consequently become more and more
morally blind. Ultimately, a politics of freedom cannot involve only one's
relationship to a discourse partner; rather—and more fundamentally—
what is at stake is one's relationship to the threatened other. In my opinion, strictly symmetrical relations of recognition never get beyond the
logic of market relations, relations of exchange and competition. Only
asymmetrical relationships, only turning to the threatened and destroyed
other, breaks the violence of the logic of the marketplace in politics. Not
a few will suspect that this emphasis on asymmetry harbors a conception of politics that is much too exacting. In fact, however, it only re-
claims the indispensable connection of politics to morality. For without
this "moral implication," politics—world politics—would end up being
nothing more than what it already appears to be in large measure today:
a hostage to economics and technology, with their so-called pragmatic
constraints in this golden age of globalization.

How "pragmatic," after all, was Ignacio Ellacuría, the philosopher and
theologian who clearly and forcefully evaluated the political reality of El
Salvador in terms of a *memoria passionis* when he called its poor "Yahweh's
suffering servant" or "the crucified peoples"? This was no mere theological turn of phrase, but a principal of profound solidarity with the victims
of our world, past and present, a solidarity that determined his life and his
deeds. As rector of the University of Central America, José Simeón Cañas,

Ellacuría, along with his Jesuit companions, strove to remake this *universitas* precisely in response to the claim that the universalism of suffering makes on us.[1] What is more, it is well known that besides his work as university administrator Ignacio Ellacuría was also very active in the political negotiations which eventually (after and, in part, because of his death) led to the end of the civil war in El Salvador. In this work nobody knew more than he that there could be no peace in El Salvador that did not arise first and foremost out of compassion. He adamantly criticized the government *and* the guerillas whenever they sought a "victory" with their backs turned to the suffering poor of El Salvador. His objectivity did not arise merely out of a respect for "the democratic process," much less from the belief that the church's representatives ought to maintain political neutrality. His objectivity arose from the most passionate subjectivity (Kierkegaard), a passionate solidarity with the suffering poor. Ultimately his "objectivity" as well as his effectiveness as an administrator and a political mediator arose not from "political pragmatism" in the above-named sense, but from a deep and profound spirituality, one that I have elsewhere called a mysticism of open eyes. I described it there as "a God-mysticism with an increased readiness to perceive, a mysticism of open eyes that sees more and not less. It is a mysticism that especially makes visible all invisible and inconvenient suffering, and—convenient or not—pays attention to it and takes responsibility for it, for the sake of a God who is a friend to human beings."[2] In a church which no longer *has* a Third-World church, but now largely *is* a Third-World church, our future will depend on our willingness to follow his footsteps in witnessing to a unique, and uniquely biblical, politics of compassion.

---

[1] For more reflections on the importance of this universalism for the university today, see Johann Baptist Metz, "Theology and the University," in *A Passion for God: The Mystical Political Dimension of Christianity,* trans. with an introduction by J. Matthew Ashley (Mahwah, NJ: Paulist Press, 1998) 133–5.

[2] Johann Baptist Metz, "A Passion for God: Religion Orders Today," in *A Passion for God,* 163.

# Bibliography
# Complete Works of Ignacio Ellacuría

*Compiled and Edited by Kevin F. Burke, s.j.*

*Early Writings*

1954–1956. "Correspondencia con Angel Martínez." *EF,* vol. 1, 1996, 197–213, previously unpublished.

1956. "El despertar de la filosofía, I." *Cultura,* no. 11, 1956, 13–28. See also, *EF,* vol. 1, 1996, 47–74.

1956. "Ortega y Gasset, hombre de nuestro ayer." *ECA,* no. 104, 1956, 198–203. See also, *EF,* vol. 1, 1996, 15–22.

1956. "Ortega y Gasset, desde dentro." *ECA,* no. 105, 1956, 278–83. See also, *EF,* vol. 1, 1996, 23–33.

1956. "¿Quién es Ortega y Gasset?" *ECA,* no. 110, 1956, 595–601. See also, *EF,* vol. 1, 1996, 35–45.

1956. "Angel Martínez Baigorri, s.j." *EF,* vol. 1, 1996, 117–25, previously unpublished.

1957. "Marcelino, pan y vino." *ECA,* no. 122, 1957, 665–9. See also, *EF,* vol. 1, 1996, 109–15.

1958. "Los valores y el derecho." *ECA,* no. 124, 1958, 79–84. Also published as "Los valores y el derecho: presentación y significado," *EF,* vol. 1, 1996, 281–90.

1958. "Bruselas, 1958, saldo negativo." *ECA,* no. 132, 1958, 527–35. See also, *EF,* vol. 1, 1996, 251–63.

1958. "El despertar de la filosofía, II." *Cultura,* no. 13, 1958, 148–67. See also, *EF,* vol. 1, 1996, 74–107.

1958. "Angel Martínez, Poet Esencial." *Cultura,* no. 14, 1958, 123–64. See also, *EF,* vol. 1, 1996, 127–95.

1958. "Posibilidad y modo de aproximación entre la filosofía escolástica y la filosofía vitalista moderna: Reflexiones ante el libro de Ramírez, *La filosofía de Ortega y Gasset,*" in *EF,* vol. 1, 1996, 223–50, previously unpublished.

1958. "Ortega, existencia desligada," in *EF,* vol. 1, 1996, 265–70, previously unpublished.

1958–1959. "Sobre la irreligiosidad," in *EF,* vol. 1, 1996, 271–80, previously unpublished.

1959. "El Doctor Zivago como forma literaria." *Cultura,* no. 17, 1959, 109–23. See also, *EF,* vol. 1, 1996, 305–28.

1959. "Santo Tomás, hombre de su siglo." *ECA,* no. 135, 1959, 84–9. See also, *EF,* vol. 1, 1996, 217–22.

1959. "El comunismo soviético visto desde Rusia." *ECA,* no. 141, 1959, 455–62. See also, *EF,* vol. 1, 1996, 291–303.

1959. "Religión y religiosidad en Bergson, I. La religión estática: su razón de ser." *ECA,* no. 145, 1959, 6–11. Also published as part of "Filosofía de la religión en Bergson," *EF,* vol. 1, 1996, 337–46.

1959. "Tomás de Aquino, intelectual católico." *ECA,* no. 146, 1959, 79–84. See also, *EF,* vol. 1, 1996, 329–36.

1960. "Suárez y la neoescolástica," in *EF,* vol. 1, 1996, 411–3, previously unpublished.

1960–1961. "Filosofía de la religión en Bergson," in *EF,* vol. 1, 1996, 337–85. Partially published as "Religión y religiosidad en Bergson, I & II" (1959, 1961); partially previously unpublished (1960).

1961. "El tomismo, ¿es un humanismo?" *ECA,* no. 157, 1961, 70–5. See also, *EF,* vol. 1, 1996, 387–95.

1961. "Religión y religiosidad en Bergson, II. La religión estática: sus formas." *ECA,* no. 159, 1961, 205–12. Also published as part of "Filosofía de la religión en Bergson," *EF,* vol. 1, 1996, 346–58.

1961. "Filosofía en Centroamérica." Review of F. Peccorini, *El ser y los seres según santo Tomás de Aquino,* in *Humanidades,* nos. 2–3, 1961, 157–68. See also, *EF,* vol. 1, 1996, 397–409.

1961. "Técnica y vida humana en Ortega y Gasset: Estudio de *Meditación de la técnica,*" in *EF,* vol. 1, 1996, 415–518, previously unpublished.

1961. "Teología del medio divino." *ET,* vol. 4, 2002, 297–330, previously unpublished; undated but written between 1958–1961.

1961. "Religiones no cristianas en K. Jaspers y K. Rahner." *ET,* vol. 4, 2002, 365–99, previously unpublished; undated but written between 1958–1961.

1961. "Christus sacerdos in ara crucis Deo obtulit." *ET,* vol. 4, 2002, 401–14, previously unpublished; undated but written between 1958–1961.

1962. "Carta abierta al autor de *Viridiana,*" in *EF,* vol. 1, 1996, 519–23. Publication unknown.

1963. "El P. Aurelio Espinosa Pólit, s.j." *ECA,* no. 178, 1963, 21–4. See also, *EF,* vol. 1, 1996, 525–33.

1963. "Religiosidad pluriforme: Carducci, Maragall, Rilke," in *EF,* vol. 1, 1996, 535–43, previously unpublished.

1963–1964. "Introducción al problema del milagro en Blondel," in *EF,* vol. 1, 1996, 545–58, previously unpublished.

1964. "Antropología de Xavier Zubiri, I & II." [See full citations under *Philosophical Writings*]

1965. *La principialidad de la esencia en Xavier Zubiri.* [See full citation under *Philosophical Writings*]

1965. "Principialidad de la esencia en Xavier Zubiri." [See full citation under *Philosophical Writings*]

1965. *Indices de "Sobre la esencia" de Xavier Zubiri.* [See full citation under *Philosophical Writings*]

1965. "Cinco lecciones de filosofía." [See full citation under *Philosophical Writings*]

1965. "Fundamentación de la metafísica." [See full citation under *Philosophical Writings*]

1965. "Reflexiones sobre la lógica estoica," in *EF,* vol. 1, 1996, 559–87, previously unpublished.

1966. "La historicidad del hombre en Xavier Zubiri." [See full citation under *Philosophical Writings*]

1966. "'Verum est declarativum aut manifestativum esse': Sobre una cita de santo Tomás," in *EF,* vol. 1, 1996, 593–6, previously unpublished.

1966. "Introducción a la filosofía," in *EF,* vol. 1, 1996, 597–624, previously unpublished.

1968. "Existencialismo ateo," in I. Ellacuría and others, *Dios-Ateismo. Tercera Semana de Teología.* Bilbao, Universidad de Deusto, 1968, 191–212. See also, *EF,* vol. 1, 1996, 625–44.

*Philosophical Writings*

1961–1963. "Conversaciones con Zubiri." *EF,* vol. 2, 1999, 19–51. Six letters to Luis Achaerandio regarding Ellacuría's conversations with Zubiri, previously unpublished.

1963–1970. "Correspondencia con Zubiri." *EF,* vol. 2, 1999, 53–70. Nine letters, previously unpublished.

1964. "Antropología de Xavier Zubiri, I." *Revista de Psiquiatría y Psicología Médica de Europa y América Latina,* no. 6, 1964, 403–30. See also, *EF,* vol. 2, 1999, 75–111.

1964. "Antropología de Xavier Zubiri, II." *Revista de Psiquiatría y Psicología Médica de Europa y América Latina,* no. 7, 1964, 483–508. See also, *EF,* vol. 2, 1999, 111–48.

1965. *La principialidad de la esencia en Xavier Zubiri.* Unpublished doctoral dissertation, Universidad Complutense, Madrid, 3 vols.

1965. "Principialidad de la esencia en Xavier Zubiri." Abstract of doctoral dissertation, *EF,* vol. 2, 1999, 149–75, previously unpublished.

1965. *Indices de "Sobre la esencia" de Xavier Zubiri*. Madrid, Sociedad de Estudios y Publicaciones, 1965.

1965. "Cinco lecciones de filosofía." *Crisis,* no. 45, 1965, 109–25. See also, *EF,* vol. 2, 1999, 177–97.

1965. "Fundamentación de la metafísica." *Razón y Fe,* 1965, 313–5. See also, *EF,* vol. 1, 1996, 589–92.

1966. "La historicidad del hombre en Xavier Zubiri." *Estudios de Deusto,* vol. 40, no. 14, 1966, 245–85, 523–47. See also, *EF,* vol. 2, 1999, 199–284.

1966. "La religación, actitud radical del hombre: Apuntes para un estudio de la antropología de Zubiri." [See full citation under *Theological Writings*]

1967–1968. "El esquema general de la antropología zubiriana." *EF,* vol. 2, 1999, 285–364, previously unpublished.

1970. "La idea de filosofía en Xavier Zubiri," in A. Teulon, I. Ellacuría and others, *Homenaje a Zubiri II,* vol. 1, Madrid, Editorial Moneda y Crédito, 1970, 459–523. See also, *EF,* vol. 2, 1999, 365–444.

1970. "Girardi y Garaudy." *ECA,* no. 259, 1970, 223.

1972. "Filosofía y política." *ECA,* no. 284, 1972, 373–85. See also, *VA,* vol. 1, 1991, 47–61.

1974. "Presentación," in *Realitas I. Seminario Xavier Zubiri.* Madrid, Sociedad de Estudios y Publicaciones, Editorial Moneda y Crédito, 1974, 5–7.

1974. "La idea de estructura en la filosofía de Xavier Zubiri," in *Realitas I. Seminario Xavier Zubiri.* Madrid, Sociedad de Estudios y Publicaciones, Editorial Moneda y Crédito, 1974, 71–139. See also, *EF,* vol. 2, 1999, 445–513.

1974. "El espacio," in *Realitas I. Seminario Xavier Zubiri.* Madrid, Sociedad de Estudios y Publicaciones, Editorial Moneda y Crédito, 1974, 479–514.

1974–1975. "Persona y comunidad." *EF,* vol. 3, 2001, 65–113, previously unpublished. [An editorial note refers to this text as "three fragments" of a larger text, the other sections of which were incorporated into Ellacuría's *Filosofía de la realidad histórica* (1990). Ed.]

1975. "La antropología filosófica de Xavier Zubiri." *EF,* vol. 2, 1999, 515–36. Partially reprinted in P. Laín Entralgo, ed., *Historia universal de la medicina,* vol. 7. Baracelona, Ed. Salvat, 1975, 109–12. Originally entitled "Antropología de Xavier Zubiri."

1975. "Introducción crítica a la antropología filosófica de Zubiri." "Introducción crítica a la antropología de Xavier Zubiri." *Realitas II. Seminario Xavier Zubiri.* Sociedad de Estudios y Publicaciones, Madrid, Ed. Labor, 1976, 49–137. See also, *EF,* vol. 2, 1999, 555–664. Partially published in *Cuadernos Salmantinos de Filosofía,* no. 2, 1975, 157–84.

1975. "Hacia una fundamentacíon filosófica del método teológico latinoamericano." [See full citation under *Theological Writings*]

1976. "Filosofía ¿para qué?" *Abra,* no. 11, 1976, 42–8. Also published as a pamphlet by Universidad Centroamericana José Simeón Cañas, San Salvador, 1987. See also, *EF,* vol. 3, 2001, 115–31. [*Writings in English Translation* (1998)]

1976. "La historización del concepto de propiedad como principio de desideologización." *ECA,* nos. 335–6, 1976, 425–50. See also, *VA,* vol. 1, 1991, 587–626. [*Writings in English Translation* (1991)]

1977. "Actualidad de la filosofía zubiriana." *Ya* (Feb. 10, 1977) 23. See also, *EF,* vol. 3, 2001, 133–37.

1978. "Historización del bien común y de los derechos humanos en una sociedad dividida," in E. Tamez and S. Trinidad, eds., *Capitalismo: violencia y anti-vida,* vol. 2, 1978, San José, 81–94. See also, *EF,* vol. 3, 2001, 207–25. [*Writings in English Translation* (1977)]

1978. "Zubiri en El Salvador." *ECA,* nos. 361–2, 1978, 949–50. See also, *EF,* vol. 3, 2001, 203–6.

1978. "Filósofo en España." *Ya* (Dec. 14, 1978) 3.

1979. "El concepto filosófico de tecnología apropiada." *ECA,* no. 366, 1979, 213–23. See also, *EF,* vol. 3, 2001, 227–50.

1979. "Fundamentación biológica de la ética." *ECA,* no. 368, 1979, 419–28. See also, *EF,* vol. 3, 2001, 251–69.

1979. "Biología e inteligencia." *Realitas III–IV. Seminario Xavier Zubiri.* Madrid, Sociedad de Estudios y Publicaciones, Ed. Labor, 1979, 281–335. See also, *EF,* vol. 3, 2001, 137–201.

1980. "Zubiri, filósofo teólogal." *Vida Nueva,* Madrid, no. 1249, 1980, 45. See also, *EF,* vol. 3, 2001, 271–3.

1980. "Zubiri, vasco universal." *El Diario Vasco* (Oct. 3, 1980) 22. See also, *EF,* vol. 3, 2001, 275–8.

1980. "Inteligencia sentiente. Libro actual, original y riguroso." *Ya* (Dec. 4, 1980) 37. Also published as "Inteligencia sentiente, nueva obra de Zubiri. Libro actual, original y riguroso." *EF,* vol. 3, 2001, 279–82.

1980. "Un tema filosófico capital." *ABC* (Dec. 27, 1980) 5–6. See also, *EF,* vol. 3, 2001, 283–9.

1980. "Una nueva obra filosófica del vasco Xavier Zubiri." *Deia* (Dec. 27, 1980) 2. See also, *EF,* vol. 3, 2001, 291–5.

1981. "El testamento de Sartre." *ECA,* nos. 387–8, 1981, 43–50. See also, *EF,* vol. 3, 2001, 319–32.

1981. "El objeto de la filosofía." *ECA,* nos. 396–7, 1981, 963–80. See also, *FRH,* 1990, 15–47, 599–602; *VA,* vol. 1, 1991, 63–92; I. Ellacuría and J. C. Scannone, *Para una Filosofía desde América Latina,* Bogotá, Universidad Javeriana, 1992, 63–88.

1981. "La nueva obra de Zubiri: *Inteligencia sentiente.*" *Razón y Fé,* no. 995, 1981, 126–39. See also, X. Zubiri, *Siete ensayos de antropología filosófica.* G. Marquinez Argote, ed., Bogotá, 1982, 191–210. See also, *EF,* vol. 3, 2001, 297–317.

1983. "La obra de Xavier Zubiri sobre la inteligencia humana, *Inteligencia y Razón.*" Book review, *El Pais* (Mar. 13, 1983) 4. Also published as an expanded text taken from previously unpublished notes under the title, "La obra de Xavier Zubiri sobre la inteligencia humana," in *EF,* vol. 3, 2001, 333–42.

1983. "La obra de Xavier Zubiri sobre la inteligencia humana." *EF,* vol. 3, 2001, 343–52, previously unpublished. [An editorial note explains that this text represents a separate draft of the text cited in the preceding entry; see *EF* vol. 3, 2001, 343. Ed.]

1983. "Zubiri sigue vivo." *Vida Nueva,* no. 1396, 1983, 55. See also, *ECA,* no. 420, 1983, 895–6; *Cuadernos de Filosofía Latinoamericana,* no. 17, 1983, 34–6. See also, *EF,* vol. 3, 2001, 353–5.

1983. "La desmitificación del marxismo." *ECA,* nos. 421–2, 1983, 921–30. Also in *VA,* vol. 1, 1991, 282–91.

1983. "Aproximación a la obra completa de Xavier Zubiri." *ECA,* nos. 421–2, 1983, 965–83. See also, *Encuentro. Selecciones para Latinoamérica,* no. 29, 1984, 137–45; I. Tellechea, ed., *Zubiri (1898–1983),* Victoria, Edita Departamento de Culture del Gobierno Vasco, 1984, 37–66. See also, *EF,* vol. 3, 2001, 365–94.

1983. "Dios, el gran tema de Zubiri." *Ya* (Sept. 23, 1983) 3. See also, *EF,* vol. 3, 2001, 357–8.

1983. "Zubiri, el filósofo más importante de España." *EF,* vol. 3, 2001, 353–5, previously unpublished.

1984. "Presentación" of Xavier Zubiri, *El Hombre y Dios,* Madrid, Alianza Editorial, 1984, i–x.

1984. "Zubiri y los vascos." *El Correo Español—El Pueblo Vasco* (Jan. 22, 1984). See also, *EF,* vol. 3, 2001, 395–8.

1985. "Función liberadora de la filosofía." *ECA,* nos. 435–6, 1985, 45–64. See also, *VA,* vol. 1, 1991, 93–121.

1985. "Presentación" of Xavier Zubiri: *Sobre el Hombre.* Madrid, Alianza Editorial, IX–XXIII, 1985.

1986. "Beitrag Zum Dialog mit dem Marxismus," in P. Rottländer, ed., *Theologie der Befreiung und Marxismus,* Münster, West, 1986, 77–108.

1986. "Voluntad de fundamentalidad y voluntad de verdad: conocimiento-fe y su configuración histórica." [See full citation under *Theological Writings*]

1987. "Zubiri, cuatro años después." *Diario* 16 (Sept. 21, 1987) 2. See also, *EF,* vol. 3, 2001, 399–402.

1988. "La superación del reduccionismo idealista en Zubiri." *ECA,* no. 477, 1988, 633–50. See also, X. Palacios y F. Jarauta, eds., *Razón, ética y política. El conflicto de las sociedades modernas,* Colección pensamiento crítico—pensamiento utópico 37, Barcelona, Ed. Anthropos, 1989, 169–95; *Congreso de filosofía, ética y religión,* vol. 4, San Sabastián, 1989. See also, *EF,* vol. 3, 2001, 403–30.

1989. "Historización de los derechos humanos desde los pueblos oprimidos y las mayorías populares," in J. Aguirre and X. Insauti, eds., *Pensamiento crítico, ética y absoluto. Homenaje a José Manzana,* Ed. Eset, 1990, 147–58. See also, *ECA,* no. 502, 1990, 589–96, LUMEN, no. 39, 1990, 9–19; *EF,* vol. 3, 2001, 433–45.

1989. "Hacia una conceptualización de os derechos humanos." *EF,* vol. 3, 2001, 431–2, previously unpublished.

1989. "El mal común y los derechos humanos." *EF,* vol. 3, 2001, 447–50, previously unpublished.

1990. *Filosofía de la realidad histórica.* A. González, ed. San Salvador, UCA Editores, 1990; prologue and conclusion from "El objeto de la filosofia" (1981). Also published by Madrid, Editorial Trotta, 1990.

1996. *Escritos filosóficos.* Vol 1. San Salvador, UCA Editores, 1996.

1999. *Escritos filosóficos.* Vol 2. San Salvador, UCA Editores, 1999.

2001. *Escritos filosóficos.* Vol 3. San Salvador, UCA Editores, 2001.

## Theological Writings

1965. "Divagaciones sobre moral tributaria." *ET,* vol. 3, 2002, 297–305, previously unpublished.

1965. "Principos teológicos sobre el problema de prensa y religión." *ET,* vol. 4, 2001, 415–45, previously unpublished.

1966. "La religación, actitud radical del hombre: Apuntes para un estudio de la antropología de Zubiri." *Asclepio. Archivo iberoamericano de historia de la medicina y antropología médica.* Madrid, vol. 16, 1966, 97–155. See also, *ET,* vol. 1, 2000, 39–105.

1967. "La juventud religiosa actual." *Hechos y Dichos,* no. 372, 1967, 124–34. See also, *ET,* vol. 4, 2002, 133–46.

1967. "Liberación en los Salmos." *ET,* vol. 4, 2002, 107–21, previously unpublished.

1967. "Hominización." *ET,* vol. 4, 2002, 331–64, previously unpublished course notes.

1968. "Carta a un ordenado vacilante." *Hechos y Dichos,* no. 385, 1968, 355–62. See also, *ET,* vol. 4, 2002, 163–72.

1969. "Violencia y cruz," in *¿Qué aporta el cristianismo al hombre de hoy? Cuatro Semana de Teología.* Bilbao, Universidad de Deusto, 1969, 261–307. See also, *TP,* 1973, 95–127; *ET,* vol. 3, 2002, 427–82. [*FMF, Writings in English Translation* (1976) 167–231]

1969. "Vida religiosa y tercer mundo." Address to Central American Jesuits in Madrid, Spain (June 26, 1969). See also, *ET,* vol. 4, 2002, 147–61.

1969. "Nuestra situación colectiva vista desde la primera semana." *ET,* vol. 4, 2002, 174–96, previously unpublished.

1969. "El problema del traslado del espíritu do los *Ejercicios* a la Viceprovincia." *ET,* vol. 4, 2002, 197–213, previously unpublished.

1969. "El tercer mundo com lugar óptimo de la vivencia cristiana de los *Ejercicios.*" *ET,* vol. 4, 2002, 215–34, previously unpublished.

1969–1970. "¿Es conciliable el análisis marxista con la fe cristiana?" *ET,* vol. 1, 2000, 509–16, previously unpublished, undated. [An editorial note indicates that this text was written in the late 60s or early 70s; see *ET,* vol 1, 2000, 509. Ed.]

1970. "Los laicos interpelan a su Iglesia." *ECA,* nos. 256–7, 1970, 46–50. See also, *ET,* vol. 1, 2000, 259–66.

1970. "Progreso y revolución." *ECA,* no. 258, 1970, 152–4. See also, *ET,* vol. 1, 2000, 267–70.

1970. "Persecución." *ECA,* no. 259, 1970, 189–90. See also, *ET,* vol. 2, 2000, 585–7.

1970. "Los obispos centroamericanos aceleran el paso." *ECA,* no. 262, 1970, 381–7. See also, *ET,* vol. 2, 2000, 603–12.

1970. "Teología de la revolución y evangelio." *ECA,* nos. 265–6, 1970, 581–4. See also, *ET,* vol. 3, 2002, 483–8.

1971. "Liberación: misión y carisma de la iglesia latinoamericana." *ECA,* no. 268, 1971, 61–80. See also, *TP,* 1973, 70–90; *ET,* vol. 2, 2000, 553–84. [*FMF, Writings in English Translation* (1976) 127–63]

1971. "¿Teología política hace 400 años?" *ECA,* no. 278, 1971, 747–9. See also, *ET,* vol. 1, 2000, 253–57.

1972. "Dimensión política del mesianismo de Jesús." *Estudios sociales,* no. 7, 1972, 81–105. See also, *TP,* 1973, 23–43; *Búsqueda,* no. 3, 1973, 24–45; *ET,* vol. 2, 2000, 33–66. [*FMF, Writings in English Translation* (1976) 41–79]

1973. "El seglar cristiano en el tercer mundo." *Búsqueda,* no. 2, 1973, 15–20. See also, *CIRD,* 1984, 293–303; *ET,* vol. 4, 2002, 123–32.

1973. *Teología política.* San Salvador, Ediciones del Secretariado Social Interdiocesano, 1973. Collection of previously published and unpublished essays.

1973. "Historia de la salvación y salvación en la historia." *TP,* 1973, 1–10. See also, *ET,* vol. 1, 2000, 519–33. [*FMF, Writings in English Translation* (1976) 3–19]

1973. "Carácter político de la misión de Jesús." *TP,* 1973, 11–22. See also, *ET,* vol. 2, 2000, 13–31; *Miec-Jesí,* docs. 13–4, Lima, 1974. [*FMF, Writings in English Translation* (1976) 23–41]

1973. "El anuncio del Evangelio y la misión de la Iglesia." *TP,* 1973, 44–69. Also published as "Anuncio del Reino y credibilidad de la Iglesia." *CIRD,* 1984, 219–63. See also, *ET,* vol. 1, 2000, 659–98. [*FMF, Writings in English Translation* (1976) 81–126]

1973. "La Iglesia, signo de contradicción." *ET,* vol. 2, 2000, 397–416, previously unpublished.

1973. "Radicalismo cristiano y educación liberadora." *ET,* vol. 2, 2000, 613–21, published previously as part of the declaration, "El Externado piensa así," *ECA* no. 269, 1973, 399–422.

1974. "Escatología e historia." *RLT,* no. 32, 1994, 113–28. Edited from previously unpublished course notes (1974). See also, *ET,* vol. 2, 2000, 95–124.

1974. "Esbozo para una carta pastoral." *ET,* vol. 2, 2000, 623–61, previously unpublished.

1974. "Lectura latinoamericana de los Ejercicios Espirituales de San Ignacio." *RLT,* no. 23, 1991, 111–47. See also, *ET,* vol. 4, 2002, 59–106. Based on previously unpublished notes from a course given in 1974 at the UCA.

1975. "Hacia una fundamentacíon filosófica del método teológico latinoamericano," in E. Ruiz Maldonado, ed., *Liberación y cautiverio: debates en torno al metodo de la teología en América Latina,* las comunicaciones y los debates del Encuentro Latinoamericano de Teología, Mexico City (August 11–15, 1975) 609–35. See also, *ECA,* nos. 322–3, 1975, 409–25; *ET,* vol. 1, 2000, 187–218.

1975. "Tesis sobre la posibilidad, necesidad y sentido de una teología latino-americana," A. Vargas Machuca, ed., *Teología y mundo contemporáneo: homenaje a Karl Rahner en su 70 cumpleaños,* Madrid, Ediciones Cristiandad, 1975, 325–50. See also, *ET,* vol. 1, 2000, 271–301.

1975. "Marxismo y cristianismo." *ET,* vol. 1, 2000, 499–507, previously unpublished, undated. [Editorial notes indicate that this was probably written in the mid-1970s; see *ET,* vol. 1, 2000, 499. Ed.]

1976. "Iglesia y realidad histórica." *ECA,* no. 331, 1976, 213–20. See also, *ET,* vol. 2, 2000, 501–15.

1976. "En busca de la 'cuestión fundamental' de la pastoral latinoamericana." *Sal Terrae,* nos. 8–9, 1976, 563–72. Also published as "La 'cuestión fundamental' de la pastoral latinoamericana." *Diakonía,* 1978, no. 6, 20–8; *ET,* vol. 2, 2000, 541–52.

1976. "Liturgia y liberación," in *CIRD,* 1984, 279–92. Previously unpublished in Spanish. See also, *ET,* vol. 4, 2002, 29–40. [*FMF, Writings in English Translation* (1976) 233–46]

1977. "Teorías económicas y relación entre cristianismo y socialismo." *Concilium,* no. 125, 1977, 282–90. Partially reproduced in "Función de las teorias económicas en la discusión teológico-teórica: teoría de la dependencia," in I. Ellacuría and others, *La Teología de la Liberación,* Ediciones Cultura Hispánica, 1990, 97–100. See also, *ET,* vol. 1, 2000, 303–12. [*Writings in English Translation* (1977)]

1977. "Fe y justicia." *Christus,* August 1977, 26–33, and October 1977, 19–34. See also, I. Ellacuría and others, *Fe, justicia y opción por los oprimidos,* Bilbao, Editorial Desclée de Brouwer, 1980, 9–78; *ET,* vol. 3, 2002, 307–73. Partially reproduced as "La contemplación en la acción de la justicia." *Diakonía,* no. 2, 1977, 7–14.

1977. "La Iglesia de los pobres, sacramento histórico de la liberación." *ECA,* nos. 348–9, 1977, 707–22. See also, *Selecciones de Teología,* no. 70, 1979, 119–34; *Encuentro: Selecciones para Latinoamérica,* no. 1, 1980, 142–8; *CIRD,* 1984, 179–216; *ML,* vol. 2, 1990, 127–54; *ET,* vol. 2, 2000, 453–85. [*Writings in English Translation* (1993)]

1977. "Notas teológicas sobre religiosidad popular." *Fomento Social,* 1977, 253–60. See also, *ET,* vol. 2, 2000, 487–98.

1977. "¿Por qué muere Jesús y por qué le matan?" *Misión Abierta,* no. 2, 1977, 17–26. See also, *Diakonía,* no. 8, 1978, 65–75; *Servir,* no. 75, 1978, 383–98; *ETM,* 1990, 25–38. See also, *ET,* vol. 2, 2000, 67–88.

1977. "El compromiso político de la iglesia en América Latina." *Corintios XIII,* no. 4, 1977, 143–62. See also, *ET,* vol. 2, 2000, 667–82.

1977. "Un mártir en El Salvador." *ET,* vol. 2, 2000, 663–5, previously unpublished.

1978. "El pueblo crucificado, ensayo de soteriología histórica," in I. Ellacuría and others, *Cruz y resurrección: anuncio de una Iglesia nueva,* Mexico City, CTR, 1978, 49–82. See also, *Selecciones de Teología,* no. 76, 1980, 325–41; *RLT,* no. 18, 1989, 305–33; *CIRD,* 1984, 25–63; *ML,* vol. 2, 1990, 189–216; *ET,* vol. 2, 2000, 137–70. [*Writings in English Translation* (1993)]

1978. "Entre Medellín y Puebla." *ECA,* no. 353, 1978, 120–9. Also published as "Entre Medellín y Puebla: reflexiones metodológicas sobre el documento de consulta." *ET,* vol. 1, 2000, 371–93.

1978. "Una buena noticia: la Iglesia nace del pueblo latinoamericano: Contribución a Puebla, 1978," *ECA,* no. 353, 1978, 161–73.

1978. "La teología como momento ideológico de la praxis eclesial." *Estudios Eclesiásticos,* no. 207, 1978, 457–76. See also, *ET,* vol. 1, 2000, 163–85.

1978. "La Iglesia y las organizaciones populares en El Salvador." *ECA,* no. 359, 1978, 692–701, under the pseudonym, "Tomás R. Campos." See also, *IPOP,* 1979, 147–61; *VA,* vol. 2, 1991, 659–77; *ET,* vol. 2, 2000, 683–704.

1978. "La Iglesia que nace del pueblo por el Espíritu." *Misión Abierta,* no. 1, 1978, 150–8. See also, *CIRD,* 1984, 65–79; *Servir,* 1979, 551–64; *ETM,* 1990, 131–43; *ET,* vol. 2, 2000, 243–355.

1978. "La predicación ha de poner en contacto vivificante la palabra y la comunidad." *Sal Terrae,* no. 778, 1978, 167–76. Also published as "Palabras de Dios y comunidad cristiana." *Servir,* no. 73, 1978, 47–60. Also published as "Predicación, palabra, comunidad." *CIRD,* 1984, 265–78; *ET,* vol. 4, 2002, 17–28.

1978. "Recuperar el Reino de Dios: des-mundanización e historización de la Iglesia." *Sal Terrae,* no. 780, 1978, 335–43. See also, *IPOP,* 1979, 79–85; *ET,* vol. 2, 2000, 307–16.

1978. "El trasfondo económico-político de Puebla." *Boletín de Ciencias Económicas y Sociales,* no. 7, 1978, 54–9. See also, *ET,* vol. 1, 2000, 365–70.

1978. "El método en la teología latinoamericana." *ET,* vol. 1, 2000, 219–34, previously unpublished.

1978. "Comentarios a la *Carta Pastoral,*" Twenty-one Radio broadcasts, *YSAX* (Aug. 30–Sept. 25, 1978). See also, *IPOP,* 1979, 163–205; *VA,* vol. 2, 1991, 679–732; *ET,* vol. 2, 2000, 705–66.

1978. "Algunas reflexiones para un proyecto de programa de teología moral fundamental." *ET,* vol. 3, 2002, 119–26, previously unpublished.

1978. "Teología moral fundamental." *ET,* vol. 3, 2002, 127–277, previously unpublished. [An editorial note indicates that this lengthy text combines an outline for a course in fundamental moral theology (1978) and an essay draft entitled "Sermón del monte" (1976); see *ET,* vol. 3, 2002, 127. Ed.]

1979. *Iglesia de los pobres y organizaciones populares.* O. Romero, A. Rivera y Damas, I. Ellacuría, J. Sobrino, and T. Campos. San Salvador, UCA Editores, 1979.

1979. "Las bienaventuranzas como carta fundamental de la Iglesia de los pobres," *IPOP,* 1979, 105–18. See also, *Diakonía,* no. 19, 1981, 56–9; *CIRD,* 1984, 129–51; *ET,* vol. 2, 2000, 417–37.

1979. "¿Es cada vez menos santa la Semana Santa?" Radio broadcast, *YSAX* (1979). See also, *ET,* vol. 4, 2002, 41–6.

1979. "Notas para una valoración de la acción pastoral de la arquidiócesis en los dos primeros años de Monseñor Romero." *ET,* vol. 3, 2002, 75–92, previously unpublished.

1979. "La Iglesia y la UCA en el golpe del 15 de Octubre de 1979." *Presencia,* nos. 7–8, 1990, 132–8, previously unpublished.

1980. "La seguridad nacional y la crucificación salvadoreña," *ECA,* nos. 384–5, 1980, 977–88.

1980. "El problema 'ecumenismo' y la promoción de la justicia." *Estudios Eclesiásticos,* no. 213, 1980, 153–5. See also, *ET,* vol. 3, 2002, 375–8.

1980. "Monseñor Romero, un enviado de Dios para salvar a su pueblo." *Sal Terrae,* no. 811, 1980, 825–32. See also, *Diakonía,* no. 17, 1981, 2–8; *ECA,* no. 497, 1990, 141–6; *RLT,* no. 19, 1990, 5–10; *ET,* vol. 3, 2002, 93–100.

1980. "La Iglesia en El Salvador." *ET,* vol. 2, 2000, 767–72, previously unpublished in its entirety; partially published as "La Iglesia en El Salvador: la salvación se realiza en la historia." *Aportes,* 1981, 34–5.

1980–1981. "Discernir 'el signo' de los tiempos." *Vida Nueva,* nos. 1258–9, 1980–1, 35–6. See also, *Diakonía,* no. 17, 1981, 57–9; *ET,* vol. 2, 2000, 133–5.

1981. "La Iglesia en El Salvador: la salvación se realiza en la historia." *Aportes,* 1981, 34–5.

1981. "El verdadero pueblo de Dios, según Monseñor Romero." *ECA,* no. 392, 1981, 529–54. See also, *Diakonía,* no. 18, 1981, 27–57; *Selecciones de Teología,* 1982, no. 84, 350–9; *CIRD,* 1984, 81–125; *ET,* vol. 2, 2000, 357–96. [Partially translated as "Persecution for the Sake of the Reign of God." *Writings in English Translation* (1990)]

1981. "Un tal Jesús." *ECA,* no. 392, 1981, 566–8. Also published as "Una obra importante," presentación del libro de María López Vigil, *Un Tal Jesús,* vol. 1, San Salvador, UCA Editores, 1982, 27–31; *ET,* vol. 2, 2000, 127–31. Also published as a chapter entitled, "Jesús, la Iglesia y los pobres," in *ETM,* 1990, 168–71.

1981. "Los pobres, lugar teológico en América Latina." *Misión Abierta,* nos. 4–5, 1981, 225–40. See also, *Diakonía,* no. 21, 1982, 41–57; *CIRD,* 1984, 153–78; *ETM,* 1990, 39–59; *ET,* vol. 1, 2000, 139–61.

1981. "Iglesia en Centroamérica." *ETM,* 1990, 159–67, as part of a chapter entitled, "Jesús, la Iglesia y los pobres," previously unpublished. See also, *ET,* vol. 2, 2000, 773–82.

1981. "Esquema de interpretación de la Iglesia en Centroamérica." *RLT,* no. 31, 1994, 3–29. See also, *Diakonía,* no. 72, 1994, 4–27; *ET,* vol. 2, 2000, 783–818, from a previously unpublished manuscript dated 1981.

1982. "Juan Pablo II y el conflicto salvadoreño." *ECA* no. 405, 1982, 633–50. See also, *ET,* vol. 3, 2002, 17–33.

1982. "Conflicto entre trabajo y capital en la presente fase histórica: Un análisis de la encíclica de Juan Pablo II sobre el trabajo humano." *ECA,* no. 409, 1982, 1008–24. See also, *ET,* vol. 3, 2002, 383–412. Also published as "Conflicto entre trabajo y capital en la presente fase histórica: un punto clave de la 'Laborem Exercens.'" *Diakonía,* no. 24, 1982, 19–42.

1982. "El Reino de Dios y el paro en el tercer mundo." *Concilium,* no. 180, 1982, 588–96. See also, *ET,* vol. 2, 2000, 295–305. [*Writings in English Translation* (1982)]

1982. "Las iglesias latinoamericanas intepelan a la iglesia de España." *Sal Terre,* no. 826, 1982, 219–30. See also, *ET,* vol. 2, 2000, 589–602.

1982. "El auténtico lugar social de la Iglesia." *Misión Abierta,* no. 1, 1982, 98–106. See also, *Diakonía,* no. 25, 1983, 24–36; *ETM,* 1990, 145–56; *ET,* vol. 2, 2000, 439–51. [*Writings in English Translation* (1991)]

1982. "Contraportada" of Jon Sobrino, *"Jesús en América Latina: su significado para la fe y la cristología."* San Salvador, UCA Editores, 1982. See also, *ET,* vol. 2, 2000, 125–6.

1982–1983. "La fe pascual en la resurrección se Jesús." *ET,* vol. 2, 2000, 89–93, previously unpublished, undated. [An editorial note indicates that this probably is an outline for a class, written in 1982 or 1983; see *ET,* vol. 2, 2000, 89. Ed.].

1983. "Luces y sombras de la Iglesia en Centroamérica." *Razón y Fe,* no. 1020, 1983, 16–26. See also, *Diakonía,* no. 26, 1983, 111–21; *Pastoral Popular,* no. 34, 1983, 50–6; *Encuentro. Selecciones para Latinoamérica,* nos. 31–2, 1984, 317–20; *VA,* vol. 1, 1991, 293–302; *ET,* vol. 2, 2000, 819–33.

1983. "El viaje del Papa a Centroamérica." *ECA,* nos. 413–4, 1983, 225–34. See also, *ET,* vol. 3, 2002, 35–44.

1983. "Mensaje ético-político de Juan Pablo II al pueblo de Centro América." *ECA,* nos. 413–4, 1983, 255–72. See also, *Diakonía,* no. 26, 1983, 144–66; *ET,* vol. 3, 2002, 45–74.

1983. "Espiritualidad," in C. Floristán and J. J. Tomayo, eds., *Conceptos fundamentales de pastoral.* Madrid, Trotta, 1983, 304–9. See also, C. Floristán and J. J. Tomayo, eds., *Conceptos fundamentales del cristianismo.* Madrid, Trotta, 1993, 413–20; *ET,* vol. 4, 2002, 47–57. Also published as "La espiritualidad cristiana." *Diakonía,* no. 30, 1984, 123–32.

1983. "Pobres," in C. Floristán and J. J. Tomayo, eds., *Conceptos fundamentales de pastoral.* Madrid, Trotta, 1983, 786–802. See also, C. Floristán and J. J. Tomayo, eds., *Conceptos fundamentales del cristianismo.* Madrid, Trotta, 1993, 1043–57; *ET,* vol. 2, 2000, 171–92.

1983. "Pueblo de Dios," in C. Floristán and J. J. Tomayo, eds., *Conceptos fundamentales de pastoral.* Madrid, Trotta, 1983, 840–59. See also, C. Floristán and J. J. Tomayo, eds., *Conceptos fundamentales del cristianismo.* Madrid, Trotta, 1993, 1094–1112. Also published as "Iglesia como pueblo de Dios," in *ET,* vol. 2, 2000, 317–42.

1983. "La paz mundial vista desde el Tercer Mundo." *Sal Terre,* no. 6, 1983, 433–43. See also, *ET,* vol. 3, 2002, 489–500.

1983. "Misión actual de la Compañía de Jesús." *RLT,* no. 29, 1993, 115–26. See also, *Diakonía,* no. 68, 1993, 33–42; *ET,* vol. 4, 2002, 235–49. Written in preparation for the 33rd General Congregation of the Society of Jesus, 1983; previously unpublished.

1983. "Misión de la Compañía de Jesús en Centroamérica." *ET,* vol. 4, 2002, 173–6, previously unpublished. [This essay mentions Archbishop Romero, the revolution in Nicaragua, and the Reagan government in the United States, indicating that it was written in the early 1980s, perhaps around the time of the preceding entry; an editorial note mistakenly identifies it as written in 1969; see *ET,* vol. 4, 2002, 173. Ed.]

1983. "Congregación General XXXIII como hecho teológico." *ET,* vol. 4, 2002, 251–5, previously unpublished.

1983. "El segundo general de los jesuitas vasco." *ET,* vol. 4, 2002, 257–61, previously unpublished; undated. [An editorial note states this essay was written "in the early years of the decade of the 1980s"; see *ET,* vol. 4, 2002, 257; the essay itself refers to "the recent General Congregation and the New General, Father Kolvenbach," indicating that it was not written before 1983. Ed.]

1984. *Conversión de la iglesia al reino de Dios: Para anunciarlo y realizarlo en la historia.* Santander, Editorial Sal Terrae, 1984. Also published in San Salvador, UCA Editores, 1984.

1984. "Recuperación del Reino de Dios," in *CIRD,* 1984, 7–19.

1984. "Historicidad de la salvación cristiana." *RLT,* no. 1, 1984, 5–45. See also, *Selecciones de Teología,* no. 101, 1987, 59–80; *ML,* vol. 1, 1990, 323–72; *ET,* vol. 1, 2000, 535–96. [*Writings in English Translation* (1993)]

1984. "Estudio teológico-pastoral de la 'Instrucción sobre algunos aspectos de la teología de la liberación.'" *RLT,* no. 2, 1984, 145–78. See also, *Misión Abierta,* no. 1, 1985, 79–99; *ETM,* 1990, 173–202; *ET,* vol. 1, 2000, 397–448.

1984. "Acoso sin derribo a la teología de la liberación." *ET,* vol. 1, 2000, 395–6, previously unpublished.

1985. "La UCA ante el doctorado concedido a Monseñor Romero." [See full citation under *University Writings*]

1985. "Relación teoría y praxis en la teología de la liberación." *ET,* vol. 1, 2000, 235–45, previously unpublished.

1985. "Teología de la liberación y marxismo." *RLT,* no. 20, 1990, 109–35. See also, *ET,* vol. 1, 2000, 461–97, previously unpublished notes from a conference address.

1986. "Voluntad de fundamentalidad y voluntad de verdad: conocimiento-fe y su configuración histórica." *RLT,* no. 8, 1986, 113–31. See also, *ET,* vol. 1, 2000, 107–37.

1986. "La teología de la liberación es más necesaria que nunca." *Diakonía,* no. 38, 1986, 186–9. See also, *Vida Nueva,* no. 3, 1987, 24–5. Also published as "La teología de la liberación más necesaria que nunca." *ET,* vol. 1, 2000, 453–6.

1986. "Pedro Arrupe, renovador de la vida religiosa," in M. Alcala, ed., *Pedro Arrupe: Así lo vieron,* Santander, Sal Terrae, 1986, 141–72. See also, *RLT,* no. 22, 1991, 5–23; *ET,* vol. 4, 2002, 263–87.

1986. "La teología de la liberación, rehabilitada." *Proceso,* no. 234, 1986, 10–1. See also *ET,* vol. 1, 2000, 449–51.

1986. "Algunas tesis sobre la doctrina social de la Iglesia." *ET,* vol. 3, 2002, 379–82, previously unpublished, undated. [An editorial note indicates that this outline was probably written between 1979 and 1986; see *ET,* vol. 3, 2002, 379. Ed.].

1987. "Aporte de la teología de la liberación a las religiones Abráhamicas en la superación del individualismo y del positivismo." *RLT,* no. 10, 1987, 3–28. See also, *ET,* vol. 2, 2000, 193–232.

1987. "La teología de la liberación frente al cambio socio-histórico de América Latina." *RLT,* no. 12, 1987, 241–64. See also, *Diakonía,* no. 46, 1988, 131–66; I. Ellacuría and others, *Implicaciones sociales y políticas de la teología de la liberación,* Madrid, Escuela de Estudios Hispanoamericanos y Instituto de Filosofía, Consejo Superior de Investigaciones Científicas, 1989, 69–90; I. Ellacuría and others, *La Teología de la Liberación,* Ediciones de Cultura Hispánica, 1990, 79–86; *ETM,* 1990, 61–89; *VA,* vol. 1, 1991, 303–30; *ET,* vol. 1, 2000, 313–45. [*Writings in English Translation* (1991)]

1987. "El origen de la teología de la liberación." *ET,* vol. 1, 2000, 249–51, previously unpublished.

1987. "Subdesarrollo y derechos humanos." *RLT,* no. 25, 1992, 3–22, previously unpublished transcript of a talk given to the 3rd International Congress of Youth in Venice, 1987.

1987. "El desafío cristiano de la teología de la liberación." *Cartas a las Iglesias,* no. 263, 1992, 12–5; no. 264, 1992, 11–3; no. 265, 1992, 14–6. See also, *ET,* vol. 1, 2000, 19–33. Transcript of a paper given at the *seminario* "Lo temporal y la religioso en el mundo actual," organizado por la Fundación Banco Exterior, Madrid, 1987.

1987. "Historia de la salvación," in *RLT,* no. 28, 1993, 3–25. See also, *ET,* vol. 1, 2000, 597–628. Also published as "Salvación en la historia," *CFC,* 1993, 1252–74. From a previously unpublished manuscript dated 1987.

1987. "Teología de la liberación." *ET,* vol. 4, 2002, 447–8, previously unpublished index.

1988. "Trabajo no violento por la paz y violencia liberadora." *Concilium,* no. 215, 1988, 85–94. See also, *ETM,* 1990, 91–102; *Reflexión y Liberación,* no. 4, 1990, 4–11; *ET,* vol. 3, 2002, 501–12. [*Writings in English Translation* (1988)]

1988. "Presencia sacerdotal en la guerrilla." *Cartas a las Iglesias,* no. 168, 1988, 7–10; no. 169, 1988, 11–3; no. 170, 1988, 5–7. Published in Italian as the preface of María Lopez Vigil, *Morto e vita in Morazán: un sacerdote nella guerriglia in Salvador,* Bologna, Italy, EMI della Coop. SERMIS, 1989. See also, *ET,* vol. 2, 2000, 835–49.

1988. "La construcción de una futuro distinto para la humanidad." *ET,* vol. 1, 2000, 347–53. From an address given in Berlin, October 1988, previously unpublished.

1988. "Memoria de monseñor Romero." "Presentación" to *Homenaje a Monseñor Romero,* San Salvador, 1988, 1–2. See also, *ET,* vol. 3, 2002, 115–16.

1988. "Hacia un desarrollo liberador de los pueblos." [See full citation under *University Writings*]

1989. "Utopía y profetismo desde América Latina: un ensayo concreto de soteriología histórica." *RLT,* no. 17, 1989, 141–84. See also, I. Ellacuría and others,

*Utopía y Profetism,* Madrid, Centro Evangelio y Liberación, 1989, 81–101; *Christus,* 1990, no. 632, 49–55; *ETM,* 1990, 103–29; *ET,* vol. 2, 2000, 233–93. Also published as "Utopía y profetismo," *ML,* vol. 1, 1990, 393–442. [*Writings in English Translation* (1991)]

1989. "En torno al concepto y la idea de liberación." I. Ellacuría and others, *Implicaciones sociales y políticas de la teologia de la liberación,* Madrid, Escuela de Estudios Hispanoamericanos, Instituto de Filosofía, 1989, 91–109. See also, *ET,* vol. 1, 2000, 629–957. Also published as "Liberación," in C. Floristán and J. J. Tomayo, eds., *Conceptos fundamentales del cristianismo.* Madrid, Trotta, 1993, 690–710. See also, *RLT,* no. 30, 1993, 213–32.

1989. "Diez afirmaciones sobre 'Utopía' y 'Profetismo.'" *Sal Terrae,* no. 917, 1989, 889–93.

1989. "El desafío de las mayorías pobres." *ECA,* nos. 493–4, 1989, 1075–80. See also, *EU,* 1999, 297–306; *ET,* vol. 1, 2000, 355–64. Address commemorating the reception of the Alfonso Comín International Prize: Barcelona, November 9, 1989. [*Writings in English Translation* (1991)]

1989. "Visión teológica del quinto centenario." *ET,* vol. 2, 2000, 517–24, previously unpublished.

1989. "Historización de los derechos humanos desde los pueblos oprimidos y las mayorías populares." [See full citation under *Philosophical Writings*]

1989. "Quinto centenario de América Latina ¿descubrimiento o encubrimiento?" *Cuadernos Cristianisme i justicia,* Barcelona, 1990. See also, *RLT,* no. 21, 1990, 271–82; *Christus,* no. 638, 1990, 7–13; *ET,* vol. 2, 2000, 525–39. Also published as "El quinto centenario del 'descubrimiento' visto desde América Latina." *Diakonía,* no. 56, 1990, 15–32.

1990. I. Ellacuría and J. Sobrino, eds., *Mysterium Liberationis: Conceptos Fundamentales de la Teología de la Liberación.* 2 vols. Madrid, Editorial Trotta, 1990. Also published in San Salvador, UCA Editores, 1991.

1990. *Ignacio Ellacuría: Teólogo mártir por la liberación del pueblo.* Madrid, Editorial Nueva Utopía, 1990.

1994. I. Ellacuría, J. Sobrino, R. Cardenal. *Ignacio Ellacuría: el hombre, el pensador, el cristiano.* Bilbao, Editiones EGA, 1994.

2000. *Escritos teológicos.* Vol 1. San Salvador, UCA Editores, 2000.

2000. *Escritos teológicos.* Vol 2. San Salvador, UCA Editores, 2000.

2000. "Filosofía y teología." *ET,* vol. 1, 2000, 37–8, previously unpublished, undated.

2000. "Magisterio y teología." *ET,* vol. 1, 2000, 457–9, previously unpublished, undated.

2002. *Escritos teológicos.* Vol 3. San Salvador, UCA Editores, 2002.

2002. *Escritos teológicos.* Vol 4. San Salvador, UCA Editores, 2002.

2002. "Moralidad de la actividad política." *ET,* vol. 3, 2002, 279–80, previously unpublished, undated.

2002. "Visión bíblica del matrimonio." *ET,* vol. 3, 2002, 281–90, previously unpublished, undated.

2002. "Moralidad de la sexualidad." *ET,* vol. 3, 2002, 291–5, previously unpublished, undated.

2002. "Conclusiones sobre la teología de la liberación." *ET,* vol. 4, 2002, 291–3, previously unpublished, undated.

## Political Writings

1969. "Seguridad social y solidaridad humana: Aproximación filosófica al fenómeno de la seguridad social." *ECA,* no. 253, 1969, 357–66.

1969. "Los derechos humanos fundamentales y su limitación legal y política." *ECA,* nos. 254–5, 1969, 435–49. See also, *ECA,* no. 267, 1970, 645–59; *VA,* vol. 1, 1991, 501–20. [*Writings in English Translation* (1991)]

1970. "Progreso y revolución." [See full citation under *Theological Writings*]

1970. "Persecución." [See full citation under *Theological Writings*]

1970. "Medallas para Cuba." *ECA,* no. 259, 1970, 228.

1971. "Estudio ético-político del proceso conflictivo ANDES-ministerio," in I. Ellacuría and others, *Análisis de una experiencia nacional.* San Salvador, 1971, 125–54. See also, *VA,* vol. 1, 1991, 523–56.

1972. "Filosofía y política." [See full citation under *Philosophical Writings*]

1972. "Un excelente psicodiagnóstico sobre latinoamérica." *ECA,* no. 285, 1972, 499–505. Foreward to I. Martín-Baró, *Psicodiagnóstico de América Latina.* San Salvador, UCA Editores, 1972.

1973. "Un marco teórico-valorativo de la reform agraria." *ECA,* nos. 297–8, 1973, 443–57. See also, *VA,* vol. 1, 1991, 567–86.

1973. "Imagen ideológica de los partidos políticos en las elecciones de 1972." J. Hernández-Pico, C. Jerez, E. Baltodano, I. Ellacuría, R. Mayorga, *El Salvador: año político 1971–1972.* Guatemala, Editores Piedra Santa, 1973, 319–62; San Salvador, UCA Editores, 1973, 321–62. See also, *VA,* vol. 3, 1991, 1487–1531.

1974. "Aspectos éticos del problema poblacional." *ECA,* nos. 310–1, 1974, 565–92. See also, *EF,* vol. 3, 2001, 19–63.

1976. "El primer proyecto de transformación agraria." Pronunciamiento del Consejo Superior de la Universidad Centroamericana "José Simeón Cañas," (June 1976). See also, *ECA,* nos. 335–6, 1976, 419–24; *VA,* vol. 1, 1991, 559–66.

1976. "La historización del concepto de propiedad como principio de desideologización." [See full citation under *Philosophical Writings*]

1976. "¡A sus órdenes, mi capital!" *ECA,* no. 337, 1976, 637–43. See also, *VA,* vol. 1, 1991, 649–56.

1976. "La transformación de la ley del Instituto Salvadoreño de Transformación Agraria (ISTA)." *ECA,* no. 338, 1976, 747–58. See also, *VA,* vol. 1, 1991, 629–48.

1977. "El problema etico de la política." *Ya,* 1977, 37.

1978. "Historización del bien común y de los derechos humanos en una sociedad dividida." [See full citation under *Philosophical Writings*]

1978. "La Iglesia y las organizaciones populares en El Salvador." [See full citation under *Theological Writings*]

1978. "El Salvador, juicio sobre el año 1978." *ECA,* nos. 361–2, 1978, 865–76. See also, *VA,* vol. 1, 1991, 353–64.

1978. "Comentarios a la Carta Pastoral." [See full citation under *Theological Writings*]

1979. "Recuperación de la universidad de El Salvador." *ECA,* nos. 363–4, 1979, 58–9.

1979. "La OEA y los derechos humanos en El Salvador." *ECA,* nos. 363–4, 1979, 53–4.

1979. "La seguridad nacional y la constitución salvadoreña." *ECA,* no. 369–70, 1979, 477–88, under the pseudonym, "Tomás R. Campos." See also, *VA,* vol. 1, 1991, 247–66.

1979. "Crece el enterés nacional por el cambio político." Radio broadcast, *YSAX* (Oct. 15, 1979). See also, *ESTE,* 1982, 558–9; *VA,* vol. 2, 1991, 801–2.

1979. "Al fin, insurrección militar." Radio broadcast, *YSAX* (Oct. 16, 1979). See also, *ESTE,* 1982, 559–61; *VA,* vol. 2, 1991, 803–5.

1979. "La proclama de la junta de gobierno: una importante toma de posición ante el país." Radio broadcast, *YSAX* (Oct. 17, 1979). See also, *ESTE,* 1982, 563–5; *VA,* vol. 2, 1991, 807–9.

1979. "Insurrección popular y hostigamiento extremista." Radio broadcast, *YSAX* (Oct. 19, 1979). See also, *ESTE,* 1982, 571–3; *VA,* vol. 2, 1991, 811–3.

1979. "La scmana fuc así (dcl 13 al 20 dc octubrc)." Radio broadcast, *YSAX* (Oct. 20, 1979). See also, *ESTE,* 1982, 579–82; *VA,* vol. 2, 1991, 815–8.

1979. "La revolución necesaria." Six radio broadcasts, *YSAX* (Oct. 22–27, 1979). See also, *ESTE,* 1982, 583–605; *VA,* vol. 2, 1991, 819–30.

1979. "La semana fue así (del 20 al 27 de octubre)." Radio broadcast, *YSAX* (Oct. 27, 1979). See also, *ESTE,* 1982, 605–8; *VA,* vol. 2, 1991, 831–4.

1979. "Las organizaciones populares ante la nueva situación." Radio broadcast, *YSAX* (Oct. 31, 1979). See also, *ESTE,* 1982, 613–5; *VA,* vol. 2, 1991, 773–5.

1979. "Pronunciamiento del Consejo Superior Universitario de la Universidad Centroamericana 'José Simeón Cañas' sobre la nueva situación del país tras el 15 de octubre." *ECA,* nos. 372–3, 1979, 849–62. See also, *VA,* vol. 2, 1991, 835–49.

1979. "El papel de las organizaciones populares en la actual situación del país." *ECA,* no. 372–3, 1979, 923–46, under the pseudonym "Tomás R. Campos." See also, *VA,* vol. 2, 1991, 733–71.

1979. "La Iglesia y la UCA en el golpe del 15 de Octubre de 1979." [See full citation under *Theological Writings*]

1980. "Universidad y política." [See full citation under *University Writings*]

1980. "En busca de un nuevo proyecto nacional." *ECA,* nos. 377–8, 1980, 155–80. See also, *VA,* vol. 2, 1991, 913–36.

1980. "La superación de un 15 de octubre fracasado." *ECA,* nos. 384–5, 1980, 929–50. See also, *VA,* vol. 2, 1991, 851–68.

1980. "La seguridad nacional y la crucificación salvadoreña." [See full citation under *Theological Writings*]

1981. "Un proceso de mediación para El Salvador." *ECA,* nos. 387–8, 1981, 3–16. See also, *VA,* vol. 2, 1991, 937–49.

1981. "Errores y sofismas de la Sra. Kirkpatrick." *ECA,* no. 389, 1981, 192–3.

1981. "¿Solución política o solución militar para El Salvador?" *ECA,* nos. 390–1, 1981, 295–324. See also, *VA,* vol. 2, 1991, 951–95; *SPP,* 1994, 13–42.

1981. "La nueva política de la Administración Reagan en El Salvador." *ECA,* nos. 390–1, 1981, 383–414, under the pseudonym "Tomás R. Campos."

1981. "La declaración conjunta mexicano-francesa sobre El Salvador." *ECA,* no. 395, 1981, 845–66. See also, *VA,* vol. 3, 1991, 1235–69.

1982. "1982, año decisivo para El Salvador." *ECA,* nos. 399–400, 1982, 3–16.

1982. "Análisis coyuntural sobre la situación de El Salvador." *ECA,* nos. 399–400, 1982, 17–58, under the pseudonym, "Tomás R. Campos." See also, *VA,* vol. 1, 1991, 365–432.

1982. "Las elecciones en El Salvador," *Razón y Fe* (March 1982) 285–94.

1982. "Las elecciones y la unidad nacional: diez tesis críticas." *ECA,* no. 402, 1982, 233–58. See also, *VA,* vol. 3, 1991, 1533–55.

1982. "Interpretación global del proceso histórico, 15 de Octubre de 1979–28 de Marzo de 1982." *ECA,* nos. 403–4, 1982, 599–622, under the pseudonym "Tomás R. Campos." See also, *VA,* vol. 2, 1991, 869–909.

1982. "Universidad, derechos humanos y mayorías populares." [See full citation under *University Writings*]

1982. "Juan Pablo II y el conflicto salvadoreño." [See full citation under *Theological Writings*]

1982. "Regionalizar la paz, no la guerra." *ECA,* no. 406, 1982, 767–80. See also, *VA,* vol. 2, 1991, 1009–23.

1982. "La independencia nacional en 1982." *ECA,* nos. 407–8, 1982, 855–64. See also, *VA,* vol. 3, 1991, 1731–40.

1982. "El Pacto de Apaneca: un proyecto político para la transición." *ECA,* nos. 407–8, 1982, 865–78, under the pseudonym, "Tomás R. Campos."

1982. "El diálogo en El Salvador como principio de solución política." *ECA,* no. 409, 1982, 981–92. See also, *VA,* vol. 2, 1991, 997–1007; *SPP,* 1994, 43–54.

1982. "Conflicto entre trabajo y capital en la presente fase histórica: Un análisis de la encíclica de Juan Pablo II sobre el trabajo humano." [See full citation under *Theological Writings*]

1982. "El Reino de Dios y el paro en el tercer mundo." [See full citation under *Theological Writings*]

1982. *El Salvador: entre el terror y la esperanza. Los sucesos de 1979 y su impacto en el drama salvadoreño de los años siguientes.* Ellacuría, I. and others, San Salvador, UCA Editores, 1982.

1983. "Mensaje ético-político de Juan Pablo II al pueblo de Centro América." [See full citation under *Theological Writings*]

1983. "La estrategia del FMLN-FDR tras el proceso electoral de marzo de 1982." *ECA,* nos. 415–6, 1983, 479–90, under the pseudonym, "Tomás R. Campos." See also, *VA,* vol. 3, 1991, 1557–73.

1983. "Análisis global de la intervención norteamericana actual en El Salvador." *ECA,* nos. 415–6, 1983, 543–56, under the pseudonym, "Ernesto Cruz Alfaro." See also, *VA,* vol. 1, 1991, 209–29.

1983. "Diez tesis sobre un proceso de negociación." *ECA,* nos. 417–8, 1983, 601–28. See also, *VA,* vol. 3, 1991, 1271–97.

1983. "La cooperación iberoamericana a la paz en Centroamérica." *ECA,* nos. 417–8, 1983, 629–40. See also, *VA,* vol. 2, 1991, 1025–40. Paper presented at the Congress "Iberoamérica, encuentro en la democracia," Madrid (Apr. 26–30, 1983).

1983. "La paz mundial vista desde el Tercer Mundo." [See full citation under *Theological Writings*]

1984. "Agonía de un pueblo: urgencia de soluciones." *ECA,* nos. 423–4, 1984, 1–12. See also, *VA,* vol. 1, 1991, 433–44.

1984. "El FDR-FMLN ante las elecciones de 1984." *ECA,* nos. 426–7, 1984, 277–87, under the pseudonym, "Tomás R. Campos." See also, *VA,* vol. 3, 1991, 1575–90.

1984. "Visión de conjunto de las elecciones de 1984." *ECA,* nos. 426–7, 1984, 301–24. See also, *VA,* vol. 3, 1991, 1591–1628.

1984. "¿Tiene solución El Salvador con el presidente Duarte?" *ECA,* no. 428, 1984, 373–96. See also, *VA,* vol. 3, 1991, 1775–97.

1984. "Los militares y la paz social." *ECA,* nos. 429–30, 1984, 475–90. See also, *VA,* vol. 1, 1991, 231–43; *VA,* vol. 2, 1991, 1041–53.

1984. "El aporte del diálogo al problema nacional." *ECA,* nos. 432–3, 1984, 729–56. See also, *VA,* vol. 3, 1991, 1327–58.

1984. "Las primeras vicisitudes del diálogo entre el gobierno y el FMLN-FDR." *ECA,* no. 434, 1984, 885–903, under the pseudonym, "Tomás R. Campos." See also, *VA,* vol. 3, 1991, 1299–1326.

1985. "Función liberadora de la filosofía." [See full citation under *Philosophical Writings*]

1985. "Seis tareas urgentes para 1985." *ECA,* nos. 435–6, 1985, 1–16. See also, *VA,* vol. 2, 1991, 1055–69.

1985. "Las elecciones de 1985, ¿un paso adelante en el proceso de democratización?" *ECA,* no. 438, 1985, 205–14. See also, *VA,* vol. 3, 1991, 1629–37.

1985. "Grave preocupación tras el primer año de la presidencia de Duarte." *ECA,* nos. 439–40, 1985, 325–44. See also, *VA,* vol. 3, 1991, 1799–1817.

1985. "El diálogo del gobierno con el FMLN-FDR: un proceso paralizado." *ECA,* nos. 439–40, 1985, 389–400, under the pseudonym, "Tomás R. Campos." See also, *VA,* vol. 3, 1991, 1359–76.

1985. "El ejemplo de Nicaragua en Centroamérica." *ECA,* nos. 441–2, 1985, 475–94. See also, *VA,* vol. 2, 1991, 1071–89.

1985. "Perspectiva política de la situación centroamericana." *ECA,* nos. 443–4, 1985, 625–37. See also, *VA,* vol. 1, 1991, 333–51.

274 Love That Produces Hope

1985. "Lectura política de los secuestros." *ECA*, nos. 443–4, 1985, 684–700, under the pseudonym, "Tomás R. Campos."

1985. "Causas de la actual situación de país y principios de solución." Pronunciamiento del Consejo Superior Universitario de la Universidad Centroamericana "José Simeón Cañas." *ECA*, no. 445, 1985, 773–86. See also, *VA*, vol. 2, 1991, 1091–1104.

1985. "El Salvador 1985: peor que 1984, mejor que 1986." *ECA*, no. 446, 1985, 883–9. See also, *VA*, vol. 1, 1991, 445–51.

1985. "FMLN, el límite insuperable." *ECA*, no. 446, 1985, 890–7. See also, *VA*, vol. 1, 1991, 197–208.

1985. "Presentación" of Rafael Rogríguez, *Oráculos Para mi Raza*. San Salvador, UCA Editores, 1985.

1986. "Hacer la paz en El Salvador." *ECA*, nos. 447–8, 1986, 5–17. See also, *VA*, vol. 2, 1991, 1139–50; *SPP*, 1994, 79–91.

1986. "Replanteamiento de soluciones para el problema de El Salvador." *ECA*, nos. 447–8, 1986, 54–75. See also, *VA*, vol. 2, 1991, 1105–38; *SPP*, 1994, 55–77.

1986. "Estados Unidos y la democratización de Centroamérica." *ECA*, no. 450, 1986, 255–74. See also, *VA*, vol. 3, 1991, 1741–59.

1986. "Dos años más de gobierno de Duarte." *ECA*, nos. 451–2, 1986, 375–87. See also, *VA*, vol. 3, 1991, 1819–30.

1986. "El Salvador en estado de diálogo." *ECA*, no. 453, 1986, 525–33. See also, *VA*, vol. 3, 1991, 1417–24.

1986. "Análisis ético-político del prodeso de diálogo en El Salvador." *ECA*, nos. 454–5, 1986, 727–51. See also, *VA*, vol. 3, 1991, 1377–1416; *SPP*, 1994, 93–117.

1986. "Centroamérica como problema." *ECA*, no. 456, 1986, 821–33. See also, *VA*, vol. 1, 1991, 123–31.

1986. "Factores endógenos del conflicto centroamericano: crisis económica y desequilibrios sociales." *ECA*, no. 456, 1986, 856–78. See also, *CINAS Cuadernos de Trabajo*, no. 9, 1987, 9–38; *VA*, vol. 1, 1991, 139–72.

1987. "La teología de la liberación frente al cambio socio-histórico de América Latina." [See full citation under *Theological Writings*]

1987. "¿Por qué no avanza El Salvador?" *ECA*, no. 461, 1987, 167–89. See also, *VA*, vol. 1, 1991, 175–96.

1987. "Lecciones del Irán-Contras para El Salvador." *ECA*, no. 462, 1987, 289–99. See also, *VA*, vol. 3, 1991, 1761–71.

1987. "Caminos de solución para la actual crisis del país." *ECA*, no. 462, 1987, 301–11. See also, *Mensaje*, 1987, 3–19; *VA*, vol. 2, 1991, 1151–69.

1987. "La cuestión de las masas." *ECA*, no. 465, 1987, 415–34. See also, *VA*, vol. 2, 1991, 777–98.

1987. "Nueva propuesta de diálogo del FMLN-FDR: los dieciocho puntos." *ECA*, no. 465, 1987, 435–47. See also, *VA*, vol. 3, 1991, 1425–48.

1987. "Análisis ético-político de Esquípulas dos." *ECA*, nos. 466–7, 1987, 599–610. See also, *VA*, vol. 3, 1991, 1681–1701.

1987. "Los noventa días de Esquípulas dos." *ECA,* no. 468, 1987, 665–73. See also, *VA,* vol. 3, 1991, 1703–11.

1987. "El proceso de pacificación en Centroamérica." *ECA,* nos. 469–70, 1987, 803–16. See also, *VA,* vol. 3, 1991, 1713–27.

1987. "Propuestas de solución en el marco de Esquípulas dos." *ECA,* nos. 469–70, 1987, 865–89. See also, *VA,* vol. 2, 1991, 1171–1215.

1987. "Subdesarrollo y derechos humanos." [See full citation under *Theological Writings*]

1987. "El desafío cristiano de la teología de la liberación." [See full citation under *Theological Writings*]

1988. "Trabajo no violento por la paz y violencia liberadora." [See full citation under *Theological Writings*]

1988. "1988: un año de transición para El Salvador." *ECA,* nos. 471–2, 1988, 5–20. See also, *VA,* vol. 1, 1991, 453–66.

1988. "Elecciones aleccionadoras." *ECA,* nos. 473–4, 1988, 151–74. See also, *VA,* vol. 3, 1991, 1639–61.

1988. "El desmoronamiento de la fachada democrática." *ECA,* no. 475, 1988, 311–27. See also, *VA,* vol. 1, 1991, 267–81.

1988. "Duarte, el final de una presidencia." *ECA,* no. 476, 1988, 461–85. See also, *VA,* vol. 3, 1991, 1831–51.

1988. "Recrudecimiento de la violencia en El Salvador." *ECA,* no. 480, 1988, 861–71. See also, *VA,* vol. 1, 1991, 467–83.

1988. "El significado del debate nacional." *ECA,* nos. 478–9, 1988, 713–29. See also, *VA,* vol. 3, 1991, 1469–83; *SPP,* 1994, 119–35.

1988. "Ambigüedad de las nuevas elecciones presidenciales." *ECA,* nos. 481–2, 1988, 995–1012. See also, *VA,* vol. 3, 1991, 1663–78.

1988. "Los partidos políticos y la finalización de la guerra." *ECA,* nos. 481–2, 1988, 1037–51. See also, *VA,* vol. 3, 1991, 1449–68.

1988. "Nuevo orden mundial propuesto por Gorbachev." *ECA,* nos. 481–2, 1988, 1099–1101.

1989. "Una nueva fase en el proceso salvadoreño." *ECA,* no. 485, 1989, 167–97. See also, *VA,* vol. 3, 1991, 1855–97.

1989. "Vísperas violentas." *ECA,* nos. 486–7, 1989, 279–84. See also, *VA,* vol. 1, 1991, 485–98.

1989. "¿Resolverá el gobierno de ARENA la crisis del país?" *ECA,* no. 488, 1989, 413–28. See also, *VA,* vol. 2, 1991, 1217–31.

1989. "El diálogo en los primeros cien días de Cristiani." *ECA,* nos. 490–1, 1989, 683–94.

1989. "El desafío de las mayorías pobres." [See full citation under *Theological Writings*]

1989. "Utopía y profetismo desde América Latina: un ensayo concreto de soteriología histórica." [See full citation under *Theological Writings*]

1989. "Historización de los derechos humanos desde los pueblos oprimidos y las mayorías populares," [See full citation under *Philosophical Writings*]

1991. *Veinte años de historia en El Salvador (1969–1989): Escritos políticos.* 3 vols. San Salvador, UCA Editores, 1991.

1994. *Seis pistas para la paz.* Bogotá, Centro de Investigación y Educación Popular, 1994.

## University Writings

1970. "Los centros privados docentes y sus problemas." *ECA,* nos. 265–6, 1970, 585–6.

1971. "Discurso de la Universidad Centroamericana 'José Simeón Cañas' en la firma del contrato con el Banco Interamericano de Desarrollo (BID)." With Román Mayorga Quirós. *ECA,* no. 268, 1971, 108–12. See also, *EU,* 1999, 19–26.

1972. "La ley orgánica de la Universidad de El Salvador: Reflexiones críticas en busca de una Universidad Latinoamericana." *ECA,* no. 290, 1972, 747–61. See also, H. Cerutto Guldberg, ed., *Universidad y cambio social: los jesuitas en El Salvador,* Mexico, Magna Terra Editores, 1990, 45–62. See also, *EU,* 1999, 27–47.

1975. "Misión política de la Universidad." *Abra,* no. 8, 1975, 2–7.

1975. "Diez años después: ¿es posible una Universidad distinta?" *ECA,* nos. 324–5, 1975, 605–28. See also, H. Cerutto Guldberg, ed., *Universidad y cambio social: los jesuitas en El Salvador,* Mexico, Magna Terra Editores, 1990, 131–66; *EU,* 1999, 49–92. [*Writings in English Translation* (1991)]

1976. "Una universidad centroamericana para El Salvador." *EU,* 1999, 93–103. Keynote address to the UCA Conference, "La UCA hacia el futuro," May 31–June 5, 1976; previously unpublished.

1978. "Funciones fundamentales de la universidad y su operativización." Final document summarizing the results of a university-wide consultation process on the role of the UCA. First published in *Planteamiento universitario 1989.* San Salvador, UCA Editores, 1989, 45–129. See also *EU,* 1999, 105–67.

1980. "Universidad y política." *ECA,* no. 383, 1980, 807–24. See also, H. Cerutto Guldberg, ed., *Modernizacíon educativa y universidad en América Latina,* Mexico, Magna Terra Editores, 1990, 35–71; *VA,* vol. 1, 1991, 17–45; *EU,* 1999, 169–202.

1982. "Una Universidad para el pueblo." *Diakonía,* no. 23, 1982, 81–8. Reedited from the English text and published as "Discurso de graduación en la Universidad de Santa Clara," *Carta a las Iglesias,* no. 22, 1982, 11–5. See also, *EU,* 1999, 221–8. [*Writings in English Translation* (1990)]

1982. "Universidad, derechos humanos y mayorías populares." *ECA,* no. 406, 1982, 791–800. See also, H. Cerutti Guldberg, ed., *Universidad y cambio social: los jesuitas en El Salvador,* Mexico, Magna Terra Editores, 1990, 45–62; *EU,* 1999, 203–19. [*Writings in English Translation* (1991)]

1985. "La UCA ante el doctorado concedido a Monseñor Romero." *ECA,* no. 437, 1985, 167–76. See also, *EU,* 1999, 229–43; *ET,* vol. 3, 2002, 101–14. [*Writings in English Translation* (1990)]

1985. "Veinte años de servicio al pueblo salvadoreño." *ECA,* nos. 443–4, 1985, 617–21. See also, *EU,* 1999, 245–51.

1985. "Los retos del país a la UCA en su vigésimo aniversario." *ECA,* nos. 443–4, 1985, 617–21. See also, *Planteamiento universitario 1989,* 152–65; *EU,* 1999, 253–72. Twentieth anniversary, foundation of the UCA: September 17, 1985.

1988. "Hacia un desarrollo liberador de los pueblos." *Planteamiento universitario 1989,* 182–91; *EU,* 1999, 273–85; *ET,* vol. 3, 2002, 413–26. UCA graduation: April 16, 1988.

1988. "La inspiración cristiana de la UNA en la docencia." *Planteamiento universitario 1989,* 195–200; *EU,* 1999, 287–95. UCA graduation: September 30, 1988.

1989. "El desafío de las mayorías pobres." [See full citation under *Theological Writings*]

1999. *Escritos universitarios.* San Salvador, UCA Editores, 1999.

## Writings in English Translation

1976. *Freedom Made Flesh: The Mission of Christ and His Church.* Maryknoll, Orbis, 1976. Trans. by John Drury from *Teología política* (1973) and "Liturgia y liberación" (1976).

1976. "Liturgy and Liberation," in *FMF,* 1976, 233–46. Trans. from "Liturgia y liberación" (1976). [*CIRD* (1984) 279–92]

1977. "The Function of Economic Theories in Theological-Theoretical Discussion on the Relationship between Christianity and Socialism," in J. Metz and J. Jossua, eds., *Christianity and Socialism,* New York, Seabury, 1977, 125–31. Trans. from "Teorías económicas y relación entre cristianismo y socialismo" (1977).

1982. "Human Rights in a Divided Society," in A. Hennelly and J. Langan, eds., *Human Rights in the Americas: The Struggle for Consensus,* Washington, Georgetown University Press, 1982, 52–65. Trans. from "Historización del bien común y de los derechos humanos en una sociedad dividida" (1978).

1982. "The Kingdom of God and Unemployment in the Third World," in J. Pohier and D. Mieth, eds., *Unemployment and the Right to Work,* New York, Seabury, 1982, 91–6. Trans. form "El Reino de Dios y el paro en el tercer mundo" (1982).

1984. "The Political Nature of Jesus' Mission," in J. Miguez Boniño, ed., *Faces of Jesus: Latin American Christologies.* Maryknoll, Orbis, 1984, 79–92; Trans. from "Carácter político de la misión de Jesús" (1973). See also, *FMF,* 1976, 23–51.

1988. "Violence and Non-violence in the Struggle for Peace and Liberation," in Küng, H. and Moltmann, J., eds., *A Council for Peace,* London, T & T Clark, 1988. Trans. from "Trabajo no violento por la paz y violencia liberadora" (1988).

1990. I. Ellacuría, J. Sobrino and others, *Companions of Jesus: The Jesuit Martyrs of El Salvador.* Maryknoll, Orbis, 1990.

1990. "Persecution for the Sake of the Reign of God," *CJ,* 1990, 64–75. Trans. from the conclusion to "El verdadero pueblo de Dios según Monseñor Romero" (1981).

1990. "The Task of a Christian University," *CJ*, 1990, 147–51. Text of the graduation address given June 12, 1982, at Santa Clara University, Santa Clara, CA. Based loosely on "Una universidad para el pueblo" (1982).

1990. "The UCA Regarding the Doctorate Given to Monseñor Romero," *Envío* 9, 1990, 15–8. Trans. from "La UCA ante el doctorado concedido a Monseñor Romero" (1985).

1990. "The Writings of Ellacuría, Martín-Baró, and Segundo Montes," in *The Jesuit Assassinations*, Kansas City, Sheed and Ward, 1990, 1–26. Trans. from brief extracts from various writings.

1991. *Towards a Society that Serves its People: The Intellectual Contribution of El Salvador's Murdered Jesuits*. Hassett, J. and Lacey, H., eds. Washington, D.C., Georgetown University Press, 1991.

1991. "Liberation Theology and Socio-historical Change in Latin America," in *TSSP*, 1991, 19–43. Trans. by James Brockman from "La teología de la liberación frente al cambio socio-histórico de América Latina" (1987).

1991. "Utopia and Prophecy in Latin America," in *TSSP*, 1991, 44–88. Trans. by James R. Brockman from "Utopía y profetismo desde América Latina: un ensayo concreto de soteriología historíca" (1989). Also in *MLT*, 1993, 289–328.

1991. "Fundamental Human Rights and the Legal and Political Restrictions Placed on Them," in *TSSP*, 1991, 91–104. Trans. by Phillip Berryman from "Los derechos humanos fundamentales y su limitación legal y política" (1969).

1991. "The Historicization of the Concept of Property," in *TSSP*, 1991, 105–37. Trans. by Phillip Berryman from "La historización del concepto de propiedad como principio de desideologización" (1976).

1991. "The Challenge of the Poor Majority," in *TSSP*, 1991, 171–6. Trans. by Phillip Berryman from "El desafío de las mayorías pobres" (1989).

1991. "Is a Different Kind of University Possible?" in *TSSP*, 1991, 177–207. Trans. by Phillip Berryman from "¿Diez años después: es posible una universidad distinta?" (1975).

1991. "The University, Human Rights, and the Poor Majority," in *TSSP*, 1991, 208–19. Trans. by Phillip Berryman from "Universidad, derechos humanos y mayorías populares" (1982).

1991. "The True Social Place of the Church," in *TSSP*, 1991, 283–92. Trans. by Phillip Berryman from "El auténtico lugar social de la Iglesia" (1982).

1993. I. Ellacuria and J. Sobrino, eds., *Mysterium Liberationis: Fundamental Concepts of Liberation Theology*. Maryknoll, Orbis, 1993. Trans. of *Mysterium liberationis: Conceptos fundamentales de la teología de la liberación*, 1990.

1993. "The Historicity of Christian Salvation," in *MLT*, 1993, 251–89. Trans. by Margaret D. Wilde from "Historicidad de la salvación cristiana" (1984).

1993. "The Church of the Poor, Historical Sacrament of Liberation," in *MLT*, 1993, 543–64. Trans. by Margaret D. Wilde from "La Iglesia de los pobres, sacramento histórico de la liberación" (1977).

1993. "The Crucified People," *MLT,* 1993, 580–603. Trans. by Phillip Berryman and Robert R. Barr from "El pueblo crucificado" (1978). Also in Ellacuría. I. and Sobrino, J. eds. *Systematic Theology: Perspectives from Liberation Theology.* Maryknoll, Orbis, 1996, 257–78.

1996. I. Ellacuria, J. Sobrino, I. Martín-Baró, *A Different Kind of University: Ignatian Voices from El Salvador.* Ed. Morgan, O., and Homer, F., Scranton, PA, Center for Mission Reflection, 1996.

1996. Ellacuria, I., and Sobrino, J., eds. *Systematic Theology: Perspectives from Liberation Theology.* Readings from *Mysterium Liberationis.* Maryknoll, Orbis, 1996.

1998. "What is the Point of Philosophy?" *Philosophy and Theology,* vol. 10, no. 1, 1998, 3–18. Trans. by T. Michael McNulty from "Filosofía ¿para qué?" (1976).

# Index

Action (see also *Praxis*), 5, 8, 13, 47, 49,
   111, 132, 135, 145, 148–60, 179,
   189, 191–2, 198, 207, 215, 224, 233
Anti-Reign/Anti-Kingdom (see also
   *Mysterium iniquitatis*), 32–7, 42, 50,
   139, 178
Apprehension of Reality, 83, 92, 93,
   96, 99–104, 113, 171
Aristotle, 21–2, 76, 78, 81, 85, 92, 94
Assassination, xiii, 46, 50–1, 68–9,
   89, 213
   Ellacuría, xiii, xxix, 52, 68–9, 89,
      213
   UCA martyrs, v, xii, xiii, 3, 8, 50,
      51, 54, 56, 57, 160, 209, 223
   Romero, xxvi, 46, 50
   Rutilio Grande, xxix, 52

Base Ecclesial Communities; Christian
   Base Communities; *Comunidades de
   base*, 20–1, 194–5, 242
Being, 92–5, 102–4, 133, 153, 156,
   205, 212
   act of being, 95–6, 156
   and relativity theory, 95–6
   as *ente* (being-as-an-entity), 94–5,
      102
   being-an-object, 95
   being real, 96

*dasein*, 92, 113
*esse*, 94–5, 257
*esse real*, 94, 95
*esse* is *percipi*, 95
*esse* is *concipi*, 95
*esse* is *poni*, 95
as *ser* (being), 94–5, 97
Ellacuría, Ignacio, 93–8, 102–4, 109
Heidegger, Martin, 92, 94–6, 113
real being, 19, 95, 96, 97, 120 note
   35
scholastics, xviii, 95
*sein-ist-Seitzung*, 95
*sein-lassen-von*, 95
substantivation of, 95–6
Zubiri, Xavier, 92, 93–8, 102–4, 113
Bondedness (see also
   *Religation/Religación*), 104, 126 note
   196, 258, 261

Cardenal, Rudolfo, xvii–xxi,
   xxiii–xxiv, xxx note 6, 267
CELAM (see also *Conference of the
   Latin American Bishops*), xvi, xxviii,
   105, 269
Central America, xv, xvi, 9, 105, 106,
   208, 213
Central American Province (of the
   *Jesuits*), xv–xxvii, 105, 145

280

ideological moment of ecclesial,
19, 110, 111, 116, 132, 170, 174
*Puebla;* Third General Conference of
the Latin American Bishops, 159,
181, 224, 225, 227–35

Rahner, Karl
and liberation theology, xxii, xxv
note 116
and Vatican II, xx–xxiii, 128–40
as teacher of Ellacuría, xv, xvi,
xix, xx–xxiii, xxiv, xxv, xxvii,
xxix, 2, 18, 22, 24, 33, 37, 44,
46, 59, 76, 105, 107, 112, 117,
128–40, 144, 146, 147, 187,
194, 195
historical reality as development
of his thought, 136, 138, 147,
156, 240
theology of symbol, xxii–xxiii,
135–7
transcendental method, xvi, 5,
130–2, 134, 137, 138, 139
Transcendental Thomism, xvi
Real, xix, 4, 8, 15, 19, 23, 37, 56,
77–83, 94–8, 99, 100, 101, 102–4,
107, 108, 113–6, 134, 136, 148,
155, 181, 182, 197, 208, 218
being real, 96
real being, 19, 95, 96, 97, 120 note
35
Realism
Christian historical, xxiv–xxv,
88, 99, 104–16, 117, 193, 199,
216
critical, post–critical, 89
historical, xxiv–xxv, 88, 99,
104–16, 117, 193, 199, 216
Reality
apprehension of, 83, 92, 93, 96,
99–104, 113, 171
constitutively dynamic, 77, 79, 80,
81, 83, 108, 156, 173

demands of, 15, 16, 24, 41, 48, 98,
104, 112, 115, 130, 171, 216,
217, 218, 230, 243
formal *r,* 88, 92, 93, 95, 96, 98, 99,
100, 101, 102–4, 105, 111, 114,
116
historical *r,* xxiv, xxv, xxviii, 20,
29, 74, 80–1, 85, 90, 104–10,
111, 113, 134, 136, 138, 147,
156, 171, 173, 174, 182, 189,
191, 199, 230, 237, 240
being real, 96
deideologizing potential of, 112–3,
242
entification of, 90, 93–8, 102, 103
Facing up to reality (see also
*Intellection, noetic, ethical, praxical
dimensions of*), 18, 19, 21, 45,
89, 113, 114, 129, 214
Intramundane, xxxiv note 98, 96,
106, 108
object of philosophy, historical,
xxv, 80, 84, 85, 95, 106, 107
philosophy of historical r, xxv, 80,
84, 85, 95, 106, 107
real being, 19, 95, 96, 97, 120 note
35
reity, 92, 93, 95, 96, 97, 98, 99,
100, 101, 103, 119–20 note 31
theologal dimension of,
theological dimension of, 103,
112, 155, 180, 182
weight of; realizing, shouldering,
taking charge of, 19, 113, 114,
115, 184 note 6
Realizing the weight of reality, 19,
113, 114, 115, 184 note 6
Reductionism, 82, 88–98, 99, 104,
108, 109, 111, 116, 117, 134
Reductionistic idealism, 82, 88–98, 99,
104, 108, 109, 111, 116, 117, 134
Reign of God (see also *Kingdom of
God*), 9, 14, 19, 32, 43, 51, 106,